Ar

CW01091634

J. P. DAUGHTON

An Empire Divided

Religion, Republicanism, and the
Making of French Colonialism,
1880–1914

Oxford University Press, Inc., publishes works that further
Oxford University's objective of excellence
in research, scholarship, and education.

Oxford   New York
Auckland   Cape Town   Dar es Salaam   Hong Kong   Karachi
Kuala Lumpur   Madrid   Melbourne   Mexico City   Nairobi
New Delhi   Shanghai   Taipei   Toronto

With offices in
Argentina   Austria   Brazil   Chile   Czech Republic   France   Greece
Guatemala   Hungary   Italy   Japan   Poland   Portugal   Singapore
South Korea   Switzerland   Thailand   Turkey   Ukraine   Vietnam

Copyright © 2006 by Oxford University Press, Inc.

Published by Oxford University Press, Inc.
198 Madison Avenue, New York, New York 10016

www.oup.com

First issued as an Oxford University Press Paperback, 2008

Oxford is a registered trademark of Oxford University Press

All rights reserved. No part of this publication may be reproduced,
stored in a retrieval system, or transmitted, in any form or by any means,
electronic, mechanical, photocopying, recording, or otherwise,
without the prior permission of Oxford University Press.

Library of Congress Cataloging-in-Publication Data

Daughton, J. P. (James Patrick)
An empire divided : religion, republicanism, and the
making of French colonialism, 1880-1914 / J.P. Daughton.
p. cm.
Includes bibliographical references and index.
ISBN 978-0-19-530530-2; 978-0-19-537401-8 (pbk.)
1. Missions, French—History. 2. Republicanism—France—
History. 3. Catholic Church—Missions—France—Colonies.
4. Missions, French—Indochina—History. 5. Catholic Church—
Missions—Indochina—History. 6. Missions, French—
French Polynesia. 7. Catholic Church—Missions—French Polynesia.
8. Missions, French—Madagascar—History. 9. Catholic
Church—Missions—Madagascar—History. I. Title.
BV2210.D38 2006
909'.0971244—dc22   2005058519

Printed in the United States of America
on acid-free paper

For K, NJ, and H

Every kingdom divided against itself is brought to desolation;
and every city or house divided against itself shall not stand . . .
—MATTHEW 12:25

Acknowledgments

This book would never have been possible without the help of an extraordinary number of people, organizations, and institutions. The bulk of my research in France was funded by a J. William Fulbright Foundation fellowship, as well as by travel grants from the University of California's Institute for Global Conflict and Cooperation, the Institute for International Studies at UC Berkeley, and Stanford University. Support from the Graduate Division and the Department of History at UC Berkeley, as well as the John Tracy Ellis Dissertation prize from the American Catholic Historical Association, made research in Vietnam and French Polynesia possible. Fellowships from the Harry Frank Guggenheim Foundation and the Woodrow Wilson Foundation supported the writing of the dissertation, and a Stanford Humanities Postdoctoral Fellowship, under the generous guidance of Seth Lerer, offered a hospitable environment in which to finish my manuscript.

This project would also have been impossible if not for the many librarians and archivists who allowed me access to their collections and provided invaluable direction. In France, I would like to thank Père Gérard Moussay and Annie Sablayrolles, both at the Société des missions étrangères de Paris; Soeur Yves LeGoff at the Archives des Soeurs de Saint Joseph de Cluny (Paris); Robert Bonfils, S.J., at the Archives Jésuites (Vanves); Claire-Lise Lombard at the Département évangélique français d'action apostolique (Paris); Odile Lolum and Laurence Brogly at the Centre national de documentation et d'archives missionnaires (Lyon); and the staffs of the Archives nationale (Paris), the Archives du ministère des affaires-étrangères (Paris), and the Centre des archives d'outre mer (Aix-en-Provence). In Rome, I benefited from the help of Alois Greiler, S.M., and Carol-Maria Schianchi, S.M., at the archives of the Pères Maristes, and the staff of the archives of the Congregatio Pro Gentium Evangelizatione. And at Stanford, Sarah Sussman provided exemplary assistance in the university library. Without their generosity, support, and bountiful knowledge of their collections, this book could never have been written.

My research in Vietnam was greatly facilitated by the gracious sponsorship of the University of Social Sciences and Humanities at the National University of Vietnam in Hanoi. In the International Cooperation Office, Pham Quang Minh made the necessary arrangements for my visa. Nguyen Van Khanh in the Department of History, as well as the staff of the National Archives No. 1, made sure my research went smoothly. I am particularly grateful to Professor Dinh Xuan Lam, who, through many discussions, shared with me his extensive knowledge of Vietnamese history and personal recollections of French colonialism. In French Polynesia, Mgr. Hubert Coppenrath and Marcelline Heitaa at the Archdiocese of Papeete, Denise Tauira at the Église évangélique de la Polynésie française, and the staff of the Archives territoriales de la Polynésie française all offered invaluable guidance, while the Gump Research Center in Moorea offered an ideal living environment. In London, I thank the helpful staff of the London Missionary Society archives at the School of Oriental and African Studies, University of London, as well as the Council for World Mission for granting access.

Personally and professionally, I have benefited immeasurably from the advice, criticisms, and insights offered by advisers, colleagues, and friends in the course of writing this book. First and foremost, I am extremely thankful to have had the chance to study at UC Berkeley under Susanna Barrows, who has had a profound influence on how I view history, understand politics and culture, and approach writing. Her extraordinary creativity, sharp wit, and boundless knowledge of all things French have challenged and motivated me over the years. She has always been an inspiring adviser and is now a cherished colleague and confidant. At Berkeley, I was also very lucky to work with Margaret Lavinia Anderson, who in fact first gave me the idea to study missionaries in the French empire. With her tireless commitment to teaching, her incisive skills as a scholar, and her warmth and energy, she has been an ideal mentor and friend. I owe both of them more than I could ever hope to repay.

A number of people generously read large portions or all of the manuscript, offering insightful suggestions and productive criticisms. For this, I want to thank Robert Aldrich, Keith Michael Baker, Edward Berenson, Julia Clancy-Smith, Nola Cooke, Robert Crews, Sarah Curtis, Susan Ferber, Brad Gregory, Eric Jennings, Ignacio Navarette, Karen Offen, Greg Shaya, Richard Roberts, Paul Robinson, Aron Rodrigue, James Sheehan, Owen White, Peter Zinoman, and the anonymous readers at Oxford University Press. I am also very grateful to colleagues who have offered direction or have engaged me in fruitful conversations: Victoria Belco, Julian Bourg, Chad Bryant, Elizabeth Foster, Gene Irschick, Tabitha Kanogo, Hee Ko, Catarina Krizancic, Thomas Kselman, Kaarin Michaelsen, Katharine Norris, Maria Riasanovsky, Jessica Riskin, Emanuel Rota, Jason Scott Smith, Robert Tombs, Patrick Tuck, and Marie-Pierre Ulloa. I am indebted to them all for having expanded and improved my project in countless ways.

This study also profited from responses from audiences or participants at the Stanford French Culture workshop, the European workshop in the Stanford History Department, the Center for Southeast Asian Studies at UC Berkeley, the roundtable discussion on "The New Religious History" sponsored by French Studies at Berkeley, and the history faculty at New School University. James Ker contributed much appreciated assistance with Latin translations and Bible references. Yen Hoang Hai adeptly introduced me to the Vietnamese language in Hanoi. Derek Vanderpool offered essential research assistance in the final stages of revision. Don Pirius produced the maps. I am deeply grateful to them all.

Finally, I would never have survived, let alone enjoyed, writing this book without the love and good humor of my family and friends. Many have helped me recover from the hours of solitude spent in archives or libraries. For that, I want especially to express my appreciation and admiration to Dan Ahern, Julian Bourg, Chad Bryant, Erin Daughton, Tom Daughton, James Ker, Kaarin Michaelsen, Hanh Ngo, Jo Park, Erin and Paul Scott, Chris Strain, and Wendy Sheanin. Michelle and Andy Lester and Alaine and Hersh Panitch have offered food and shelter on many occasions, for which I am forever thankful. Max Lester made sure I kept to my writing schedule. Sally and Don Daughton have been ideal parents: supportive, loving, and wise.

Most important, my wife, Karyn Panitch, and sons, Nathaniel and Henry, have been the greatest sources of inspiration, humor, and happiness. For their love and patience, I dedicate this book to them.

Contents

THEY SHALL CAST OUT DEVILS

Introduction: Empire in an Age of Discord

And he said to them: Go ye into the whole world and preach the gospel to every creature. He that believeth and is baptized shall be saved: but he that believeth not shall be condemned. And these signs shall follow them that believe: In my name they shall cast out devils. They shall speak with new tongues.

— Mark 16:15–17

The republican party has shown . . . that [France] cannot just be a free country; that it must also be a great country exercising all the influence it has on the destiny of Europe, that it must spread this influence in the world, and carry everywhere it can its language, its customs, its flag, its arms, its genius.

— Jules Ferry, 1883

For what is wedlock forcèd, but a hell,
An age of discord and continual strife?

— William Shakespeare, *Henry VI, Part 1*

In late 1899, Monsieur Julia, a minor colonial administrator in rural Madagascar, was having trouble with a local French Jesuit missionary named Père Delmont. In a series of reports to his superior, Julia complained that Delmont had repeatedly interfered with official colonial business. First, Delmont obstructed the administration's pursuit of justice by telling witnesses to give false testimony to help clear two Catholic converts accused of theft. The priest went so far as to sit in the courtroom to make sure the witnesses stuck to the fictitious script, even though the evidence against the accused was overwhelming.[1] Several weeks later, Julia discovered that for five months Delmont had been assuring local villagers that, by working to build the mission's new church, they were fulfilling their labor obligations to the colonial

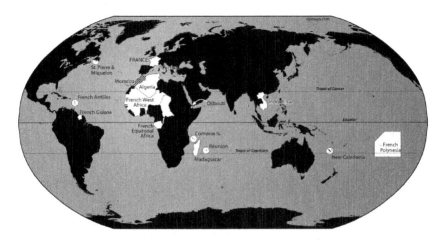

Map 1.1. The French empire, c. 1914

government. One Malagasy Christian told Julia that the people worked for Delmont because "like cattle, [we] go where we are led when we are told it is for the government."[2] The administrator was disgusted by the missionary's presumptuousness. He penned a letter to his superior pointing out not only that Delmont had unlawfully exploited these laborers but that the missionary had not even received official permission to build the church in the first place.

Julia's troubles with Delmont did not end there. He accused the priest of stealing a pile of telegraph poles—property of the French colonial government—to use in the construction of a chapel.[3] This crime carried with it symbolic, as well as practical, significance: not just a means of colonial communication and control, telegraph poles were emblems of French progress and technology. Making matters worse, Delmont perpetrated the crime in order to build what many French republicans in 1899 saw as a temple to clericalism and superstition. The missionary, on the other hand, believed he had put the wood to excellent use, erecting a building where France could pursue the one true *mission civilisatrice*—or "civilizing mission"—by converting one soul at a time.

By Christmas of 1899—just a month after Julia had started his investigation—relations between the mission and the colonial administration, the two most powerful French influences in the region, had broken down. This dispute in a relatively remote corner of Madagascar eventually involved both the governor-general of the colony and the regional bishop. Julia's immediate superior expressed exasperation to Governor-General Joseph Gallieni, writing that he, too, had tried to find common ground with the Jesuits, though they "clearly indicated their desire to inflame the questions I wanted to conclude amicably."[4] Nor could he stop Julia from threatening the mission. Gallieni ordered Julia not to pursue any charges against the priest and asked the bishop to rein in Delmont. After three months of negotiations and heated exchanges, Julia and Delmont finally made peace. The missionary wrote the administrator a conciliatory letter, praising him and offering to work with him. "And why should it be otherwise?" Père Delmont asked. "Are we not Frenchmen working for the greater good of our common mother, dear France? *Vive, vive, vive la France!!!*"[5]

The archives of French colonialism are filled with stories of disagreement, conflict, and reconciliation like these exchanges between Monsieur Julia and Père Delmont. From 1880 to 1914, the French empire was a place of many uneasy relationships, not just between Europeans and indigenous populations. As this incident in Madagascar shows, French men and women—officials, merchants, colonists, officers, soldiers, and travelers—were regularly divided both on basic questions of colonial policy and on issues of national allegiance and patriotism. No altercations were more heated (nor ideologies more divergent) than those between Catholic missionaries and their critics. In the case of Julia and Delmont, from what seem to have been minor disagreements over law, labor, and lumber emerged starkly different views of communication, civilization, and ultimately colonialism.

In his peacemaking letter, the missionary posed a rhetorical question that this book will explore in detail: between 1880 and 1914, were all Frenchmen in the colonies working for a "common mother" called France? If so, was the *mère-patrie* a religious Catholic or a secular republican? Did France want to convert pagans to the glory of Jesus Christ or to the possibilities of technology and rational economics? And what of France's colonial populations: were converted indigenous Christians—such as the ones Delmont tried to defend in court—friends or foes of the French colonial administration? When Delmont cheered, "*Vive la France!*" just *which* France—and *whose* France—did he have in mind? The answers that men and women, in both France and the empire, supplied to these questions had significance well beyond the colonial world, reflecting broader attitudes about France's political and cultural heritage and its moral role in world affairs.

This book tells the story of how French people with markedly different backgrounds, moral codes, and political perspectives shaped colonial and national politics between 1880 and 1914, the most intense period of colonial expansion in French history. The anger and animosity felt by the likes of Julia and Delmont resulted from a great paradox at the heart of French colonialism during the early Third Republic. Starting in the 1880s, the colonial lobby—a rather haphazard group of republican politicians, businessmen, adventurers, and scholars—invoked a *mission civilisatrice* as a rallying cry to motivate an ambivalent nation to acquire and invest in overseas possessions.[6] A promise to reform, educate, and improve the livelihoods of France's new colonial populations, the civilizing mission embodied the spirit of the French Revolution and the specifically rational, secular ideals of the Enlightenment. But as the boundaries of the empire expanded, few politicians or colonial lobbyists were willing to pay (or ask taxpayers to pay) for the programs they promised. Instead, they regularly turned to the most convenient and inexpensive alternative to implement their programs: Catholic missions.

While in some ways logical, the decision to rely on Catholic missionaries was politically and ideologically fraught for everyone involved. The new interest in colonial conquest coincided exactly with the climax of republican anticlericalism in France. Many republicans who tirelessly sought the eradication of all Catholic influence at home found themselves depending on missionary expertise to facilitate—and even justify—their rule abroad. For their part, most missionaries were less than enthusiastic about their new partnership, as well. But a variety of factors motivated leaders of the divided groups to nurture an informal, if rocky, entente. Thus, from the 1880s to the First World War, the daily operation of the so-called republican civilizing mission in the French empire was regularly carried out by the republic's sworn "enemies"—Catholic religious workers—many of whom not only had serious reservations about colonialism but also were openly hostile to republicanism.

Administrators concerned with political harmony in the possessions tried to repress their distrust of all things Catholic by repeating a popular republican dictum of the day: "Anticlericalism is not an item for export." Officials in Paris and high-ranking administrators abroad concealed, either willingly or under orders, any misgivings they might have had about Catholic workers. But, as the following chapters will show, such official repression of anticlericalism was not always effective, especially among lower-ranking administrators in the field, as in the case of M. Julia. Nor could the official position effectively control the many "nonofficial" or "third-party" critics of the Catholic missions, such as journalists, Freemason and radical colonists, and Protestant missionaries. A similar dynamic governed missionary behavior: bishops and missionary superiors regularly instructed their workers to stay clear of the administration altogether. As Père Delmont deftly exemplifies, however, many religious workers in the field still protested policies and undermined colonial authorities by writing inflammatory letters, newspaper articles, and books, and by organizing demonstrations. Such sparring reveals the competing concerns of distinct groups of Frenchmen who struggled for influence and moral authority over the same colonial populations.

While upper echelons of both the administration and the mission hierarchies strove to keep relations amicable despite long-standing differences, the lines from an old missionary song—"When a Frenchmen in a foreign land sees a Frenchmen, he feels his heart beat"—often rang flat in the early decades of the Third Republic.[7] Indeed, as this book will show, distrust and disagreement led Frenchmen to level the most serious of charges at one another—accusations that included slave trading, sexual impropriety, treason, murder, and the physical destruction of entire societies. The divergent, often antithetical motivations of missionaries and their critics led to heated— even violent—disagreements over the nature of France's relationship to the world, the form colonialism would take, and the very meaning of French civilization. In the first thirty years of its republican incarnation, the French empire was a place of unexpectedly deep divisions.

The friction between missionaries and republicans can only be fully appreciated against the backdrop of the long history of religious conflict in modern France. Starting in the eighteenth century, reformers scornful of the power and wealth of the monarchy and the Catholic Church imagined a society freed from the yoke of these conservative institutions. They aimed to build a new society governed by liberty and based on secular moral codes, rituals, and icons. While they wanted their new nation to have a culture all its own, ironically many secularists impressed by the pomp, ceremony, and liturgy that Catholicism offered turned to religious practices for inspiration.

In the wake of the French Revolution, early incarnations of a republican vision took shape with remarkable speed.[8] In terms of political legitimacy, the power of the people replaced divine right. National holidays, such as the Fête de la Fédération, competed with Christian holy days. In one of the more famous images of the revolutionary era, the Declaration of the Rights of Man appeared as new commandments, inscribed on two great stone tablets, and trumpeted by an angel of reason. Revolutionaries converted the church of Sainte-Geneviève in Paris into the Panthéon, which would act as a secular shrine of the nation. In its hallowed crypt, secular France would honor its own prophets, heroes, and martyrs. The republic that the Revolution had brought to life was France's messiah; accordingly, calendars started anew at Year I.

The republican desire to create a secular nation that emulated Catholic practices was born not of admiration but of resentment and often hatred of everything the Church stood for. The historian Owen Chadwick tells how one such critic dreamed of strangling the king with the intestines of the last cleric.[9] While such violent fantasies were perhaps not the norm, virulent republican opposition did not wane after the era of revolution. The process of sanctifying republican ideals lasted for more than a century and encountered countless bumps along the way.[10] In place of the Father, Son, and Holy Spirit, republicans offered the promise of liberty, equality, and fraternity. Even when not in power, republicans intervened in religious education, encouraging students—as one midcentury political cartoon showed—to memorize Voltaire instead of the catechism.[11]

For modernizing republicans, the Church opposed everything they cherished, most notably Progress itself. Standing before the legislative assembly in 1849, Victor Hugo condemned the Catholic Church for this very reason: "Every step made by the European mind has been made in spite of it," he insisted. "Its history is written in the annals of human progress, but it is written on the reverse side." The more religious corners of the audience groaned with astonishment.[12] Nonetheless, Hugo's assessment was not completely unreasonable; fifteen years after the speech, the papal *Syllabus of Errors* denounced much that the modern world had to offer, including liberalism.

By the second half of the century, Catholicism had become the largest front in a Franco-French war. Struggles between Catholics and secularists came to the fore of French politics from the beginning of the Third Republic. The very concept of "anticlericalism" was an invention of the 1870s—an indication of how politicians considered the Church to be their main political, social, and cultural adversary.[13] Republican rhetoric shifted gears, accelerating from contempt and critique to all-out battle, gaining venom and vitriol. In 1877, Léon Gambetta, a towering figure in the founding of the Third Republic, changed the nature of the debate by thundering, "Clericalism—there is the enemy!" before the National Assembly. Many historians suggest that Gambetta's anticlericalism had more to do with unifying republicans against a common foe than with attacking the Church. But while divisions in town squares may have been characterized more by "second-rate insults" than by serious ideological debate, the result of Gambetta's war cry was to turn Frenchmen against one another for decades to come.[14]

Gambetta's call signaled the beginning of what James McMillan has termed a French Kulturkampf. Two Frances—one religious, one republican—coexisted in the same country, under the same law, but subscribed to significantly different values.[15] The list of offenses that republicans leveled at clerics was long, often colorful, and severe. They considered clerics to be anti-individual, antiliberal, superstitious, and irrational. *Religieux* were said to be products of the Middle Ages, servants of the Inquisition, slavers and torturers who lived in a dark and distant past and answered to a foreign prince at the Vatican. As ultramontanists, they were said to be traitors incapable of patriotism, offering their allegiance only to the pope. Republican criticism grew even more intense when Alfred Dreyfus, a Jewish captain in the French army, was wrongfully accused of espionage in 1894, pushing France to the brink of civil war. The ensuing "affair" drove many republicans to blame the retrograde institutions of the ancien régime—the army and the Church—for being out of step with the ideals of the modern republican nation. The polemics of the Dreyfus affair emboldened radical republicans to demand the complete separation of Church and state in 1905, a year before Dreyfus was fully exonerated.

Many Catholics, particularly clerics, were no more charitable in their assessment of republicanism. From the age of revolution forward, antirepublican Catholic commentators argued that liberal gains were a sign of France's fall from grace. France's defeat in the Franco-Prussian war in 1870 and the ensuing violence of the Paris Commune were proof that God was punishing the nation for its rampant immorality. With the founding of the Third Republic, Catholics struck back at the attacks of Gambetta and his supporters, driving the political wedge between the two camps even deeper. Priests denounced republicans as godless sinners who served Satan by sullying France's traditional role as "the eldest daughter" of the Catholic Church.

During the years of the Dreyfus affair, right-wing polemicists, of whom Édouard Drumont is only the most notorious, often stooped to xenophobia and racism, accusing the republican left of cowering to its own foreign influences, namely, Freemasonry and a manipulative international Jewish elite. The growing wave of reaction, however, proved to be more a symptom of political desperation than a sign of a strengthening ideological movement.

By the late 1870s, moderate republicans had won legislative power and launched an offensive to dismantle the Church's hold on the nation. To help solidify their gains, republicans replaced the Virgin Mary with Marianne, secular France's beloved symbol, and started to populate every village and government building with statues of republican saints. No battleground was more pivotal than education; and creating primary schools that were compulsory, secular, and universal became *the* republican priority. In the early 1880s, under the leadership of Jules Ferry, the government forced religious workers out of public schools and expelled the Jesuits—as well as more than five thousand teachers from other male orders—from France.[16] It was a first step in a project to achieve what Pierre Chevalier calls "the separation of Church and school."[17]

The goal of republican education policy was not to put teaching orders out of business altogether, a move that many feared would lead to serious social unrest. Rather, republicans embraced a policy of *laïcité*—the desire to remove all symbols of and references to religion from public education, and to teach moral lessons based entirely on secular values to the nation's future citizens. More than a question of political preference, Ferry deemed *l'école laïque* to be a necessary condition of the republic's survival.[18] It was central to the republican goal of conquering the French countryside. Public schools would teach peasants to speak proper French and to appreciate the political ideals necessary for citizenship. History and science would cleanse children of the superstitions of their parents and village priest. Liberating France from the outdated hierarchy and dogma of the Catholic Church was an essential component of the government's civilizing process. For more radical republicans, a degree of comfort came only in 1905 when the Church was formally separated from the state. Only then did it seem that secular republican civilization had proved victorious in the war of the two Frances.

For the republican faithful, the desire to see secular civilization trammel the regressive practices of Catholicism was not simply a domestic goal; civilization belonged everywhere and to all mankind. Just as pious men and women believed God had chosen France to deliver Catholicism to the world, ardent republicans considered their own liberal ideas to be the nation's gift to humanity. Republican values were every bit as universal—or so their sponsors claimed (regularly turning a blind eye to the women and non-Europeans excluded from its most basic promises)—as faith or salvation. And, like their Christian forebears, these values were eminently exportable. Spreading them became the central tenet of the ideology behind republican colonialism.

By the 1880s, many republicans saw colonialism as an important yardstick (along with weakening the Church) of their political success. What France accomplished abroad reflected the nation's potential at home. "The conservation of the colonies," Alexis de Tocqueville had written in the 1840s, "is necessary to the strength and greatness of France."[19] This line of reasoning gained adherents after the Prussian defeat of 1870 and the subsequent loss of Alsace and Lorraine. Eager to rebuild French prestige, pro-colonial republicans argued that imperial expansion would make or break France.[20] "It is through expansion, through influencing the outside world," Gambetta said, "that nations persist and last."[21] In 1882, Paul Leroy-Beaulieu, a leading colonialist commentator of his day, wrote that success in the colonies was "for France a question of life or death." Should it fail, he prophesied, France would be as insignificant in European affairs as Romania or Greece.[22]

But not all republicans, nor all Frenchmen, were so sure. Many on the left saw colonies as a waste of money and effort that distracted attention from pressing social issues at home. In the early 1880s, a republican deputy in the Assembly shouted that colonies were "a hallucination, a deceptive, perilous dream" that heaped an unnecessary burden on the nation.[23] Conservatives concurred, though for very different reasons. They deemed strength on the continent—including the recovery of Alsace and Lorraine, and facing down British and German industrial might—to be the best recipe for national rejuvenation.

To persuade these critics, colonialists pointed to the benefits of developing French industry and commerce overseas. The bible of French colonialism was Leroy-Beaulieu's *De la colonisation chez les peuples modernes*, first published in 1874. Leroy-Beaulieu, who drew on John Stuart Mill's *Principles of Political Economy*, argued that colonization was an inevitable by-product of economic, political, and cultural development.[24] "Savages and barbarians emigrate sometimes," Leroy-Beaulieu wrote, but "only civilized people colonize."[25] France needed colonies, he continued, both as economic and demographic outlets for expanding markets (which would in turn make France competitive with its continental rivals) and as destinations to which excess capital and labor could emigrate (to help ease social tensions at home). Leroy-Beaulieu's work had a deep impact on political debate. It was the sort of background reading that led Jules Ferry to proclaim, "Colonial politics is the daughter of industrial politics."[26]

Talk of industrial politics might have convinced a few capitalists' minds, but it captured no one's imagination. In 1889, colonialists met at the Universal Exposition in Paris to discuss how best to inspire an apathetic nation to adopt a vigorous imperial policy. In addition to educating the public about colonialism's political and economic benefits, the colonial lobby determined to appeal to Frenchmen's love of country and their belief in the value of spreading civilization.[27] They adopted the rhetoric Ferry had used for almost a decade: as a "superior race," France had a right to conquer "inferior races" because it had a *duty* to civilize them.[28] Ferry's somewhat awkward equation, promoted by the colonial lobby, formed the basis of the republican civilizing mission.[29] Spreading republican ideals, culture, know-how, and technology was inseparable from colonialism itself; putting "uncivilized" regions of the world on the road to progress was, according to colonialists, France's chief goal.[30] Beneficiaries of French science, reason, business, and politics, the new possessions would be what Tocqueville had called "monuments to the glory of our fatherland."[31]

The appeal to civilization was politically expedient in the 1880s for it provided both a moral justification of and a patriotic motivation for expansionism. It was also a familiar concept. With its origins in the eighteenth century, the idea of civilization had influenced republican social programs throughout the nineteenth.[32] By the founding of the Third Republic, according to Eugen Weber's famous assessment, republicans viewed the process of forging a new nation as "the civilization of the French by urban France."[33] The concept would be no less important to the forging of a new empire.[34] The colonial civilizing mission promised to abolish slavery, to advance humanity through education, to reform immoral cultural practices, to stamp out superstition, and to equip colonial societies with political and economic institutions and laws.[35] Pro-colonial politicians and writers were less forthcoming about specific ways of implementing their mission, that task being ultimately left to administrators in the field.[36] But that made it no less important: for many, the depth of the nation's republican roots would be best measured by the successes of the civilizing mission.

Republicans were by no means alone in their desire to export French values around the globe. Throughout the long nineteenth century, France led the world in the production of Catholic missionaries. Century's end was the golden age of the missions, when two-thirds of the approximately 14,000 priests working outside of Europe were French.[37] These priests were joined by other French *religieux*, such as teaching brothers and sisters, bringing the total number of Catholic religious workers abroad to approximately 58,000 in 1900, according to one missionary estimate.[38] Assisting in the French effort were many thousands of indigenous priests, brothers, and sisters. This considerable undertaking was supported by more than a million French men, women, and children who, according to the rules of subscription to missionary organizations, donated money and prayers to religious workers around the world. With networks of churches, schools, orphanages, leper colonies, and hospitals, Catholic missions were engaged in one of the single largest private French endeavors outside of Europe.

Missionaries worked and lived side by side with large groups of indigenous people, typically building far closer relationships with local peoples than administrators, merchants, or colonists did. It was common for individual missionaries to work in a single town or region for years and even decades, becoming fluent in local languages and customs, and immersed in politics. To millions of converts worldwide, missionaries were confidants, teachers, doctors, and nurses. They offered spiritual guidance and participated in the rituals that helped define communities, such as baptisms, marriages, deaths, and funerals. And they were often leaders in their communities, acting as advisers and advocates.

Not all missionary work, of course, was benevolent. Some missionaries—as later chapters will make clear—dominated their neophytes under what can be best described as a regime of terror, resorting to intimidation, violence, and even slavery to defend their local power. Missionaries' mere presence in a community often led to devastating social unrest, as conversions could turn neighbors against one another and split villages and towns. Local political authorities regularly felt threatened by the relative wealth and power of the missions and responded by violently attacking their Christian converts. In Indochina, for example, conflict between Christian and non-Christian villages cost 40,000 lives in the 1880s alone.[39] Whether loved and respected or detested and targeted, French missionaries were at the forefront of their nation's encounter with the world. Weighing the supposed benefits of missionary work against its apparent drawbacks became one the most volatile political issues in the empire in the decades before the First World War.

Catholic missionary goals around the world often mirrored republican ones, but their motivations were drastically divergent. Like those of their secular compatriots, missionaries' agenda included working to educate converts, to reform "immoral" practices like bigamy and cannibalism, to end slavery, and to improve the spiritual and economic lots of the communities in which they worked. But collaboration with republican authorities was always complicated. Religious workers were traditionally driven neither by liberal ideals of progress nor, initially, even by a desire to spread civilization. Rather than prophets of revolutionary values, missionaries saw themselves as "soldiers of God"; instead of agents of colonial enterprises, they were "colonizers of souls."[40] Missionaries wanted first and foremost—not surprisingly—to save souls by converting people to Catholicism. In so doing, they carried on old Christian traditions that stood starkly at odds with the beliefs of their secular republican compatriots. Religious workers sought to expand the frontiers of Catholicism and establish the Church's hierarchy across the globe—an apocalyptic vision to many a devout secularist.

In view of their sheer numbers, organizational support, and the profound impact they had on indigenous communities, a history of the French empire without religious missionaries is akin to a history of the Great War without the trenches. And yet missionaries remain either ignored or greatly misunderstood in most histories of French colonialism. Despite a recent fascination with empire, historians have not addressed the many paradoxes of religious work in an era of republican anticlericalism, or the complex relations between missionaries and colonial regimes.[41] This trend is particularly striking in the work of many scholars influenced by the concept of cultural imperialism, who have portrayed missionaries as simply one of a litany of forces that helped establish a distinctly "modern," bourgeois form of European hegemony.[42] For such scholars, missionary sources are indistinguishable from other journals, novels, and reportage produced by lay Europeans, all of which reflect the dominant bourgeois interests that drove Europeans to categorize, understand, and ultimately control non-European societies.[43] As a result, French missionaries are regularly—and, considering the political context of the fin de siècle, ironically—lumped together with efforts to establish secular republican rule in possessions around the globe.[44]

A central contention of this book is that ignoring missionary work or conflating it with secular programs has resulted in an overly uniform, monolithic image of French power and colonial relations. For anticlerical republicans who worried about their own colonial authority, Catholic missionaries posed a considerable threat. Many argued that missionary work would not aid expansion but rather threatened to undermine it. Certainly, both missionaries and republicans sought "an appropriation of the world," but their aspirations for that world were in many ways antithetical.[45] More than simply differences of outlook, divisions among Frenchmen influenced not only the shape of colonial policies but also how colonialism was experienced. Indigenous populations understood and experienced colonial rule not as an undifferentiated force but as one filled with contradictions, uncertainties, and even overt discord. As the following chapters demonstrate, to consider religious missions as indistinguishable from colonial power is to ignore the deep fissures in the foundations of colonialism that indigenous societies exploited in their interaction with their European rulers.[46]

This story does not begin and end with missionaries. Rather, by focusing on Catholic evangelizing, it contends that missionaries are essential to understanding *republican* attitudes toward colonialism, as well. A number of studies have portrayed the French colonies as "laboratories of modernity" where scientists, architects, and theorists experimented with liberal projects of social change.[47] But, in practice, policies were far from systematic or scientific. From the 1880s to the First World War, administrators in the empire, who both followed orders from Paris and responded to events on the ground, were infrequently guided by ideology. No example makes this more apparent than the policy dealing with missionary work.

Regardless of the anticlerical tone of domestic politics, pro-colonial republicans quickly learned that France had a history of using Christian missions to further national interests abroad that could be traced as far back as Charlemagne's commitment to protect the Holy Lands. More recently, the Vatican granted Napoleon the role of protectorate of the missions under the Concordat of 1801. Virtually every nineteenth-century French government used the protectorate as a convenient moral and political justification of foreign policy. The Third Republic, despite its anticlericalism, was no exception: as the imperial race heated up in the second half of the nineteenth century, France's commitment to its Catholic missionaries became a key issue in international affairs. Merchants and businessmen often supported the protectorate, believing that official intervention on behalf of missionaries would open up new lands to French business and political interests. As a result, pro-colonial republicans who fought for legislation that would limit religious work at home found themselves arguing that missionary efforts abroad strengthened France's position in world affairs. Gambetta himself respected the long-standing "diplomatic traditions" in regions where France had a religious protectorate.

As the historian Pierre Guillen points out, for supporters of colonial expansion, any reason for French involvement in foreign affairs was a good reason. Thus, in 1876, Gambetta could announce apparently without irony that France must support its "Catholic clientele in the world"—the world, that is, outside of France.[48] The man who would thunder that clericalism was the enemy would add the caveat that "anticlericalism was not an item for export." In the mid-1880s, the equally anticlerical Jules Ferry argued, with his mind on Indochina, that the protectorate of the Catholics "was a foot that we must keep in the affairs of the East, a serious tradition, a moral power." Ferry even called on France to expand its Catholic clientele by extending its protectorate to Egypt and Ethiopia in an attempt to counter British and Italian influence.[49] Some of the most avid cleric baiters apparently saw no hypocrisy in voicing their devotion to the protectorate of the missions if it served the imperial needs of the day.

Despite the certainty with which Gambetta and Ferry spoke, attitudes of republican politicians in Paris toward missionaries were as divided as republican support for the colonies. In fact, imperialism forged strange political alliances in the 1880s, as no single party claimed a policy of expansion as its own.[50] More fervently anticlerical deputies and commentators condemned what they considered the "clerical spirit" at the Quai d'Orsay, France's Ministry of Foreign Affairs.[51] It was not a hard accusation to make: in the first decades of the Third Republic, the Quai d'Orsay did not simply tolerate Catholic projects; it actively funded them. The Quai d'Orsay regularly paid for missionary travel to and from the colonies, particularly for teachers and nursing sisters, and helped finance missionary schools, orphanages, leper colonies, and hospitals around the globe. Such subsidies were meant to underwrite humanitarian services, not evangelizing. But officials certainly knew that, for missionaries, the two were never separated.

Facing staunch criticism, the foreign ministry steadfastly defended the logic of its position. From a political standpoint, supporting missionaries avoided unnecessary conflict, not only with the large indigenous Christian populations in the empire but with the Vatican, as well. It also placated the republic's military, as many officers imagined their own work abroad to be historically and ideologically linked with the Church's overseas missions.

The protectorate also had undeniable economic advantages: missionaries taught French, making commercial interactions easier and limiting the influence of the English. The Quai d'Orsay believed the missions spread French influence not only in the empire but also in other regions of the world. For example, the Quai d'Orsay supported the missions in the Ottoman Empire, one of the most developed Catholic enterprises in the nineteenth century, as key tools for spreading French influence there. The investment paid off: the presence of 150 French Jesuit schools in Syria and Lebanon helped justify the French mandate after the First World War.[52] Best of all, missionaries worked almost for free. In 1896, Foreign Minister Gabriel Hanotaux restated what others had said for at least a decade: to replace missionary workers around the world with lay staffs would come at a price the state could little afford to pay.[53] For the foreign ministry, anticlericalism was not for export in large part because the tariff was far too high.

But for critics of religious proselytizing, the Quai d'Orsay's rationale made no sense. In their minds, the republic could ill afford *not* to shut down the Catholic missions. While anticlerical republicans might have welcomed the exodus of religious Catholics from French soil, a wide range of politicians, journalists, and colonists argued that, just as clerics endangered the authority and prestige of metropolitan France, missionaries in the possessions threatened republican colonial rule. Establishing and maintaining control in the colonies, these critics insisted, was already difficult enough without having to worry about plots and conspiracies devised by antirepublican missionaries and their crowds of converts. Echoing other colonial anxieties, republican criticism of missionaries often drew on racial imagery. Across the empire, critics insisted that missionaries were more "savage" and "barbaric" than even the most uncivilized indigenous populations. In retort, Catholic missionaries often vaunted their converts' behavior as far more civilized than that of the radical, Freemason, and Protestant riffraff that peopled the empire.

More than mere differences of opinion, this book argues that the criticisms and condemnations that shaped much of the interaction between missionaries and their detractors are essential to understanding the formation of colonial policies. As missionaries and anticlericals coexisted in the possessions, the views and projects of each shaped and informed the other. Republican critics of religious workers regularly defined their own goals largely in opposition to missionary work. In response, the missions often challenged the morality and practical benefits of certain republican proposals. Equipped with a language of discord dating back at least to the French Revolution and given new vitality during the Dreyfus affair, missionaries and republicans continually assessed the moral and political authority of their adversaries' actions. Colonial administrations were often in the middle, playing the role of mediator: holding to the policy of religious neutrality, officials encouraged missionaries and their critics to respect one another, intervening only in the most serious affairs.

Colonial administrators rarely escaped these conflicts unscathed. Finding it impossible to enter the fray without becoming targets of criticism themselves, administrators often ended up having to defend their policies to their own colonists. For example, critics of the missions regularly demanded to know why laws implemented to limit Catholic projects in France were not applied to the colonies, as well—a complaint aimed at the administration more than the missions. And when criticism from Protestants or radicals pushed colonial officials to take steps to weaken the missions, missionaries demanded to know why the administration was undermining the civilizing work—being carried out by religious workers—at the heart of the government's own colonial rhetoric. Far from being local complaints, such criticisms of the colonial administration were regularly picked up in the metropolitan press, spurring angry letters to editors and becoming fodder for speeches on both sides of the political aisle.

This uncomfortable symbiosis—between missions, their critics, and administrators in the middle—reveals the extent to which colonizing and civilizing were far more convoluted than a simple application of universal truths and ideological goals. For example, when radical critics of the missions called for the opening of secular schools in places like Indochina and Polynesia in the early 1900s, they were not only expressing their age-old commitment to *laïcité* and spreading republican *civilisation*. The call for secular schools was also a direct critique of missionaries and the religious education they offered. Critics railed that corrupt missionaries, concerned wholly with catechism and personal power, failed on every level—to form colonial citizens, to spread French authority, and even to teach their students French. Critics insisted on more secular schools not only as a means of educating children but also as a way to undermine the worrisome power of the missions.

This book argues, therefore, that the main impetus for developing republican civilizing programs was neither a purely liberal ideological nor a "humanitarian" one. Rather, civilizing policies were commonly wrought in the fires of religious resentment and political confrontation. Clashes between missionaries and their critics abroad spurred republican politicians in Paris to call for policies to defeat the missions. Anticlerical republicans in the National Assembly, for example, jumped at the opportunity to denounce publicly the alleged missionary dictatorship over the inhabitants of the Gambier Islands in Polynesia, or to excoriate missionaries in Vietnam for teaching their students Latin but not French. Such invective lent further legitimacy to the republican tirade against the Church in France. Radical politicians could use accusations of missionary wrongdoing not simply as an opportunity to reflect on the state of colonial policies but also as a chance to wax about morality, progress, and other liberal concerns.

Starting in the 1900s, with the polarization of French domestic politics during the Dreyfus affair, attacks on the missions pushed the colonial and foreign ministries to give ground on their "anticlericalism is not for export" policy. Support of missionary endeavors gave way to new, increasingly restrictive policies (such as ending colonial subventions for missionary schools or eliminating sisters from the ranks of nurses in colonial hospitals). But most colonial administrators still refused a full-scale assault: missions in many parts of the empire, after all, enjoyed the support of thousands, sometimes tens of thousands, of followers—a portion of local populations they did not want to alienate. Officials and politicians, therefore, often responded to the outcry against the missions by demanding better funding for state-run schools and health care programs—two fields missionaries traditionally dominated. Republicans took steps not to outlaw missionaries but to minimize the empire's reliance on them by creating more official or overtly republican programs to provide services alongside the missions. In this way, the controversy over Catholic missionaries' presence in the empire actually precipitated republicans' commitment to civilize on their own secular terms.

By examining the array of factors that shaped the civilizing mission, this book argues that what is often called French "colonial ideology"—the ideas behind, motivations for, and implementation of programs designed to reform and develop colonial societies—was in fact much less an extension of revolutionary republican values than a set of individual projects defined by degrees of dissent, debate, competition, and collaboration between people both at home and abroad. Differences of opinion over strategies of colonizing—in the Delmont-Julia case, whether poles should be used for a chapel or a telegraph system and whether labor should be used to build a church or a colony—forced administrators, missionaries, colonists, local inhabitants, and others to present, critique, and defend plans for expansion and control. Thus a multiplicity of voices and influences—not a single set of political ideals—shaped French rule. The civilizing policies ultimately adopted were neither strictly republican nor Catholic. Instead, they were shaped by the anxieties and aspirations of a variety of French men and women faced with the challenge of living with one another and ruling large indigenous populations.

The missionary movement also played a vital role in shaping popular perceptions of the empire at home. As the century came to a close, the republican impulse to eradicate clerical influence increased rather than diminished, forcing all Catholic organizations to respond to the radicalization of France's political leadership. The campaign against Catholic organizations culminated in three particularly devastating laws. First, the 1901 Law on Associations shut down dozens of religious organizations, and a 1904 law prohibited *religieux* from teaching in France. These laws left thousands of priests and nuns without work or homes and drove some 30,000 into exile abroad.[54] Then, in 1905, a parliament dominated by radical republicans definitively separated Church and state. An array of historians has examined the political divide between reactionary Catholics and anticlerical republicans at this time.[55] But the colonial context adds a new dimension to the study of this period that witnessed both the political triumph of secular republicanism and a renaissance of Catholic spirituality. The combined effects of colonial divisions and a polarized political climate pushed the major French missionary organizations to redefine their long-standing traditions and motivations or else face legislation that would put an end to their work.[56]

With an increasingly loud call to outlaw Catholic religious work in the empire, missionaries could no longer afford to remain neutral in matters of colonial politics. At stake was far more than the careers of thousands of missionaries. Religious workers considered themselves to be modern-day apostles. In the tradition of Saint Paul, missionaries believed they proved the vitality of Jesus' church on earth by spreading "truth"; thus they interpreted any threat to their work as an attack on Catholicism itself.[57] The response of missionaries to the challenges of anticlericalism and imperialism was in some ways unexpected in this era of discord. Under the guidance of the Oeuvre de la propagation de la foi, France's leading missionary organization, the movement rewrote its rhetoric and redefined its goals to coincide more closely with the republican colonial project.

In a massive campaign to reshape the image of the movement, organizations produced travelogues, histories, and journals, and sponsored public ceremonies and exhibitions that showed Catholic missions committed to serving republican projects. Spreading civilization, which missionaries had long considered simply a fortunate by-product of evangelizing, came to the fore in Catholic propaganda as the movement's chief goal. From the 1890s forward, missionary publications increasingly chronicled the lives and tribulations of missionaries committed not only to God but also to the *patrie* and a specifically French civilizing mission. Unlike the antirepublicanism and anti-Semitism of reactionary Catholics in France, missionaries ultimately helped shape the language of *ralliement*—the pope's call to France's Catholics to accept the nation—as they moved into national politics by embracing the cause of colonialism.

The rapid metamorphosis of a centuries-old movement traditionally concerned only with questions of conversion, spirituality, and faith reveals the power of the colonial experience to change even the most intractable of European institutions. As many of the debates in the following chapters will reveal, patriotism became a potent force in the colonies. Accusations that missionaries were traitors to France often inspired long and emotional defenses. Whether or not their patriotism was genuine, missionaries quickly realized that colonialism was a reality, and that administrators had the power either to aid greatly the cause of evangelizing or to put an end to it entirely. Suspicion over missionaries' allegiance to the nation, therefore, was one of the driving forces behind the effort to redefine religious work to coincide with the official effort. The retooling of the missionary movement into a colonizing, as well as evangelizing, force reverberated well beyond the missions. By addressing new realities, the movement brought hundreds of thousands of its supporters in France into colonial politics, as well.

The huge community of Catholics represented an important political body in fin de siècle France. Historians of France have long argued that the empire never had a large popular following. But when measuring attitudes toward empire, historians have ignored how missionary supporters viewed France's interaction with the world, opting instead to focus solely on popular secular and official republican representations.[58] Pious supporters of Catholic missionaries represent a significant, unexplored dimension of how Frenchmen understood their empire as well as their *mère-patrie*. From the early nineteenth century, readers of missionary journals, annuals, and books understood the non-European world as a place to be evangelized. As missionaries redefined their role within the new colonial order, supporters at home saw France's place in the world in a new light.

With the shift of focus from evangelizing to civilizing, missionary publications became more overtly patriotic, increasingly extolling the links between the greatness of God and the glory of France. Readers were encouraged to admire missionaries as both Christian and national heroes. The shift in missionary rhetoric also included a more blatantly racial conceptualization of evangelizing. For much of the nineteenth century, missionaries associated "savagery" primarily with "paganism." Nonbelievers could be "saved" from their debauched ways through conversion to the One True Religion and the moral transformation that followed. But with the introduction of civilizing as a central part of their vocation, missionaries increasingly portrayed savage behavior as being linked to culturally and racially determined practices, not simply to a lack of faith. As a result, readers of missionary publications began to see and understand the empire as a place in need of both evangelization and civilization. Now readers learned that many of the world's populations needed Christ to overcome not only their paganism but also their cultural and racial inferiorities. The redefinition of missionary goals, therefore, represented a significant shift in the popular perception of the empire for a large number of French men, women, and children.

In August 1914, when France went to war, the cacophonous wrangling of the Catholic right and the republican left was overwhelmed, if not entirely silenced, by the thunder of artillery. Historians still debate the sincerity of the *union sacrée*—the unspoken agreement between longtime political foes to work together for the war effort—with some casting doubt on whether animosities were truly put aside for the greater good of the nation.[59] But there is reason to believe that the *union* in the colonies was more genuine. Missionaries working abroad volunteered to return to France to work as chaplains or translators for colonial troops—a move welcomed by many government officials. A good many missionaries paid for their new commitment to the *patrie* with their lives. In the years before the digging of trenches on the western front, missionaries had faced an organized, outspoken, and empowered opposition calling for their demise. During the war—and certainly in its aftermath—missionary allegiance to the colonial effort and France was less often questioned.[60]

Conflicts between missionaries and their critics continued into the 1920s and beyond. But the features that made for such intense conflict between 1880 and 1914—republican anticlericalism, the heated polemics of the Dreyfus affair, the financial and political pressures of a vigorous republican policy of expansion, and the climax of the Catholic missionary movement—changed significantly after the war. The fact that many soldiers turned to religion to understand and cope with the destructiveness of the war helped pave the way for more peaceful relations between the Church and the republic.[61] In the interwar years, debates over missionaries continued, but in a different key, lacking much of the intensity of the prewar period and revolving around new issues and concerns, such as the rise of nationalist and anticolonial movements.

While the point of departure is discord, this story ultimately explores one venue—the empire—where, in an age of division and polemic, Frenchmen chose reconciliation and cooperation, if not mutual admiration. Despite vocal criticism from many anticlerical republicans, the colonial administration ultimately defended the presence of Catholic missionaries abroad. And, as a result of the retooling of the missions' chief goals, by the First World War, there was a considerable portion of the French population committed to both Catholicism and the republic's colonial cause. Historians have long focused on how the polemics of domestic politics locked Catholics and republicans in an intractable confrontation. But, by looking to the empire, a new picture emerges. The challenges of colonial expansion in the years 1880 to 1914 reveal not how solid but rather how malleable and fragmented Catholic and republican ideologies really were. Though rife with dissension and aggravation, the experience of colonialism forced French men and women to redefine their nation's moral goals and objectives in ways that helped bridge the most important political and cultural divisions in France—divisions that had plagued French society since 1789.

Finally, this book reconsiders the formation of the French nation within an international context. Since the publication of Eugen Weber's *Peasants into Frenchmen*, studies of how the French came to define their nation in the nineteenth century have been firmly rooted in the soil of metropolitan France. Weber has inspired endless debate and a library of studies on the effects and limits of the modernization of a rural country into a polity of cosmopolitan sophistication.[62] Complementing a body of literature that has tried to relocate the locus of debate, this study insists that French identity was shaped not only by experiences at home but also in a variety of locations where men and women defined their moral and political positions within an international and often contentious context.[63] Conflict over colonial policy and the meaning of civilization was ultimately not only about buttressing power over indigenous populations; it was also an exercise in defining the values of the *patrie*, how Frenchmen were to think and behave—in short, what it *meant* to be French. The process of forging the French nation was limited by the vagaries, contradictions, and eccentricities of its citizens, but not by its European borders.

In order to capture the tone, complexity, and consequences of the controversy over missionary work, this book examines three colonial case studies, framed by two accounts of changing metropolitan views of Catholicism and empire. In addition to providing some background on the history of the Catholic missionary movement, chapter 1 sets the stage by exploring how drastically missionary and republican perspectives on colonialism diverged throughout much of the nineteenth century. Its central assertion is that, until the 1880s, missionaries rejected liberalism and nationalism and remained committed to Christian traditions that had informed their religious vocation for centuries, seeking personal redemption through hardship and even martyrdom, and pursuing the spiritual transformation of societies through evangelization.

From this overview, the study turns to three very different regions—Indochina, Polynesia (especially Tahiti and the Marquesas Islands), and Madagascar—that all witnessed serious conflicts over missionary work. These cases allow the opportunity to explore the varieties of contexts with a level of detail that would be impossible in a general study. Indochina, Polynesia, and Madagascar are in many ways obvious choices, as they represent the three possessions with the longest and richest traditions of Catholic evangelizing by French missionary societies. In the seventeenth century, Indochina was the destination of missionaries from the Société des missions étrangères de Paris, France's oldest and most respected missionary organization. In the same era, Lazarists, under the directorship of the famous French missionary Saint Vincent de Paul, ventured to Madagascar. Though a failure, the Lazarists' early attempt was followed by others until Jesuits established a permanent mission on the island in the mid–nineteenth century. Finally, starting in the 1830s, Polynesia—especially the Gambier Islands, Tahiti, and the Marquesas—was the destination of *religieux* from three French missions: the Congrégation des Sacrés Coeurs, the Marists, and the Soeurs de Saint Joseph de Cluny. The islands of the South Seas were a major front in the battle against Protestantism, as missionaries competed island by island to win converts to their faith.

By the 1880s, French missionary publications celebrated the long Catholic commitment to each of these regions and promoted the need to continue the work to win more souls, from either paganism or heresy. Missionaries did not turn away from any country where Christ was unknown, but no missions in the French empire enjoyed such a lauded position as those in Indochina,

Polynesia, and Madagascar. By the late nineteenth century, France's old colonies—such as Réunion, Guadeloupe and Martinique, and Guyana—were receiving far less attention in the missionary press, due largely to the fact that their era of evangelization had passed.[64] In Algeria, the Church was first and foremost a servant of the European community. Catholic missionary efforts across Islam had long been frustrated by what they considered the spiritual intractability of Muslims. These notions combined with concerns about social upheaval to discourage missionaries in Algeria from working extensively among the Arab Muslim population, though they did evangelize among Muslim Berbers.[65] And missionary work in France's newer possessions in West and Central Africa was still in an early state of development. The White Fathers, for example, founded in 1868 to evangelize across Africa, were just starting to move into the interior of the continent in the late 1890s.[66] Thus, when publications heralded the long commitment of French missionaries in the colonies, they naturally turned to their accomplishments in Indochina, Polynesia, and Madagascar.

These three were also among the most important possessions consolidated and developed as colonies during the early Third Republic: Indochina was integrated administratively in 1887, Tahiti (the center of French activity in Polynesia) was declared a colony in 1880, and Madagascar came under direct French control after 1895 when French troops took the island by force. The three also had political and strategic significance. French expansion in Indochina was key to the republican opportunists' colonial agenda, earning Jules Ferry the label *le Tonkinois* for his support of involvement in the region. Indochina was seen by many to be France's India, as well as a stepping-stone to China. Polynesia had long captured the popular imagination of the French public, thanks in large part to the writings of the philosophes and Pierre Loti. In addition to the appeal of the exotic, the islands were strategic ports in an expansive ocean crisscrossed by British and American ships. And in Madagascar, the military campaign of 1895, extensively reported in French newspapers, came at the height of both the Dreyfus affair and imperial competition with Britain. Across Europe, the success of France's "pacification" of the island would measure the republican regime's political weight.

These cases also provide a sense of the extraordinary variety of experiences within the French empire. Part II, on Indochina, focuses on missionary struggles with low-level administrators and radical Freemason colonists over the meaning of and strategies for spreading "French influence." Thus, chapters 2 and 3 show how slowly a civilizing program developed, changing from one concerned primarily with security to one inspired by ideological goals designed to assimilate the indigenous population. Part III considers the considerable challenges Frenchmen faced in trying to devise a civilizing mission in Polynesia, especially in Tahiti and the Marquesas. As chapter 4 reveals, the French administration's use of missionary sisters as teachers in the Marquesas and Society Islands exposed the gender dynamic of official projects to improve the morality and hygiene of islanders, particularly girls. Chapter 5 explores how the devastating depopulation that resulted from French colonialism in Polynesia became the focus of conflict between missionaries and the republican administration.

The final case examines the role of religion and nationality in the French conquest of Madagascar (1895–97). In the wake of the "pacification" of the island, conflict between French Catholics and British Protestants forced officials to define French nationality in terms of religion, bringing questions about colonial violence, liberty, and indigenous rights to the fore. In the midst of these debates, as chapter 6 shows, official France—which, in the case of Madagascar, was heavily represented by military officials—reevaluated the suitability of revolutionary republican ideals in a colonial context. Chapter 7 explores the international consequences of applying anticlerical metropolitan laws, such as the 1901 Law on Associations and the 1905 separation of Church and state, to the empire. The implications of exporting anticlericalism included empowering indigenous religious figures and organizations to an extent few colonial officials were willing to consider.

While Indochina, Polynesia, and Madagascar offer the most vibrant examples of colonial division, similar conflicts between missionaries and Freemasons, administrators, and Protestants could be found across the empire at this time. Whether missionaries strengthened or undermined French influence and whether missionary schools served colonialism were crucial questions in literally every possession acquired in the nineteenth century. In the 1880s and 1890s, Freemason attacks on missionaries like those in Indochina were also orchestrated in New Caledonia, Madagascar, and West Africa. Competition between British and French missionaries was endemic from West Africa to the New Hebrides. These other cases could offer this book more actors and further evidence but not a significantly different picture of discord in the empire. While Indochina, Polynesia, and Madagascar offer exceptionally rich and relevant stories of colonial discord, they were by no means atypical of relations in France's divided empire.

These cases also reveal the cast of republican characters who attacked the missions. This book does not pit the Third Republic against the Church; rather, it explores how a host of republican figures argued that missionaries were detrimental to French prestige and power. In Indochina, it was primarily vocal Freemasons and radical colonists who criticized missionary wrongdoing. In Polynesia, denunciations of missionary influence came largely from local colonial officials spurred on by the anticlerical tirades of the Dreyfus affair in distant France. In Madagascar, it was Protestants—both French and British—who made the most inflammatory accusations, charging that Catholic missionaries used violence and intimidation to force cowering local populations to accept their religion. These cases, therefore, offer the chance to see just how fragmented and diverse republican opinion about colonization and civilization was. They also provide insight into the various strategies that different missions used in deflecting criticism and proving their value to the colonial effort.

The final part of the book shifts from the colonies back to France to navigate how religious tensions at home, coupled with the divisive experiences in the colonies, changed the ways missionaries represented their work to their supporters. By looking at popular missionary journals, political pamphlets, and works of mission history from the 1890s to 1914, chapter 8 traces how conflicts between Catholics and anticlerical critics drove leaders of the missionary movement to redefine their vocation to dovetail with republican goals of colonizing and civilizing. The result was an imperial ideology defined exclusively by neither republicans nor missionaries but rather by a combination of two competing traditions faced with the tasks of justifying expansion and keeping control in France's overseas empire.

The Origins and Traditions of the Nineteenth-Century Missionary Movement

Oh Félix! Can you believe it . . . ! Martyrdom is here, at my door. A few hours more, and it is possible that I will be taken, that is to say, burned, massacred, torn into a thousand pieces. Ah! What a situation, brother! What joy, on the one hand; but also what sorrows, what tortures of the heart!

—Père Honoré Dupont, 1885

Et d'abord! La grande raison de cette vocation, c'est la foi!
—Père Augustin Aubry, 1888

In 1888, a Catholic missionary stationed in Kibanga, in the Upper Congo, wrote a letter to the superior general of his mission in Algiers. Père Guillemé's letter described the countryside in which he traveled—in this case, the region around Lake Tanzania—and recounted the tribulations of a lone European missionary evangelizing in a land far from home. As was common practice from the 1820s onward, the missionary's superior sent the letter on to the Oeuvre de la propagation de la foi (the Society for the Propagation of the Faith) in Lyon, a lay organization that raised money for Catholic missionary work overseas.[1] The directors at the Oeuvre liked the account enough to publish it in the organization's *Annales*. Within a few short months, the letter went from the African bush to the pages of one of France's leading religious publications, circulated to more than a million French supporters of the Catholic missionary movement.

In the missionary parlance of the day, Père Guillemé was a lone soldier of God who taught the lessons of Christianity, won souls to Catholicism, and cared for the sick, elderly, and dying. For Guillemé, Africa's heat, rugged terrain, "tigers," and other constant dangers mirrored the moral disorder of the continent's inhabitants. While dense forests and steep mountains tried the

Figure 1.1.   The cover of *Missions Catholiques*. The image of Jesus and his apostles illustrated the Oeuvre's desire to situate contemporary missionary work in biblical lore. (Reproduced with permission from the Oeuvres pontificales missionnaires—Coopération missionnaire, Lyon.)

missionary's physical stamina, his incorrigible African porters tried his patience. He encountered bands of Muslim pirates who proved themselves worthy of Allah's paradise, Guillemé noted, by robbing from pagans and cutting off Christians' heads.[2] The missionary's letter guided his European readers on a trip into a heart of darkness, where the treacherous grandeur of the countryside was matched only by the poverty of its miserable inhabitants. "Everywhere amid these black peoples with different morals and varied customs," he wrote, "I saw the devil across humanity, and the *bon Dieu* across creation."[3]

At one point in Guillemé's travels, some villagers assured him of their undivided attention if he could stop a troop of monkeys from stealing their crops. Confident of his failure, a small crowd gathered to watch the missionary look the fool. The priest had no choice but to accept the challenge, though he knew he put himself in a most tenuous position. Success would win him an audience; failure would bring him humiliation.[4] Guillemé took his rifle in hand and, with the laughter of the crowd ringing in his ears, approached a tree full of monkeys. "Believing themselves safe from my shot," he wrote, the monkeys "played, leaped about, made a thousand gymnastic turns."[5] Guillemé aimed at the largest and fired. The animal fell.

At the sight of the dead monkey, the villagers broke into an excited frenzy and pummeled the corpse, yelling things, according to Guillemé, that would have made a soldier blush. A villager explained that local folklore considered monkeys powerful creatures, for spears not only failed to reach their perches in tall trees but endangered bystanders on the ground as they fell back to earth. In the shade of a large tree with his promised audience, Guillemé used the death of the monkey to show the foolishness of popular beliefs. It was a lesson equally valuable for his readers at home. "Here as well as in Europe," he wrote, people understood the futility of superstitions but failed to abandon them.[6] For the moment, he was triumphant and basked in the opportunity to teach the Ten Commandments and the glory of God. What impact this conversation had, he dared not venture to guess. A tiny skirmish in an epic struggle had been won; but he knew his next challenge lay just beyond the next knoll.

Missionary letters, both published and private, along with a host of other sources, such as allocutions, reports, poems, and songs, offer a window into the traditions, motivations, beliefs, and sensibilities of Catholic missionaries abroad and their supporters at home. What is most striking about Guillemé's letter—and thousands of missionary publications like it—is its complete indifference to European politics and imperialism. Guillemé toured in 1888, at a time when European expansion into foreign lands advanced at a pace unprecedented since the founding of the New World. Three years earlier, European powers had convened in Berlin to lay down guidelines for the "scramble" to claim African possessions. To the west of where Guillemé traveled, King Leopold II of Belgium had recently founded the Congo Free State with the help of the journalist, explorer, and unabashed self-promoter Henry Morton Stanley. Together, the two men were making the Congo one of the most profitable and murderous African colonies.[7] To the east of Guillemé, Germany faced armed indigenous resistance, as well as competition from Britain, in its bid to secure the possession of Tanganyika. France, discouraged by competition in the region, had turned its attention to African acquisitions to the west and the north. Here was a missionary writing literally from the front lines of imperial expansion, yet Guillemé made no reference to conquest, colonialism, or even his nation of origin in the pages of his letter.

Historians of colonialism have overwhelmingly portrayed missionaries—Protestants as well as Catholics—as agents of national empires.[8] So how to explain Guillemé? He was certainly aware of the colonial storm closing in around him. Was this freewheeling evangelist living in denial or blissful ignorance? Or did he simply keep his true imperial motivations hidden? Despite the jingoism of the era, as a Catholic missionary, Guillemé did not describe himself as a patriot working for French colonial expansion. Guillemé—like many Catholic workers devoted to a vocation steeped in long and rich traditions—measured victories not in swaths of territory won for the *mère-patrie* but in a handful of potential converts gathered beneath an old shade tree. His eyes were trained not on the prize of territory or national glory but on souls saved by Christ.

Such motivations made missionaries no less culpable for the momentous, often devastating changes wrought by European intervention in non-European communities. Nor, however, did they make missionaries simple agents of their nation's empire. Rather, it is instructive to see late nineteenth-century missionaries as they saw themselves: as agents first and foremost of an empire of God. The history of this religious empire long preceded Europe's recent imperial expansion and shattered its boundaries. God's spiritual empire was not contiguous with France's worldly possessions, but spread over the globe. If missionaries shared with their lay compatriots certain ideas about France, patriotism, and race, their primary preoccupation was evangelizing and opening wide the reach of Christianity—a point often too quickly brushed over by contemporary scholars.

Guillemé's story offers a snapshot of relative peace before a momentous collision of traditions, not only between Europeans and Africans but between two very different and, at times, antithetical French visions. For more than two centuries, French Catholic missionaries had evangelized on six continents. They had faced hostile opposition from indigenous rulers, sought assistance from European traders, and relied on occasional protection from the French military. But they hardly ever defined themselves in terms of the French—or any other—state. Indeed, in their correspondence, they very rarely mentioned their national roots well into the era when most historians suggest that national identity trumped all other forms of self-definition. An analysis of the traditions and development of the nineteenth-century missionary movement reveals that, even as late as the 1890s, for thousands of Catholic missionaries there was no glory in working for France or any worldly entity. Glory came only in serving God.

Early Versions of the Apostolic Life

The lives of Père Guillemé and his religious colleagues were rooted in an old and vibrant apostolic culture that long predated the Age of Empire and the era of the modern nation. As the opening line of an 1894 mission history pointed out, "The work of the missions was born with the Church." Père Adrien Launay, in his massive 1,800-page chronicle *Histoire générale de la Société des missions-étrangères*, linked modern-day missionaries directly with Jesus' call to "preach the word to all creatures, go, teach the nations."[9] Missionary literature was littered with references to the New Testament, constantly relating contemporary experiences to biblical passages. In addition to Jesus, missionaries looked to apostles and saints for role models. Perennial favorites were Saints Paul, Augustine, and, perhaps most important, Francis Xavier, the sixteenth-century Jesuit whose tireless apostolic zeal led him, within the span of a decade, to preach in India, Southeast Asia, the Philippines, and Japan.

While missionaries found many lessons in the long and colorful history of European evangelization, two seventeenth-century innovations in very different parts of the world were particularly influential in shaping the modern Catholic missionary movement. The first of these was the new way of defining and promoting the apostolic life to supporters in Europe that emerged from the largely unsuccessful attempt to spread Christianity among the Hurons, Iroquois, Algonquins, and other groups of North America. By the mid-1640s, with the assistance of missionary sisters, French Jesuits had established outposts across a significant portion of New France, where they worked to convert local peoples.[10] These missionaries understood conversion to be a process that reached beyond the adoption of religious faith and included the purging of local customs and beliefs, and the learning of French language, customs, and morals. The French crown soon considered converting, teaching, and moralizing to be an integral part of colonization, but it did little to support the Jesuit missions.[11] So from the beginning, since both their finances and their political position in New France were uncertain, the Jesuits began depicting their lives and goals for a readership in Europe.[12]

With the aim of raising money and support from both individual donors and the French monarchy, Jesuit missionaries began publishing annually their *Relations* after 1632. The reports and letters in the *Relations* were widely read by the literate French public for their colorful accounts of travel, ethnographic descriptions of native groups, and missionary tribulations among the natives of North America.[13] The Jesuits depicted the raw and often gruesome details of a missionary life full of suffering, sacrifice, fear, and violence. Choosing to live among the native populations, they were forced to learn difficult languages and to endure privations ranging from sleeping in bark huts during the icy Canadian winter to relying on hunting and gathering for their food. Ill prepared for the harsh environment, many missionaries lived in a chronic state of semistarvation.[14] Using guerrilla-like tactics, Native Americans kept Europeans constantly on edge. One priest, for example, complained that it was not safe to pick vegetables in his garden, not to mention collect firewood in the forest.[15] By the end of the 1640s, after a decade of expansion, the unforgiving conditions had forced the Jesuits either to focus most of their efforts on defending the missions from armed attacks by native peoples or to retreat to areas populated by white settlers.

Though New France seemed wholly inhospitable to Christian proselytizing, missionaries never questioned the importance of spreading the word. They remained militant, disciplined, and eager for martyrdom should God call them to make the sacrifice. And they were not to be disappointed: the fifteen years following 1645 became an Age of Martyrs, when native people killed missionaries in a variety of ways, including drowning, burning, and boiling.[16] In the 1650s, infighting among politicians and *religieux* in both France and North America finally weakened the influence that the Jesuits held in colonial society. Nonetheless, the *Relations* left behind a systematic record of peoples to be converted, allowing other missionaries eventually to continue the Christianizing mission.[17] Through its detailed accounts of missionaries being tortured, mutilated, and martyred, the Jesuit *Relations* also left an indelible image of the apostolic life: evangelizing with unflagging zeal and piety in the grips of deprivation and terror remained a prevalent image of Catholic missionary existence.[18] Documenting and promoting this life to an eager readership in Europe would become a central feature of the Catholic missionary movement that took shape in nineteenth-century France.

The experiences of seventeenth-century Jesuits far from North America were responsible for a second significant innovation. While French Jesuits and sisters were at work in New France, missionary endeavors in Asia expanded as well, prompting the departure of many Catholic workers to the east. Among them was Alexandre de Rhodes, born in Avignon in 1591, an ambitious missionary who would prove influential in shaping a new method of—and new interest in—Catholic proselytism. A Jesuit who shared with many of his fellow missionaries an appreciation of the high cultural achievements of Chinese society, Rhodes rejected as cruel the idea that Europeans should force their languages and cultural practices onto the peoples of Asia. Rather than expect converts to adopt European habits, clothing, and manners, he argued that missionaries should, as much as possible, leave established social, familial, and cultural practices in place. He considered living among the local population and being able to read and write the local language to be essential for all missionaries. (He himself was a noted linguist, could preach in Vietnamese after six months of lessons, and was a major force in transliterating Vietnamese into the Roman script.)[19] According to Rhodes, having learned the language and the culture of a community, the missionary could then adapt lessons to the mentality of the congregation by molding Christian tenets to local beliefs, rituals, and ceremonies.

Rhodes's method broke with some existing Jesuit practices, such as the targeting of elites for conversion. His experiences in Vietnam in the 1620s, where elites regularly cracked down on or expelled European missionaries, led him to devise a system of evangelizing that focused on common people and sought the training of catechists who could continue religious teaching even in the absence of missionaries. His method also drew on a mixture of reason and spectacle. He suggested that missionaries appeal to people's inherent understanding of morality and their need to live according to certain rules, such as the Ten Commandments. From this base, missionaries could explore the more spiritual aspects of Christianity, such as the immortal soul, God, and the Holy Trinity. He then relied on religious spectacles and festivities, such as the adoration of the cross, singing in the local language, and Nativity scenes at Christmas, to attract the curious. Such spectacles, he argued, were even more effective if incorporated within local festivals and rituals.

In the early 1650s, Rhodes returned to Europe, hoping to turn religious fervor in France into financial and political support for missions in Asia. In publications of his travels in Armenia, Persia, China, and other Asian kingdoms, Rhodes told of Christian martyrs who had gladly spilled their blood for Jesus Christ. Like the *Relations*, these dramatic accounts of missionary work in Asia found an audience in France and drew the support of religious and lay people alike. Eager to see his evangelizing work spread, Rhodes sought more missionaries and set to work encouraging the creation of missionary organizations in France. At first, he encountered resistance from Rome, which was both pressured to leave missionary work under Spanish and Portuguese control and fearful of further conflict between feuding missionary orders. But by 1653, with many Frenchmen eager to go to Asia, Rhodes had found aristocrats willing to fund seminaries at home and missions abroad.[20] Rome finally gave its support, allowing the formation of the secular Société des missions étrangères de Paris, the first French apostolic organization.

The first three apostolic vicars from the newly formed Société des missions étrangères departed for regions in Asia—Tonkin, Cochinchina, and Nanking—between 1660 and 1662. To map out the non-Christian world for future missionary enterprises and to avoid attracting the attention of the Portuguese, the vicars decided *to walk* much of the way from Paris to Vietnam and China.[21] Crossing most of Persia and India on foot took close to two years. These "travelers for Christ" had no experience in the apostolic life and little understanding of the cultures they met. As Launay's history of the Missions étrangères explains, the missionaries adopted the discipline and tactics of an army, "the skill of the attack and the secrets of defense."[22] The expedition helped solidify the icon of the deeply spiritual nomadic man of religion that had also been found in the writings of Rhodes and the Jesuits of New France—an image that would still be prominent in missionary correspondence more than two centuries later.

Two of the apostolic vicars, François Pallu and Pierre Lambert de la Motte, edited the *Instructions*, a guidebook to help prepare future missionaries, outlining the challenges and emotions newcomers were likely to encounter.[23] The *Instructions* reflected on all aspects of the missionary's spiritual life. They drew heavily on the life of Jesus as their model—"Jesus was then led away by the Spirit into the wilderness, to be tempted by the devil" (Matthew 4:1)—an indication that they were based as much on religious idealism as on lived experience. First and foremost, the *Instructions* warned that resisting temptation and bodily pleasures—concerns not just of the body but of faith as well—required constant vigilance. The authors encouraged missionaries to see their own temptations as indistinguishable from the ones with which

Satan challenged Jesus. To give in to avarice, vainglory, or corporeal pleasures was to weaken one's love of God, and one's ability to spread the gospel.

To counter Satan (who played a key role in the *Instructions*—an entire section, for example, is entitled "The Missionary Must Prepare to Fight the Devil")—the missionary had to pray regularly and make his life "a continual penitence." Meager food and clothing were sufficient sustenance; simplicity in all aspects of existence was the goal; satisfaction was to be avoided. In the same vein, suffering was a plus. Linking contemporary missionary work to that of the earliest Christian evangelists, the *Instructions* said to heed the advice of Saint Paul to suffer from hunger and thirst, and to wear only rags in the burning sun or cold wind (1 Corinthians 4:11). Should this life still be too comfortable, missionaries could take a cue from Saint Francis Xavier and inflict bodily mortifications.[24]

The *Instructions* also addressed very practical issues, outlining a method of winning converts. Like Alexandre de Rhodes, this method broke with the Jesuit strategy of targeting and living among elites, emphasizing a more broad-based approach to evangelizing. The authors reflected on problems ranging from the training of catechists to how to ensure the continued practice of Catholicism in villages without resident priests. They provided a step-by-step list of how to convince converts to accept the True Religion: prove first that there is only one God; demonstrate that the soul is immortal; show that happiness is a part *not* of this life but of another; and so on.[25] Profane methods were to provide little help to these full-time religious combatants. After all, "The weapons we wield are not merely human, but divinely potent to demolish strongholds" (2 Corinthians 10:4).

As servants of Christ, missionaries were to rely on Providence, not politics, commerce, or even wisdom. While critics were to accuse missionaries of every kind of impropriety over the centuries, the *Instructions* explicitly forbade missionaries from getting involved in any form of business, using violence, or abusing their good reputations to manipulate communities for personal gain.[26] Although evangelizing was inherently a political act—even Rhodes did not deny the benefits of baptizing powerful figures—nowhere in the *Instructions* were kings, states, or nations explicitly mentioned. In the wilderness, there was no place for worldly politics. Instead, the *Instructions* described a life shaped entirely by the missionary's relationship with God. Every moment of this life, from the day of departure until death, was to be dedicated to the work at hand—proselytizing, teaching, and establishing an indigenous clergy. According to the *Instructions*, evangelizing was to be a purely spiritual pursuit for each missionary: spreading the gospel helped the missionary better understand God; a better understanding of God made a more effective missionary.

An indication of their lasting impact, the *Instructions* remained standard issue for all departing missionaries of the Missions étrangères until the twentieth century. As a result, the essential concerns, guidelines, and goals of the apostolic life changed very little in two centuries. Throughout the nineteenth century, the complete dedication, self-denial, and bodily suffering reflected both in the *Instructions* and in the Jesuit *Relations* appealed to French clerical—and especially missionary—sensibilities. The century after the French Revolution witnessed a renaissance of many Tridentine traditions, including the concept of *contemptus mundi*, or the rejection of worldly things.[27] Seminaries in France tried to distance themselves from what they perceived to be the profanity of modern life. As the 1864 *Syllabus of Errors* made plain, French society—especially in its bourgeois, republican incarnation—provided pious society with nothing more than misguided aspirations, immoral thoughts, and degenerate impulses. For missionaries, the deserts and forests of distant continents were not the only places haunted by Satan.

How the Catholic Missionary Movement Became French

In the more than two centuries between the seventeenth-century *Relations* and the travel narrative of Père Guillemé, the institutional forms of the Catholic missionary project underwent significant trials and transformations. After flourishing throughout the seventeenth century first in the New World and then in Southeast Asia, French evangelizing suffered decline and defeat in the eighteenth century. The ascendancy of Britain and Holland helped spread Protestantism around the globe, often in parts of the world once considered Catholic fields of action (such as Canada). Local resistance to Catholicism, especially in Japan, China, and Indochina, put a violent end to many missions. These international concerns were coupled with theological divisions in Europe and the suppression of the Jesuits starting in 1750. Throughout the eighteenth century, Rome had been losing its political sway in Catholic Europe, and the French Revolution was the crowning blow.[28] The sheer destructiveness of the Revolution had devastating effects on French Catholicism, including the killing of priests, the division of the clergy into rival factions, the closing of seminaries, and the secularization of Church properties. To revitalize the missionary movement in the nineteenth century would require a complete overhaul of the organizations supporting global Catholic evangelizing.

While the Napoleonic Era brought some improvements, it remained a period of uncertainty for missionaries. The Concordat of 1801, which Napoleon negotiated with Pope Pius VII, helped ease the divisions caused by the French Revolution by regulating the place of clergy and Church property within the state and guaranteeing France's commitment to protect Catholic missionaries abroad—a protectorate that would last into the twentieth century. In 1804, Napoleon reestablished France's three primary organizations, the Lazarists, the seminary of the Saint-Esprit, and the Société des missions étrangères, but he ordered that they be merged and placed under the control of the archbishop of Paris—and, by extension, the French state. In March 1805, Napoleon decreed the missions' freedom as spiritual organizations, though five days later he named his uncle, Cardinal Fesch, protector of the missions.

Napoleon's support of missionary efforts could not undo the devastation wrought by the Revolution. In 1808, an investigation by Napoleon's minister of religion revealed that the Pères du Saint-Esprit were diminished to 12 missionaries, the Missions étrangères to 39, and the Lazarists to 21 at home and 33 abroad. In the twenty years since 1789, the Missions étrangères had been able to send only 15 priests to the Far East.[29] Even when missionary organizations slowly started to function again under Napoleon, there remained the ever-important question of money. In France, donations from the faithful dried up, leaving missionary organizations unable to train new missionaries or support those already working. Napoleon shut down the Propaganda fide (Congregation for the Propagation of the Faith) in Rome, which since its founding by Pope Gregory XV in 1622 had organized and supported overseas missions. The Propaganda fide's archives were sent to Paris, and some of its property was sold off. It was 1817 before Pius VII could reopen its doors, but even then he could offer only scant funding to the handful of missionaries eager to go abroad.

Ironically, the violence of the French Revolution and the Napoleonic Era was instrumental in shaping the reemergence of a Catholic missionary movement dominated by French men and women. After the final defeat of Napoleon, Rome attempted to rebuild the missionary project. Pius VII approved two new French missionary organizations, the Congregation of Sacrés Coeurs, called the Picpuciens, and the Marists, which would evangelize in Canada and the Pacific over the course of the century. These two male orders joined the Soeurs de Saint Joseph de Cluny, founded in 1806 by Anne-Marie Javouhey, which would send *religieuses* to French Guyana, West Africa, and the South Pacific primarily as nurses and teachers. With Rome weak and unable to fund missionary endeavors, and with the influence of Catholic Spain and Portugal greatly diminished, a French organization that was to be instrumental in funding evangelization was founded to fill the gap.

In 1822, Pauline-Marie Jaricot, a devout Catholic in her early twenties, inspired the opening at Paris and Lyon of the most important French missionary organization of the century, the Oeuvre de la propagation de la foi. The Oeuvre was a lay organization and guarded its independence from Rome. Most who participated in its founding—including Jaricot herself—were laypeople; and, until 1860, its fifteen-member council counted only one member of the clergy.[30] The Oeuvre tried to avoid distinctions between categories of "lay" and "clerical," and, in fact, it took steps to veil the identity of its council members in a shroud of mystery, hoping to attract the largest possible following. While the Oeuvre aimed to attract a large lay audience, it relied heavily on parish priests to raise awareness of and money for missionary endeavors.[31]

Although the idea to raise money for the missions reportedly came to Jaricot as a vision from God, the founding of the Oeuvre reflected a general movement among the philanthropic and religiously minded French public to revive the missions in the wake of the Revolution. Three years before the founding of the Oeuvre, a member of the Missions étrangères noted that Catholics in several French towns, such as Lyon, Nancy, Metz, Le Havre, and Rennes, had formed societies in which each member donated one sou per week, or two francs sixty per year, to help carry "the good news to the idolatrous peoples" of the world.[32] The one-sou-per-week subscription was typical of how religious organizations in nineteenth-century France adopted entrepreneurial schemes to draw small donations from the broadest spectrum of society.[33] But from its founding, the organization had a spiritual, as well as financial, goal. The Oeuvre required all supporters to give prayers, not just money. Members agreed to recite once a day the Pater, the Ave, and the invocation "Saint Francis Xavier, pray for us."[34] The Oeuvre, therefore, was not purely occupied with funding foreign missions; it equally aimed to inspire piety in its European supporters.

The founding of the Oeuvre came in the midst of a Catholic revival in which missionary work played a profound historical and spiritual role. France was itself—both past and present—a *pays de mission*. For many French Catholics, Gaul was born when missionaries traveled beyond the boundaries of Rome and introduced Christianity to barbarians who knew only how to pillage, burn, and kill. When Clovis placed himself under the banner of Christ, France became "the eldest daughter" of the Church.[35] Once saved, this daughter turned her eyes abroad to spread the word and, when necessary, protect Christianity. Throughout the medieval and early modern periods, successive French elites considered the defense of Christians in the Levant to be a God-given duty—a divine covenant that tied France to the very birthplace of Christianity.

The French Revolution, however, had brought the eldest daughter under the "idolatrous" (that is, secular and anticlerical) influences of republicanism.[36] For many Catholics, the process of recovery would require a revival of Catholic spirituality both at home and abroad. In the 1820s, at the very moment of the Oeuvre's founding, the clergy was sending missionaries into the French countryside. These "missions to the interior" brought French men and women back into the fold of Catholicism and tried to purge society of the ungodly morals that had brought the Revolution in the first place.[37] The historian Sheryl Kroen has shown that, in the wake of the Revolution, many Catholics believed France to be a "spiritual desert" in need of conversion. The clergy hoped not only to save individuals from damnation but also to "resacralize" the restored monarchy. Catholic renewal thus had deep political implications; imbedded in counterrevolutionary politics, it steeled the nation against future lapses into the chaos caused by secular government.[38] Many Catholic commentators described the foreign missions as an extension of this pledge to fortify the nation's piety. By spreading the gospel to the world, France was helping to cure the spiritual ills that had caused the horrors of the Revolution and that gave rise to a century of republican anticlericalism.[39]

Despite the reactionary origins of the movement, counterrevolutionary rhetoric found no place in the columns of the vast majority of late nineteenth-century foreign missionary publications. The Oeuvre de la propagation de la foi was, after all, primarily a fund-raising organ and, as such, avoided ostracizing potential supporters with divisive politics. By its own estimations, it was remarkably populist, appealing to a wide array of social and economic groups, with the majority of subscribers coming from the laboring classes, such as peasants, factory workers, tradesmen, and domestics.[40] The appeal to supporters' spiritual, rather than political, needs proved extremely effective.

The Oeuvre viewed religious concerns, namely, the conversion of nonbelievers, as inextricably linked with certain humanitarian causes, notably, the rehabilitation of former slaves, the teaching of morality, and providing care for the sick and elderly.[41] Though it remained "devoted" to the Propaganda fide in Rome, it defended its autonomy. Leaders at the Oeuvre viewed their organization's role as fundamentally different from that of the Propaganda fide. As one of its publications recounted in 1905, the Oeuvre did not involve itself with "the intimate life of the Missions"; it did not send missionaries or name apostolic vicars. "Having a more modest role," the Oeuvre sought "to furnish missionaries their daily bread" and to help them build necessary establishments abroad.[42] Regardless of the modesty of its stated objectives, the Oeuvre's independence remained a point of contention, particularly for leaders at the Propaganda fide, who lobbied to bring it under the pope's direct authority. The Oeuvre's unparalleled financial successes, however, ultimately protected it from Rome's influence.[43]

While French men and women were the force behind the rebuilding of the nineteenth-century Catholic missionary movement, Rome provided essential administrative guidance after 1830. Gregory XVI, who had served as the prefect of the Propaganda fide, was named pope in 1831. Aside from his experience working with missionaries, Gregory XVI was inspired by a number of contemporary events of the day: France had taken Algeria, parts of Africa were being explored by Europeans, Europe's involvement in China was on the rise, and improvements in shipping made travel to once-isolated Oceania considerably easier. Five new societies came into existence over the following ten years, sending missionaries to Syria, the South Pacific, Peru, China, West Africa, and Madagascar. The hierarchy of the Church abroad developed extensively, especially in Africa and Southeast Asia—in all, seventy dioceses, apostolic vicariates, and prefectures were created over a fifteen-year period.[44] The Propaganda fide reasserted missionary duties that it had first outlined in its directive of 1659: besides the establishment of local clergy, Rome warned missionaries to steer clear of politics and to focus on education as the best way to root Catholicism in local societies.[45] Thus, echoing the methods of the *Instructions*, the Propaganda fide instructed that bishops and priests were to organize much of the evangelizing effort, while teaching brothers and sisters were to be essential in making religion permanent.

A potent combination of factors—a new European age of exploration, Rome's renewed interest in aiding missionary endeavors, and a popular movement in France that provided both manpower and funds for international missionary work—led to an unprecedented growth of French missionary zeal in the latter half of the nineteenth century. Between 1850 and the founding of the Third Republic, a number of organizations, including the Missions africaines de Lyon and Cardinal Lavigerie's Pères blancs, were founded, with the goals of opening up Africa to missions, funding Catholic education in the Levant, and training future missionaries. In 1865, a French Jesuit, Père Albéric Foresta, opened in Avignon a seminary—an *école apostolique*—exclusively to train missionaries. Similar schools followed over the next ten years in Amiens, Poitiers, and Bordeaux.

The Oeuvre de la propagation de la foi was not the only organization successful at raising money and awareness of the plight of Christians in the world—a measure of French Catholic desire to support evangelization. In 1843, Bishop Charles-Auguste-Marie-Joseph Forbin-Janson founded the Oeuvre pontificale de la Sainte-Enfance to help combat infanticide and the mistreatment of children around the world. Forbin-Janson turned to the young people of Europe, and especially of France, to raise funds to help efforts to baptize children across the globe. Unlike the Oeuvre de la propagation de la foi, the Sainte-Enfance was largely clerical, shaped by the ecclesiastical hierarchy, and championed by the pope. Within a few years of its founding, it was raising more than three million francs per year, over a third of which came from France.[46] By 1846, the organization was firmly established in sixty-one French dioceses and counted 660,000 subscribers, about half that of the Oeuvre de la propagation de la foi. In the latter half of the century, the organization witnessed phenomenal growth, due in large part to sustained support in France. In the early 1880s, the Sainte-Enfance supported 2,336 schools, 179 ateliers, and fifty-four farms worldwide; in 1911, it funded more than 10,000 schools, 5,619 workshops, and nearly 2,000 orphanages.[47]

Other French organizations had more specific goals, though no less lofty aspirations. In 1856, the Oeuvre des écoles d'Orient (Association for Schools of the Orient) was founded in Paris to raise money for Catholic education in the Levant. In its first three years, it raised more than 100,000 francs. And in 1860, when 200,000 Lebanese Christians were killed in religious warfare, the organization raised more than three million francs in a single year. The Oeuvre des écoles d'Orient never reached great prominence but still managed to raise 300,000 francs per year until the end of the century.[48] The success of such small organizations reflected the vitality of Catholic associational life throughout the century.

Although smaller organizations made significant contributions, the Oeuvre de la propagation de la foi remained the dominant supporter of French missionary work. Its growth was nothing short of remarkable, as the Oeuvre quickly became one of the very largest associations—religious or not—in all of France, with membership well over one million from the mid–nineteenth century until the First World War. As French support for Catholic missionaries blossomed over the course of the century, so too did the Oeuvre's influence. Bringing in nearly 23,000 francs its first year, the Oeuvre's fund-raising efforts steadily rose to more than 6.8 million francs by 1884.[49] Though it assisted an international Catholic movement that worked in tandem with Rome, the Oeuvre was an overwhelmingly French organization. In 1900, despite the Oeuvre's efforts to develop a support base across Europe, South America, and the United States, more than two-thirds of its funds still came from France.

The second half of the century also witnessed a boom in the number of Frenchmen answering the missionary call. In Lyon, a traditional stronghold of Catholicism, the number of missionaries ordained to work abroad was almost as high as the number of priests ordained to work in France.[50] By the 1890s, twenty-eight of the forty-four Catholic missionary congregations working in the world were French. A full two-thirds of all European priests, brothers, and *soeurs* working in Catholic missions were French—making for a total of more than 50,000 French religious workers abroad by 1900. By the end of the century, the Missions étrangères alone boasted 1,100 priests in East Asia, thirty-two of whom were bishops; thirty seminaries with a total of 2,000 students, and 3,000 schools with 90,000 pupils. In Africa, there were more than 1,000 priests, 1,600 schools, and 230 hospitals; in the Middle East, 80,000 students received a Catholic education.[51] Having funded a mere ten foreign missions in the 1820s, the Oeuvre de la propagation de la foi distributed money to some 370 missions worldwide by the late 1880s. A century after the Revolution had inflicted a dizzying blow to Catholicism, the Third Republic boasted an apostolic system with the resources to recruit, train, place, and support missionary work on six continents.

Representing the Missionary Landscape

Despite the proliferation of geographic societies, adventure magazines, and travel books in the nineteenth century, more French men and women, by far, viewed the outside world through the lens of missionary journals than any other source. From its inception, the Oeuvre documented its work in its publications, especially the *Annales de la Propagation de la Foi* and, later, the *Missions Catholiques*. The *Annales* got its start in 1826, with a bimonthly run of 10,000 copies, an impressive output for its first year. By 1839, 16,000 copies

Figure 1.2. "Oubanghi—Enfants de Brazzaville." A missionary at work in equatorial Africa. (Reproduced from *Missions Catholiques* with permission from the Oeuvres pontificales missionnaires—Coopération missionnaire, Lyon.)

were being produced, the same circulation as the *Constitutionnel*, one of the most popular French newspapers of the day.[52] The *Annales'* readership reflected its deep French roots: though the journal appeared in German, English, Spanish, Italian, and seven other language editions, the majority of readers were French.[53] In the mid-1880s, 165,000 of the nearly 255,000 copies of the *Annales* printed were in French, and over 6,000 more were in Breton (the number of the Breton-language edition printed slumped only slightly from the 1880s to 1914, a fact that must have rankled republican reformers bent on making French the language of the land).[54] As support for the Oeuvre expanded to Catholics around the globe, the percentage of editions published in French dropped off in the years leading to the First World War. But the French-language edition still accounted for more than half of the 340,000 copies printed in 1912.

Directors at the Oeuvre estimated that each edition of the *Annales* passed through the hands of, at least, between 1.5 and nearly 1.8 million French supporters in the three decades leading up to the First World War.[55] Even if only half of those who received the *Annales* in 1880 actually read it, the journal still would have been more widely read than the most popular daily of the era, *Le Petit Journal* (the circulation of which was four times greater than its closest competitor).[56] By comparison, the Société de géographie de Paris—one of

Figure 1.3. "Arizona—Indian of the Yuma tribe." A face from the missionary's world. (Reproduced from *Missions Catholiques* with Permission from the Oeuvres pontificales missionnaires—Coopération missionnaire, Lyon.)

France's most famous geographic and pro-colonial organizations—had a comparatively paltry membership of 2,000.[57] No lay organization concerned with France's position in the world could boast a popular following comparable to the broad-based support that missionary organizations enjoyed.

Running reports of Catholic experiences abroad and outlining the year's successes and tribulations, the *Annales*, along with the later weekly spin-off the *Missions Catholiques*, chronicled evangelizing in every region of the world and among every imaginable society and culture. Started in 1868, the *Missions Catholiques*, with a large, tabloid format and illustrated with etchings and photos, was particularly effective at capturing an international feel. Its editors made little effort to group articles and pictures of similar themes together on the page, making for a hodgepodge of images and stories from distant corners of the globe. Flipping through a tome of the *Missions Catholiques* from a single year—1903 (though a similar impression would emerge from one from 1873 or 1893)—reveals, on one page, an image of two Asian buffalo dueling with their horns and, a few pages later, the new apostolic vicar sitting for a portrait in Hunan, China. From Egypt, the silhouette of a mosque rises above the Cairo skyline, a charmer entices his snake, and a pile of exhumed mummies stands in the open air. Scattered among these images are indigenous people of the Bas Niger, a grand mandarin of Tonkin, and two heads on stakes in Nigeria. Disparate pictures stare each other down on a two-page spread: a town in Syria next to a landscape of Saskatchewan; an Apache chief facing a Pima "squaw." One page reveals the dunes of the Sahara, another a temple in Siberia. Here three children play on an immense tree trunk in the *pays Fang* of Gabon. There the wind blows silently across a frozen Norwegian fjord.[58]

By their very appearance in the *Annales* and the *Missions Catholiques*, the mixture of cultures, rituals, histories, and landscapes gained unity and meaning in relation to a single overarching theme—namely, the truly *international* drama of the Catholic Church in action. The journals offered a coup d'oeil of the progress accomplished, of each "new path" cut by the apostolate. They built on the traditions of the Jesuits' *Relations*, depicting the missionary as "persecuted or triumphant, but always glorious."[59] The work of today called to mind the missionary heroes of the past: in 1891, for example, the *Annales* claimed that Asia had witnessed "the triumph of Saint Francis Xavier, the great apostle of the Indies and Japan," and that Africa had heard Saint Paul's call "Advance! Advance!"[60] The conqueror of newly won lands was thus, now as before, Jesus Christ and his *église universelle*. This spiritual empire was one of constant conflict, of "battles and victories for truth." For hundreds of thousands of French readers of missionary journals, the outside world was not a stage where common heroes acted out mundane colonial dramas. Rather, it was a place engaged in cosmic battles, fought between pagans and Christians, Satan and God, and the damned and the saved.[61]

Catholicism, Race, and Secular Civilization

Many historians have argued that nineteenth-century Protestant missionaries carried into the field not only Bibles but also Enlightenment ideas about individual liberty and the perfectibility of society.[62] Catholic missionaries' relationship to "civilizing" work, by contrast, was far less straightforward. Before the 1880s, Catholic missionary journals did not focus on spreading civilization, a concept that, in France, had links to republicanism (and its anticlerical traditions). The historian Yannick Essertel argues that, as late as the 1890s, many Catholic missionaries took offense at the idea that their chief occupation was spreading civilization, believing it cheapened the true and spiritual vocation of the missionary.[63] Instead, when Catholic missionaries mentioned civilization, it was described as a natural by-product of conversion, not Enlightenment ideals. Readers of the *Annales* and the *Missions Catholiques* met missionaries who changed repugnant practices, morals, and beliefs by teaching the benefits of a Christian life. Converts were not expected to speak, dress, and act like Frenchmen. Rather, local cultures could stay intact, at least in theory, while "unchristian" practices, ranging from sexual depravity to cannibalism, fell into disregard. True Christians, missionary publications insisted, would never commit infanticide, torture their enemies, or eat human flesh. Conversion, therefore, civilized and developed communities through spiritual awakening.

Missionary views of civilization stood starkly at odds with the secular republican notion that civilization was defined by revolutionary values, progress, and science. In 1885, an article called "Le Missionnaire" in an Oeuvre de la propagation de la foi publication claimed that the spreading of the word was like the planting of crops; the missionary was a farmer of new souls and of a renewed, plentiful Christian civilization. Missionaries, the article continued, had brought civilization to Europe by turning somber forests into "happy harvests," and pestilential swamps into "a plain for cultivation." Through evangelism and lending a hand, Benedictine missionaries had "made our old Europe into the *foyer* of civilization." Their initiative and perseverance could only inspire religion, and similar work continued in the nineteenth century. "Le Missionnaire" cited the accomplishments of modern-day Benedictines who, in Australia, worked in a place where the soil was good but the people "savage." Within a few years, however, "working under the direction of the *pères*," the local population became shepherds, cultivators, and artisans.[64] Good Catholics, it seems, made good farmers.

For much of the nineteenth century, because of this belief that civilization sprang from Christianity, religiosity more than race shaped how missionaries viewed potential converts. Individual missionaries were by no means above the prejudicial attitudes of their era. Père Guillemé is a fine example. In addition to showing his distaste for the "savage" behavior of the Africans he met, Guillemé noted that when discussing the Ten Commandments, he spent a little extra time on stealing, "for the blacks, it must be said, are a bit thieving."[65] Other reports in the *Annales* and *Missions Catholiques* depicted, as various writers put it, the gross, repugnant, and beastly habits that missionaries faced in their apostolic rounds. Non-Christians' penchant for infanticide, cannibalism, torture, and human sacrifice were common subjects of interest in letters and reports. One French priest formulated pagan behavior particularly bluntly: in an 1891 allocution, Abbé F. Marnas said that pagans were by definition loveless, self-satisfying, and utterly lacking in respect for life, a fact proven by the tortures they inflicted on one another.[66] Considering that the vast bulk of the world's non-Christians possessed, to paraphrase the novelist Joseph Conrad, darker complexions than Frenchmen, missionary depictions surely fed more scientifically racist attitudes prevalent in Europe since the Enlightenment.

Whereas scientific racism held "savagery" to be linked to unalterable biological and cultural characteristics, missionaries generally associated immoral or reprehensible practices with an absolutely alterable lack of faith.[67] The entire missionary enterprise hinged on the redemptive power of evangelizing. Indeed, in his discussion of paganism, Abbé Marnas argued that the missionary's zeal alone could "transform" pagan souls, pull them from their abject ways, and "purify" them.[68] Savagery could be cured by faith—or, at least, by faith and continued vigilant oversight. Well after conversion, missionaries were regularly portrayed in a position of spiritual control, directing and correcting their inferior neophytes' behavior. This was a dynamic that priests experienced everywhere in the nineteenth century. The clergy in France constantly complained of the impious thoughts and shocking actions of even the faithful. As Eugen Weber notes, country priests in France were always telling their childlike parishioners "no" to correct their behavior.[69] So, too, abroad: as one missionary in Indochina observed, "Vicious humanity is very much the same at all latitudes."[70] Priests everywhere judged their followers with the eye of a disciplinarian patriarch—they were not called *pères* for nothing.

Missionaries' use of race as a defining dimension of converts' behavior was further complicated by the constant blurring of distinctions between Europe and the rest of the world. Europe itself, they argued, was not civilized as a result of its inherent biological or cultural superiority but because it was Christian. After all, as one priest put it, it was the apostles of Rome, Athens, and Judea who brought "to our ancestors the religion that civilized us."[71] Missionaries themselves blurred racial differences by crossing the linguistic and cultural boundaries that traditionally separated Europeans from the rest of the world. Moving across the globe, they adopted cultural practices foreign to their own ways. As one missionary noted, they had to become "more indigenous than the indigenous" in order to plant the roots of Christian faith.[72]

By the late nineteenth century, for many missionaries, the greatest danger to European society was not racial degeneration due to exposure to non-Europeans. Rather, it was the triumph of anticlerical republicanism and heretical British and American Protestantism that threatened the very civilization Catholicism had made possible. Because they had declared war on the One True Religion, so went the argument, Protestants presented a significant "peril" and were aggressively criticized by Catholic religious workers.[73] Catholics had no problem condemning republicans and Protestants for being "agents of the spirit of evil" and asserting that, should they fail to return to the flock, they would face damnation.[74] Just as cannibals in the darkest jungles needed the guiding light of faith, so, the *Annales* argued, Protestants in England, Scotland, and Switzerland needed to be brought back under the influence of Rome.[75] Missionaries celebrated the conversion of Dutch "heretics" just as much as Asian "pagans."[76] In the cosmic battle between good and evil, the front lines were only imperfectly drawn along the contours of racial, cultural, or even regional identities.

Qualities of the Modern Missionary

In describing and documenting evangelization, missionary journals hoped not only to inspire supporters but also to recruit future apostles. Consequently, descriptions of the missionary endeavor reveal much about the hopes, concerns, and spiritual aspirations of the men and women who decided to commit their lives to evangelizing. Missionaries were the vanguard of nineteenth-century Catholicism—and allocutions, lectures, and publications provide evidence of this important point. French priests commonly drew from stories and letters published in the *Annales* for inspiring sermon material.[77] While young boys or girls were entranced by the stories of distant, heroic religious workers, they also learned about the characteristics necessary for the apostolic life. By their own description, missionaries were engaged in an epic, supernatural struggle, far from the comforts of home, faced with deadly foes, and willing to give their lives for Jesus and his Church. It was a calling for the young and energetic committed to a life at the cutting edge of Catholicism.

Apostle, traveler for Christ, Christ's witness, prince of souls, saver of souls, winner of souls, hunter of souls—such were the terms used to describe the nineteenth-century missionary. These appellations revealed the simplicity of the missionary's central aim in life: to teach and convert as many people as possible to Catholicism. From conversion, all else followed. Missions provided humanitarian services, such as orphanages, leper hospitals, and care for the sick and the elderly, but such services also aided in conversion. Those in the twilight of life—the elderly and the dying—as well as children and recently freed slaves were the easiest souls to win over. Converting other segments of the population took considerably more time and effort, and generally was far less effective. Again drawing on missionary methods of old, the 1885 article "Le Missionnaire" explained that the missionary could only preach by example, winning followers "by putting under their eyes" the virtues of a Christian life.[78] According to one Jesuit who worked in Madagascar, the missionary imposed his ideas on his followers through his discretion, dignity, experience, devotion, and affection.[79] With such a method, patience was more than a virtue; it was obligatory.

As the vanguard, the missionary had to possess three characteristics: faith, zeal, and readiness for sacrifice. No commentator better dissected the duties and sacrifices of the late nineteenth-century missionary than Jean-Baptiste Aubry, a missionary renowned for his zeal who wrote extensively on seminary training and who ultimately died in China in 1882. Aubry, who reasserted many of the core ideas found in the seventeenth-century *Instructions*, argued that the central concern of the modern missionary was developing the "interior life"—a process that brought one closer to God and the "supernatural." He encouraged missionaries to "embrace nobly" the prospect of a life of solitude, of suffering, tears, contempt, and misunderstanding. Such conditions would test the missionary's closeness to God. Faith and prayer were his weapons to defend against these opposing forces.[80] Considering the importance of zeal, it is not surprising that nineteenth-century seminaries provided future missionaries almost exclusively with spiritual training. Missionaries waited to learn local languages and cultures until they arrived at their posts abroad.[81]

While faith was an essential condition, sacrifice was the linchpin of the missionary existence. Aubry wrote that missionaries had to accept a radical form of sacrifice in order to prove a love of God: "Yes, I want to sacrifice everything, I want to be detached from everything, and, like the apostles, give up everything for you, oh my God."[82] Such sacrifice was a divine privilege that helped the missionary penetrate the mysteries of faith and become closer to God.[83] Aubry penned a prayer for missionaries to recite in times of doubt; it called on God to offer a better understanding of the interior life in exchange for sacrifice. The exchange helped the missionary "better taste the supernatural things" and revealed God to the missionary's soul.[84]

Sacrifice meant withstanding unspeakable spiritual, emotional, or physical torment and, if need be, giving one's life. Throughout the nineteenth century, missionaries reveled in descriptions of agony, dismemberment, and death. Missionary publications had a remarkable penchant for gore. Promises of being torn asunder abounded: missionaries were sheep sent among wolves; they worked in murderous lands where much blood had already spilled. A hard life followed by a tortured death was the ultimate rejection of bodily comforts. The "Chant pour le départ des missionnaires," sung on the occasion of missionaries' departure from the Paris seminary of the Missions étrangères, expressed their ethos of the unflinching acceptance of hardship:

> Be full of apostolic zeal;
> Poverty, work, combat,
> Death: there's the magnificent future
> That God holds for his soldiers. . . .
> Yes, if we must die, we will die.

> Leave, friends, adieu for this life,
> Carry far the name of our God,
> We will meet again one day
>   in the *patrie*,
> *Adieu*, brothers, *adieu*.[85]

The "Chant" described a life that certainly not everyone would find "magnificent," but it clearly had its rewards for the faithful. In language that foreshadowed the rhetoric of the fallen soldier of the First World War, bodily sacrifice in God's battle on earth won missionaries eternal glory. But it was not secular, nationalist glory.[86] The song guaranteed the missionary a final resting place in the *patrie*—not the terrestrial *mère-patrie* of France but the *patria aeterna*, the medieval idea of the celestial city.[87]

Christ's own experiences provided a powerful model for the apostolic life. In 1888, on the occasion of the departure of six missionaries for Asia, a French priest noted in his allocution that, before entering the seminary, these men had looked upon the crucifix and asked themselves if they could withstand Christ's suffering. Although the question had spiritual significance— they had asked themselves whether they were willing to walk in Christ's footsteps and to drink from his bitter chalice—the speaker took special care to describe the physical pain. "Look at his crown of thorns," the priest waxed. "His flesh bruised, crushed and streaming with blood! . . . His limbs nailed to the cross!" Only by accepting a future of pain could seminarians become members of the "avant-garde" of Christ's soldiers. "The apostle falls," the priest concluded darkly, "he does not grow old."[88] From the first days of seminary, the life of the missionary was doomed—gloriously, triumphantly, beautifully doomed.

Martyrdom Celebrated

Throughout the nineteenth century, martyrdom—the ultimate sacrifice and the clearest sign of spiritual salvation—remained the crowning glory of any missionary's life. Religious workers were not supposed to be motivated by the desire for martyrdom, but many clearly were. Martyrdom appealed to Charles-Martial-Allemand Lavigerie, the eventual archbishop of Algiers, founder of his own missionary organization, and one of the most famous members of the clergy in nineteenth-century France. Lavigerie agreed to go to North Africa in 1867 instead of pursuing what was assured to be a successful career at home in large part because of the increased possibility of meeting a glorious death.[89] The attractiveness of martyrdom was not unique to Lavigerie. Seminaries taught students about the heroes who had passed through the program before them, the most notable of whom were martyrs. Many organizations had (and still have) private or public museums displaying the ropes, chains, and blades that, as it were, sent their missionaries' souls to heaven.[90] Missionary journals vividly chronicled the tribulations of martyred missionaries. Such coverage greatly benefited the movement: in the wake of martyrdoms, even late in the century, applications to seminaries increased.[91] Martyrdom was a major draw.

Ironically, by the second half of the nineteenth century, missionaries who worked outside France could expect to live longer than the average Frenchman. And when missionaries did die, it was usually due to infectious diseases, heart attacks, cancer, or accidents—not at the hands of persecutors hungry for Christian blood.[92] But that did not keep missionaries from celebrating martyrdom as the climactic moment of any religious life. In 1853, Père Retord, a persecuted missionary in Tonkin, gave voice to his aspirations in "The Martyr's Desire," a rhyming poem repeatedly republished in late nineteenth-century journals:

> When will I fight in the arena
> Against the tyrant's fury,
> When will I see the chain at my feet,
> The yoke around my neck?
> My friends are covered in glory,
> And I can only bemoan.
> In order to gain victory, I want
> To die, to die, to die.[93]

The poem—which was put to music in 1889—described a missionary who accepted death not as a professional hazard but rather as the ultimate triumph of the Catholic worker.[94] It was also the clearest indication of God's desire to see the martyred missionary in heaven—a fact that explains its powerful appeal. Reportedly impatient for his own death, the priest-poet Retord had once complained of his martyred colleagues, "Oh! I am more than sad, I am *jealous* to see you leave before me to the celestial *patrie* by the surest and shortest route."[95]

If martyrdom signified God's highest approbation, then a number of French missionaries in the mid-1880s showed themselves to be blessed. Between 1884 and 1886, anti-European uprisings destroyed a number of missions in China and Indochina. In Annam and Tonkin (central and northern Vietnam) the regions most struck by violence, French military and political pressure inspired anti-Catholic movements.[96] With the French navy threatening invasion, the Vietnamese regent turned on the 350,000 indigenous Catholics who lived across the kingdom at the time. In the regent's opinion, if the French were able to know the roads, the rivers, and everything that happened in the kingdom, it was "solely thanks to the Christians and their priests." As part of the broader royalist Can vuong ("Save the King") movement, the regent called on his fellow Vietnamese to dedicate themselves to "the extermination" of the Christians. This accomplished, the French would be reduced to "complete immobility," he concluded, like a crab with its legs torn off.[97]

The Société des missions étrangères had survived martyrdoms and violent conflicts over the course of the nineteenth century, but its *Compte-Rendu* for 1885 reported that "no year has witnessed so many disasters . . . none has seen so much Christian blood spill." That year, persecutors killed ten European missionaries, twelve indigenous priests, sixty catechists, 300 indigenous *religieuses*, and at least 30,000 Christians. One entire mission, 200 Christian hamlets, and 250 churches and chapels were all torched, along with two seminaries, forty schools, seventy missionary residences, a printing house, and the houses of 55,000 Vietnamese Christians.[98] Not surprisingly, the report failed to mention that Vietnamese Catholics had themselves caused bloodshed by attacking non-Christian communities and burning pagodas.[99] Rather, letters that arrived in Paris from missionaries focused solely on Catholic losses and described the horrors the Christians had faced. Lamented one missionary: "All is reduced to ashes."[100]

The movement's response to the events of the mid-1880s reveals just how tenaciously missionaries remained true to their age-old traditions and beliefs. Like Père Guillemé's failure to mention the colonial storm closing around him in Africa, the missionary reporters in Indochina and China made only the most fleeting references to the French government's handling of the affair. Instead, reports of the events focused on martyrdom, explaining the massacres in terms of religious battles and spiritual turmoil, not secular politics. Missionary celebration of dying for God struck secular witnesses. For example, an expert on China, Jean Bessières, in an article on religious turmoil in the region, expressed horror at the fact that a bishop had described to him the glories of being martyred. For Bessières and others, this attitude toward martyrdom was the clearest example of how missionaries were driven by a religious zeal incompatible with modern, secular sensibilities.[101]

Regardless of whether missionary attitudes were out of touch with the modern world, the movement embraced modern technologies of mass communication. Publications transmitted news and reproduced images in what was a modern twist on the medieval tradition of documenting martyrdom in words and woodcuts.[102] With text and images, the Missions étrangères's *Compte-Rendu*, as well as the *Missions Catholiques*, described each fallen missionary's youth, spiritual development, and—often, in gruesome detail—final moments.

For example, the *Compte-Rendu* offered the testimony of a witness to the missionary Jean-Marie Poirier's demise in East Cochinchina. As the "cutthroats" pressed through the church garden in search of the priest, Père Poirier remained "always on his knees, turned toward the altar; he did not move and his gaze remained fixed on the holy image." It was in this position that his attackers shot him with a gun. His body on the floor, the journal reported, the mob tore at his beard, split open his chest, and finally cut off his head.[103] Death was not so easy for the thirty-one-year-old missionary André-Marie Garin. Though Père Garin was in hiding when the violence broke out, a mob ultimately found him, tied him to a post, and tortured him before he died an excruciating death by "a hundred cuts." His tormentors came daily, "armed with hooks and tongs, and tore from him shreds of throbbing flesh."[104] After three days of this "atrocious torture . . . the soul of the martyr flew away toward the heavens." Another missionary was publicly decapitated, his body then grilled like "butchered meat"; a further one was stabbed and hacked to pieces.[105]

Missionaries regarded these deaths as supreme acts of faith—a sign that the fallen was expressing his love of God by making the ultimate sacrifice for his converts. This point was made finer by the good deeds he performed during his final moments. According to the *Compte-Rendu*, Père Henri Macé saved a child from a burning church but decided to remain praying before the altar as the flames enveloped him.[106] A number of missionaries and other *religieux* comforted their fellow Christians by taking confessions and offering final absolution even as bands of murderers approached.[107] Missionaries' complete faith in God was proved by how willingly they embraced their own deaths. In 1885, a martyr in Cochinchina was said to have responded to assailants who wanted his head, "Come take it, if you want." His tormentors obliged with three blows of the sword.[108] An article from one of the Oeuvre's 1886 publications explained that the martyr defeated his murderers by taking pity on them at the very moment of death: "He prays for those who are his executioners, and it is in asking for grace and mercy for them that he exhales his last breath." By asking for forgiveness for his captors and willingly shedding his blood in the soil of his flock, the article concluded, the missionary plants a "firm and assured" step for Christianity.[109]

For journal editors, the events in China and Vietnam were also shrouded in mystery, even miracle. Père François-Xavier-Louis Barrat's obituary included a letter he had written to his hometown curé in which he described the danger around him. In a passage that the journal treated as prophecy, Barrat mentioned the possibility of his own death, begging the curé to tell his mother little by little if indeed God called him to heaven. Barrat's premonitions would come true: "Toward the end of the month of July, Our Lord Jesus Christ asked him for the sacrifice of his life."[110] In a vague allusion to the supernatural, the journal reported that nothing other than the date was known of the final death of apostolic missionary Louis-Marie-Charles Guégan. Without elaboration or comment, it recorded that the missionary's sister and mother back in France might have heard the missionary ascending to heaven around the estimated time of his death.[111] Such miraculous stories showed these fallen soldiers as not simply martyrs but saints as well.

Missionaries were not the only Christians who died the martyr's death, and when information permitted, stories of fallen indigenous clerics graced the pages of the *Missions Catholiques*. In a description that highlighted the missionary fascination with detailing physical pain, a letter from Bishop Puginier, the apostolic vicar in Hanoi, chronicled the final days of a curé named Câp, a Vietnamese priest killed by a group of Chinese mercenaries. Puginier reported that the priest was made to walk to five or six different Chinese forts. Sixty years old and weakened by hunger, thirst, and fevers, Câp endured a *cangue*, an awkward wooden vice around his neck that he was forced to carry night and day.[112] The bishop insisted that Câp's faith did not waver. Reports claimed that the priest carried a small crucifix with him. When the Chinese asked what it was, the priest replied: "It is my Master, and yours also." For his beliefs, Câp was sentenced to death: the Chinese buried him alive, head first, with his feet above ground, dangling a sign from his feet reading, "This is how followers of the perverse religion will be treated."[113] In another instance, a ninety-year-old Vietnamese man burned to death with a number of other Christians. Like Saint Lawrence, just moments before death, the man reportedly called on his companions to repent for their faults, to pardon their enemies, and to accept the death the Lord requested. "It was only when his soul left his body," the *Missions Catholiques* reported, "that this true servant of God stopped speaking."[114]

Like their missionaries, Vietnamese Christians benefited from supernatural intervention. One of Bishop Puginier's letters told of a young Vietnamese girl who was tied by her captors to a column in her home. The invaders set the house alight, but just before she would have been burned alive, she broke free of the rope binding her and fled. "She said herself that the holy Virgin saved her." Another woman was thrown on a pile of corpses and set ablaze. She remained unburned, as the bodies around her protected her from the flames. Puginier refused to "make a miracle" of the facts, choosing instead to leave that decision to God, and to be content believing in his Providence.[115] For readers, such stories were inspirational, demonstrating the power of God to save the faithful. But the unflinching spiritual strength of such indigenous Christians also revealed the piety and faith of converts, and offered a clear measure of the depth of Catholicism's roots. While the torment of martyred missionaries reflected commitment to God, the resilience of indigenous Christians living under extreme circumstances proved the success of the missionary movement in instilling true Christian belief in lands still under the rule of nonbelievers.

Though journals emphasized the tragedy of missionaries' and converts' deaths and suffering, there remained the consolation that these Christians had died for their savior and would be welcomed into heaven. By highlighting the piety and devotion of the fallen, obituaries transcended earthly trials such as personal pain and loss. Martyrs were also clearly held up as inspiration to common Catholics. As Brad Gregory has shown for the early modern period, martyrs were less fanatics than exemplars of the suffering that all missionaries were willing to endure in their love of God.[116] This basic tenet still held true in the late nineteenth century. Reports in 1880s missionary journals conformed to the traditional image of the martyr, reminding readers of Christ on the cross and the long line of martyrs who had fallen in his name. Like martyrs of old, a modern missionary's final demise represented not defeat but a step toward victory: "The apostles," the *Annales* encouraged its readers in 1885, "will not fail in their task; for, in the army of Jesus Christ, when one soldier falls, ten rise up to replace him."[117] The death of God's soldiers proved the vitality of those left behind and the growing strength of Catholicism. No need to pity the dead missionaries, be they strangled, dismembered, or burned: God had called his children to heaven.

Apostles in a Secular World

In nineteenth-century France, it is often said, the light of reason, spread by republican schoolmasters and government officials, penetrated the darkest corners of the most remote villages. Railroads and newspapers brought urban tastes, sensibilities, and political values to the most backwater towns of the nation. Modernity hit religion with a resounding thud: in Owen Chadwick's famous phrase, this was the era of the secularization of the European mind.[118] Superstition gave way to the cold truth of science. Church attendance across Europe slumped; piety wore thin. By the 1880s, a favorite topic of debate, for everyone from café conversationalists to novelists, was religious skepticism. A new level of pluralism made agnosticism and atheism fashionable religions for the modern world.[119] And, at the same time, missionaries like Père Guillemé, wandering alone along the shores of Lake Tanzania, followed in the footsteps of Saint Francis Xavier, dreaming of hardship, exile, torture, and—if they were one of God's chosen—a bloody death in the name of Christ.

It is tempting to meet the anomalies offered by a nineteenth-century movement more interested in religious conversion and faith than in secular notions of progress and patriotism with grave skepticism. Were missionaries and their supporters really sincere in their descriptions of the apostolic life, or were they just playing on the emotions of the faithful in an attempt to raise money? Like any large group, the ranks of God's soldiers undoubtedly included opportunists and frauds. But the evidence that many were pious and deeply committed to their vocation reaches well beyond publications aimed at raising money. Private letters, seminary traditions and songs, and publications designed for missionary, not public, consumption (such as the *Instructions*) are too copious to deny. These documents overwhelmingly corroborate the evidence of a religious sensibility profoundly influenced by faith, zeal, and sacrifice found in fund-raising material. This is not to put Catholic missionaries on a pedestal but rather to emphasize an obvious point too often ignored by scholars of empire: missionaries were deeply religious people, devoted to a project of evangelizing with traditions and goals that differed radically from national programs of colonial expansion.

On the question of traditions, some fruitful distinctions can be made between French Catholics and British Protestants. While complex, relations between Protestant missionaries and officials in the British empire were far less fraught than in the French possessions. In addition to the fact that many Protestant missionaries were openly pro-empire, there were strong historical links between Protestant evangelizing and British expansion: the birth of the Protestant movement at the end of the eighteenth century coincided directly with a vigorous period of British commercial ventures. British missionaries and merchants often shared common social backgrounds and sensibilities. And, especially during the Victorian era, British missionary work seems to have informed a distinctly "bourgeois" vision of British imperialism.[120] Equipped with middle-class sensibilities, British Protestants played an instrumental role in converting non-Europeans to "modernity" as well as Christianity.[121] In addition to the word of Christ, Protestant missions brought to the empire modernizing reforms, from capitalist practices and bourgeois values, such as notions of self-improvement, to desires for consumer goods.[122] As a result—and despite some disagreement over the day-to-day challenges of empire building—by midcentury, it is possible to say that "the bible and the flag" formed a dual impetus for British overseas endeavors.[123]

The case of Catholic missionaries in the French empire offers striking contrasts to the British example. Unlike in Britain, the Catholic missionary movement did not grow with French expansion but as a response to the devastation of the French Revolution, largely before the renewed republican imperial impulse of the 1880s and 1890s. As the century progressed, French missionaries and merchants were not from common socioeconomic backgrounds, nor did they share common politics or sensibilities. Missionaries increasingly came from humble rural upbringings; colonial entrepreneurs tended to be middle-class and liberal, and often active in Masonic lodges and republican politics, where anticlericalism thrived. Many missionaries, as the following chapters will show, were openly antagonistic to republican colonialism and the liberal, modernizing reforms it aimed to bring. If their religiosity alone was not enough to separate missionaries from many staunch republicans, then their fascination with Satan, corporeal suffering, and martyrdom, as well as their desire to spread wide the reach of the Catholic hierarchy, put them completely at odds with what most historians would consider "modern" bourgeois sensibilities. Until the early 1900s, few Catholic missionaries considered themselves agents of imperial expansion; in fact, many worried that French colonialism, driven by anticlerical republicans, would spell the end of evangelizing.

The sensibilities of Catholic missionaries require historians to reexamine not only French identities in the empire but also the very methods they use to understand colonialism. Influenced by colonial studies, many scholars have privileged class, along with race and gender, as an essential rubric of European identity abroad.[124] While class distinctions no doubt played an important role, such an approach is problematic when applied to French imperialism. In these first decades of republican expansion, class was a less influential force than religion in shaping one's allegiances. A middle-class pious Catholic and a middle-class Freemason likely had far less in common—in terms of their political perspectives—than a republican peasant and a republican businessman. As Maurice Agulhon has observed, religious divisions in France had no clear correspondence to class differences.[125] To understand what issues truly divided Frenchmen in the empire between the 1880s and 1914, no factor is more critical to consider than faith. The divisive relations between French men and women who debated religion in the empire were no mere tensions; they represented fractures and, at times, ravines.

This does not mean, however, that the Catholic missionary movement should be dismissed—as many secularist critics did at the time—as a throwback to a distant world, the embodiment of reactionary and antimodern fanaticism. Missionary supporters were not the only nineteenth-century Catholics to embrace the spiritual and supernatural with vigor. Support for missionaries bloomed at a time of popular religious revival, when miracles, visions, and prophecies were increasingly common.[126] This was the same era when many gave their savings and even their lives to defend the symbolic power of the Sacred Heart of Jesus Christ. It was the same decades when an illiterate shepherd girl's vision of the Virgin Mary drove tens of thousands of visitors to Lourdes every year to seek supernatural cures for what ailed them. Marian apparitions and pilgrimages both helped shape Catholics' belief in divine power and, as the historian Ruth Harris has shown, reflected a "changed devotional culture" in France.[127] To these varied believers can be added more than a million supporters of the Oeuvre de la propagation de la foi and other organizations that considered missionaries to be exemplars of Catholic faith, zeal, and sacrifice. Supporters and missionaries may have been religious fanatics. But if so, then fanaticism was a common affliction, for they were not few in number. In the late 1800s, the light of reason may have shone brightly across the hills and fields of the French countryside, but so, too, did the light of faith.

Like other forms of popular religious expression at the time, the missionary movement complicates the often-used dichotomy of "modern" and "traditional." Missionaries drew on *and* stood at odds with what might be called the modern, secular world. To help answer Jesus' call to evangelize, the Oeuvre de la propagation de la foi and similar organizations used sophisticated entrepreneurial schemes and campaigns to raise money. Full of biblical lore and saintly legends, missionary publications reflected the times in which they were mass-produced, complete with illustrations and, later, photographs. The *Missions Catholiques* published missionaries' geographic, ethnological, and other scientific reports (alongside its stories of evangelization) in a conscious effort to compete with popular scientific and travel publications of the day. By applying modern strategies to old narratives and even older spiritual concerns, the landscape of proselytizing, first sketched in the seventeenth century, took on greater texture and deeper contours. Rather than being antimodern, with its triumphant conversions and tragedies of martyrdom, the missionary movement was, as Thomas Kselman has said of miracles and prophecies, "part of the process through which Frenchmen dealt with modernity" and, it should be added, the world around them.[128] Steamships, military technology, and improved communication systems opened up vast tracts of the non-European world to commerce and colonialism. For pious Catholics, these lands also beckoned God's soldiers. The modern world offered new obligations, and chief among them was the duty to evangelize.

Missionary journals defined evangelizing as a movement that existed alongside, and distinct from, the expansion of Europe's political, military, and economic influence. Catholic intellectuals, commentators, and members of the Church hierarchy made much of the political—usually counterrevolutionary—potential of missionary work. But to accept the New Catholicism of late nineteenth-century France in purely political terms is to deny many French men and women their deeply felt religious beliefs. What is striking about the missionary movement up until the 1880s is how *little* concerned its soldiers and supporters seemed to be with the profane politics of national and international policy. Despite the involvement of clerics at all levels—from town priest to the pope—in politics, most missionaries (and the organizations that supported them) described their objectives in strictly spiritual terms until the late 1880s.

Many commentators and politicians often held up missionaries as patriotic heroes and their work as signs of the profound Christian roots of the French nation. But, for missionaries themselves, in both private letters and published reports, there is a striking lack of references to their nations of origin or to current European political issues. Yet evangelizing and conversion were inherently political processes, requiring religious workers to become enmeshed in local power struggles. The arrival of Christianity disrupted social relations and often gave rise to violent antagonisms. Missionaries were by no means naive spectators to this: although they may have been sent among wolves, they certainly were not sheep. But throughout much of the nineteenth century, on topics ranging from imperial rivalries to Church-state relations, Catholic missionaries remained surprisingly silent. Working alone in places Europeans considered dark, uncivilized, and dangerous, they saw themselves as soldiers in an epic struggle between the powers of God and Satan. By comparison, party politics and international squabbles were somehow less pressing. Considering the scope and aspirations of their movement, missionaries were far from being simple agents of republican imperialism. Throughout most of the century, the "empire of God" was much larger than that of France.

Such were the centuries-old traditions and motivations that enabled Père Guillemé to travel across Africa without mentioning the European imperial storm closing in around him. But in 1888, when Guillemé penned his report, a blind, all-engrossing commitment to apostolic work was increasingly a luxury. For many religious workers, it was becoming impossible to avoid the disruption of European expansion and interaction with colonial regimes. From those days on, relations between missionaries and administrators would be deeply influenced by the exigencies of establishing power in each colonial possession and by a long history of enmity between Catholic and republican in the *mère-patrie*. The two ideas of France and the civilization it exported to the nation's new possessions—one deeply Christian, the other equally secular—would come into conflict. By the late-1880s, Catholicism was not the only proselytizing religion in France: the other was republicanism, particularly in its more radical incarnations. And many pious republicans had their own ideas about which devils needed to be cast out.

II

INDOCHINA

Defining French Influence in Indochina

No corner of the French empire offers a better example of how Catholic missionaries could see republican colonizers as Johnnies-come-lately than Indochina.[1] In the 1870s, when republicans started showing an interest in expanding France's hold on Southeast Asia (Cochinchina was already a possession and Cambodia a protectorate), missionaries of the Société des missions étrangères de Paris had been working in the region for more than two centuries. Despite their conflicts with Catholicism at home—this was the decade Gambetta declared clericalism to be the enemy—republican supporters of colonial expansion celebrated the missionary legacy. As the historian Stephen Roberts put it, "France successfully raked history for proofs of her interest in Indo-China."[2] Even Jules Ferry, who spearheaded the campaign to limit Catholic influence at home, pointed to the long history of missionary work as evidence of a proud "French" tradition in the region.[3] Abroad, it seemed, France had no greater champion than the Catholic missionaries of Southeast Asia.

Throughout the nineteenth century, in times of religious conflict, Catholic workers regularly sought French diplomatic and military support to defend what they considered to be their right to evangelize. By the second half of the nineteenth century, to expedite official intervention, apostolic vicars often described their converts as wholeheartedly devoted to the French cause. A particularly vigorous advocate of Catholic converts' love of France was Mgr. Paul François Puginier, arguably the most politically engaged apostolic vicar of Tonkin that Hanoi ever saw. In 1884, at a moment when the missions faced particularly violent opposition, Puginier warned French officials that mandarins—Vietnamese officials who administered much of the day-to-day functioning of the protectorate—wanted to "exterminate Christians" because they saw them as friends of France. In his correspondence with officials, Puginier turned his converts into dedicated patriots. "Yes, I can say it," he wrote in one report, "our neophytes have always loved and still love France." In return for their mistreatment, he added, his Christians deserved the justice that only French gunships could deliver.[4]

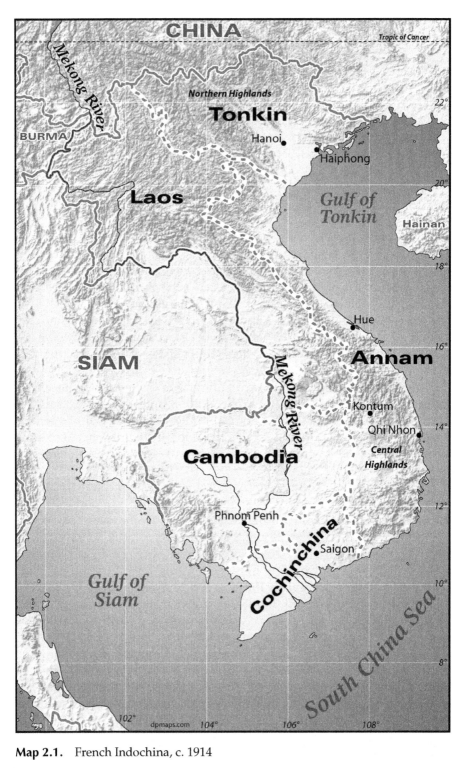

Map 2.1. French Indochina, c. 1914

Such patriotic declarations have led historians of French Indochina to portray missionaries as crucial facilitators of colonial expansion.[5] In the years before an official colonial presence in the region, it is often argued, French missionaries were their nation's de facto representatives.[6] At times of violent resistance, missionaries counted on French military intervention to protect them. In return, missionaries often offered military and, later, colonial officials key services as translators, cultural intermediaries, and guides. Protection of missionaries gave French officials a justification for intervening in Vietnamese affairs, and—most historians concur—led to a permanent colonial presence in Indochina. There is, no doubt, much validity to this story: throughout the nineteenth century, the more French troops defended against anti-Christian violence, the more likely they were to stay in the region. But in portraying missionaries as eager collaborators of colonial expansion, historians take for granted that religious workers wanted to live under French colonial rule—a fact, as this chapter will show, that many Frenchmen at the time doubted greatly.

In the late 1880s, with the founding of the Union of Indochina, the expanding ranks of French civil administrators in Indochina brought the prospect of a long coexistence of republicans, colonists, and missionaries, provoking concern on all sides. For missionaries, a sustained official presence raised the specter of government interference, regulation, or, worst of all, prohibition. Administrators, in turn, wondered whether missionaries, with their considerable knowledge of Vietnamese society and sway over many Christian villages, benefited the colonial cause or made French rule all the more precarious. Although anticlerical critics questioned missionary allegiance in literally every possession in the French empire, the deep regional roots of Catholicism made the issue most pressing in Vietnam. At the founding of the Union of Indochina, the Missions étrangères counted more than 270,000 Catholics in Tonkin and Annam, and more than 90,000 in Cochinchina.[7] Nowhere did French missions possess a longer history or a more developed operation.

From the mid-1880s to the mid-1890s, when Frenchmen in Indochina debated missionary contributions to the colonial effort, it was always in terms of whether they helped spread "French influence"—always a nebulous phrase. While the pro-colonial politicians in France spoke of the nation's civilizing goals, officials in Indochina focused on the practical necessities of establishing colonial rule. As a result, security and allegiance trumped all other concerns, from fulfilling abstract colonial aspirations like the civilizing mission to exporting the anticlerical policies propounded by republicans at home. In the colony, high-ranking officials and bishops vowed to keep conflict between local administrators and missionaries to a minimum. But the awkward alliance did not hold everywhere. Away from the major towns, beyond the shadows of the cathedrals and halls of government, relations between missionaries and administrators in the countryside were plagued by ideological differences, mutual suspicion, and even petty jealousies.

These debates over Catholic influence heralded significant changes in both long-held missionary and republican attitudes and practices. In the 1880s, when officials increasingly questioned missionary allegiance to France, religious workers were forced to abandon their self-styled image as homeless soldiers of God and to enter the profane realm of public opinion. When pressed, missionaries on the defensive associated the spread of influence with providing intelligence, helping official expeditions and scientific missions, and acting as guides and translators. They often embellished their records of cooperation with declarations of patriotism. Nowhere was this better exemplified than in the central highlands of Vietnam, where a mission under suspicion of committing treason defended itself with flamboyant proclamations of love for France. Such a formula ultimately sufficed for the colonial government. But a group of critics, composed of lower-ranking officials and colonists, suspected—often with good reason—that when the missions professed love for the *patrie*, it was not for the republic but for a potentially subversive counterrevolutionary vision of a bygone France.

Past and Present: Religious Violence and French Colonialism

When Jules Ferry invoked the long history of French missionaries in Indochina, he was referring in large part to the waning years of the eighteenth century.[8] In 1787, Pigneau de Béhaine, a French bishop working in Cochinchina, traveled to Versailles to elicit support from Louis XVI for Nguyen Anh. A struggling prince who had lost his family's patrimony to a domestic rebellion, Nguyen Anh remained neutral toward Christianity but held Pigneau in high regard, hoping he would help him regain his power.[9] Pigneau's trip to Versailles was perhaps most memorable because he brought with him Nguyen Anh's young son, Prince Canh, whose presence caused much talk and amusement. A century later, many Frenchmen—Catholic and republican alike—mythologized the bishop's visit as proof of a deep bond between France and Vietnam.

Bishop Pigneau's turn to his native France for help, however, was primarily made out of despair for the future of Christianity, not out of his desire to see his *patrie* spread its political influence in the region. The bishop had in fact first turned to the Portuguese for military assistance. The Portuguese military presence in the region, combined with their sympathy for the Catholic cause, made them an obvious choice. But the Portuguese refused the bishop's request. Louis XVI—Pigneau's second choice—ultimately signed a treaty offering military assistance for Nguyen Anh, a pledge that was never honored. Upon returning to the region from Versailles, Pigneau found Nguyen Anh struggling. In haste, the bishop raised his own small army and helped the Vietnamese leader defeat his foes. Pigneau de Béhaine died before seeing Nguyen Anh take the title of Emperor Gia Long, but he left behind an ambiguous partnership between Catholic missionaries, the Vietnamese throne, and the French crown—a history of collaboration that rested largely on a memorable appearance at court by a Vietnamese child and on an unfulfilled promise for military assistance.

It was not until the 1840s that the protectorate of the Catholic missions drove France to significant political and military involvement in eastern Asia. For the next two decades, anti-Christian violence witnessed the killing of tens of thousands of Vietnamese converts, as well as the imprisonment, torture, and execution of missionaries. Such violent episodes, combined with increasing French interest in the economic possibilities of trade with China, brought French ships into confrontation with Vietnamese forces and inspired French policymakers, including Napoleon III, to seek a permanent foothold in the region. By 1862, French attacks resulted in the taking of Saigon and outlying provinces in Cochinchina. Within two years, the French had declared a protectorate over neighboring Cambodia, as well. A small group of pro-colonial commentators started envisioning Indochina as France's answer to the British Raj.

While military men and merchants interested in political prestige and economic profit drove French expansion into Indochina, the plight of Vietnamese Catholics remained a looming issue throughout the period. In some instances, such as during Francis Garnier's 1873–74 invasion of Tonkin, Vietnamese Catholics fought on the side of the French.[10] The attack on Hanoi was ultimately a failure for French colonizers, costing Garnier his life. But the cause of Catholicism was rewarded: the Treaty of 1874 that the French and Vietnamese signed guaranteed, as Patrick Tuck notes, "virtually unfettered" freedom of religion.[11] A decade later, when Prime Minister Jules Ferry ordered troops to invade Tonkin, France gained a protectorate, but with a price. French troops suffered humiliation—Henri de Rivière, who led the French assault, was captured and beheaded—and the move threatened war with China, which remained uneasy about having a European colony along its southern border. Although Tonkin became a protectorate, the French military's less-than-stellar performance cost Ferry his job.

The religious violence that accompanied the invasion of Tonkin resulted in the death of between 30,000 and 40,000 Vietnamese Christians and brought to light the role of Catholic missionaries in a new republican empire. While missionary publications reported the events in almost exclusively spiritual terms, focusing heavily on the glories of martyrdom, the general question of the political impact of missionary work in the empire became a salient issue for a variety of commentators in the French press. French newspapers addressed the killing of Christians and their missionaries with outrage and horror, but a political agenda shaped the analysis. Clerics wrote editorials to garner political and financial support from both the French government and local congregations. For other commentators, be they supporters or critics of missionary work, the issue showed the extent to which international affairs could be colored by domestic religious politics and the civilizing rhetoric of French imperialism.

Many on the Catholic right—generally *not* friends of colonial expansion in the 1880s—used the violence in Asia to paint republican policymakers as cold and even murderous for ignoring the missions' plight. In 1885, one expert on the Far East, Frédéric Romanet du Caillaud, wrote that, by remaining indifferent to the anti-Christian violence, the republic was carrying on a dangerously anticlerical tradition that stretched from "the horrors of '93" (when many members of the French clergy were killed in the Terror) to the Paris Commune.[12] An article in the *Semaine Religieuse* claimed that the deaths of the "true Christians" of Vietnam laid bare the Jewish and Masonic roots of the republic. "Ah! If it had only concerned some Jewish groups, expelled . . . by populations tired of their monstrous usury," the article ranted, "what cries of indignation, what violent reclamations, in the name of humanity and civilization, would have been heard from all sides!" But unfortunately, complained the *Semaine Religieuse*, the *libre-penseurs* and Freemasons of the republican camp seemed unmoved by the blood of 30,000 Asian Christians.[13]

In addition to their critiques of republicanism, both editorials emphasized that Catholic converts were, to use Romanet du Caillaud's words, "naturalized Frenchmen" sympathetic to the colonial cause. For the *Semaine Religieuse*, the deaths of the Vietnamese were "an irreparable loss" for France. Other writers concurred. In his newspaper *Liberté*, the notorious anti-Semite and reactionary Édouard Drumont hailed missionaries' role in spreading French influence. Missionaries "who seem to work only for God," he wrote, "have been the most marvelous instrument of civilization, incomparable workers for French power overseas."[14] In neglecting the missionaries and their civilizing influence, Drumont surmised, republicans showed they were not committed to making France a country of greatness. "If we want France to retake its rank among peoples," he wrote, "we must return to French tradition and not persecute the religion that made France what it was, that is to say, the premier nation in the world."[15]

Missionaries, all these articles agreed, pushed wide the boundaries of empire. For a writer in the *Avenir Militaire*, missionaries represented important footholds in regions of the world hostile to European intervention. Missionaries, the paper insisted, provided a shared religion and a superior education that "destroyed in these converts [their] hatred of foreigners." The author continued, "what was drowned in blood" in the violence in Indochina "was a political force favorable to Europe." With the loss of the Christians came the loss of France's only friends. "Their blood has spilled," the article concluded, "not only for God, but for France; their death is a defeat and a threat to us."[16]

Just as supporters of the missions argued that evangelization spread French power by "naturalizing" converts, critics believed that religious work inevitably led to violence. In 1886, for example, a number of articles in

Indochinese newspapers debated whether missionaries laid or destroyed French inroads in China. The issue had particular relevance to readers in colonial centers where Frenchmen were asking the same questions of local missionaries. A serialized article in *L'Avenir du Tonkin*, a paper sold in Hanoi and Haiphong, was clear in its criticisms of the danger of missionary "zeal"—a state of mind that stood at odds with the rationalism required for international politics.[17] The article, written by Jean Bessières, insisted that anti-Christian violence in China was not a by-product of Chinese intolerance but rather retribution for missionary meddling. Horrified that missionaries saw martyrdom as felicitous for the Catholic effort, Bessières condemned Catholics for using the threat of French military reprisals to manipulate Chinese governors. One instance of missionary scheming, he claimed, led to a military skirmish that cost twenty-seven French soldiers their lives.[18] For Bessières, missionaries were all guilty of "inopportune intervention" into affairs that did not concern them; "their ambitions, holy or profane, their imprudence, their excess of zeal" were all sources of continual French embarrassment.[19]

Other articles supported Bessières's conclusions. The *Courrier d'Haiphong* seriously scrutinized whether France's protectorate over the Catholic missions of China had brought any good.[20] In a piece in *L'Avenir du Tonkin*, a former French consul in China named Eugène Simon stated plainly that missionaries were responsible for the most serious conflicts between the two countries.[21] Under such circumstances, France could not achieve its political and civilizing aims. In Vietnam, French readers of these articles on China's missions could not help but have questioned the intentions of the missionaries in their midst. There, much of the discussion of Catholics avoided inflated talk of civilization and French greatness, focusing instead on the far more practical concerns of security and allegiance—not surprising, since, throughout the 1880s, piracy and rebellion remained a part of daily life.

Bishops, Officials, and the Uncertain History of Missionary Commitment

Officials in Indochina had good reason to want to believe that Catholic missionaries and converts were sympathetic to their plans. In 1884, when France added a protectorate over Annam and Tonkin to its possessions in Cochinchina and Cambodia, not only had French Catholic missionaries been in place for two centuries, but they also influenced considerable numbers of Christian villages. In its estimates that year, the Société des missions étrangères de Paris, the missionary organization in the region, counted more than 350,000 Catholics in Indochina, the vast majority in Vietnam. In addition to souls, the missions had an extensive physical and administrative infrastructure, including six apostolic vicars, more than 150 French missionaries, and 225 indigenous priests who could preach in more than 700 churches or chapels. To prepare future generations, they ran nine seminaries and more than 600 schools and orphanages that taught well over 10,000 students.[22] With the exception of the Philippines, French Indochina was the most Christian region in Southeast Asia.

Few things could please French officials more than to think that hundreds of thousands of indigenous Christians were their friends. In 1880s and 1890s Annam and Tonkin, where most administrative duties remained in the hands of indigenous elites, French officials avoided involvement in religious troubles, playing the part of mediator only when conflicts became particularly heated. The administration took an official stance of religious neutrality from the beginning of the protectorate. In 1886, responding to requests made by Minister of Foreign Affairs Charles de Freycinet (a Protestant, missionaries liked to point out), the colonial administration voted a new subsidy of 10,000 piastres for the missions to help spread "French influence."[23] The government also paid varying subventions to the missions to teach the French language and to run schools, orphanages, and other facilities.

Despite the policy of neutrality and the paying of subventions, official reservations about missionaries still loomed. Even de Freycinet's call to subsidize the missions' efforts to spread "influence" met with some consternation in the colony. But officials in Paris easily swayed the doubters, who ultimately agreed that it would be "impolitic" to alienate Catholic communities.[24] The administration refused to arm Christians, as many missionaries had asked. But it turned a blind eye to independent Catholic militias organized to combat mandarins whom missionaries deemed aggressive or corrupt.[25]

Catholic bishops were no less ambivalent about their new partnership. Stationed in the main cities of the region—Hanoi, Saigon, Hue, Phnom Penh—bishops represented the missions in all official business and, for that reason, had far more regular interaction with the administration than did missionaries in the field. When troubles arose between missionaries and local officials, mandarins, or colonists, it was the local bishop who went to the administration to help smooth over the problems.

From very early on, some bishops showed themselves eager to prove their commitment to help France catch pirates, stave off rebellion, and avoid war. The nineteenth century had been a tumultuous one for the Missions étrangères in Indochina: from the 1830s, every decade brought stories of missionary persecution and death. Mission leaders hoped that a French colonial presence—provided it was partial to the missionary endeavor—would bring a level of social and political stability that could serve evangelizing. Colonialism could help conversion in less tangible ways, as well. As Frenchmen, missionaries could tell their followers—with much truth—that they enjoyed close relations with the new power. The French administration, if it acted in ways that complemented missionary goals and that benefited Christian communities, could enhance the missions' prowess in the countryside.

Bishops' communications with administrators therefore showed their eagerness both to assist colonization and to guide officials to act in the missions' best interests. From the mid-1880s, for example, Mgr. Puginier sent regular reports—sometimes more than one per week—to the residents-general of Annam and Tonkin. Puginier's correspondence was rich with colorful details: talk of "secret enemies" with "perverse designs" to foment "internal revolts" was not out of the ordinary.[26] In one report from 1888, for example, Puginier warned that Chinese troops were waiting at the northern border of Tonkin for the perfect moment to invade, while pirates within the protectorate were swaying villagers to be "hostile to the French cause." "Careful! It is time to take precautions," he warned. The colonial government, his letters seemed to say, was in grave danger.[27]

Mgr. Puginier's apparently primary allegiance to France allowed him to influence the government to help the cause of evangelization. For example, in 1888, Puginier suggested two steps that the administration could take to avoid social unrest: it could ban census taking and put an end to the corvée, the colonial system of requiring labor of the indigenous population. He argued that both systems allowed local mandarin administrators to manipulate and intimidate peasants. Some indigenous administrators in the countryside, he wrote, would demand difficult physical labor of a starving population and then blame the corvée on the colonial administration, effectively turning the population against the French. Regardless of whether Puginier's recommendations were logical or sympathetic, they directly benefited evangelizing. Missionaries' chief adversaries in Tonkin were mandarins who, Catholics complained, used census information to target Christian communities for extortion and violence. Corvées were also a common point of contention for missionaries who believed that the missions alone should influence, and in some cases dictate, converts' work habits. Puginier argued that limiting the reach of indigenous administrators would help win over a population already suffering from famine. He most certainly also hoped it would further empower Catholics and free the missions from mandarin interference.[28]

Mgr. Puginier was a more adept politician than his fellow bishops. Some bishops could not accept easily the potential benefits of colonization, choosing instead to harp on the hardships it caused for the missionary and his followers. Especially contentious issues were taxation and justice. Taxes required a poor population to work harder, meaning that, as one bishop put it, the Christian "has neither the time, nor the leisure of studying prayers and Christian doctrine."[29] In addition to concerns about prayer time, the mandarin intermediaries who collected taxes undermined missionaries' political sway in their communities, often pitting the mission against local administrators. A heavy tax burden, combined with corvée, also limited the amount of work the missions could demand of their converts—a serious concern, since Christian labor helped missions function.

The law commonly stirred controversy as well. Missionaries in Indochina regularly became embroiled in questions of justice when Christians were involved. In less divisive cases, the colonial government allowed missionaries to help settle local disputes. But officials often found priests overstepping their bounds and threatening domestic order. Serious altercations led to official reproach of missionary behavior. In 1891, for example, a group of missionaries in Cambodia overruled indigenous judicial officials, or *balat*, in order to impose punishments for crimes ranging from tax evasion to murder. According to the resident-superior of Cambodia, missionaries had "a very marked tendency to assume power that they do not have." Calling Christian villages "veritable independent states," he complained that missionaries intervened "almost daily and always with impunity." Even in a case of murder, one local priest took it upon himself to pass sentence, excluding the local judge and failing to notify French officials a few miles away in Phnom Penh.[30] According to one indigenous observer, the missionary's "French nationality" and "intelligence" gave him "great prestige before the people and the mandarins, the latter of whom are not permitted to intervene in an affair in which the *Père* will be involved."[31] Such influence, in the minds of many French officials, could either buttress their rule or undermine order and lead to ethnic conflict, as the vast majority of Christians in Cambodia were ethnic Vietnamese.

Missionary intervention in local politics regularly drew in—and was mediated by—men at the highest level of government. In 1889, conflict between Christians and non-Christians in the troubled province of Nghê An threatened, as the resident-superior of Annam noted, "to lead to the return of the events of 1885." Despite calls from the administration to back down, a number of priests attempted to oust mandarin leaders and pursued charges against a Vietnamese army officer. In a letter to the governor-general, the resident-superior argued that the protectorate "must, without hesitation, remind the mission of the truth of their role to stop their encroachment in the domain of administrative authority." But, in the end, the government's response lost much of the resident-general's initial ire. Rather than reprimand the priest directly, the resident-general advised the regional bishop to respect the established chain of administration; the existing system, he said, was the best way to ensure tranquillity for the mission and the region.[32]

In addition to disagreements over policies, there was the problem of compatibility: many missionaries and republican officials just did not like one another. In one 1890 report, the bishop of West Cochinchina wondered why it seemed increasingly difficult to convert the local population. He attributed the mission's difficulties to the growing influence of French officials and colonists in the region. In his words, there was a perceptible "feeling of incredulity that penetrates the *indigènes* with knowledge of the French."

"Everywhere," he continued, there was "hate and contempt . . . for our com-patriots." The bishop clearly sympathized with these emotions, seeing his compatriots as an unimpressive bunch. "*Och!*" he lamented. "If France had only sent honest and Christian men to Indochina!"[33] But in his correspon-dence with the administration, the bishop dutifully held his tongue, trying to make the best of what was quickly becoming an inevitable fate. While the partnership between bishops and officials had become far more intimate and complex than in the days of Pigneau de Béhaine's visit to Versailles, the am-biguities of their relationship were very slow to fade.

The View from the Field

While bishops and high-ranking officials in Hanoi, Saigon, and other major colonial towns strove to keep relations amicable, missionaries in the country-side were often more hostile to colonialism. From the mid-1880s forward, the arrival of new local administrators armed with regulations forced missionar-ies to come to terms with a new predicament. Bishops ran into officials with great regularity at meetings, at social events, or even on the street. Missionar-ies in the countryside, on the other hand, saw their new *chefs* with far less frequency and often actively avoided interacting with them. This lack of regular interaction likely did more to breed suspicion than to minimize mis-understandings and gave rise to a climate of accusation, denial, and counter-accusation. Despite bishops' assurances that all missionaries spread a love of France, many local administrators remained doubtful.

A look at missionary attitudes in one remote Catholic outpost suggests that officials had good reason to be dubious. In the late 1880s and early 1890s, there was no more controversial mission in the region than the one in the highlands of central Vietnam. Its headquarters was at Kontum, a village that was an arduous 200-kilometer trek from the coastal town of Qui Nhon, capi-tal of Binh Dinh province. If Frenchmen knew much of the plateau of the central highlands, they knew of its reputation for dismal weather, dense forests, fever, tigers, and unwelcoming inhabitants. The people who lived in the region, such as the Sedang, the Bahnar, and the Jarai, were both ethni-cally distinct from the majority Vietnamese population and fiercely au-tonomous, causing many Frenchmen to invoke the derogatory Vietnamese term *moï*, or savage, to describe them. Catholic missionaries were the only Europeans who had any prolonged experience in the "Pays moï," having had an established mission there since 1852.[34] They faced a life of physical hardship and sometimes violent confrontation that led them to call their Kontum headquarters—with great pride—the "Mission des sauvages."[35]

Père Jean-Baptiste Guerlach, a missionary who spent most of his apostolic career in the central highlands, left a vivid picture of how missionaries func-tioned in societies where Europeans rarely ventured, much less settled.[36]

Like most missionaries, Guerlach imagined his vocation as a continuation of the work of Saint Paul, Francis Xavier, and Alexandre de Rhodes. He often worked alone, guided by the long-established methods of his trade. In his correspondence, the priest described how he lived within the norms and traditions of the local population. He became fluent in local languages and wrote detailed ethnographic studies of the highland minorities. He was a teacher, doctor, and moral tutor for dozens of Christians. He also immersed himself in local politics for the sake of the mission, working hard to make alliances with local groups.

In the spring of 1887, for example, conflicts with the Sedang, longtime rivals of his Bahnar converts, made an attack on the Bahnar mission likely. Before war broke out, the missionary mediated an accord between the groups. In addition to minimizing the chances of future bloodshed, Guerlach hoped that contact with the Sedang would bring them under the influence of the mission and the One True God. To accomplish this, the missionary chose a man named Bat to help him arrange a meeting with the Sedang chiefs. Bat informed Guerlach that it would be necessary to make a blood pact with the chiefs to guarantee an indissoluble union. "That disgusted me a little," Guerlach admitted, "but force made me submit to necessity." The blood pact would make the two chiefs, as the missionary understood it, his sons. On the appointed night, a group of Sedang arrived in Guerlach's village, which was appropriately decked out "*à la mode* Bahnar."[37] Through the night the two groups drank wine to the beat of drums; they slaughtered and feasted on a buffalo, reminding Guerlach of scenes from *The Iliad*. The missionary presented his new sons—"one of whom," he quipped, "could certainly have been my grandfather"—gifts of drums, bells, cotton, and pearls. Bat made a short speech saying that the two groups were now one village and one family, with one father—Père Guerlach.[38]

The next morning, Guerlach set up an altar with a large crucifix surrounded by burning candles and a statuette of the Holy Virgin. As musicians played their gongs and drums, Guerlach stood between the two Sedang chiefs, while each of them placed a hand on the crucifix. "Oh God," the priest pronounced, "I make today an alliance of father and son with Peu and Léo of Kon Run." The priest asked Jesus Christ to "reward my sons if they are good and judge them according to your severe justice if they dare to break their promises." Then the three men—two Sedang chiefs and one French priest—cut their thumbs and dripped blood into a cup of wine, which Bat stirred with a chicken bone. Closing his eyes, Guerlach took a sip of the blood and wine, and his two "sons" finished it off. The cup was then refilled with wine so everyone present could drink from it.[39]

The differences between this scene and official European diplomacy are obvious; it is hard to imagine colonial officials agreeing to drink bloody wine stirred with a chicken bone. But Guerlach was a missionary who typically accepted "as much as possible" the practices of the local culture. His mingling of local practices, Christian prayer, and a masslike ritual were in the tradition of Alexandre de Rhodes and other early missionaries who molded Christianity as need dictated. Guerlach later claimed that he had brokered the alliance for the benefit of French influence, an idea he certainly believed insofar as he thought Catholicism was a core French tradition. But in form and function Guerlach's approach could not have differed more from the republican style of colonialism. His goal was not to bring the Sedang under French rule but to lead them, as he put it, "to quit the devil in order to give themselves over to the good Lord."[40] Even the justice that Guerlach promised to deliver was not the Third Republic's but rather that of Jesus. With the strange communion complete, the reach of Catholicism's influence now extended to a new highland ethnic group.

Not only did Guerlach fail to see his work tied to French rule, he was openly hostile about many of his lay compatriots. Despite his isolation, Guerlach's work in the highlands often stirred his resentment for the immorality of contemporary French society. The story of Pierre, a young highland neophyte, was one such case. Ignoring Guerlach's admonitions, one day, while working in the hot sun, Pierre drank some wine, sending him down a long and unfortunate path. Over the previous few months, Pierre had been able to rebuff the unwanted advances of a local pagan girl. Tipsy, however, Pierre was doomed. "My unfortunate young man," wrote Guerlach, " '*let one thing lead to another*,' as one vulgarly says, and he succumbed."[41] When the wine vapors cleared, Pierre realized his mistake, wept, and swore never to drink again. Rather than a story of moral weakness, Guerlach held up Pierre as a model for decadent French society. "How Europeans don't have this delicacy of conscience," the missionary complained. He decried the French attitude that said, "one peccadillo more or less, what's that? Youth must have a good time!" By contrast, the punishment for adultery in Pierre's society was harsh: the guilty paid a penalty of one buffalo to the village. Had the adultery resulted in "complications," Guerlach added, the two would have been enslaved or forced to pay five to nine buffalos. "Try then to pass this law in the Senate or in the chamber of deputies," Guerlach wrote. "Civilization is a beautiful thing; but how many of the civilized have a more obliterated moral sense than [that of] the Savages!"[42]

Time and again, when Guerlach thought of France he became convinced that "a good number of savages will have a higher place in heaven than many Frenchmen."[43] If the republic had fallen into a general state of moral degeneracy, Guerlach considered its radical politicians to be the true savages—an observation that lent a racial dimension to his criticisms. For example, the missionary turned a discussion of Sedang sorcery into political commentary about Freemasonry. While he believed that the devil intervened in sorcerers' work, the priest found Freemasonry to be even more demonic. "Our unfortunate savages," he wrote of his neophytes, indulged in "diabolical practices, but they are a thousand times less criminal than the Occultist

Masons" who committed "the most ignoble blasphemies and the most horrible profanations."[44]

By attacking Freemasons, Guerlach made reference to a prevalent political issue in the colonies, where many of the most vocal proponents of expansion (and the most outspoken anticlericals) were Freemasons. Under the influence of Freemasonry, French colonial rule endangered all that Guerlach worked for—Christianity in Vietnam. He had particular scorn for Governor-General Jean de Lanessan, a Freemason and critic of Catholic proselytizing. As governor-general, de Lanessan followed Paris's policy of religious neutrality. But Guerlach found the governor-general's anticlericalism obvious. He criticized de Lanessan for letting mandarins' "hatred of the Christian religion" go unbridled. Like a modern-day Pontius Pilate, de Lanessan had "abandoned the Christian princes to the hatred of their persecutors" and had furnished the rod with which the mandarins beat the Christians.[45] Far from championing the arrival of French colonialism, Guerlach was deeply concerned about its potential destructiveness. Thousands of miles away in France, supporters of the republican empire were blowing the trumpet of civilization. From where this missionary stood, it was unclear which savages needed civilizing—the inhabitants of the Pays moï or their supposed republican saviors.

Beyond the Pale No Longer

Guerlach's antagonism toward many of his countrymen makes clear that he would have preferred to remain beyond the legislative reach of the administration, a lone evangelist in his beloved Mission des sauvages. But soon after France declared its protectorate over Annam, the central highlands aroused serious official concern. The mid-1880s witnessed a number of events that led to French unease about the security of Annam's western border in the central highlands. Under the guidance of mandarins, thousands of peasants revolted with widespread violence aimed at overthrowing French rule. In his history of Vietnamese anticolonialism, David Marr marks 5 July 1885— the day Ham Nghi, the sitting emperor of Vietnam, fled his capital—as "a turning point in the history of Vietnam's response to foreign intervention."[46] The day signaled the real start of the Can vuong movement of widespread, violent resistance to French rule. General de Courcy, who led the French forces, believed he lacked the troops to defeat the rebellion and restore order. Ham Nghi remained in hiding in the mountains of northern Annam, seeking assistance from Muong minority villagers. French officials feared he might stir up further rebellion until his capture in November 1888.[47]

The central highlands witnessed episodic violence, though not on the scale of regions to the north and south (which made martyrs of missionaries that led to debates in the French press). In central Annam, French administrators relied on collaborating mandarins to help put down local scholar-gentry rebellions. The relative security in this region, however, was undermined by international politics when Siam increased its influence over territory east of the Mekong River. French officials believed the British to be behind Siam's encroachment. Suspicion grew even deeper in 1886 when the British moved into Upper Burma. Uncertain of their power over the Vietnamese population and worried by menacing neighbors, Frenchmen in Indochina saw their rule threatened from all sides.[48] By the late 1880s, the central highlands had ceased to be a terra incognita; instead, many officials now saw the region as a vulnerable frontier where the Siamese, British, or even—as some rumors suggested—Germans could stage an invasion of the French protectorate. The French were thoroughly unprepared to battle both foreign invaders and Can vuong resistance fighters.

Though nominally part of the French protectorate of Annam, the central highlands remained politically autonomous. Local and regional mandarins were entirely absent from the region, with Vietnamese authority not stretching beyond An Khe, a town less than halfway to Kontum from Qui Nhon on the coast. Traditionally, highland minorities had fiercely defended their independence from the Vietnamese, occasionally fighting with and even enslaving Vietnamese who entered their territory. The French had little interest in challenging these groups' claims of independence. The Catholic mission was a powerful force in these communities, and the administration happily accepted it as a sufficient representative of French influence. But against this backdrop of instability, the essentially unchallenged independence of the mission was to come under scrutiny.

In 1888, Charles-David de Meyréna, a ne'er-do-well adventurer and explorer, arrived in the central highlands.[49] Claiming to be on an official mission for France, Mayréna enlisted the help of two local missionaries, Père Guerlach and one of his coreligionists, Père Irigoyen. Using the missionaries as guides and translators, Mayréna spent more than two months meeting with local chiefs, making agreements defining villages' relations to French authority, and regulating trade between the region and the rest of the colony.[50] But in June 1888, during a bout of severe fever, Mayréna started making modifications to the agreements already in place.[51] In a constitution signed on 3 June at the Sedang village of Kon-Gung, in a region the French considered most vulnerable to foreign attack, Mayréna proclaimed himself king of the Sedangs.[52]

The new "king," who assumed the throne as Marie I, had a brief but notorious reign. Though he had no aristocratic blood in his veins—"de Mayréna" was an affectation—he was a master of royal pretensions and grandiose gestures. Marie I ordered royal stationery, flags, medals of honor, postage stamps, and even European-style military uniforms for his Sedang soldiers.[53] To the embarrassment of some and the amusement of many, the king granted interviews to European journalists and wrote confident letters to heads of state, including the president of the French republic. He spoke flamboyantly of his commitment to defending *his* people despite not being able to speak his people's language. Stories of Mayréna's adventures circulated in cafés from the rue Catinat in Saigon to the boulevards of Paris, and filled columns of national and colonial papers.[54] His kingdom was a European fantasy that only imperialism could have made real.

Not all, however, was harmless showmanship. Out of cash, Mayréna threatened to turn to Britain, Siam, or even Germany—this from a man awarded the Chevalier of the Legion of Honor for his part in the Franco-Prussian War—if the French failed to recognize and invest in his Sedang kingdom. Concerned that the highlands could fall under the influence of their adversaries, colonial officials monitored Mayréna's movements carefully and treated him as a serious threat. The government spurned his requests to meet with officials, including the president of the republic, and waited for his options to run out. Broke, he soon left his kingdom for Hong Kong and Europe in search of investors in his new country. In November 1890, on the island of Tioman off the Malaysian peninsula, while plotting his surreptitious return to the highlands, the king of the Sedang died, allegedly from a snakebite, though other theories, including suicide, abounded.[55] "I believe he was at the end of his resources," wrote the French consulate in Singapore. "This adventure is therefore finally finished."[56]

For the Catholic mission, however, the Mayréna affair had just begun. From the moment they heard of his coronation, French officials began asking how Mayréna came to power in the first place. Quick to acquit themselves of wrongdoing, a number of administrators who had dealt with Mayréna denied ever having officially sponsored his expedition. Suspicions shifted to Guerlach and Irigoyen. For the Catholic missions in Indochina, it was the first time their commitment to colonization came into serious question. The entire mission—from the missionaries who had assisted the king of the Sedangs to regional bishops—became embroiled in what grew into a very public affair.

Sorting Out Facts, Assigning Blame

Mayréna may have been, in the words of one biographer, nothing more than a "mediocre adventurer, a swindler, and worse still, nearly a traitor," but he was also an adept opportunist.[57] Playing on anxieties about Ham Nghi's flight to the highlands, and despite being a suspected criminal without money or connections, Mayréna ultimately won the support of the administration for an expedition to look ostensibly for gold in the area.[58] Most officials who met him had reservations—even grave doubts—though time and again they assisted him.[59] The lieutenant governor of Cochinchina believed that an expedition like Mayréna's could be beneficial for "developing French influence in this region" on the condition that it be entrusted to a man "of irreproachable morals and perfect honesty." He was skeptical that Mayréna was such a man.[60] But in the early spring of 1888, the administration deemed Mayréna good enough, and gave him permission to go, though without the status of an official expedition.

Mayréna also impressed, if deceptively, Mgr. Van Camelbeke, the bishop in Qui Nhon. Believing that Mayréna was on an official mission, the bishop contacted his priests in Kontum and appealed to (as he later put it) their "patriotism" to facilitate the explorer's project.[61] The assistance proved essential. Mayréna's entourage included a European associate, two Vietnamese concubines, a cook, four Chinese merchants to help locate gold deposits, an interpreter, eighteen *miliciens*, and eighty coolie porters, and by the time it arrived in the highlands, it was in trouble.[62] Many of Mayréna's porters had abandoned him because of brutal treatment and work left unpaid.[63] He immediately sent a message to Guerlach requesting elephants and Christian porters. Upon the missionary's arrival, Mayréna had signed two treaties of friendship with local chiefs, including a particularly influential chief named Pim.[64] Mayréna seemed to be establishing what officials called "amicable alliances between tribes," something both missionaries and French administrators had championed for some time.[65] With letters of introduction from officials and the bishop, Mayréna seemed completely legitimate.[66]

For much of the following three months, Mayréna traveled and lived side by side with the missionaries of Kontum, particularly Père Guerlach. In addition to acting as interpreter, Guerlach transcribed and translated the agreements Mayréna signed with local chiefs.[67] In his reports to officials, Mayréna repeatedly spoke of the influence the missionaries held over the local population, stating that their involvement would be essential in any further negotiation.[68] At the same time, Guerlach later reported, Mayréna increasingly spoke of his royal aspirations, assuring the missionary all along that the government had condoned his plans.[69]

What exactly happened in the weeks after Mayréna named himself king remains, as *Le Temps* put it at the time, "a little obscure."[70] Later accounts by Guerlach, Mayréna, and others were colored by the accusations and defenses of the ensuing affair. Two facts caused great embarrassment and called into question the missionaries' actions. On 1 July 1888, Mayréna revised the constitution of the Sedang kingdom to make Catholicism the official religion. It was but one of many articles in the document, but it raised officials' eyebrows.[71] And cementing the impression that the mission had conspired with the king of the Sedangs, on nearly every treaty Mayréna signed were the signatures of the missionaries who acted as translators and witnesses. In addition to such cold facts, Mayréna's flamboyant praise of his missionary assistants by no means helped the Catholic cause. He assured the administration that the mission was the only real force in the region. "Who furnished the maps that the Ministry of Foreign Affairs has?" Mayréna asked in one letter. Answer: "The Missions. Who today can say where Annam begins and ends? The Missions."[72] In the same vein, a thought must have struck many French officials: Who must have helped Mayréna, a potential traitor, become the king of the Sedangs?

Resident Charles Lemire, the ranking French official in Qui Nhon, was the first to finger missionary culpability. Lemire was a classic colonial type, part bureaucrat who bounced from one imperial post to another, and part explorer, traveler, art collector, and guidebook writer.[73] He had initially shown excitement for Mayréna's project, asking the explorer to collect flora, fauna, and minerals for the Exposition de Paris, and to keep logs describing the expedition's travels, the daily weather, and other information to be presented to the Congrès géographique the following year.[74] After the king's ascension to the Sedang throne, however, Lemire was eager to shed his erstwhile enthusiasm.

In November 1888, Lemire blamed the mission of the central highlands for Mayréna's successes and questioned missionary allegiance to France. In his opinion, Guerlach and Irigoyen had actively supported Mayréna's royal designs in the hope of establishing an independent Catholic kingdom like the Jesuits of seventeenth-century Paraguay—a stock criticism leveled by anticlerical republicans in the fin de siècle.[75] Lemire offered evidence of the mission's intentions: he reported that *after* Mayréna had returned from the highlands as Marie I, priests in Qui Nhon had honored the renegade with a special prie-dieu, a private prayer desk, fitted with red drapery and a special cushion. Surrounded by such finery, the resident added, Mayréna had been the guest of honor at a mass given by none other than Père Irigoyen, the translator of the Sedang constitution.[76] In France, *Le Temps* printed Lemire's accusations that missionaries had blessed the newfound kingdom. The newspaper, which took the entire affair lightheartedly, joked that, considering Mayréna's desire to find investors in Europe for his new enterprise, Guerlach might now bless dividends as well as the king's flags.[77]

The resident-superior of Annam and Tonkin, Paul Rheinart, was not amused. He took Lemire's claims seriously and oversaw an investigation of the mission's involvement in the affair. He demanded that Guerlach and Irigoyen be removed from their positions in the region—a request that drove Guerlach to travel to Hanoi to clear his name.[78] And he asked Mgr. Van Camelbeke in Qui Nhon to explain the mission's position on French influence in the highlands. When Van Camelbeke said that the region was largely independent of colonial administrative influence, Rheinart strongly rebuked him—"the political map of Indochina," he snapped, "contains no 'blanks'"— and expressed concern that the mission "took the side" of a man who planned to turn the region over to foreign domination.[79] As the issue moved up the administrative chain, however, the language describing the mission's actions became notably more circumscribed. Governor-General Richaud, in a report to Paris, described the mission's interaction with Mayréna as "very regrettable" and echoed Resident-Superior Rheinart's concerns about the mission's allegiance.[80]

Criticism of the mission was not restricted to the halls of government; the Mayréna affair, from the beginning, was also an *affaire de presse*. In late June 1888, Mayréna turned over a copy of the 3 June constitution of the Sedang kingdom to the *Courrier d'Haiphong*, one of the major newspapers in Tonkin. News of Mayréna's royal ascension brought about a rich exchange of articles reflecting an array of opinions about the king, the French administration, the pays moï, and the Catholic mission. Mayréna appreciated the power of public opinion, and many of his subsequent articles were submitted in the hope that "public opinion would provoke a solution."[81] A solution based on public opinion, however, was just what the mission hoped to avoid.

The Mission Responds

To the accusations made against the missionaries of the central highlands, the mission responded at all levels—from Guerlach to regional bishops, from private meetings to letters published in colonial newspapers. In conversations and correspondence with the administration, Bishop Van Camelbeke repeatedly denied the claim that the mission had knowingly collaborated with Mayréna. He dismissed as "pure fable" Lemire's assertion that the church had given a special mass in Mayréna's honor and outfitted a prie-dieu for royal use. Lemire, in the bishop's view, believed too many of the extravagant things that came from Mayréna's mouth. Instead, the bishop assured officials that he and his missionaries had spurned the king's requests for assistance. "We refused equally," Van Camelbeke added, "to give him the denominations of Sire, Majesty, King . . . etc."[82] The bishop's denials were padded with proclamations of patriotism. Avoiding passionate claims about a love of country, he nonetheless reasserted what he called "the rectitude of my feelings" regarding the *patrie*.[83]

In addition to offering denials and patriotic promises, apostolic vicars described the highland missionaries not as potential traitors but as assets of colonial control. If the colony wanted to spread its influence in the highlands, the missions argued, it did not need to fund adventurers like Mayréna. Rather, as Van Camelbeke wrote to the governor-general in late 1888, the mission would do: "France can, when it wants, recognize its protectorate over these savage tribes, since the missionaries displayed the French flag well before M. de Mayréna."[84] The regime's biggest error of judgment, in other words, was not relying more on missionaries in the first place.

No one made a more masterful case for missionary assistance than

Mgr. Puginier, whose vicariate did not include the central highlands. In some "secret and private notes" shared with the governor-general, Puginier reflected on the mistakes that officials had made in trusting the treasonous Mayréna. The public, he warned, would find it "strange" that the government had not only allowed Mayréna to become king but also failed to respond quickly to the affair. People would "find it inexplicable that this man guilty of committing a crime so grave" had, first, been received as a guest by the resident of Qui Nhon and then been allowed to go to Hong Kong, where, it was rumored, he had sought financial support from the British. With the balanced tone of a seasoned adviser, Puginier suggested two ways of settling the affair, thus saving the government further embarrassment. The first "less noble" option was simply to pay Mayréna "in secret" 100,000 to 200,000 francs to give up his possession. A second, preferable option was to convince the Sedangs to remove Mayréna from office. "I think," the bishop added, "that this could be done in secret and that the missionaries would be able effectively to help obtain this goal."

Acting as if officials had never accused the Kontum mission of wrongdoing, Puginier encouraged the government to confer with the bishop at Qui Nhon to find the best way to involve the mission in this "delicate" undertaking. He wrote that the mountain populations would have to retain some autonomy from the colony and that the missionaries in the highlands would be best able to "give practical information" on how to foster relations with the "tribes" of the highlands.[85] Puginier's advice was a brilliant bit of political maneuvering. His analysis of the Mayréna affair turned the missionaries suspected of treason into the most logical saviors of the government's reputation. Even more important to missionaries protective of their autonomy from administrative meddling, it made a case for letting the minorities of the highlands—and the mission of Kontum—remain outside the watchful eye of French authorities.

Père Guerlach's defense followed a tack very similar to that of his superiors. Bishops generally did not endorse missionary forays into public debate. In the case of the Mayréna affair, however, Père Guerlach was allowed to defend himself both in private meetings with officials and in print. In late 1888, as the story became a sensation in the colonial press, Guerlach penned lengthy letters in rapid succession that appeared on the front page of the *Courrier d'Haiphong*. The priest's published accounts were studies in the arts of evasion, denial, and excuse. "My signature," he wrote, referring to Mayréna's treaties and constitutions that he and Irigoyen had signed, "implies no engagement or cooperation whatsoever." He reassured a skeptical public: "I signed as an eye-witness, that's all."[86] Père Guerlach became most animated—and melodramatic—when defending his patriotism. Time and again, he insisted that his work as a missionary "planted the French flag" in faraway regions. And he showed himself to be deeply sensitive to accusations that the mission was "hostile to our *patrie*" and to rumors that questioned "the patriotism and honor of the missionaries."[87]

Sensitive one minute, he lashed out the next. Guerlach reserved his most toxic venom for Charles Lemire, who, he claimed, should not have allowed a man like Mayréna to venture into the highlands in the first place.[88] He denounced Lemire as a poor judge of character for befriending Mayréna. "In this circumstance, as in many others," the missionary railed, "M. Lemire did not prove the qualities necessary of a Resident."[89] By contrast, Guerlach championed the resident-general who he believed had looked benevolently on the mission. Perhaps aware that higher-ranking administrators were more tolerant of the missions, Guerlach waxed that the resident-general knew "that the missionaries established among the savages love France with all their hearts and are disposed to serve it with all their power. May M. le Résident-Général receive here publicly evidence of my respectful devotion."[90]

Like Bishops Van Camelbeke and Puginier, Père Guerlach used the affair to promote his mission. Had the administration given the Catholic mission an official diplomatic and political role in the first place, he argued, French rule would not be so unstable in the region. To support his case, he pointed to a number of agreements he had made with highland villages that, he insisted, benefited France. He told Resident-General Rheinart that he had been involved in the creation of the Bahnar-Rongoa Confederation, a defensive alliance of two major highland ethnic groups. While the confederation was initially developed to defend the region against Vietnamese encroachment, Guerlach now argued that it had been ready to put itself under the protectorate of France when Mayréna arrived and complicated matters. He lamented that the mission—"the sole presence that had planted the French flag" in the region—had no official authority and, therefore, could not help build an alliance between the confederation and the French. Guerlach encouraged the administration to give the mission an official status so that Père Vialleton, the superior in Kontum, could start negotiating with "the savage chiefs" who remained beyond French reach.[91] Like Puginier, Guerlach promoted a plan that would have the administration rely on the mission, and would have the mission remain independent.

The Vagaries of French Patriotism

One of the things Père Guerlach loved most about his Mission des sauvages was its remote and inhospitable location, where he enjoyed what he called "the calm of the apostolic life."[92] But in the wake of Mayréna, his mission was invisible no more. In the spring of 1889, Vice-Resident Guiomar in Qui Nhon was dispatched to the central highlands to investigate the mission's influence. Like other administrators before him, Guiomar filed a report that focused heavily on the question of missionary allegiance to France. Though he acknowledged being more or less at the mercy of the missionaries during his travels, Guiomar was skeptical throughout about the mission's patriotism and commitment to aiding colonization. He noted that he saw French flags flying in every village he visited, but he remained uncertain whether these were permanent displays or simply put up by Guerlach and his coreligionists for the vice-resident's benefit.[93]

Guiomar was struck by the tremendous power the mission at Kontum had over both the Christian and non-Christian populations. Its influence was not necessarily excessive, but the impression worried him. "The missionaries," he wrote, "consider the country they occupy as their property, and they never voluntarily favor the settlement of any European whatsoever." The realization lent credence to Lemire's accusations: in the vice-resident's opinion, the missionaries had found in Mayréna a man who would act at their discretion, "a docile instrument" who would help them in the creation of an independent state, like that of the Jesuits of Paraguay. When it became apparent that Mayréna had ideas of his own, Guiomar determined, the mission turned on him because "they preferred to abandon their projects before giving in to a master."[94]

In Guiomar's estimation, patriotism had nothing to do with the missionaries' behavior throughout the affair; he even refused to believe that the mission ever thought Mayréna was an envoy of the French government. "In the interest of their work," Guiomar wrote of the missionaries, "and in order to justify their conduct that followed, they said and repeated that their patriotic sentiments had been abused." Why were the missionaries so concerned about their reputations, he wondered, "if their conduct had not been dubious?" Guiomar questioned whether the mission would prove so patriotic in the future as the administration strengthened its presence in the highlands and used its authority to regulate the mission's activities.[95]

Vice-Resident Guiomar's criticism struck at some basic truths about the missionaries in the central highlands, and more generally about religious workers in French Indochina. Père Guerlach's claims that he blindly followed Mayréna in the belief he was helping an official envoy of France simplified more complex motivations. In a private letter written *after* the affair, Guerlach candidly recounted how Mayréna's visit had benefited the mission in a number of ways. Generally, by traveling with Mayréna across the region, Guerlach had "an occasion to explore foreign villages and to build with them relations of good friendship"—thus laying the groundwork for future evangelizing.[96]

More specifically, Mayréna offered a solution to what both Mgr. Van Camelbeke and Père Guerlach called "the famous Jarai affair."[97] The Jarai were particularly aggressive neighbors of the Bahnar and had long menaced evangelizing efforts by attacking and pillaging Christian villages and convoys. Upon his arrival, Guerlach persuaded Mayréna to lead an expedition of 1,400 Sedang and Bahnar warriors against the Jarai. Guerlach, who went along "as the chaplain," boasted that the Jarai "received a severe lesson"; they were made to pay a ransom equivalent to the goods they had stolen from the Bahnar, he reported, and they knew not to bother the mission again. The area secure, the priest said that the mission could now "more easily extend and develop our work." In this instance, the missionary admitted, "the Mission des sauvages greatly prospered" from Mayréna's work.[98]

The fact that Guerlach was eager to see Mayréna's military power benefit the mission does not necessarily mean that he supported the adventurer's royal aspirations, however. Guiomar's observation about the relative political and social power the mission enjoyed over the population undermined his allegation that it hoped to establish an independent Catholic state. With European visitors a rarity in the highlands, missionaries were essentially independent as it was—a belief Van Camelbeke betrayed to the administration. Declaring the central highlands an independent Catholic state would have attracted more official attention, not less, especially at a time when the administration was intensely aware of security weaknesses. The mission had nothing to gain by putting its faith in a feverish Frenchman.

Officials had little time to study the nuances of missionary motivations and appeared interested in answering only one question: Were missionaries patriots or pariahs? Conflicts between missionaries and officials—be they bishops and residents-general, or rural religious workers and local administrators—forced missionaries to express their patriotism in a way that ran counter to the spiritual traditions of their vocation. For some, like Bishop Puginier and Père Guerlach, declarations of love for France seem to have come naturally and were likely heartfelt. Even so, missionary definitions of patriotism were strikingly different from those of republicans. The republican criticism that missionaries worked to spread the love of God, not French influence, did little to clarify this difference: to missionaries, French influence could only begin in a land that loved God.

In the early Third Republic, one Frenchman's patriot could be another's pariah. No missionary better exemplified this phenomenon than Guerlach. With a background more suitable to a prime minister than a priest, he was born on Bastille Day in 1858 (a coincidence he might have lamented) in Metz, Lorraine. In 1870, still a child, Guerlach took to the battlefield to defend French soil against the Prussian invasion.[99] After France's defeat, he spent his youth in what he called a *patrie mutilée*, resentful of the Prussians and praying to "God the Protector" to "save France in the name of the *Sacré Coeur*."[100] Throughout the nineteenth century, the Sacré Coeur was a powerful political symbol of counterrevolutionary thought in France. The basilica in Montmartre built for the Sacred Heart of Jesus set in stone many Catholics' disdain of French republicanism. Guerlach undoubtedly loved France, though not the France that Lemire and Guiomar served.

Guerlach's decision to become a missionary was closely linked to his patriotism—but it was by no means a love of the republic. By living among the "savages," learning their languages and customs, and making treaties with them, he believed he was fulfilling France's duty to God. For Guerlach and many missionaries like him, evangelizing was in itself a patriotic act: the separation of French influence and the mission's influence was, in his mind, not possible. A country evangelized by missionaries, France now had a duty as the eldest daughter of the Church to evangelize abroad. Despite the rise of the anticlerical republic, he wrote, "France still remains the soldier of God and the kingdom of Mary. *Regnum Galliae, Regnum Mariae.*"[101] Guerlach described himself as a soldier in a "holy war" in the "Kingdom of God" who fought the devil, paganism, and sin with the teachings of Christ.[102] In his mind, nothing could better serve France, its traditions, or its influence in the world than the triumph of Catholicism. Lemire, Guiomar, and many other republicans in the empire could not have disagreed more.

A Complicated Collaboration

While Guerlach's counterrevolutionary patriotism would have perplexed and appalled legions of secularist republicans in France, it sufficed to alleviate anxieties in 1880s Indochina. As far as Resident-General Rheinart was concerned, the declarations of patriotism made by Catholic missionaries in the wake of the Mayréna scandal cleared them of further suspicion. Considering the Quai d'Orsay's position to support French missionary work, Rheinart needed little convincing. Writing to Van Camelbeke of his "esteem and sympathy for our missions," Rheinart commended what he called the "sentiments of ardent patriotism" that missionaries had shown "many times in the face of danger." Even constricted by the stale genre of the official letter, the administrator's correspondence gushed with admiration, expressing his happiness "that nowhere is more patriotism shown than in [the bishop's] beautiful mission." Van Camelbeke's "so loyal declarations," he commended, had helped "destroy and annul" all accusations made against the missionaries of the central highlands.[103]

Rheinart lauded Guerlach as well. "I thank you infinitely for this new sign of patriotism you have given us," the resident-general wrote. "Believe that I am very touched by it, and that I am very happy to have seen entirely disappear the misunderstanding that had sprung up during the Mayréna Affair." He also commended Guerlach for his wise advice regarding the highland confederations and for helping organize "the defense of the country."[104] Rheinart demonstrated his approbation with administrative action. He instructed Lemire, whose behavior he called "tactless," to cease further investigation of missionary wrongdoing.[105] The following month, in January 1889, Lemire was removed from his post and reassigned to Vinh. Lemire left office convinced the mission was guilty of duplicity, saying that one missionary had supported Mayréna at Qui Nhon while another repudiated the king of the Sedang at Hanoi.

Though insightful and powerfully worded, Vice-Resident Guiomar's report on Guerlach's mission failed to change French policy toward the missions of the central highlands or anywhere else in Indochina. Further investigation determined that building a permanent administrative post in the region would be too difficult and too costly. For the administration in both Indochina and France, the missionaries were accepted as effective tools for spreading French influence. During the years that followed, the Kontum mission encountered only occasional travelers. In 1898, after years of informally relying on his help, the French government named Père Vialleton, the superior at Kontum, as the official representative of the protectorate in the highlands.[106] The government congratulated the priest, who was once implicated in the Mayréna affair, for using the mission's influence to benefit the administration. The protectorate had the representation it needed without building expensive new posts. The highland mission had won the administration's trust to fulfill the political and diplomatic functions of the colony. As a result, the region, its ethnic minorities, and its missionaries remained outside the reach of republican administrative officials for the following decade.

The Mayréna affair reveals how Catholic missions across Indochina—and, indeed, the empire—came to interact with the French administration in the 1880s, during the first ten years of republican colonial expansion. There was, as many historians have suggested, a level of collaboration between missionaries and republican officials. But this collaboration was far more complicated than historians have suggested. The fiercely competing traditions, goals, and political sensibilities of the two groups involved expose the problems of seeing religious missionaries and republican colonizers as simple partners. Despite the Quai d'Orsay's policy to support French missionary efforts and bar the exportation of anticlericalism to the empire, local colonial officials often raised the thorny—and valid—question of whether missionaries worked to spread French influence or purely to fulfill their apostolic goals, even to the detriment of the empire. In extreme cases, such accusations drove high-ranking administrators like Rheinart to investigate and motivated bishops to reassure officials of the benefits the missions had to offer the colony. Missionaries insisted that their work helped spread a love of France among the indigenous population. In most instances, bishops and high-ranking officials tried to smooth over conflicts between missionaries and local administrators, but the deep enmity between the two was suppressed only with difficulty. Far from being eager servants of empire in Indochina, missionaries remained acutely suspicious of colonial authority. Even as they made declarations of patriotism—proof, it would seem, of their commitment to the colonial cause—they maneuvered to safeguard their autonomy and increase the missions' influence over local communities. For missionaries in the 1880s, spreading French influence was still, at best, a fortunate by-product of spreading Catholicism.

While missionaries may or may not have benefited French colonial authority, they quickly learned that the Catholic cause could flourish under the new regime. Despite some significant political bumps along the way—the Mayréna affair being the most jarring—the arrival of republican colonial rule witnessed a dramatic growth of evangelizing. A decade after the protectorate of Annam and Tonkin had been added to France's empire, the number of Catholics in Indochina had increased by 60 percent to more than half a million. The missionary ranks swelled, and mission schools, hospitals, and orphanages expanded. Such services gave the administration more reason to tolerate Catholic workers, and high-ranking officials became increasingly defensive of the policy of religious neutrality in the colonies. They became more adamant about keeping conflicts between local administrators and missionaries to a minimum. But with the successes of the missions mounting and the number of republican colonists expanding, the climate of conflict did not calm. The 1890s and early 1900s witnessed a new anticlerical force emerging in French Indochina: Freemasons. As French control of the countryside became more assured, the question of French influence was no longer at issue. For Freemasons, Catholic missionaries posed a much graver threat—to civilization itself.

Civilizing and Its Discontents

If the French come to settle in your territory, you must know that it is not at all with the thought of seizing your land or your crops, but, on the contrary, with the intention of augmenting the general wealth by increasing the value of your property, by facilitating your agricultural cultivation, . . . by creating easy means of communication, by developing the riches hidden in your mines and protecting your commercial transactions with foreign nations.

—Paul Bert, resident-general of Annam and Tonkin, 1886

In the spring of 1886, amid continued fighting in the countryside, the newly arrived resident-general Paul Bert made his first proclamation to the people of Annam and Tonkin. Bert, who had taken leave of a successful career as a republican lawmaker in Paris to accept leadership of France's most promising new territory, was a master of imperialist rhetoric. And on 8 April 1886, he endeavored to explain why France had come to Southeast Asia. Colonialism, he announced, was not about exploitation but assistance. French rule was not about domination but new partnerships. The French came not to steal but to cultivate, to develop, and to bring economic prosperity. And France, he noted, had "the capital, the tools, the engineers, and the great experience in business" that the Vietnamese lacked. Like the Chinese, who had once brought to the region their governors, philosophers, and literature, Bert pledged that now the French would enrich the Vietnamese intellect "by instruction." Possessing the cultural and moral wherewithal to accomplish the task, France had come to civilize.[1]

Bert's towering pronouncement soon crumbled under the weight of its own hubris. In the years that followed, Frenchmen showed themselves far more concerned with capturing rebels and developing local resources than with disseminating the insights of French philosophers and novelists. Before administrators could contemplate Bert's civilizing goals, they had to delineate the boundaries of their control. Before they could teach French to the Vietnamese, they had to organize an effective military to maintain internal stability and protect against the possibility of British, German, and Chinese aggression. While official efforts focused on security and achieving basic fiscal goals, services such as schools, hospitals, orphanages, and other ostensibly humanitarian operations were left in the domain of the well-established Catholic missions. Missionaries' significantly different motivations, traditions, and definitions of patriotism—though regularly highlighted in reports from republican administrators in the field—failed to cause much anxiety at the resident-general's office or in Paris. Considering the serious challenges facing the colonial administration, missionary promises of allegiance and patriotism sufficed to reassure republican officials.

After a decade of uncertainty, things started to improve. In the history of Indochina, 1897 stands as a watershed of sorts. That year, Paul Doumer, a reform-minded republican politician, became governor-general of Indochina. Doumer promised to expand the civil administration and to make Indochina economically profitable.[2] After a decade of episodic violent rebellion, the French captured the leaders of the Can vuong movement, sentencing many Vietnamese rebels to imprisonment or death and forcing collaborators' villages to pay reparations.[3] In this somewhat calmer climate, officials could turn to fundamental questions about how to develop Indochina's material and moral condition.

The new hope that Doumer's government brought to the region only reignited internecine fighting among Frenchmen of differing religious and political orientations. At the center of these conflicts, once again, were Catholic missionaries. But the terms of disagreement that emerged had changed from the time when establishing "influence" ruled the day. From the late 1890s, debates over the role of missions in the empire were deeply influenced by events in France. In the years since Paul Bert made his proclamation to the people of Tonkin, relations between republicans and conservative Catholics in France had steadily deteriorated. Paul Doumer's arrival in Hanoi in 1897 came in the wake of the conviction of Captain Alfred Dreyfus, a Jewish officer in the French army wrongly imprisoned for treason. Dreyfus's controversial conviction fanned already smoldering hostilities in France. The ensuing affair pitted republican Dreyfusards, who believed an outdated military hierarchy had framed the captain, against conservative anti-Dreyfusards, who sought to protect the reputation of one of the nation's oldest and, in their opinion, most revered institutions.

These domestic conflicts were not confined to the boundaries of France but accompanied Frenchmen wherever they settled. As a result, the late 1890s saw renewed attacks on Catholic missions around the empire. Indochina, widely considered a jewel in the republic's Phrygian cap, particularly drew the attention of critics. As in the days of Mayréna, lower-level officers continued to complain about missionaries they confronted in the field. But in the era of the Dreyfus affair, the most vocal criticism in Indochina came from a new source: colonists, particularly members of the Freemason lodges flourishing in major towns across Indochina. Drawing on the anti-clerical fervor at home, radical Freemasons launched a systematic campaign asserting that the Catholic missions undermined the great republican *mission civilisatrice*. The missions were not the only ones that needed to respond: critiques of the civilizing mission—or lack thereof—were equally uncomfortable for the colonial administration. The anticlerical polemics of the Dreyfus affair, reformulated in the colonies as distrust of and disgust for missionary work, most forcefully brought the issue of civilization to Indochina.

The Dreyfus Affair in the Empire

The volatility and confrontation that stirred colonial society in Indochina during the two decades leading up to the First World War paralleled contemporary discord in France. By the 1880s, with the Third Republic looking ever more permanent, many Catholics had become, in the words of one commentator, "exiles in their own country."[4] As Réné Rémond points out in his classic study of the French right, conservative Catholics, many of whom were faithful monarchists, faced the unlikelihood of ever seeing another restoration. In 1890, Cardinal Lavigerie made his famous "toast of Algiers" to the French republic, a signal step in reconciling relations between the Church and the new state. Lavigerie's toast was the beginning of the *ralliement*, a call to Catholics to work within the republican system, not in opposition to it. Two years later, Pope Leo XIII's encyclical encouraged Catholics to participate in French political life, essentially sending legitimists and other conservatives on two paths: one that accepted the papal decree and moved to conservative republicanism, and another that resisted the order and embraced extremist, right-wing nationalism, hoping for a monarchical restoration or the arrival of a new Bonaparte.[5] By the mid-1890s, conservative republicans, also known as *ralliés*, had become essential partners of moderate republicans in government—an alliance that temporarily held off radical, anticlerical demands from the far left.[6]

The Dreyfus affair exposed a deep rift in French society. At stake was more than the fate of an army captain. Catholic commentators denounced republicans as hypocritical sinners who touted individual liberty and respect for all religions, save one. The Dreyfus affair helped anti-Semitic reactionaries pull public debate into the mire of intolerance; for right-wing commentators, Jews like Dreyfus plotted to destroy the "true"—that is, conservative and Catholic—France. What emerged was *les deux France*—the phrase many historians use to describe the era's divided political landscape. Each side embraced competing concepts of French identity: defenders of Dreyfus exalted

Enlightenment and revolutionary ideals such as the supremacy of rationalism and the triptych of *liberté, égalité, et fraternité*, while conservatives championed the illustrious traditions of Old Regime institutions, notably the army, the Church, and the crown.[7]

By the end of the 1890s, a bloc of radical republicans had gained prominence, radicalizing French domestic politics. In July 1901, republicans in Paris passed the Law on Associations, requiring all religious congregations to be registered with the government. In 1902, Prime Minister Émile Combes and his radical and radical-socialist supporters gained control of the French parliament. Though Combes had once considered joining the priesthood, his political reputation was now so fervently anticlerical that one observer deemed him "the national antipope."[8] In the hands of anticlericals, the Law on Associations allowed republicans to shut down dozens of nonauthorized organizations—most notably, the Jesuits and the Assumptionists—which they considered particularly dangerous to the republic.

Combes and his supporters attacked Catholics with deliberate bravado; on one occasion, they closed eighty-one congregations of nuns with a single vote. They bent the law to shut down thousands of religious schools run by authorized congregations, showed no sympathy for elderly priests and nuns left broke and homeless, excluded *religieux* from state exams, and restricted soldiers' access to religious ceremonies.[9] Anticlericals stated their goals with frank prejudice: as one Freemason put it in 1903, "The congregations must be radically destroyed."[10] By New Year's of 1905, the separation of Church and state seemed inevitable; it was put into law later that year, signaling the end of the century-old Concordat, as well as of government funding of all religious activity. Across the empire, the most immediate impact of the separation was on the least threatening component of the Catholic missions: nursing sisters were removed from military and colonial hospitals, and the minority of teaching brothers and sisters who worked at state-run schools were excused from their duties. Most mission schools and medical facilities continued to operate.

Though French lawmakers did not immediately apply them to the colonies, the religious laws posed a serious long-term threat to missionary efforts. Were the Law on Associations to be applied abroad, requiring authorization of foreign missions, a number of the largest missionary groups could have faced closure. The Jesuits, the White Fathers of Africa, and the Trappists were all among the organizations that were unauthorized in 1901. Criticisms of missions were nothing new, but never had missions faced such a clear legislative onslaught. Throughout the 1890s, colonial administrators in France had stuck to the guiding principle that anticlericalism was not for export. But with new standards and regulations set in France, the missions' most ardent critics demanded a colonial policy that was consistent with the law of the *patrie*. It was left to the missions to prove their importance to the future success of colonialism.

Freemasons at Home and Abroad

Along with the spread of Protestantism, Catholic missionaries regularly identified Freemasonry as posing the greatest threat to their work. Freemasonry had a profound connection with republican politics throughout the second half of the nineteenth century; towering figures like Léon Gambetta, Jules Ferry, and Jules Simon were all members of lodges.[11] Though a wide array of republicans belonged to lodges, the core Masonic ideals reflected a left wing, anticlerical vision of society that formed the platform of radical politics.[12] From the beginning of France's renewed interest in imperial expansion, Freemasons had been at the forefront of republicans calling for the regulation of evangelizing. For instance, an 1885 pamphlet that discussed Masonic views on colonialism focused almost entirely on the dangers of missionaries. Produced by the "Travail et perfection" lodge of Angers, the pamphlet rued that colonial policy could be described as "everything by missionaries and for the Propagation de la foi." Contending that Catholic missions spread nothing but embarrassment and hatred for France, the pamphlet warned that missionaries would use colonialism to augment their influence—and that of Rome.[13] In place of the "baneful consequences of religious proselytism," Freemasons called for a balance of security, commerce, patriotism, and secular education.[14]

The influence of Freemasons soon spread as lodges opened around the empire.[15] The first lodge in Indochina was founded in Hanoi in 1886, and over the following twenty years, *fraternités* met in every major French urban center, including Haiphong, Saigon, Tourane, and Phnom Penh.[16] By 1906, there were some 200 active lodge members in Indochina, though an estimated 500 colonists and administrators in the colony had at some time been Freemasons.[17] Masonic influence on colonial politics ran deep. Many colonial officials, including several governors-general, were either active or onetime Freemasons. Those who had no official position in colonial government took an active role in expressing opinions about policy. Ardently committed to secular, republican government, these colonists pounced on any aspect of colonial society or policy they deemed improper or ineffective. Their favorite targets were reaction, clericalism, and anyone who threatened *libre pensée*, including army officers and, of course, missionaries.[18]

Freemasons also dominated the journalism profession in Indochina. The publishers and editors of *Le Courrier d'Haiphong*, *L'Indépendance Tonkinoise*, and *Le Mékong*—three of the four major French papers—were active members of their lodges in Haiphong, Hanoi, and Saigon, respectively.[19] Newspapers were principal forums of public discourse; testimony to their power over opinion is the effort the administration made to monitor the publications. From the early 1890s, these papers regularly ran stories about missionary abuses, sparking heated exchanges, accusations, and denials in the form of letters to the editor. Some articles were incendiary pieces meant to provoke more than to inform. One newspaper, *Le Mékong*, accused nursing sisters of prostitution and claimed that missionaries had "massacred natives, and pillaged, and stolen and burned down houses." Based on rumor and innuendo, these stories embarrassed the mission and undermined its public reputation and moral authority. Mission policy was to avoid conflict in the press, but by 1897 the attacks had become so incendiary that a bishop was driven to write scathing letters to the editor of *Le Mékong*. The mission also threatened legal action.[20] In these cases, the colonial administration encouraged tolerance and goodwill on all sides, hoping things would blow over.

Missionaries were not the only targets in Freemasons' sights. Lodge members regularly penned critical reviews of the colonial government's policies. In 1887, for example, only a year after the first lodge opened, Freemasons in Tonkin railed against bureaucratic interference that left private commercial efforts "crushed by a meddlesome, timid administration without political views." Tonkin lodge members argued that unfair tariff policies had left commerce "hard put," had spread "misery everywhere," and had rendered sterile a country once "so fertile." They chastised the "miserably trained" administration for thinking it could run a colony of twenty million inhabitants "like an old department of France."[21] These complaints, written in the form of published letters, garnered a response from Masons at home who continued the battle. From France, the solution to the possession's problems seemed easy: minimize the role of the military in colonial affairs and expedite the creation of a true civil government. Only civil rule, one Mason concluded, would bring "the Progress and Emancipation" that colonialism promised Indochina.[22]

While their anticlerical diatribes willingly incorporated unsubstantiated rumors and stock slander, radical critics championed an ideological colonial agenda. As one publication described it, Freemasons wanted "to republicanize, to laicize, to emancipate Indochina."[23] Another lodge member asserted that France's goal in the colonies must be "the pacific spreading of its flag, its ideas, its genius, and its civilization."[24] Freemasons demanded the secularization of education, the teaching of French history and language, the replacement of all local missionary representatives with republican ones, and the dissolution of Church-owned plantations. Some demanded taxation of the mission; others asked for the ousting of the mission altogether. In waging war on the missions, Freemasons offered a new vision of "French influence" in Indochina with an increasingly moral and ideological flavor. In short, they wanted to see the civilizing mission in action. This demand went beyond anticlericalism: it also hit hard at a republican government that was not living up to its own civilizing ideals.

The Freemason Campaign

The arrival of Governor-General Paul Doumer—himself a Freemason—in 1897 coincided with the start of roughly a decade of sustained critique of the missions and often, by extension, the colonial administration. New denunciations—which usually came from colonists, not officials—not only addressed the hopes for a productive colony that Doumer embodied but also reflected (and redefined) mounting tensions in French domestic politics. The year after Doumer arrived, Émile Zola would publish his famous "J'accuse," an exposé of military and political corruption, that stoked the flames of the Dreyfus affair. Indochina, like other overseas possessions, was in no way isolated from the polemics of metropolitan France. As the bishop of West Cochinchina reflected in 1903, the mission felt "almost instantaneously the repercussions of events that result from the political and religious battles waged in France."[25] And, in turn, the turmoil of colonial politics found its way into newspapers and books in France, and into debates on the floor of the National Assembly.

Radical colonists were certainly inspired by the mounting anticlericalism at home, but their attacks on the mission were also tailored to the concerns of Frenchmen living in the uncertainty of the empire. Freemasons accused missionaries of nearly every evil imaginable. For most commentators, missionaries were dangerous enemies of France. A former Hanoi bureaucrat, for example, denounced them as "an army of sappers in black robes" and warned that it would be "at the decisive moment, when we think we're victorious, that we will lose the ground beneath our feet."[26] But for most Freemasons, the goal was not simply to expose dangerous, immoral, or unpatriotic behavior. Rather, accounts of abuses showed how the missions undermined France's efforts to create the conditions necessary to build a stable and prosperous colony and to implement civilizing reforms. By exposing how missionaries' supposedly savage behavior went unpunished, Freemasons also revealed the extent to which the republican government neglected its own colonial ideology.

In 1897, a short diatribe that revisited the Mayréna affair signaled a new wave of Freemason attacks and missionary countermoves. No single individual more vehemently detested missionaries than the pamphlet's author, Camille Pâris. A planter and a bureaucrat who worked for the telegraph service from the mid-1880s, Pâris was a loyal Freemason who wrote newspaper articles, pamphlets, and books, two of which—one a travel journal, the other a study of tea and coffee production in Vietnam—won awards. Among his fellow colonists, he was perhaps equally well known for his temperament, which was once described by his wife's divorce lawyer as violent, brutal, and contemptuous.[27] By his fellow Freemasons, however, Pâris was admired for his tireless attacks on clerical intrigue. In his 1897 *Du rôle néfaste joué par les missions en Annam*, which he had in fact penned years earlier at the height of the Mayréna affair, Pâris first started to outline the themes that were to shape a new generation of Freemason critiques of the missions.

Like other commentators during the Mayréna episode, Pâris questioned missionary patriotism and, drawing on the oft-used anticlerical charge, accused the highland mission of founding a kingdom under the puppet Marie I reminiscent of that founded by the Jesuits of seventeenth-century Paraguay. If Pâris added anything to the ink already spilled on Mayréna, it was to highlight the violent nature of missionary power. The mission was particularly dangerous because it threatened to arm its "intolerant Catholic savages" in the hopes of destroying their Buddhist brethren, causing war and instability to reign.[28] Pâris expanded on the themes of violence and instability in another book, *Les Missionnaires d'Asie*, that he coauthored with Alfred Barsanti. The authors claimed that missionaries used murder, torture, and slave trading to intimidate and manipulate non-Christian populations. "But the most ignoble recruitment," Pâris wrote, "is the stealing of children," many of whom were driven from their homes, and made to walk eight hours a day, causing four-fifths to die of exhaustion. Such horror was not rumor, Pâris insisted; on one occasion, a priest had even offered to sell a child to him.[29]

Other Freemasons echoed, if not corroborated, Pâris's allegations. An article in a French Freemason publication criticized missionaries for always demanding that the Vietnamese kneel before them (an act of submission, in fact, that many French officials expected of the Vietnamese, as well). "The audacious ones," Armand Séville added, "who dared raise their heads were, without pity, tortured, decapitated, exiled, their goods confiscated for the profit of the mission or of the indigenous Catholics."[30] Another Freemason pamphlet described how missionaries turned their Christians against nonbelievers and peasants against mandarins, making neighbors into enemies, tearing the very fabric of indigenous society, and risking persecutions and massacres.[31] In a book called *Les Missions et leur protectorat*, the Freemason, prolific writer, and former governor-general of Indochina Jean de Lanessan recounted how, in 1891, missionaries had converted a prince in the royal family and then tried to stage a coup to make him emperor. The mission, he wrote, "was always looking for a Constantine who would force the Vietnamese population to convert to Christianity." Had they succeeded, nothing would have been more dangerous for France: de Lanessan speculated that it would have "very probably" resulted in a general rebellion of the population.[32]

While colorful and detailed, few Freemason claims were fully substantiated by evidence. The more extreme accusations—such as torture and murder—were just the sorts of crimes that the colonial administration would have investigated. And, though authorities occasionally reprimanded missionaries, it was never for the sordid behavior Freemasons attributed to them. But the accusations were effective at attracting republicans' attention to what they saw as the clericalism of the colonies. Though their allegations pertained directly to colonial life, the Freemasons' polemic bore all the markings of metropolitan political discord in the 1890s, especially during the Dreyfus affair.

In most of their accounts, Freemasons wanted to show that missionary misdeeds stemmed from intolerance. Camille Pâris claimed that he had met catechists whose hatred of Vietnamese non-Christians ran so deep that they refused to bury their corpses, leaving their skulls and bones littered on the ground. Who taught them "these principles of intolerance," he wondered.[33] For his part, de Lanessan regretted how the colonial administration had stood by and allowed Buddhists to be the object of Catholic "contempt and incessant profanation."[34] The theme of missionary intolerance echoed criticisms of Catholic anti-Semitism in France, of republican distaste for slogans such as Édouard Drumont's *"La France aux français!"* Missionaries, it seemed, rallied behind the cry *"Les colonies aux catholiques!"*—an outrage that drove many Freemasons to reach for their pens.

Intolerance stood at odds with colonial goals in two key ways. Intolerance begot violence against the non-Christian population, which, as Pâris asserted, strongly accentuated "the Vietnamese hatred of the European" and inspired insurrections.[35] As France's primary goal was to establish social and political stability in order to better develop Indochina's economic resources, Freemasons had reason to be wary of insurrections. Further, intolerance depicted missionaries as unable to embrace the "associationist" ideology that was emerging at the time in French colonial thought. Freemasons had long critiqued the hopes of "assimilationism"—the belief that France could transform its vast colonial populations into Frenchmen.[36] Instead, by 1900, Freemasons, along with many colonial officials, were insisting that colonialism should aim to forge partnerships with its subjects. Civilizing, they claimed, included building schools, improving hygiene, and eradicating the more objectionable moral practices (cannibalism, bigamy, political systems deemed outdated). But association, in theory, aimed to leave the social and political fabric of the possessions undisturbed where possible. For Freemasons, by insisting all non-believers convert or face decapitation, missionaries were, to say the least, at odds with the spirit of cooperation that the republic championed.

A Civilizing Mission Unfulfilled

Violence and intolerance were not the only dangers missionaries apparently posed; Freemasons also accused Catholics of obstructing the *mise-en-valeur*— the program of developing the economy—of the colony. Critics drew on an old and rich cache of images that helped them portray the missions as archetypal Old Regime institutions that enslaved, terrorized, and dominated the local population. They highlighted missionaries' history of close friendship with the monarchy, especially Louis XVI (here, the story of Mgr. Pigneau de Béhaine's visit to Versailles became an example of missionaries' long ties to the monarchy, not of France's first official relations with Vietnam). They repeatedly complained that the missions used converts as forced laborers in the fields and remained exempt from property taxes by declaring their farms to be Church property.[37] They ridiculed the popular perception that missionaries led lives of devotion and abnegation.[38] Reminiscent of stock complaints about the power of the Church in France, Freemasons still held that clerics gained wealth through the impoverishment of their flock.[39] Had they chosen to illustrate their image of the Catholic missionary, Freemasons in Indochina could have easily reprinted Revolution-era cartoons of a portly, self-satisfied curé resting on the back of an overburdened peasant.

Within the context of colonial development, alleged missionary greed was more than just another case of clerics padding their pockets. The missions posed, so insisted Freemasons, an economic threat to colonists struggling to survive. In 1900, a pamphlet claimed that the missionary came to Indochina with the intention not of preaching door-to-door but of amassing power, wealth, and property—"in a word, to render himself a moral master of the people and become a proprietor of land."[40] In Camille Pâris's view, they succeeded: he complained that missionary planters outnumbered colonists, especially in Annam, where the *Annuaire de 1900* reported that there were eighteen missionaries compared with only three *citoyens*—one of whom was Pâris. This imbalance, he argued, stemmed from missionary manipulation and intimidation. In one instance, in "Village D . . . ," Pâris reported that missionaries simply stole hectares of gardens as well as surrounding buildings from their owners. In the "Village of C . . . ," despite a tiny Catholic population, missionaries staked a claim to half the village and the entire waterfront where fishing was done.[41]

For Pâris, mission plantations that broke the law with abandon undermined the entire colonial project, threatening lay planters who had to hire workers, pay taxes, and comply with colonial regulations. He despised the fact that indigenous Christians showed little respect for, and absolutely no desire to work for, the likes of Pâris. Missionaries, he railed, trained their Christians to avoid contact with lay Europeans (with anticlerical neighbors like Pâris, it is easy to understand why). A convert, he lamented, is "a worker lost to the French colonist." It was even difficult, according to Pâris, for a traveler to find help in a Christian village. In a number of examples, the Freemason described how planters' efforts to work with missionaries or their followers ended not with reliable labor but in lawsuits. "The missionary," he concluded, "is the enemy of the colonist."[42]

While many of Pâris's complaints were very personal in nature—how missions kept him from finding laborers—he and other critics tied their experiences to the fate of the nation. The alleged economic successes of missionary ventures, they complained, helped to enrich neither France nor the empire. "Weren't the colonies conquered," asked one Freemason, "to assure the flow of products from the *métropole* and to bring it, in exchange, the riches of their still virgin soil?"[43] Another complained that "Jacques Bonhomme," the typical French worker whose labor funded the colonial effort, gained nothing at all from possessions where missionaries and the *caste plutocratique* reigned.[44]

Growth of the economy was more than a matter of francs and centimes for honest French workers; it was also a central component of republican civilizing rhetoric. As Pâris put it, republican colonialism's "duty to humanity" was to bring justice to "peoples ignorant of their social rights" and to give them a better life through economic prosperity. Colonists were not, he insisted, merely "avid capitalists" who exploited the colonial population. Instead, through working fairly with colonial populations, colonists inspired "an adaptation" of society that helped put the indigenous "on the march to progress."[45] According to this line of thinking, the Catholic mission sought to make the local population into followers, or worse—slaves; they would commit any atrocity to "impose their hegemony."[46] In a climate of such economic unfairness, critics claimed, colonial *mise-en-valeur* would remain an unfulfilled dream.

Freemasons seemed unfazed by the obvious hypocrisy of their criticism of the Catholic missions. Regardless of missionary culpability, Freemason colonists were themselves avid imperialists who hoped to profit personally from their nation's forceful "imposition of hegemony" in Indochina. Vietnamese accounts of labor conditions on French plantations described violence and hardship not unlike those that Pâris insisted were found only on mission plantations.[47] But a realistic picture of colonial life was clearly not the Freemasons' intention. Instead, their rhetoric was aimed more at drawing unequivocal, idealized distinctions between retrograde clerics and the liberating potential of republican colonialism.

Time and again, the fundamental question Freemasons posed was whether missionaries served republican France's goals. Not surprisingly, considering the picture of intolerance, violence, instability, and greed already painted, the answer was a unanimous no. What had changed in the years since the Mayréna affair were the terms of defining influence. No longer simply concerned with security and spreading "a love of France," after 1900, Freemasons harped on the fact that missionaries taught neither French ideas that facilitated colonization nor even the French language in their schools. Instead, they insisted, the Catholic schools of Indochina had but one goal: conversion. And conversion, they insisted, was antithetical to colonization.

Freemasons complained that the most common misconception in France about missionaries was that they were the primary teachers of the French language in the empire. Freemasons insisted it was not true. With certain hyperbole, numerous commentators made it seem that a French word never passed a Catholic lip. Priests, reported one article, "teach their catechists Latin under the pretext that it is the liturgical language and *never* teach them French." The shortcomings of such a curriculum, the author concluded, "need no commentary."[48] In similar style, Pâris claimed that missionaries had "no interest" in teaching French because it would weaken their own domination by enabling their students to communicate with "French atheists."[49]

The accusations were somewhat overstated. Missionaries did teach some of their students to speak French—mission estimates showed that about a quarter of students learned French around 1900—but admitted that they did not have the time or the inclination to teach them all.[50] By the late 1890s, the dissemination of the French language had become an essential aspect of colonization. Gone were the early *colons* who spoke some Vietnamese and who often took the time to learn local history and customs. The "New Frenchmen," as historian Philippe Devillers calls them, had only a simplistic understanding of the local culture around them.[51] French bureaucrats and colonists increasingly demanded that French be taught in primary and secondary schools. By showing outrage at the missions' limited effort to teach French, Freemason critics hit on the linchpin issue of the civilizing mission—one that was sure to attract attention at home as well as in the possession. How, after all, could the Vietnamese profit from the philosophy, the literature, in short, the genius of France if they were not fluent in the language?

For critics, the neglect of the French language was the most obvious sign that missionaries felt no sense of duty to France. For Jean de Lanessan, saying that missionaries did not serve France was not a critique; it was a simple truth. In his estimation, missionaries were preoccupied with one thing only. "After the conquest as before," he wrote, "the missionaries have only one goal: to make Christians. Need this be surprising? Isn't that why they became missionaries?"[52] Other critics agreed but described the divisions between nation and mission in starker terms. One writer, reflecting the political equations of the Dreyfus era, insisted that "it would be absurd to ask these people whose doctrines are, whatever they may say, anti-democratic and anti-liberal, to spread the ideas that they make a profession of combating."[53] And, of course, Camille Pâris summed up missionary contributions to colonialism with typical subtlety: believing that missionaries spread a love of France was "one of the biggest errors of the century." The truth for him was the opposite: "*missionaries make us hated in the countries they invade.*"[54]

The wave of critiques of missionary behavior in Indochina embodied more than a wholesale denunciation of Catholic workers. The corrupt black robes and their marauding neophytes provided poignant evidence of the failure of colonial officials and their policies. Freemasons were dumbfounded by an administration that appeared not only to condone missionary work but also to defend and nurture it. Georges Piermé, Cochinchina's delegate to the executive committee of the radical and radical-socialist party, lamented that Paul Doumer, the ex-Freemason governor-general and "ex-eater of *curés*," had maintained "very intimate, very cordial" relations with the "Roman faction." In so doing, Doumer fraternized with common panderers: Piermé claimed that the missions "civilized" the country by "selling '*congaïes*' (girls) and 'boys' " to "lovers of fresh flesh."[55] It was a matter of time, he warned, before the indigenous population believed this to be officially sanctioned behavior. The "entente cordiale" between government and mission, in his opinion, showed official France to be complicit in all the missionaries' sordid misdeeds.

Inspired by the gains made by Émile Combes and radical republicans in France, Freemason critics had one end in mind: to demand the application of metropolitan anticlerical legislations to the colonies. If clericalism was so "detestably bad" for Europe, wondered radical-socialist Armand Séville at the height of the Dreyfus affair, was it not all the worse when exported? Séville bewailed the irony that missionaries stole land and became wealthy under the "complaisant eyes of bureaucrats of the radical-socialist Third Republic."[56] Georges Piermé asked why, at the height of laicization and the war on congregations in France, officials in Indochina funded missionary schools and hospitals instead of founding their own.[57] Jean de Lanessan, in the wake of the 1905 separation of Church and state, demanded to know why colonial governments continued to respect the protectorate of the missions.[58] One pamphlet published in Tonkin explained the position of Freemasons with admirable honesty. If asked the question "Is anticlericalism an article for export?"—referring to the dictum that governed much of France's overseas policy regarding missionaries—"we will respond resolutely in the affirmative."[59]

Freemason criticisms ultimately gave shape to a vision of what French colonialism should be—at once civilizing and respectful of local traditions (a core "associationist" ideal). The work of missionaries, at odds with both core republican ideology and current metropolitan political realities, made attaining this vision impossible. By converting non-Christians to a foreign religion, missionaries reaped misery wherever they went. Echoing other Freemasons, de Lanessan asserted that France's "premier duty" was "to respect, in an absolute way, the traditional beliefs of the *indigènes*." This ideal was not just essential to the interests of colonialism but rather reflected the universal values republicanism promised. Missionaries needed to be combated not only for the benefit of France but "in the name of the peace and tranquility of humanity."[60] François Nicol, an influential republican voice on colonial matters, complained that France had not remained true to its ideals in the empire. "In the colonies, as elsewhere," he wrote, "only the principles of 1789 and of 1848, conforming to the spirit and genius of our nation, must guide us. Has it not always been thus? Unfortunately, no!"[61] For critics like Nicol, more worrisome than the proliferation of Catholic missions in the empire was the fact that the once-robust belief in the republic's power to civilize had withered and grown pale on distant shores.

Progress, Civilization, and Faith

The Freemasons' assault on the missions did not fall on deaf ears. Their articles, pamphlets, and books—combined with reports from France of the polemics of the Dreyfus affair—gained an audience beyond a fringe of radical colonists and shaped general opinions in the colony. In his correspondence with the Missions étrangères' *maison* in Paris, Mgr. Lucien Mossard, bishop of West Cochinchina, wrote regularly of the impact anticlerical critiques had on the reputation of the missions. In the early 1900s, he described the commonly held view that missionaries worked "first, to enrich themselves, [and] second, to dominate and exploit the indigenous." For many in the colony, missions were little more than "vast commercial and industrial companies" that used converts "in order to operate in the best possible condition."[62] Camille Pâris could not have put it more succinctly. The image, Mossard insisted, was completely false, noting that without the assistance of fund-raising organizations in France, the missions would not be able to continue their work.[63] In other letters, Mossard described attempts to reclaim church property and end the school subvention as being motivated by anticlerical critics. Missionaries clearly felt the pinch of their adversaries' polemic.

In the midst of Freemason attacks, the Catholic missions had their defenders. In 1897, Joseph Chanel, a member of the Société académique indochinoise de France, published a study of the central highlands in a reputable geographic bulletin. From its first line, Chanel's "Voyage chez les Moï" expressed "profound gratitude" for the missionaries who made his expedition run with "as much facility and much more enjoyment than a promenade in France." In a section called the "Influence of French Missionaries," Chanel commended religious workers for playing the roles of doctor, arbiter, and judge.[64] Missionaries had rid the highlands of slavery and taught agricultural and economic methods that reduced hunger and stabilized the economy in the region.[65] Most of all, he argued, the missionary taught by example, living "an existence entirely consecrated to doing good," showing his followers what could be expected of Frenchmen. "This love and this respect that [the French missionary] instills by his abnegation and devotion, contributes more than a little to give these savages a great and noble idea of the country from where similar men come."[66] Chanel's glowing report from the central highlands must have pleased missionaries who, the very same year, suffered Camille Pâris's rekindling of the Mayréna affair.

But it was becoming clear to a number of missionaries that countering mounting anticlericalism with praise alone would not suffice. In the decade of the Freemason onslaught—from the late 1890s to about 1907—the missions retooled their rhetoric and redefined their position vis-à-vis the colonial regime. The missions did not respond to the myriad pressures put on their work in the way that many conservative Catholics in France did. While they often addressed Freemason criticisms head-on, they did not don the clothes of anti-Dreyfusards—anti-republican, anti-Semitic, and counterrevolutionary. Though many missionaries still felt deep reservations about colonialism, they usually kept quiet. Instead, bishops, who in the 1880s had once guarded the missions' autonomy and interacted with officials only when necessary to smooth out problems, took an increasingly active role in promoting the value of missionary work to the colonies. In the era of Mayréna, missionary allegiance was defined in terms of the basic services they provided the administration, their patriotism, and their ability to spread a love of France. In the cutthroat age of the Dreyfus affair, when cries for anticlerical legislation could put the missions out of business, religious workers increasingly emphasized their ability to implement a project that looked suspiciously like the republican civilizing mission.

In the early morning of 10 March 1901, the Catholic missions of Indochina had a remarkable opportunity to redefine their role in the colony. That day, a considerable crowd of colonists, French and Vietnamese dignitaries, and local Christians gathered in front of the Saigon Cathedral. A witness reported it was "one of those beautiful days in the Far East, when the light of the sun brings a special clarity"; flowers and palms, as well as countless French flags, covered the pavilion set up for the occasion. At exactly seven o'clock, Governor-General Paul Doumer arrived, was first greeted by Mgr. Mossard, who hosted the event, and then joined other guests such as the mayor of Saigon, admirals, commandants, and members of the administration. A military band and a church chorus played patriotic music as the guests took their places. Then, with the crowd quieted, a veil covering a new statue fell to the ground, revealing a nearly three-meter-tall figure of Bishop Pigneau de Béhaine. For the mission in Cochinchina, Mossard reported, it was the most important day of the year.[67]

The plans leading up to the unveiling of the statue of Pigneau de Béhaine—the bishop who had traveled in 1787 to Louis XVI's court in search of support for the struggling Nguyen Anh—had been in the making since the late 1890s. Just as colonial lobbyists like Jules Ferry had drawn on Pigneau as a historical basis for France's colonial aspirations in the region, missionaries used the centenary of the bishop's death to defend and justify their own work. In the hands of missionary writers and speechmakers, Pigneau's legacy underwent a radical makeover. For most of the century since his death, the Catholic mission remembered Pigneau as a diligent missionary who worked to spread the power of the Church in Southeast Asia. In 1884, for example, Père Adrien Launay, the official historian of the Missions étrangères de Paris, wrote a history of Annam that made nothing of Pigneau de Béhaine's role in assisting future French colonial endeavors.[68]

But only a dozen years later, amid growing anticlerical clamoring, the mission resurrected Pigneau as both a hero for Catholicism and a dedicated servant of French colonialism. In 1896, Louis-Eugène Louvet, another Missions étrangères historian, published a biography in anticipation of the erection of a statue and what he called a "religious and national ceremony" to commemorate Pigneau's contribution to Franco-Vietnamese relations.[69] In a rousing preface to an otherwise straightforward biography, Louvet considered Pigneau's current-day importance in a way that contrasted starkly with traditional images of the missionary. Louvet's preface did not even mention conversion, nor did it even explicitly associate Pigneau's work with bringing

Christianity to Vietnam. Instead, Louvet focused on the bishop's work as a civilizer and politician. "Nation" shared equal prominence with "God" in most of the preface's formulations. Pigneau strove, in Louvet's words, "to achieve civilizing work." Now, France (and not Catholicism) continued to harvest "the fruit . . . of his wise politics."[70] For enriching the colony in so many ways, Louvet claimed, France owed Pigneau "the debt of national gratitude and patriotism."[71]

Louvet did not just use words like "civilization"; he showed fluency with republican means of implementing it. One of the more striking examples is how the biographer venerated Pigneau's work as a facilitator of French commercial interests. Aside from wrenching Vietnam from the grips of civil war (a rebuke to critics who claimed the missions caused disharmony), Pigneau worked "in the name of France," opening Vietnamese ports "to us, despite the ill will and avarice of our rivals for influence in the seas of China: the English in India, and the Spanish of Manila."[72] Associating Pigneau with France's commercial hopes and anxieties over international trade reflected the political and economic concerns of Louvet's era as much as Pigneau's. The biographer showed the bishop to have been concerned with British imperial competition and with fundamental questions of *mise-en-valeur* a century in advance of republican colonizers.

Louvet's biography reproduced an 1896 letter from Mgr. Dépierre (the bishop in Indochina who had first conceived of the centenary) that linked France's civilizing impulses with Christianity. To Dépierre, Pigneau had acted with a mixture of force and goodness, wisdom, moderation, and prudence— values that combined political know-how and Christian morality.[73] Dépierre continued that France, like Pigneau, was on "a mission of peace and progress, of justice and fairness," in short, a mission "inspired by Christian faith." The "superior men" who subscribe to these ideas, and who understand colonial issues, "know that Christianity is the great factor of all true civilization."[74] Dépierre's linking of Catholicism to civilization echoed Jules Ferry's famous formulation that republican France would export its ideas, language, and genius to the world. But Dépierre's vision included a spiritual dimension: the honor of noble France, he wrote, was not to exploit the people it conquered but "to bring before them all [France's] ideas, its civilization, and its faith."[75]

For Louvet and other missionary commentators, Pigneau's crafting of the Versailles treaty was also a model of "associationist" colonialism. The bishop of Adran emerged as a man who worked with Nguyen Anh to calm a society in the grips of "profound anarchy," while at the same time securing territorial and economic benefits for France.[76] "This, it must be recognized, was truly Christian and civilizing politics"—the kind of politics, Louvet added, that "present day governments rarely show us, respectful of people's rights and the honor of the weak." In rendering services and clarifying duties, Pigneau's work offered a recipe for peaceful colonial existence: his political

Figure 3.1.   Statue of Pigneau de Béhaine in front of Saigon Cathedral. (Reproduced from *Missions Catholiques* with permission from the Oeuvres pontificales missionnaires—Coopération missionnaire, Lyon.)

goals, "far from oppressing and dividing hearts, brought together two civilizations, until then strangers and enemies, by opening to them magnificent prospects of prosperity and grandeur."[77]

If there was a single theme to the centenary it was patriotism. In his first preface to Pigneau's biography, Louvet used the word itself, in its various forms, more than once a page. In defining Pigneau's patriotism, Louvet gave shape to a new form of missionary patriotism that inextricably linked a love of God with a love of France. Louvet, in a clear response to radicals' ciriticisms, rejected what he termed "laic" claims that Pigneau's religiosity minimized his patriotism.[78] Rather, in Louvet's opinion, by symbolizing "the indissoluble alliance of patriotism and religion," Pigneau worked both for the "reign of God" and to open "to French influence this rich and populous peninsula of Indochina."[79] The theme of patriotism was so key to the memory of Pigneau that Louvet changed the title of his biography. In the first edition published in France in 1900, the publisher dropped the lackluster title *Mgr. D'Adran, notice biographique* for the more poignant *Mgr. D'Adran, missionnaire et patriote*.[80] The latter book went through at least two editions in its first year, and another in 1902.

What is striking about the unveiling of Pigneau de Béhaine's statue in Saigon is just how *republican* it was. Commemorations and monuments were central to republican culture in the 1880s and 1890s. Continually on the defensive against both the monarchist right and the radical left, moderate republicans in France made an art of publicly professing their political ideals. Public ceremonies and monuments gave shape to a vision of a France based on the promise of liberty, justice, and the power of the people. In 1880, the *14 juillet* became a national holiday, commemorating the unity of the Fête de la Fédération of 1790, not the mobs that took the Bastille in 1789.[81] From the 1880s on, busts of Marianne, the symbol of the republic, began appearing in town halls across France; statues of heroes of the nation were erected in squares and parks.[82] With the death and entombment of Victor Hugo, hero of the Third Republic, the Pantheon became the undisputed secular church of the nation, thus dividing republican "great men" from religious and royal ones.[83] Such statues and landmarks, as Philip Nord has observed, turned the nation into a "great outdoor classroom, bristling with moral lessons for youth."[84]

The centenary of Pigneau's death performed a similar function for the missions. From beneath the statue's veil emerged a new image of Catholic missionaries in colonial and French politics. The new Pigneau symbolized a bridge between France and its colonial peoples, between a love of nation and a love of God, and even between republican civilizing ideals and the goals of Christian charity. The tall statue had Pigneau standing straight in a bishop's robe and cross, his right hand extended from his body, holding a copy of the Treaty of Versailles he brokered in 1787. In his other hand, he guided the young Prince Canh. Pigneau's massive figure nearly enveloped the young prince; the sculptor placed Pigneau behind Canh, but with his foot and hand

131. Tonkin - HAIPHONG — Monument Jules Ferry

Collection de l'Union Commerciale Indochinoise

Figure 3.2.   Statue of Jules Ferry, Haiphong. Postcard, c. 1912.

forward, as if also guiding the boy. The speeches that morning echoed the symbolism of the statue. Pigneau was a Frenchmen who supported and led a generation of Vietnamese.

Mgr. Mossard, who by the 1890s had emerged as one of Indochina's most politically savvy bishops, was the main speaker. Addressing the arrangement of the statue, Mossard explained that Pigneau had appeared to the Vietnamese "as the most perfect model of a master, as a loyal, wise, and devoted friend."[85] Pigneau saved the life of Nguyen Anh, he recounted, and inspired his followers. Pigneau united France and Cochinchina, obtaining "for his royal *protégé* the help of his country of origin, of the generous nation, France, always helpful

in hardship, for centuries protector of civilization and the Catholic apostolate."[86] In describing Pigneau, Mossard could not have better described the relationships of associationist colonialism: France, as many Freemasons
clamored at the time, was not a conqueror but a partner and friend.

Mossard's speech left no room to doubt that the celebration of Pigneau's
life was as much about the Dreyfus affair and mounting anticlerical attacks
on the missions as it was about history. The statue, he said, would be "like an
open book" for future generations: "It will say aloud that the battles of parties, the political dissensions, in a word, all that excites the spirits these days
in the *mère-patrie*, cannot divide, in this colony, the hearts of true Frenchmen.
Yes, Gentlemen, it will say that we all were united to offer this bronze to an
illustrious compatriot, the bishop of Adran, a name long famous, and henceforth the most honored and the most popular in Cochinchina."[87]

In Pigneau, Catholic missionaries saw an opportunity to express their commitment to *ralliement*, not to polemics. Mossard's words—stripped of all talk of
God and conversion—spoke of reconciliation, of a missionary project willing to
join, rather than challenge, colonialism. But the bishop insisted on one point:
that republicans had no monopoly on civilization. "For us, Frenchmen abroad,"
he announced, "we salute this man of large and fertile ideas who wanted, in
this Far East, the name of Frenchmen to be synonymous with progress, civilization, and true liberty."[88] A decade earlier, such a public proclamation by a
bishop would have been unthinkable. Considering the centuries-old tradition
in missionary writing of portraying religious workers as lone, homeless apostles, the recasting of Pigneau as a front man for French commerce and civilization represented a major departure. But the heat of conflict and critique—in
both Indochina and France—had driven missionaries like Louvet, Dépierre,
and Mossard to wax patriotic in a way they hoped both moderate republicans
and *religieux* could accept. The missions' future rested on it.

Precious Auxiliaries of Colonization

Pigneau's centenary might have been the most eloquent and public expression of missionaries' views on colonialism, but it was not the last. Throughout the early 1900s, missionaries increasingly defined their work in terms
that many Freemasons used—spreading influence through disseminating
French ideas, language, and economic programs—that is, the recipe for civilization. Working out the right balance between mission, administration, and
civilization, however, was not always easy. Even Mgr. Mossard, who had
shown himself so adept a speaker at the unveiling in 1901, made some false
steps along the way.

In 1901, the Conseil colonial, the body that, among other duties, monitored the colonial budget, threatened to end its annual subvention of 15,000
piastres to Mossard's mission of West Cochinchina due to its failure to teach

French in its schools. Mossard later complained to his colleagues in Paris that anticlericalism, not concern over schools, motivated the Conseil to act. In defense of the mission, he wrote a long letter—more than twenty printed pages—to the administration to explain the mission's commitment to teaching. In it, he reminded officials of the importance of the protectorate of the missions, arguing that to end the subvention paid to the missions would be "anti-liberal." He denied any suggestion that the missions were enemies of colonial expansion, calling them instead "precious, if not indispensable auxiliaries" in the colony's educational efforts. Losing the funding, he warned, would mean the mission would have to close one-third of its schools, leaving children uneducated and causing resentment among parents.[89]

Mossard then tried to make the difficult case of explaining why missions did not teach more French. Teaching French, he argued, required better-trained teachers, and many students attended schools for too short a time to learn. He reassured the administration that the missions did teach French to as many as made sense—about a quarter of all students. But Mossard's reasoning took a terribly wrong turn: he questioned, in print, the value of teaching French across the possession. What was the benefit, he asked, of producing so many bilingual peasant children when neither the administration nor industry had places for them except in the rice fields? Such an educated class would no longer be peasants willing to work but bitter *déclassés* who would pose a serious danger to the stability of French influence. The argument had validity and was later essentially adopted by republicans. But it was not an opportune moment for a missionary to voice such views. "Dare I add," Mossard stated bravely, "that the Vietnamese who know French are, with rare exception, those who love the French the least, who respect them the least, and who, fundamentally, are the most hostile to them?"[90]

Mossard's candidness would haunt the mission for some time. In 1904, as politicians in Paris discussed missionary funding in the empire, critics read Mossard's words aloud in the National Assembly, inciting exclamations of disbelief from the far left.[91] But the most immediate effect came closer to home. At a meeting of the Conseil colonial, a Vietnamese councilman named M. Diep took issue with the bishop's presumptuousness. His protest revealed the extent to which questions of civilization ruled the day, even in the minds of some Vietnamese officials. Reading from Mossard's *Mémoire*, Diep called the bishop's words an attack on "all Vietnamese who, like me, received the benefits of French civilization. Mgr. Mossard clearly is accusing us of being traitors." Diep, who showed himself to be no great supporter of the missions, went on to conclude that the French-speaking Vietnamese who had such disdain for Frenchmen must be "creatures of the mission." After all, he asserted, the only Vietnamese whom Mgr. Mossard knew well were Catholics.[92] In time, the Conseil colonial voted. The subvention that the West Cochinchina mission had received for fifteen years came to an end.

The incident led Mossard to write a second long letter on the mission's position on teaching French. While the bishop might have hoped to salvage the subvention, this was primarily an exercise in damage control. Mossard now emphasized the benefits of missionary education to French influence, ringing notes that officials wanted to hear. He insisted that teaching French could be accomplished only within a broader plan to develop the country, materially and morally. The administration served material concerns. The missions, he argued, accomplish France's "moral conquest": "Missionaries work for it, by speaking French to those who speak it, by speaking Vietnamese to all. By their instruction, by their conversations, they make stick, surely and profoundly, the ideas that France has a real interest in propagating abroad"; these ideas, he added, cemented the union between the two peoples. With clear reference to the growing chorus of critics, he added that to challenge missionary work was to hurt France's colonizing effort. Mossard felt the need to conclude by asserting that no one spoke to the Vietnamese "with more passion of the true glories of France" than the missionary, who cried "with joy" when recounting "the triumphs of the *Patrie*."[93] A healthy dose of patriotism never hurt anyone's cause in the empire.

While teaching French and encouraging morality were two of the most obvious ways missionaries could (or failed to) assist the colonial effort, they were not the only ones. In the early 1900s, missionaries increasingly highlighted how the mission could bring the political and economic reforms to the countryside that the administration wanted. In 1903, for example, Mgr. Marcou sent a detailed report to the governor-general describing how missionary work could develop the Muong ethnic minorities living in the remote mountains of Tonkin.[94] Mgr. Marcou wrote his "Note Relative to the Muong People of the Provinces of Thanh-Hoa and Hoa-Binh" at a moment when local resistance to Catholic work was intense. At stake, insisted the bishop, was not just religion but colonization and the success of French civilization.

Marcou began with a description reminiscent of how travelers saw the central highlands around Kontum in the 1880s. "Completely outside the influence of France," the Muong were a people full of "latent but real hostility" and "feelings of hatred toward France," he wrote. This ill feeling originated with the *tri-chau*, or petty chiefs, in the region, who feared that the moment their people had "real contact with the French administration" and were exposed to civilization, their "absolute power" would diminish. For this reason, the bishop continued, many chiefs over the previous few years had blocked the establishment of missions in the area, using all forms of intimidation to achieve their goal, resorting even to beating and fining members of the community who welcomed missionaries.[95] Considering the nature of many criticisms against the mission, Marcou made a rather unorthodox suggestion: Catholic missionaries could help end the absolutist tendencies of local chiefs and help solidify republican rule.

Marcou's "Note" presented the governor-general with a point-by-point explanation of why missionary work served the civilizing goals of France. In rebuking the missionary, Muong chiefs had rebuked France itself; the Muong people, said the bishop, wanted to benefit from "French civilization," which had shown itself "so protective to the weak and oppressed." Marcou's description of civilization's supposed benefits paralleled colonizing policies around the French empire. The mission, for example, sought to end the nomadic existence of the population, teaching them to cultivate the land and to develop agriculture practices. The mission would bring stability to the region, putting an end to pirates and the insurrectional movements they inspired, and thus providing a secure setting where sedentary agricultural communities could grow. Missionaries would be "the first workers for a slow but progressive transformation of an entire country."[96]

The Muong mission would bring both security and progress: by sending missionaries, the government would have French "partisans" in the region, who could watch out both for foreign invasion and for any internal *mécontents* who might try to profit from complications caused by foreign forces. If missionaries could establish an outpost there, they could build schools, maintain relations with the population, and make sure that "French influence" would extend from "deep roots." Marcou emphasized that occasional apostolic trips to the region and meetings with chiefs no longer sufficed; it was necessary to make contact with an entire population "to seat French influence solidly in the country." As long as such contact was limited, the bishop asserted, the chiefs' hatred of France would go unabated.[97] The mission offered all these services, with little expected in return, despite criticisms that missionaries benefit from the hardship of their converts. "The missionaries who exercise their ministry in this region," he reflected, "at the price of privation and unspeakable fatigue, fulfill an eminent patriotic role." A good number of them, he added, would succumb to the task, but others would replace them. Putting a new spin on martyrdom, Marcou wrote that all his missionaries were sustained by "the thought that they suffer and die not only for their religious faith" but also for "their double *patrie*": France and the "Annamite-Laotian country that they would like to see united with France by indestructible links."[98]

Bishops were not the only religious workers who retooled the missions' aims to dovetail with republican goals; the language of civilization trickled down to missionaries in the field, as well. Freemason attacks inspired many missionaries to reply to the accusations, either in letters to high-ranking officials or in print. For example, the incendiary assaults of Camille Pâris led to a heated published exchange with Père Guerlach of Mayréna affair fame. Guerlach berated Pâris for hating and persecuting the missions, hypocritically "in the name of free-thought and freedom of conscience."[99] Like Mossard, Marcou, and others, Guerlach infused his reply with civilizing rhetoric about the mission's contribution to the livelihoods of its followers.

Another missionary felt the need to defend his reputation and actions, which were attacked in a series of newspaper articles. In a letter to the governor-general, Père Artif insisted that for him, like all missionaries, "patriotism is not only an affair of the heart, it is also a means of achieving a set goal: 'To infuse in the Vietnamese the French mentality.' "[100] Missionaries were just as capable of championing their selfless contributions to French civilization as the Freemasons were of portraying them as sinful traitors.

An Impetus to Civilize

To destroy, enslave, and steal; or to teach, moralize, and civilize? Those were the contradictory images of missionaries that the administration had to grapple with. The ruckus over missionary work could not have offered more complications for officials. The veracity of Freemason claims and missionary counterclaims was only part of the question. There were also the problems of the mounting expense of *mise-en-valeur* and of rectifying the failures of the administration's own civilizing mission. These concerns mingled with growing anxieties about political unrest. Though officials wanted to believe that the conquest had been completed in the 1890s, they remained anxious, vigilantly pursuing a wide range of threats to social stability, including political activism.[101] And there were mixed messages from Paris. After 1902, the Ministry of Colonies showed itself sympathetic to Freemason cries to laicize the colonies, encouraging officials to minimize the influence of the all-too-powerful missions.[102] But the Ministry of Foreign Affairs remained concerned about respecting the protectorate, while mending relations with Rome, and called for caution.[103]

A certain amount of laicization was a fait accompli. Subventions were cut; teaching brothers and sisters were removed from government schools; nursing sisters were dismissed from colonial hospitals; crucifixes came down from public spaces. But beyond that, despite pressures from colonial critics and from politicians in France, the administration in Indochina defended its policy of neutrality regarding the missions. With more than 500,000 Catholics in Indochina at the turn of the century, attacking the mission posed a potentially considerable threat. Another major concern, as always, was expense. A wide range of services, from schools and hospitals to orphanages and leprosaria, were in the hands of the missions. According to one official, missionaries ran these facilities ten times more cheaply than the colony could.[104] In 1903, the governor-general added that, even if the administration could afford to replace missionary workers with lay ones, some of the "particularly repulsive" jobs, such as working with lepers, would be hard to fill.[105] External threats also loomed. With the Japanese defeat of the Russians in 1905, and with political disturbances mounting in China, the security of French interests in Southeast Asia again appeared uncertain. Considering that "the yellow peril is becoming more and more menacing," as a resident-superior of Annam pointed out in 1905, "it is important to meet all new intrigues by developing as much as possible every French interest without concerning ourselves as to its source, whether commercial, agricultural *or religious.*"[106]

In June 1908, *Le Temps* published an article announcing the arrival of Governor-General Antony Klobukowski to his new post in Hanoi. It quoted the promises that the new official, like his predecessors, had made upon his appointment. They were all very familiar: to bring liberty and security, to associate the Vietnamese in the governing of the possession, and to offer intellectual and moral instruction. Such were, the article noted, the ideas that "we represent in the world." But, the piece continued, the governor-general's work would not be easy: the Vietnamese population felt overburdened by the "tyranny" of colonial taxes and humiliated by officials' love of "marking their superiority" through "mockery" and "vulgar familiarity" with the population. The article quoted Phan Chu Trinh, an imprisoned dissident, who had described in a famous letter the "profound contempt" the French had for the Vietnamese: "In your eyes, we are only savages, foul brutes incapable of distinguishing between good and evil." The article lamented the rising feeling among the Vietnamese that the French had no respect for the population. Klobukowski's task would be to face these difficult fiscal and moral issues.[107]

The *Le Temps* article did not sensationalize Governor-General Klobukowski would later reflect that, in 1908, the possession was in "a crisis": there were plots being hatched in Hanoi, bandits in the delta, reformist groups near the Chinese border, discontentment everywhere about taxation—all this despite the "works of peaceful influence" such as economic development, schools, and the creation of a postal service.[108] The most worrisome new challenge to colonial rule was the development of an anticolonial movement, designed in part by exiles in Japan, and inspired by one of Vietnam's early nationalist figures, Phan Boi Chau. Born into a scholar-gentry family, Phan was a poet, patriot, and political organizer who denounced French oppression and called for the end of colonial occupation.[109] In 1908, Phan and a famous anticolonial militant named De Tham plotted a rebellion of Vietnamese troops in Hanoi; the plan was ultimately uncovered, but it was disturbing evidence of growing Vietnamese animosity to French rule.

Amid these new threats, Klobukowski's first order of business was to stifle discord between Frenchmen in Indochina. Before even leaving France, Klobukowski stressed the need to put an end to the "complete freedom" of the "imprudent" colonial press, including the journalistic efforts of the Catholic mission. Missionaries had recently attempted to shape public opinion on political issues by acquiring two influential newspapers in Tonkin, including the *Courrier d'Haiphong*, a onetime pro-Freemason publication that had run some of Camille Pâris's diatribes.[110] Concerns over missionary meddling in the arena of public opinion soon boiled over when it became apparent that some indigenous Catholics favored the nascent reformist movements. In late 1908, a bishop was even implicated in a case where Vietnamese priests had raised money for Phan Boi Chau. Mgr. Mossard quickly stepped in, organized the removal of the bishop, and assured the governor-general that the mission did not want to harm the "[religious] neutrality that until now has been full of advantages for it."[111] With Mossard's agreement, Klobukowski accepted the missions as a patriotic tool for spreading French influence and deterring nationalist uprisings, and agreed to block antimissionary legislation.[112] But officials were clearly growing weary of the endless intrigues.

Although the colonial administration did not declare war on missionaries in the way that many Freemason colonists would have liked, the decade of critique and political polemic did change colonialism in Indochina, including relations between the regime and the Catholic missions. In weighing questions of missionary mischief or contribution, increasingly colonial officials dealt with controversy by sidestepping the missions entirely. The most effective way of minimizing their influence—and of dodging critiques that the administration failed to punish Catholic corruption—was to make sure that religious workers were not essential to fulfilling France's colonizing and civilizing goals. In the wake of the Dreyfus affair and the furor it had inspired in Indochina, the administration answered its critics by pursuing its own ostensibly civilizing efforts with new vigor. These included new programs to develop the economy, to take over medical facilities, to develop official education, and to establish outposts in more remote areas to assure the spread of French justice. While most of these programs functioned independently of the missions, some directly challenged missionary autonomy.

A window onto the change of administrative mind-set was opened in 1908 when a missionary in Tonkin requested permission to take over a government-funded leper facility that served both Christians and non-Christians. The priest requested that the mission receive directly the government subvention that maintained the facility.[113] More than twenty years earlier, the resident in Hanoi had championed the mission's "charity" for volunteering to take care of lepers.[114] But in 1908, the field administrator (echoing common Freemason concerns) determined that the missionary wanted control of the facility only in order to "extend his influence" over the local population by winning more converts. As the missionary's goal was clearly "proselytism," the official suggested that the administration refuse the offer. In his brief reply, making reference to similar incidents elsewhere in Tonkin, the resident-superior in Hanoi wholly agreed with the official's assessment, saying that the government fared better by avoiding missionary involvement entirely.[115] Whether the missionary was sincere in his desire to help lepers or was simply seeking new converts—a question made so murky by the religious conflict of the previous decade—was no longer at issue. The administration would deal directly with the leper community and would not involve the mission in official programs.

The administration dealt similarly with the much thornier question of education. In the wake of the scandal over missionaries' failure to teach French, Governor-General Klobukowski made no effort to crack down on missionary education, choosing instead to isolate it as a private enterprise. In a 1910 speech to supporters of laicization, Klobukowski showed himself to be no fan of religious instruction, deeming it out of step with "modern ideas." But he advised those in the audience to turn their attention away from combating mission schools for, after the separation of Church and state, they were no longer a concern. Instead, it was time for the administration to develop an effective laic educational system in Indochina that would cultivate its own ideas—most notably, as he put it, reason, not superstition—and serve its own goals. The audience, made up of many men and women who had fiercely fought missionary influence in the empire, applauded the governor-general.[116]

Reforming education was no small task. Official education, while often touted as a key component of republican colonization, remained more a concept than a reality, even in the early 1900s. Since 1896, the Ministry of Colonies had expressed concern that education in parts of Indochina left much to be desired. That year, the minister insisted that it was important to develop an educational system that would help shape "young indigenous generations" in a fashion consistent with "the needs of our colonization."[117] In 1906, the governor-general admitted to an audience that included the emperor of Annam that French efforts had been "paralyzed," but he reasserted the need for European colonies to transform the "protected or conquered races."[118] Despite reorganization of the system in 1906 and 1907, government education was still struggling when Klobukowski arrived. In 1909, an inspector of education, a M. Péralle, outlined new goals of colonial education, ones that more clearly reflected associationist policies. More immediately important than moral reform was the need to teach students basic hygiene as well as commercial and industrial skills. In a move that must have raised a few eyebrows at the cathedral in Saigon, the inspector's report argued that *quoc ngu* (Vietnamese in roman script), and not the French language, would serve as the "vehicle for our ideas" for the majority of students. Only an elite would learn French.[119]

The main problem facing the administration's impetus to educate remained a lack of trained teachers and money. Here, Klobukowski turned to independent organizations: to the Alliance française to expand its efforts to teach French, and to the Mission laïque to provide more trained teachers. The Mission laïque, founded in 1902 by the director of education in Madagascar and a handful of university professors, was from its inception deeply influenced by Freemasonry and republican ideology. It worked, according to its own literature, for the "defense and progress of laic education" primarily by running the École Jules Ferry, where instructors were trained for careers in the colonies and abroad.[120]

The Mission laïque also organized programs that brought Vietnamese students to France. A 1909 article in *Le Siècle* by Alphonse Aulard, the organization's director and renowned historian, described one such visit. In order to give the students a real taste of France, the organizers took them on a balloon ride and showed them factories and a republican *colonie de vacance*; they even had the opportunity to see a monument to Jules Ferry and meet Mrs. Ferry. The young Vietnamese students, Aulard wrote, sensed firsthand "the superiority of the French," which led them to comparisons with their own country, and to realize that their civilization was behind, "but perfectible." Such a program, Aulard continued, made the Vietnamese love France.[121] Shortly after his arrival in Hanoi, Klobukowski called on the Mission laïque to increase its efforts in Indochina, to train and send more *instituteurs*, and organize more exchange projects. Aulard hailed Klobukowski for implementing a rational, systematic "civilizing policy" in place of the old routine based more on theory than on practice.[122]

By calling on the Mission laïque for help, Klobukowski showed the administration's commitment to a core ideal of republican civilization—education—without paying the price of religious conflict. Missionary schools continued to exist and, indeed, thrive. And with organizations such as the Mission laïque contributing to and championing the administration's program, Klobukowski was congratulated for jump-starting this important aspect of the republican civilizing mission in Indochina. In 1911, Klobukowski linked successful education reform to somewhat improved relations between European and indigenous people. He declared that his new school programs had shown France's "friendly intentions" to lift the "moral and intellectual level" of the Vietnamese. They now understood the French willingness to open, to an elite, the horizons that a French education offered.[123]

But Klobukowski's optimism did little more than expose the deep gulf between civilizing rhetoric and the actual results of reform. The following year, inspector of education Péralle filed his own assessment of the state of education, painting a less than promising picture of both white and indigenous children's experiences. He spent considerable ink describing how wholly unsatisfactory education in Indochina was for French children; prolonged contact with the indigenous population, Péralle feared, had unfortunate effects on the moral and intellectual formation of "the French of France." More pertinent to recent reforms, he attacked the practice of sending some secondary Vietnamese students to France to study. Though these students earned degrees, they did not assimilate "our ideas and our civilization" well. Echoing the warnings of Mgr. Mossard a decade earlier—observations that had been deemed unpatriotic when uttered by a missionary—Inspector Péralle confessed that these students returned to the colony with expectations that could not be fulfilled: "unhappy, bitter, they become our worst enemies," he warned. The result was "a profound disdain for the French."[124] Such were the uncertain dividends of the civilizing business.

The Ghost of Mayréna

One aspect of Klobukowski's plan to streamline administrative efforts to bring stability to Indochina did affect some missionaries directly. In addition to increasing official independence in the development of health and education projects, the administration undertook to establish more posts across the possession. "From the administrative point of view," Klobukowski wrote in one report, there remained "very serious imperfections": authority was too greatly dispersed, with local administrators, agents, and *chefs de provinces* often giving contradictory direction to an increasingly confused population.[125] This was particularly true in more remote regions heavily under the influence of missionaries. Officials viewed establishing effective administrative posts as key to the republican dual vision of colonizing and civilizing: they ensured security, creating environments where political, economic, and judicial reforms could be introduced. In regions where missionaries enjoyed relative autonomy, the stage was set for conflict.

As in the 1880s and 1890s, missionaries and low-level officials continued to step on one another's toes well into the twentieth century. French missionaries and indigenous priests continued to complain of unfair taxation, corrupt policies, and religious persecution. Officials reported that uncontrolled zeal drove Catholics to overstep their proper roles while resident-superiors and bishops intervened in more serious cases and smoothed over differences. *Plus ça change.* But in some cases, official policies to reform local practices and to introduce French notions of liberty and justice to isolated townships brought missionaries into direct conflict with the administration.

The Catholic mission at Kontum was, again, a case in point. Some fifteen years after Mayréna had returned from his adventures as the king of the Sedangs, the central highlands were still an administrative uncertainty. In 1904, an inspector named Dulac toured the region and reached the same conclusions as many officials before him: in choosing Père Vialleton to represent France, the administration had "accorded its confidence to adversaries" who "were resolved, if not to combat openly, then at least to neutralize our influence," to the benefit of their own. Dulac described a mission that dominated local communities, pronouncing laws, imprisoning people, charging fines, and seizing property. Père Guerlach, aging but still battling, fared prominently in the condemnations. On one occasion, the report stated, Guerlach had set up a hut and a church in the village of Pley-Klou to convert the inhabitants. When the villagers refused to give up their traditional practices, the missionary decided to leave, but demanded payment of twenty buffalo to cover the expenses he had incurred.[126] In this era of a rational, centralized colonial regime, such arbitrary use of authority by the mission disturbed Dulac.

More important, Dulac highlighted the failure of missionary work to bring significant moral reform. In particular, the mission's approach to slavery ran counter to republican ideals. The mission encouraged the slave trade, he argued, by buying slaves their freedom; instead of ending slavery, the practice gave groups a financial incentive to capture more and more slaves to sell to the priests. The mission's "civilizing role" was further damaged, he suggested, by the fact that bought slaves did not win real freedom but were forced to remain at the mission, working as unpaid laborers, earning their food and board. Dulac addressed this issue with one missionary, Père Alberty, but without effect: "I understood that we did not have the same ideas on the slavery question," the administrator wrote, "and I did not have the poor taste to insist, contenting myself to cut short my visit."[127]

Dulac never returned to complete his report, and concern over the highlands mission may well have faded had it not been for Camille Pâris's blistering personality. By 1907, Pâris's assaults on Catholic workers grew so intense that the mission accused the Freemason of defamation. The case drew the governor-general's attention to the Kontum mission, its relation to the state, and its alleged illegal activities.[128] Other branches of the administration had already started work when the request from the governor-general was made. A month earlier, the resident-superior of Annam expressed concern that the number of missionaries working in the central highlands had ballooned to nineteen since the Mayréna years. The sheer number of missionaries, coupled with the longevity of the project (Vialleton had been there more than thirty years), represented an entrenched clerical presence that the government might need to limit.[129] Then an official investigation confirmed many of Pâris's accusations: the mission was the "master" of the region and desired only "the creation of a Vietnamese colony entirely at its devotion."[130] Pâris's most sensational claim—that the highland mission had been behind the murder of a number of government officials who had traveled through the region—was never proved. The following year, in one of the more bizarre twists in the story, Pâris was killed while traveling in the central highlands. His brothers at the lodge accused the mission.[131]

After Klobukowski's arrival in Hanoi, the administration developed its own post in the highlands, building contacts and winning the confidence of the local population. Relations between the French delegate at Kontum and the mission soon broke down. Léopold Sabatier, the delegate, was an astute and driven bureaucrat who pursued claims against the mission with simmering determination.[132] He took depositions of local residents who had experienced problems with the mission and examined even minor incidents that belied missionary attitudes.[133] In 1911, a man named Yo'n from the village of Dak Drei complained that a missionary named Kemlin had entered his hut where Yo'n and some family members were mourning the loss of his grandmother in the traditional fashion—by getting drunk with the corpse. The missionary interrupted the ritual and demanded to know why they were drinking, then took the jar of wine and smashed it. Yo'n testified that he was poor and could not afford to lose the expensive jar.[134]

Sabatier brought the case to Père Kemlin's attention and provoked a revealing response. Far from denying the events, the missionary used the case to instruct the official on local ways. When rules were broken, Kemlin wrote, those responsible had to be severely reprimanded; the only punishment they understood was monetary. The missionary added, "even slavery itself is only—if I can express it this way—a fine pushed to the extreme limits, for only those who cannot pay an imposed fine become slaves." Kemlin explained that the mission imposed fines when necessary in Catholic villages. In the case of Yo'n, Kemlin said that all converts took public oaths that they would no longer practice superstitions, especially *mut kiet*, the practice of drinking with a corpse. The broken jar was his punishment. Kemlin refused to pay for the broken items.[135] In some ways, the missionary's perspective conformed to the relativism of "associationist" doctrine promoted by many republicans. Like other missionaries, Kemlin was "as much as possible" trying to conform to the mores of the local community. But, for Sabatier, such an interpretation of "associationism" was unacceptable.

Two approaches to "civilizing" were about to come into conflict. Sabatier moved up the chain of command, asking Père Guerlach to force Kemlin to pay for the destroyed property, but without luck. "There is a question of principle," Guerlach told him, "an antecedent of very great consequences for the future." Were the mission made to pay, a host of other accusations would follow. According to local practice, he concluded, converts gave the mission permission to inflict punishment as it saw fit.[136] But Sabatier was not to be dismissed so easily. "I share perfectly the opinion of M. Guerlach," Sabatier wrote to a colleague in Qui Nhon. Sabatier hoped that rendering justice to Yo'n would be "an antecedent full of consequences" that would open "the door to a crowd of others." Not investigating complaints against the mission, the official worried, "would compromise forever the work of civilization and justice undertaken by the French administration."[137]

In January 1912, a far more serious charge came to Sabatier's attention. A group of men testified that they had converted to Catholicism out of fear because, in their words, "the missionaries made war on those who did not want to become Catholic, they trapped them and made them slaves."[138] As Sabatier took more depositions, a particularly serious incident took shape. A missionary named Hutinet insisted that the inhabitants of a village arrest chief Drio from the village of Kon Bu'ng or else face having ten of their villagers enslaved. Once captured, Drio was put in a *cangue* and bound by the hands and feet. According to witnesses, the missionary then held Drio for a month to punish a local village that had rebuked his attempts at proselytism. In order to win the chief's freedom, the village had to pay a 100-franc ransom.

Out of fear of the missionary, the village ultimately paid the ransom. In the days before the administration arrived, they said, the missionary controlled everything: "It's because of fear that everyone became Catholic."[139]

With this information, critics of the highland mission had finally attained the evidence to support their longtime suspicions. According to Sabatier, Père Hutinet had no complaint against Drio except that his village did not want the missionary evangelizing there. The missionary in fact had acted within the boundaries of local customs; but "in their apostolic zeal, they do not hesitate to put into practice [such customs], even when the most elementary moral condemns it." If immoral behavior were not enough, the missionary's actions also drove Drio's village to wage war on those villages that had helped the missionary capture the chief. "It remains now to French justice to follow its course," Sabatier wrote.[140] Père Hutinet was found guilty, condemned to six months' imprisonment, and fined 500 francs. Because the missionary had no prior criminal record, his sentence was suspended.[141] Sabatier was not ignorant of the historical precedent of this case, for it challenged a missionary program *"en vigeur* for such a long time in the region."[142]

But he did not seem to relish the victory. Illegal methods had won many conversions to Catholicism, allowing the missionaries, he added with irony, to improve the morals of the "savages."[143] By bracketing *savages* in simple quotation marks, Sabatier expressed serious doubts about missionary influence: considering the violent and demeaning behavior of Père Hutinet, who could tell whether the savages were the people of the Pays moï or the missionaries of Kontum? Sabatier's systematic pursuit of justice reveals just how entwined republican civilizing ideology was with the politics of anticlericalism. While the administrator undoubtedly believed in the ideals of bringing French liberty and justice to the secluded highlands, his mission was both prompted and deeply influenced by an equally compelling desire to undermine the worrisome power of the mission. The official brought a republican civilizing mission to the highlands. Ironically, it was Catholic missionaries—not the ethnic minorities—who were the first to bask in its reforming rays.

Between Secular and Catholic

The years from the mid-1890s to about 1907 witnessed significant, yet very different, changes in metropolitan French and colonial Indochinese society. With the Dreyfus affair and the struggles over the religious laws of 1901–5, politics in France grew so divisive as to teeter perilously near civil war. Indochina and other colonial possessions were not sheltered from the din. Freemasons and radical republicans both in France and abroad pressured colonial administrators to implement a secular, republican civilizing mission that they hoped would lead to a crackdown on Catholic missionary work. The exchange of antimissionary ideas—evident in Freemason letters in Vietnam, political speeches in Paris, and both colonial and metropolitan publications—reveals how permeable the boundaries of the French empire were. Anticlericalism may not have been for export, but it poured out of France all the same. Abroad, it took on new contours and returned to France to fuel fires already raging.

The example of Indochina demonstrates how intricately questions of civilizing were linked to religious politics. In the hands of anticlerical factions, calls to tighten security, to develop economic programs, and to open schools that would disseminate the ideas and language of France—cornerstones of both the civilizing mission and the practical needs of colonization—were not only about improving the lot of indigenous people or convincing them to trust French authority; the implementation of this republican mission also aimed to undermine what many feared was the violent, corrupting power of the Catholic missions. While many republicans undoubtedly believed fervently in their civilizing aims, their programs were nonetheless wrought in the fires of religious conflict.

In the wake of a decade of religious bickering, the colonial administration responded not by taking sides—a move that promised to bring more unrest to the possession—but by pursuing a more vigorous policy to open government schools, to lobby independent republican organizations like the Mission laïque to become involved, and to broaden the reach of the administration and the justice it aspired to ensure. While anxieties over nascent anticolonial movements made these new efforts wise, they were also inspired by an official desire to defuse potentially divisive clashes between missionaries and their critics. The impetus for official civilizing projects, then, was not purely ideological; high-ranking French officials had long crafted inspiring speeches to describe their plans to lift up the unfortunate colonial masses, but it was not until after the First World War that reality began to reflect their rhetoric. Anticlerical opposition to Catholic missionaries in Indochina, with its unwelcome political pressure and worrisome social instability, motivated Klobukowski and other officials to pursue a civilizing policy that was truly republican and did not rely on missionary involvement.

The missions, however, did not go away. Even at the height of the antireligious movement in France, some missionaries in Indochina remained confident that the colonial regime would not turn on them. Colony and mission, despite serious differences of orientation and goals, had more to gain from entente than from divorce. What was less certain was whether radicals in France would demand the "ruin" of Catholicism in the empire.[144] Rather than mounting the political barricades that so divided Frenchmen at home, the missions opted for *ralliement*. Declarations of patriotism and the retooling of religious goals to correspond with republican civilizing policies were aimed at deflecting criticisms and protecting the missions from damaging legislation. For missionaries whose vocation had for centuries rejected such worldly concerns as patriotism, the process of redefining evangelizing was a major undertaking.

While Klobukowski assured his laic friends that he had isolated the missions as inconsequential private enterprises, he obviously knew that they continued to exist and, indeed, prosper. In 1911, for example, when he touted the relative successes of his efforts to develop secular education, the colonial regime still ran considerably fewer schools, particularly outside the main urban centers, and taught thousands fewer students than the missions. By its own count, the government taught just shy of 5,500 male students in Tonkin, fewer than a third of the number taught in Missions étrangères schools.[145] Thus, the administration's decision to pursue its own secular programs while leaving the missions to their own devices was no victory for anticlericalism. Leaving the missions in business meant that efforts to spread national ideals—to spread, in *Le Temps*'s terms, what France stood for—were far from uniformly secular and republican. In the three decades following the founding of the Union of Indochina, for hundreds of thousands of indigenous Catholics, interaction with Frenchmen meant catechism, not *Candide.* In allowing religious workers to pursue their vocations (within the hazy boundaries of colonial law), the administration tacitly accepted the formulation that missionaries had made on the centenary of Pigneau de Béhaine's death: in Indochina, France stood for progress, civilization, and the Catholic faith.

The outbreak of war in Europe in August 1914 temporarily doused the embers of strife between the missions and their critics. In the 1920s, Freemasons would renew their criticisms of missionaries, again failing to win the sympathy of the administration.[146] During the war, the colonial administration called on the Vietnamese people to prove, as one proclamation put it, their "attachment to the great nation" that had made them "its beloved sons."[147] By 1916, forty missionaries from the Société des missions étrangères de Paris had been mobilized to go to war. At the request of the government, the Catholic mission used what one bishop called its "moral influence to facilitate the recruitment of soldiers and colonial workers destined for France."[148] The government and the Military Office agreed to send Vietnamese-speaking missionaries to act as chaplains in indigenous units in France, both to assist with translation and to perform religious rites.[149] Missionaries who had once traveled to Indochina with little thought of ever returning home now found themselves serving alongside Vietnamese soldiers and workers in France. In 1916, after thirty years of trying to convince the French administration that they were committed to the cause of the *mère-patrie*, missionaries and Vietnamese Catholics had the dubious honor of proving it with their lives.

III

TAHITI AND THE MARQUESAS

Silent Sisters in the South Seas

Reading missionary publications from the nineteenth century can leave the overwhelming impression that Catholic missionaries, by definition, were men. Although the nineteenth century was the heyday of women's congregations in France, missionary sisters remained relatively invisible and nameless within the public image of the movement and were relegated to a role markedly subsidiary to that of their male counterparts.[1] Between 1880 and the First World War, only a tiny percentage of the articles in the Oeuvre de la propagation de la foi's journals, the *Annales* and *Missions Catholiques*, were written by, or even specifically about, missionary sisters. On the infrequent occasion that a letter from a sister in the field made its ways onto the pages of these journals, the editors often chose not to print the woman's name, instead labeling it, simply, a "letter from a *soeur missionnaire*"—a practice never used with men's correspondence.[2] As one scholar has noted, "missionary"— as an evangelist, a representative of his followers, and a force in the community—was a distinctly masculine noun.[3]

With few exceptions, sisters did not embody the ideal of the crusading soldier of Christ waging war against Satan's handiwork—sin, paganism, and heresy. Instead, in her typical capacity as teacher, nurse, and caregiver to orphans and the elderly, as well as cook and maid of the missions, the sister personified gentler, more subservient qualities. Sisters' lives brought to mind images of piety, docility, simplicity, gentleness, and fervor. In an 1897 letter printed in the *Annales*, for example, an apostolic vicar in Gabon described the difficult work of helping children and tending to the sick or injured. "Who does this work?" he asked. "If one wants it done gently and properly, then it's a *Soeur*." The letter went on to tell of one sister's life, starting each day before dawn, including caring for children, cleaning wounds, enduring mistreatment from the local population, and looking for people to help.[4] A sister received little thanks or succor. Rather her rewards were spiritual: she chose to leave her family, to live in remote and often inclement locales, and to die in obscurity in the Lord's service.

Sisters themselves did little to counter the image. In fact, the qualities

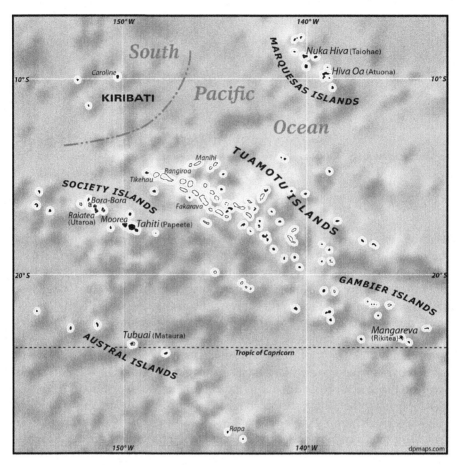

Map 4.1.   French Polynesia (EFO), c. 1914

regularly associated with them may well have been what drew many women to the vocation in the first place. A biographical sketch of a missionary sister of the Congregation of Saint Joseph de Cluny, for example, provides contours to the life of the committed *religieuse*. " 'Faithful servant,' " her biography began, "such was Marie Perrine Raguénès from a young age." The daughter of "hardworking and honest peasants," Raguénès took the name Sister Saint-Othilde and, at age twenty-four, made the five-month voyage to New Caledonia in the western Pacific. Once there, she won the adoration of women deportees, the sympathy of schoolchildren, and the respect of her fellow *soeurs*, who admired her "sweet charity" and her commitment to sacrifice.[5]

Saint-Othilde's characteristics were common to both men and women religious workers. Male missionaries certainly experienced, and, in their dispatches, even reveled in, sacrifice and hardship; when not crusading for

Jesus, they needed patience, charity, and compassion. But notable distinctions remained: men could be soldiers of Christ, women were servants; men often battled, women always endured; men were mobile preachers, women stayed and took care of the children, sick, and elderly. While women's typical characteristics differed from male missionaries' more active, apostolic, martial inclinations, sisters like Saint-Othilde saw their work as an essential service of the divine, but often in very practical terms. For Saint-Othilde, spiritual rewards came only after the hard work was finished; she encouraged the nurses in her charge to remember that "the meek shall inherit the earth."[6] Such a fate was as apropos to missionary sisters as to the poor and sick they aimed to serve.

The qualities that missionary sisters cherished were reflected in the impressions many colonial officials had of them. In the 1880s and 1890s, these officials regularly praised sisters for their work and commitment. A letter from the governor of Saint-Pierre and Miquelon, for example, said that a recently deceased sister at the military hospital had won "the sympathy of everyone for her affability and devotion." Functionaries, officers, and others, he reported, came together to say a few words at her grave.[7] From the other side of the world, a report from Diégo-Suarez requested that the administration make a special dispensation to cast a gold medal of the first class to honor a sister who had worked for more than thirty years as a nurse and teacher. Though the medal was too expensive for the local budget, the governor emphasized the value of this *soeur*'s "career of unfailing devotion." Officials in Paris agreed that it was a worthy recognition of the woman's contribution.[8]

Sisters offered colonial officials a double blessing: they were hardworking, and they avoided confrontation. Unlike male missionaries, who often assailed administrators with ink and paper, missionary sisters' letters to officials typically were mundane exchanges about travel arrangements, upcoming events, and official visits. Rarely did colonial officials in the field complain, as they often did with male missionaries, that sisters had overstepped their bounds or interfered with colonial business. Fixtures of many colonial societies—one sister in Saint-Pierre, for example, worked as a nurse for forty-nine years—sisters were inexpensive, useful, and, it would seem, nonthreatening servants of the French cause.[9] Considering their vast numbers in the empire—by the late nineteenth century there were some 10,000 French sisters working worldwide—they provided French officials an ideal workforce to employ in difficult jobs in often remote locations.[10]

Although they did not garner the attention that their male counterparts did—in the form of either adulation from missionary publications or consternation from officials—sisters were an essential component of Catholic evangelization. Nowhere was this more the case than in the islands of Polynesia. Unlike in many of France's possessions in the late nineteenth century, missionaries in French Polynesia—especially the Marquesas, Gambier, and

Society Islands—did not face populations that they felt were prone to violent political resistance. The populations of most of these islands had, by that time, largely or completely converted to either Catholicism or Protestantism. The task at hand was, therefore, not winning pagan souls but rather changing the sinful ways of the converted. Teaching sisters, renowned for their patience and tenderness, were considered the perfect candidates to instruct generations of children in how to be good Catholics.

For colonial officials concerned about the immoral, insalubrious habits of the Polynesian, teaching sisters were fleeting glimmers of civilization in a dark and sordid sea. Official support of missionary sisters' work reflected the particularly gendered nature of the civilizing mission in Polynesia. Because the French saw venereal disease and sexual debauchery as closely linked to the demise of the Polynesian race, officials believed missionary sisters to be indispensable to the process of forming young indigenous women into responsible, moral, and pious mothers. It is not surprising that republican officials in the 1880s would look to missionary sisters to prepare future mothers, for religious schools continued to educate a majority of girls in France.[11] Despite the rise of anticlericalism in the 1880s, many republicans continued to believe that girls' education needed to include religious and spiritual formation to guarantee they would eventually become moral mothers—the keystone of a strong republic.[12] Even in republican schools in France, girls were taught obedience, thrift, modesty, and cleanliness, all traits traditionally stressed in Catholic schools, minus the references to God.[13]

The fact that sisters were often championed in official civilizing plans, however, did not render them free of opinions about colonialism. One of the more remote groups of teaching sisters, the Soeurs de Saint Joseph de Cluny in the Marquesas Islands, left a detailed record of correspondence that gives shape to their lives, concerns, and motivations between the 1880s and the early 1900s. The reticence of the sisters, who were widely considered to be dedicated servants by republican officials, should not have been mistaken for allegiance to the colonial cause. Like their republican compatriots, sisters viewed colonialism in explicitly gendered terms, though what they saw was a far darker picture. To officials, missionary sisters represented hope for future Polynesian mothers and their families. But, from the sisters' perspective, colonialism symbolized immoral and destructive male impulses that threatened to turn innocent Catholic children into impious sinners.

Catholicism and the French Presence in the South Pacific, 1838–80

As in so many corners of the empire, the plight of missionary sisters in Polynesia can only be understood against the backdrop of relations between the missions and the French state. Starting in the 1830s, religion played a central part in justifying an official French presence in the South Pacific. Early in the century, the Pacific became a major battleground both in the struggle for souls between French Catholics and British Protestants and in the growing imperial competition between France and Britain, with Britain enjoying a decisive edge in both cases. Such a state of affairs was particularly evident in Tahiti, the largest and, for would-be colonizers, the most attractive of the Society Islands, in eastern Polynesia. In 1838, Queen Pomaré, of Tahiti, under the influence of George Pritchard, a Protestant missionary who also served as London's consul in Papeete, expelled two French missionaries who had come to Tahiti, and refused to allow any future Catholic missionary work on the islands under her reign. The French admiral Abel Aubert Dupetit-Thouars, who was to play a key role in establishing France as a power in the Pacific, came to Catholicism's defense, forcing the queen to apologize for the affront.

But British missionaries continued their efforts to block Catholic missions. And, in 1842, Dupetit-Thouars returned to the region, this time with a more aggressive colonial agenda. With the help of a Catholic missionary interpreter, the admiral annexed the Marquesas Islands—a Polynesian archipelago northeast of the Society Islands—and declared a French protectorate over Tahiti. The move aroused vocal protests from the British, but conflict between the two European powers was averted. By the following year, France had established a military presence in the Society and Marquesas Islands, but it faced strong local resistance, and the following four years witnessed violent clashes with local chiefs. The Franco-Tahitian war lasted until 1847, when, after considerable effort, the French forced the Pomaré monarchy to acknowledge their protectorate.[14]

Despite the annexation and protectorate, Catholic missionaries often represented the only French presence in many parts of Polynesia, especially in the more remote archipelagos. In the late 1840s, French Catholics were no strangers to the Pacific. A decade earlier, French Marist missionaries had set out for the western Pacific and within a few years were evangelizing in Wallis and Futuna, New Caledonia, Tonga, Fiji, Samoa, New Guinea, New Zealand, and elsewhere.[15] At the same time, missionaries from the Congrégation des Sacrés Coeurs, known as the Picpuciens, started working in the Society, Gambier, and Marquesas Islands. Political instability and competition from Protestant missionaries undermined Catholic efforts in the Societies and Marquesas, allowing them to make only slow, if steady, progress converting islanders. The Picpuciens met much quicker success in the Gambier Islands, where, by the mid-1840s, they had strong political influence over the population. There, missionaries offered to secure an official French protectorate of the islands—more in the hope that a protectorate would undermine British Protestant evangelization than in the service of French prestige. Though the government showed little interest in the proposal, many officials recognized that the Gambiers were a de facto protectorate, as French Catholic missionaries established a veritable theocracy over the local inhabitants.[16]

By the 1880s, increased competition with Britain and a renewed interest in colonial expansion had led republicans to broaden their power in the Pacific, making Tahiti, Moorea, and the Tuamotu Islands into colonies. The Gambiers, which were formally annexed in 1881, also came under civil administration, as did other islands in the Society and Austral archipelagos over the following twenty years.[17] The republic appointed a civilian governor in Papeete, by then the headquarters of the Établissements français d'océanie (or EFO)—France's colonial territories in the region—and the center of the French presence in Polynesia, as some 90 percent of Frenchmen in the South Pacific lived on Tahiti.[18]

While Papeete was the center of French officialdom, it was also ardently Protestant—the legacy of a long British Protestant presence. The ascendancy of French colonial power on the overwhelmingly Protestant island made for a complicated—and often divisive—religious climate. Protestant Tahitians pushed the French government to recognize Protestantism as the official religion. The awkward arrangement of having Catholic France as protector of Protestant Tahiti meant that the ruling government did not officially endorse its own Catholic missionaries. The administration appointed a curé to serve the French population in Papeete, but it did not officially acknowledge the two apostolic vicariates that the Vatican had founded in 1848—one in Tahiti, the other in the Marquesas.

The French government did, however, subsidize Catholic missionary work through the end of the century.[19] Despite the strength of Protestantism in Tahiti, the outlying archipelagos of the Marquesas and Gambiers were almost entirely Catholic by the 1880s. French officials looked to missions to provide education and health services, and to be a settled source of French influence, a particularly important contribution in a colony that lacked government schools and permanent administrative posts, and where transportation and communication were at the mercy of wind, current, and tide. Missionaries obliged: in the 1890s, in the Marquesas, for example, nine teaching sisters and a handful of teaching brothers ran ten schools, with between 400 and 500 students. There were no government schools. With forty posts on six islands, the twenty-six French religious workers in the Marquesas were the largest single block of Frenchmen. The large majority of the islanders were Catholic—some 3,300, compared with 150 Protestants and 300 non-Christians.[20]

Officials had no choice but to see the missions as crucial allies, considering that there was little that was even vaguely French about late nineteenth-century French Polynesia. Frenchmen still made up only a minority of the already tiny number of Europeans in the region. French colonists were almost nonexistent. In 1887, fewer than 320 native-born Frenchmen had settled in all of the EFO—which spread over more than 4 million square kilometers of sea—and most of them lived in Papeete, leaving dozens of outlying islands entirely uninhabited and unvisited by Frenchmen, save missionaries.[21] On a map awash in so much blue, officials welcomed any kind of French outpost, including religious ones.

The Uses of Missionaries

From the beginning of the 1880s, French officials who visited mission outposts in the South Pacific focused on two issues: missionaries' work to spread French influence, and their success at displacing traditional beliefs and practices deemed distasteful or immoral by European standards. As in Indochina, impressions of the effectiveness of religious workers on various islands differed from official to official, with lower-ranking, local officials being more prone to criticism than administrators in Papeete or Paris. But unlike Indochina, there was also a notable difference of opinion between naval officers, who often made quick inspections of the social and political conditions of islands, and civil administrators, who sometimes spent extended periods of time in close proximity to missionaries.[22] Civil administrators, for example, were more likely to point out missionaries' excessive power and their proclivity to abuse their positions to the detriment of local inhabitants. They also tended to be more skeptical of the missions' successes at civilizing and reforming the Polynesians. But, in general, these criticisms were minor. Through the 1880s, naval officers and civil administrators alike overwhelmingly endorsed missionary work, especially on more remote islands where an official French presence was impossible.

Constantly concerned about influence, officials took steps to ensure that missions were staffed exclusively with French men and women. In 1880, the commander in chief of the Pacific naval division found that there were three Germans in the ranks of the Picpuciens working in the Marquesas. The commander reported to Paris that he had suggested to the regional bishop that it would be "useful and opportune" if all the missionaries in the Marquesas "were exclusively French." Someone in Paris, perhaps the minister himself, agreed, scribbling "that's indispensable" in the margin of the report.[23] Three years later, however, German missionaries were still there, drawing much stronger criticism from the archipelago's official resident. The resident reported that one German missionary, who had told his followers not to pay taxes, "took pride in defending the *indigènes* against the (I censor the qualifiers he used) Administration."[24] The bishop agreed to send the Germans off to the Hawaiian Islands, and from that point forward the resident reported excellent relations with the missions.[25]

But even French-born missionaries were not given free rein. Though few suggested limiting Catholic work, some administrators pushed to better define the role of missionaries in order to help the official effort to colonize the region. One administrator suggested that the government pay the Catholic mission for teaching their students to speak French. This approach, the argument went, had a double benefit: it would give missionaries some official authority on the islands where they worked, and it would also give officials more direct control over the missions. As a naval commander in 1881 wrote, "I think it would be very useful for the future of the Marquesas that the missionaries be placed under the dependence of the local authority either as Ministers of religion or as schoolmasters." The government could then, he reasoned, impose certain standards of behavior on the missions "in order to avoid the abuses that it has the liberty of committing under its present regime of independence." The idea appealed to an administrator in Paris who jotted in the margin an enthusiastic "*bien!*"[26]

Officials who lived nearby and regularly interacted with missionaries were often openly critical of missionary excesses, but they still fell far short of calling for the end of the missions. In 1884, for example, the head of the EFO described reports from administrators in Moorea and the Marquesas that signaled "the unfortunate consequences . . . of the incontestable influence that the Protestant pastors and Catholic missionaries exercise over the *indigènes*." While the indigenous population seemed uninterested in wage labor, he lamented, they were particularly attracted to the festivals, ceremonies, and singing found at the missions. Naval authorities had traditionally encouraged French missions to develop their influence on these islands. But the arrival of the new civil administration in 1880 signaled a change in policy with what the head of the EFO considered to be "the fortunate consequence" of freeing islanders, "at least legally, from the despotism of the Catholic missions."[27]

Despite criticisms of missionary abuses of power, residents and officers alike considered missionaries to be rare beacons for a population in need of economic, social, and, especially, moral direction. But they equally realized that the obstacles to any significant social change were daunting. This challenge was perhaps best described in an 1880 report by the commandant of the ship *Victorieuse*. The commandant argued that missionaries deserved certain freedoms that would help develop the remote Marquesas, including letting missionaries get involved in commercial ventures. He commended the missions' successes at raising livestock that allowed the navy to procure fresh meat. And he suggested that missionaries' constant exchange with the "*indigènes*" won their confidence and introduced them to the benefits of European agriculture, such as the production of cotton.[28]

But, livestock and cotton crops aside, religious workers had little reason to celebrate. The commandant reported that the missionaries themselves recognized "that their efforts have been ineffectual" when it came to moral reform. The 1880 report offered an account of Marquesan life that was to become a familiar narrative for the next thirty years. The report mixed moral condemnation of indigenous behavior with a fleeting acknowledgment of France's culpability: "The coconut *eau-de-vie*, the debauchery, the opium that we introduced just recently by our own hands, as there is a government farm, has driven all these *malheureux* to a horrifying state of demoralization, and I exaggerate nothing by saying that . . . they see us coming among them to put an end to them."[29] The report hinted at French responsibility for the population's moral decay, but the brunt of the problem was cultural. Most shocking to French observers was the apparent Polynesian appetite for sex, intoxicants, and violence. While the commandant had little hope for the future, he encouraged further support of missionary efforts—particularly their schools—as the only hope to reform Polynesian behavior.

Officials agreed that education was key to moral reform in Polynesia. In the early 1880s, missionaries were the only realistic candidates to run schools, especially on less populated islands. Because of the nature of Polynesians' assumed deficiencies, teaching sisters took a leading role in the reform effort. Officials were particularly convinced of the efficacy of Catholic girls' schools. Threatened by lascivious Polynesian men, girls were in need of the physical and moral protection that the sisters could offer. Once the girls were enrolled in school, religious workers could set to the difficult work of eradicating their more savage inclinations. Official reports from this time regularly ended with requests that Paris fund more *soeurs* to augment existing schools or to run newly built ones. In his 1880 dispatch, the commandant wrote that "the influence" of new girls' schools "will be promptly felt" by the local Marquesans.[30] Another touring officer claimed that swelling the ranks of religious teachers with new recruits would make mission schools all the more effective—a point that led an official in Paris to concur with a "*sans doute*!" in the margin.[31]

At the forefront of officials' concerns was, as usual, money. Missionaries were eminently affordable: Catholic schools were primarily *écoles libres*—independent schools—that received no direct administrative support, relying instead on donations from France. The colonial government did provide an annual subvention to the missions with the aim of subsidizing their civilizing enterprises, including schools, but it was largely a symbolic gesture. In 1883, it paid subventions to both Catholic and Protestant missions totaling just over 30,000 francs, an amount that did not come close to paying the expense of mission schools.[32] The two Catholic schools in Papeete alone cost 15,000 francs a year to run.[33] By comparison, the same year, the governor of the EFO estimated it would cost 350,000 francs to run government schools in Tahiti and Moorea, another 200,000 to build schools in the Marquesas, and an equal amount to keep them staffed and running.[34] Then there would be the even more difficult question of finding lay staffs. Officials did not, however, see the mission as a viable long-term solution. The governor asserted that the cost of state schools was a small price to pay considering how much of the population was estranged from the ways of the French, remaining instead under the influence of American and English Protestant missionaries.[35]

But in the short run, missionaries—especially teaching sisters—served the government's purposes. By the time the republic arrived in the colony, girls' education in the Marquesas was well established, having been started in 1864 with the arrival of the first Soeurs de Saint Joseph de Cluny. The Parisian order was founded by Anne-Marie Javouhey and established by Napoleonic decree in 1806. Javouhey, who from an early age committed herself to teaching young peasant girls about God, is said to have experienced a dream in which she was surrounded by—in the words of one biographer—"a multitude of children, blacks, mulattoes, and of the yellow race," and heard an interior voice say, "these are the children that God gives to you."[36] During the Restoration, the government called upon the Soeurs de Saint Joseph de Cluny to provide teachers and nurses to French posts abroad. The order made its reputation in Guyana, where sisters worked with liberated and fugitive slaves. In the early twentieth century, missionary commentators regularly celebrated Javouhey's work of spreading civilization in the French possession. But in the 1830s, her method of choice was deeply rooted in evangelism. In her words, she hoped to found in Guyana "a new Paraguay, where the Lord must be served, loved, glorified."[37] Such principles accompanied the sisters of the order across the globe. By the late nineteenth century, teaching and nursing sisters were busy "glorifying" the Lord in Senegal, Madagascar, Saint-Pierre and Miquelon, New Caledonia, and the South Pacific.

With decades of evangelizing behind it, the Marquesas mission enjoyed enough influence to convince many skeptical islanders to put their children in school. An 1881 report stated that the entire population was either Catholic or on the road to conversion.[38] At that time, the schools of the Soeurs de Saint Joseph de Cluny on the islands taught 435 students, that is, most of the children there.[39] Missionaries were also efficient, working with small staffs at large schools. At Taiohae on Nuku Hiva, for example, all the children of the island were brought together in a boarding school run by three *soeurs* and a teaching brother. Said one official report: the students' parents, "who come to visit often, are pleased by their good behavior, their health, and by what they are learning."[40] The missions' experience and reputation for good schools made them a useful partner for administrators working to develop educational policy.[41]

Officials were pleased with the progress missionaries made. They were impressed by missionaries' ability to speak Polynesian, a talent that one official called "indispensable" to teaching—especially to teaching French, a vital facet of colonization.[42] The 1880 *Victorieuse* report noted that pupils in the Marquesas spoke only a little French, pointing to the lack of materials needed to teach the language effectively.[43] But, four years later, the governor of the EFO toured the same missionary schools and was impressed by the students' ability to speak "our language." Curriculum was not limited to French class: in the girls' school on Nuku Hiva, some sixty to seventy girls learned French as well as arithmetic, geography, and sewing. At the boys' school on the same island, the ninety students recited a French dialogue that

Figure 4.1. The mission at Atuona, Marquesas Islands. (Reproduced from *Missions Catholiques* with permission from the Oeuvres pontificales missionnaires—Coopération missionnaire, Lyon.)

lasted more than half an hour; the single missionary who ran the school expressed interest in providing "professional instruction," such as trade skills, as well.[44]

By the mid-1880s, classes at all six Catholic *écoles libres* in Tahiti were conducted in French, garnering praise from the local press and drawing more students than the government schools.[45] In 1888, an article in the *Messager de Tahiti* announced the results of recent exams that proved the "marked superiority" of the *écoles libres*—especially the girls' schools of the Soeurs de Saint Joseph de Cluny—over the official schools. The author called for the government to support these schools instead of the *école laïque* that was "very expensive to the budget." While the official school faced certain understandable problems—a higher student-to-teacher ratio, and a higher percentage of non-French-speaking Polynesian students—the article encouraged the administration to learn from the successes of the mission schools. Particularly admirable, it said, was the missionaries' *phono-mimique* method of teaching French whereby all students were forced, with threat of light punishment, to speak only French, both in class and at recess. The article ended with a gendered flourish, encouraging all teachers—religious as well as secular—to continue their "so nobly generous" occupations of "forming men useful to their country and mothers of little Frenchmen of the future."[46]

Missionary Lives in the Marquesas

Considering the nearly complete isolation of the *soeurs'* schools, the truth is that few officials or colonists had any idea whether Catholic schools were forming mothers of future Frenchmen or not. This was particularly the case in the Marquesas; of all the populated islands under French control, none was more remote or more challenging to missionaries and colonizers alike. Geographically, they were 1,400 kilometers—at least a ten-day journey by boat—from Tahiti. Once in the archipelago, even neighboring islands were separated by significant distances, meaning a whaler, or equally large ship, was needed for interisland travel. Currents and reefs made navigating treacherous, forcing ships to anchor offshore and launch smaller, much slower boats to carry passengers into port. When the winds were strong, a voyage from one end of the Marquesas to the other, even by steamship, could take two weeks.[47] And once on land, high mountains made terrestrial travel no less arduous.

Throughout the nineteenth century, Frenchmen believed six of the eight main Marquesas Islands to be inhabited by a population prone to cannibalism. As one missionary report noted, as late as 1881, many Marquesans "knew only three things: to get drunk in the morning, to fight each other in the evening, and to eat each other at night." Thus, when they started arriving in the 1840s, missionaries believed they had to be "pacifiers before apostles" in order to achieve any improvements. In 1890, according to the apostolic vicar, "the legendary ferocity" of the cannibals was "nothing more than a memory. They listen willingly to the word of God, convert in great numbers, and want to live as Christians. We harvest with joy," he concluded, "what our predecessors planted with tears."[48] Such poetic optimism befitted a report such as this one—to the Oeuvre de la propagation de la foi, a chief patron of the missions—and certainly belied the much more desperate conditions of a local population facing illness and low birth-rates and of missionaries enduring physical and emotional misery.

Religious workers across Polynesia drew on age-old missionary techniques, as a bishop in Tonga put it, in order to "plant the flag" of Catholicism.[49] Missionary priests were regularly on the move, traveling from village to village and island to island, celebrating mass, hearing confessions, baptizing children, and fulfilling all other ritual functions. Stretched thin, priests were often able to visit some regions only a few times each year.[50] By contrast, the teaching sisters and brothers represented the most stable aspect of the missions. At the center of the mission's operation were the schools, three for boys and two for girls, which in 1891 taught some 640 boarding students, about two-thirds of whom were girls. The methods of the *soeurs'* schools were in the same tradition as those they had used elsewhere, from Guyana to Senegal: they emphasized Christianity as the only road to moral and material salvation. In schools, the young came together to undertake the slow process of learning how to live as Christians.

In the Marquesas, girls' education was deemed most important, for entwined with teaching was the larger project of forming future mothers of stable, Christian families. Rather than instill a love of France—indeed, France was rarely mentioned in the sisters' correspondence—the goal of the missionary school was to convert and lay the groundwork for the creation of what the local bishop called, "if not fervent, at least honest and Christian families."[51] Well-taught girl students, the mission hoped, would eventually seek legitimate Christian marriages and give up what *religieux* considered to be depraved and dangerous sexual practices. The effectiveness of the *soeurs* won them a reputation. By the 1890s, they had earned the enthusiastic support of bishops around the Pacific who considered their schools fundamental to evangelization.[52] And the French government supported their efforts, providing *soeurs* with transportation costs and in some cases a salary for their work.[53] One French official said the sisters were the only "civilization and justice" present on the islands. The *soeurs* agreed. A 1914 in-house history recalled that their arrival in the Marquesas had been "like a rainbow after the storm."[54]

Rainbow or not, letters from the *soeurs* who lived in the Marquesas painted a picture of a place where dark clouds constantly loomed. Regular correspondence from Atuona, on the island of Hiva Oa and the site of the largest girls' school in the Marquesas, tells of lives long on hardship and short on spiritual and educational successes.[55] Illness was a constant problem literally from the day the sisters left France. The journey to the Marquesas took months, requiring passage first across the Atlantic to New York, then by land to San Francisco, and then across the Pacific. One sister complained that the ocean crossings entailed unending seasickness.[56] Conditions did not improve much upon arrival. One *soeur* described a life of "privations upon privations" where there was little time to do religious exercises and even less to rest.[57] The tropical climate fostered diseases; letters regularly listed the latest victims of dengue and other fevers, toothaches, and wounds that would not heal. Such was the price paid for living in an island paradise.

Despite the male-dominated hierarchy of Catholicism, women who decided to join orders like the Soeurs de Saint Joseph de Cluny had opportunities seldom afforded to lay women. In the late 1800s, it was rare for women to travel and live abroad, particularly in Polynesia. For women who wanted to live outside of France, being a missionary sister was one of the only occupations that offered travel to places radically different from home. It would be wrong to suggest that a desire for adventure alone inspired many women to join missionary orders. But for deeply pious women seeking to remove themselves from the confines of French domestic life, the missionary vocation offered an alternative, if not entirely liberated, existence. While well outside the normal routine of French life, missionary sisters abroad lived in enclosed, highly regulated religious communities. The *soeurs* were largely left to their work, but the mission was a male-dominated world. Although the superior of the order directed her sisters, apostolic vicars heavily influenced what sisters did and where they lived.

From surviving correspondence, it is difficult to know much about individual sisters' lives, let alone their personal motivations. As with male missionaries, sisters entering the apostolic vocation required a deep commitment to God and spirituality. Sisters gave up their names when they were accepted into the order and stripped themselves of any vestiges of their previous worldly lives. Many of their letters explored the links between their vocation and personal religious awakening. "I had to come to this land lost in the middle of the ocean," Sister Saint Prix Moindrot wrote, "to find such devotion and goodness."[58] Sister Aldegonde summarized her rewards in similar terms. "I am," she wrote, "content and happy to devote myself to these poor savages, or still half-savages. It seems to me that the good God has graced me so much by employing me in this work that seems to me so beautiful; I was very far from meriting such a favor. Deign this God of mercy and love give me the zeal and the devotion that I lack to carry out with dignity this great mission."[59] If hardship brought spiritual rewards, then the *soeurs* themselves were likely the greatest benefactors of their efforts. Much to their disappointment, the good word they brought failed to transform Marquesan society in the ways they had hoped.

An Enclosed Garden

The education that the sisters offered in the Marquesas was not unlike that provided by thousands of *religieuses* at girls' schools in France. At the heart of the sisters' teaching method was a Catholic pedagogy similar to the one that the historian Sarah Curtis describes as "religious, logistical, societal."[60] In nineteenth-century Catholic schools in France, order and regulated daily activities provided a structure for learning prayers and Christian rituals—a practice linked not just to personal growth and piety but also to the salvation of the society as a whole. In addition to teaching catechism, the most important element of a Catholic education, girls' schools aimed to provide the basic instruction needed to live a healthy life. Both in France and in the South Pacific, sisters taught girls good hygiene and skills such as sewing and knitting that would be useful in their lives as mothers. They also provided a smattering of "secular" know-how such as reading, writing, history, math, and French.[61] Perhaps more important, they made sure that girls received a moral education that stressed devotion and virtue—what one historian has called a Catholic woman's primordial quality in the nineteenth century.[62]

Catholic pedagogy, regardless of latitude and longitude, was more than educational; it was a total formation of thought, belief, and activity. Schools were places of both learning and surveillance. Not simply teachers, sisters *monitored* children in every aspect of their daily lives.[63] Watching over Marquesan girls was among the greatest challenges the sisters faced. Soeur Aldegonde noted that she had to improve her understanding of the local language, "not to speak with them, but to listen in on their conversations."[64] More than a decade later, Aldegonde again wrote that a group of children were never left without at least two sisters watching them. Lessons, mealtimes, and bedtime, she explained, were all choreographed to facilitate surveillance.[65]

Sisters' attitudes toward what they considered the Polynesian "mentality" informed their pedagogical and disciplinary tactics. The sisters were quick to form opinions about the racial characteristics of the local population. Correspondence spoke of Marquesans as lazy, unhealthy, ill-mannered, prone to immorality, and spiritually adrift. "These poor children are still entirely savage, entirely peasant," wrote one *soeur*.[66] Such characteristics helped missionaries explain their limited successes at inspiring real faith after years of evangelizing. Race also informed their treatment of incorrigible students. When poor behavior was discovered, punishment could be harsh. One sister warned, "With the *canaques* [the islanders] you must have an iron hand."[67] Discipline, however, was a fine art in the Marquesas; indigenous students could—and did—voice their disapproval with their feet. Children punished too severely left school, sometimes to study with the Protestants where, one sister lamented, "discipline is not as severe."[68]

The schools' primary function was twofold: to produce good Catholics, and to protect students from corrupting forces that might undermine their piety. In 1883, Bishop Jaussen reminded the teaching brothers of Tahiti of a fact equally applicable to teaching sisters in the Marquesas: the goals of mission schools were religious, and nothing but. He put it simply:

Our schools are Catholic.

The missionary will take care to see that his pupils do their religious exercises Sundays.

A difference will be made between those who miss in order to go to [Protestant] temple and [those who] are simply absent.

The missionary must above all teach catechism.[69]

The bishop, who was known for his goodwill toward colonial officials, spoke most eloquently in his omissions. School was not for teaching math, the French tongue or—God forbid!—the glories of the Revolution. School was about conversion to Catholicism and combating the gains of Protestantism. The colonial state, the republic, its culture, its language, all went conspicuously unmentioned in the bishop's note—just as they did in the *soeurs'* schoolrooms.

When the writer Robert Louis Stevenson visited the Marquesas and toured a number of missionary establishments, he described an average day at school as "prayers, and reading and writing, prayers again and arithmetic, and more prayers to conclude."[70] It was little exaggeration. In Atuona a typical day started early, at 5:00 A.M., for prayers and mass.[71] Morning lessons included reading exercises in French, usually using religious texts and common letters sent from the Saint Joseph de Cluny *maison générale* in Paris. These lessons were followed by catechism. Students stopped their studies during mealtimes because it was difficult for the sisters to eat, teach, and keep discipline at the same time. In the mid-1880s, Soeur Aldegonde added physical work to the curriculum of the Atuona school, supplementing class time every day with work in the mission garden, where students tended corn, coffee, manioc, bananas, and coconut trees.

Even the garden was a spiritual, as well as practical, exercise. "A means to preserve their morals," the garden would teach students what Aldegonde called the rewards of toil, for the *"kanaques* don't work the land" if they could help it. Digging dirt and pulling weeds with her students, Aldegonde did not miss the opportunity to impart religious wisdom. She wrote to her *mère générale*: "The other day while carrying some rocks to make a wall around this enclosure, they brought one rock that was not quite like the others, and they told me: Sister, this rock used to be the god of the *kanaques*. I started laughing and I said to them: well then, bring all the gods of the *kanaques* and we will put them in the wall. They laughed well and went out to find others."[72] The garden grew quickly; a year later, another *soeur* described it as "a vast piece of land." In addition to helping the students learn to work, the garden provided much-needed variety to the local diet—something the sisters appreciated at least as much as their students.[73]

The garden, with its rock walls surrounding the budding crop, could have been a metaphor for the school as a whole. In addition to inspiring faith, piety, and good morals, the sisters' schools were essentially enclaves that defended girls' chastity from the predatory society outside. Even more than educators, sisters in the Marquesas viewed themselves as a moral barrier between children and the outside world. They did not like their students even to leave school, for they were convinced that when a girl was out of their sight, God was certainly out of the girl's mind. Though vacations offered the sisters a few weeks' respite, they considered them the most dangerous time of the year for their students. As some sisters told Robert Louis Stevenson, "The annual holiday undoes the whole year's work."[74] Even on vacations of a few days, girls got married, joined the Protestants, succumbed to familial pressure to stay home, or simply never returned, causing sisters to be relieved when pupils asked to stay at school during vacation.[75] Far from responsible protectors, parents were seen as their children's "first corrupters."[76] Soeur Aldegonde recounted a conversation she had had with her students after vacation, mimicking her pupil's ungrammatical French: "I had recommended to them to be wise, some of them told me: 'Me, my Soeur, no *mikéa* (no sinning) and do my prayers.' They are very afraid of the *tiaporo* (devil) but this does not keep them from committing sin. They tell me sometimes: 'papa [says] to me much *mikéo* and no prayers.' "[77] While sisters tried to plant the fear of the devil in students' hearts, they feared it was little defense against parents' encouragement to sin. Even a visiting brigadier noticed this, Aldegonde reported: "These children, with their parents, lose the little good that they have learned," he pointed out to the all-too-aware sisters.[78] One sister lamented that after leaving school "the children end by becoming again what their parents are"—that is, "pagans."[79]

Dangers were not limited to Polynesian society; the mission also feared European colonists. More specifically, in the sisters' opinion, all European men were dangerous sexual predators.[80] European colonists in Polynesia were overwhelmingly male: the gender ratio of Tahitian colonial society in the 1880s was one European woman to every ten European men, dropping in the 1890s to one to five. And in the outlying islands, like the Marquesas, there were even fewer white women.[81] The majority of men remained single and sought sexual gratification with Polynesian women—unions that sometimes, but certainly not always, included marriage. Prostitution on the islands was more than an institution; said one Frenchman: it was a religion.[82] Mission schoolgirls were by no means immune, and sisters like Aldegonde saw Europeans as waiting to corrupt the "poor children" of the mission. Immoral colonists regularly encouraged parents to take their children out of mission schools, sisters believed, so they could more easily persuade them to sin.

Throughout the 1880s and 1890s, to save girls from the sordidness of parents and colonists, the sisters' main goal was to convert and educate young girls in preparation for marriage. The bishop of the Marquesas regularly officiated at weddings, for religious workers believed the Marquesans to be particularly fond of Catholic pomp and ceremony.[83] Yet the sisters had little hope that even marriage would do the young women any good. Aldegonde wrote, "Our children who have left school are for the most part in disorder. Monseigneur employs every means possible to marry them well and to make them stay happy, and despite this many among them are unfaithful. There is only hope in the generation to come, as long as these old pagans live they are rooted in their ideas and very difficult to convince."[84]

Sisters did what they could to make marriages work. In addition to protecting their young students from external temptations until they were of marrying age, they made sure that newly wed girls had some money to support their new families. It was a considerable expense for a mission short on funds, but it was far better than seeing former pupils turn to prostitution.[85] As the 1890s progressed, the Marquesas mission became increasingly aware of its failure to change the habits of the local population, to instill in them a true Christian faith, and to stem the trend of disease and immorality. In 1894, the apostolic vicar of the Marquesas noted a turn in the local population's response to the mission: a lack of religious fervor, increasing social disorder, drinking, obscene songs, and dancing had returned.[86] Despite the wall built around the mission's garden, the seedlings continued to struggle.

Avoidance, Repugnance, and Partnership

While missionaries remained insecure about their own efforts to protect children from the corrupting forces around them, the missionary hierarchy tried to reassure the colonial regime of the missions' successes. Throughout the 1880s, in particular, regional apostolic vicars gently pressed the administration to help further develop mission schools. In an 1884 letter to the governor, Bishop Dordillon expressed his appreciation for the support that the missions in the Marquesas had received from the government and asked the administration to help him bring more teaching missionaries from France. Emphasizing the hardship of the task, the bishop noted that it was extremely difficult to find even missionaries willing to work on some of the more remote islands.[87]

The following year, Mgr. Verdier sought financial support from the president of the Alliance française for Catholic schools in Tahiti, Moorea, the Gambiers, and the Tuamotus. Playing to his audience, Verdier stressed that teaching French was the mission's priority, and that Catholic schoolchildren were considered by everyone, even the local Conseil supérieur of public instruction, to be the best in the colony. Neither the Protestants nor the administration, he asserted, could compete with the Catholic schools' "superior results in what concerns the diffusion of the French language in the colony of Tahiti."[88] Speaking on behalf of their missions, bishops were happy to show their workers to be France's greatest asset—Catholic or Protestant, religious or secular—in the South Pacific.

Despite apostolic vicars' proclamations of goodwill, in the faraway classrooms of Catholic girls' schools, the Soeurs de Saint Joseph de Cluny refused to champion republican France, finding colonialism to be distasteful at best. Like missionaries around the empire, sisters were wary of the French administration and avoided interaction with officials whenever possible. For much of the 1880s, this was not a difficult task, since the center of Catholic activity was on the island of Hiva Oa, not on Nuku Hiva where the resident lived. But as the 1890s progressed the number of both visiting and resident officials increased in the Marquesas. The sisters spent considerable effort determining administrators' political leanings, whether they were Catholic, Protestant, or Freemasons—a simple schema that indicated whether an administrator was on the mission's side or not. Such a formula was perhaps necessary under a colonial administration in constant flux. No fewer than thirty-four different men held the post of governor between 1880 and 1914.[89] But sisters met all visits—from commandants, brigadiers, and even the governor of the EFO—with foreboding. While it was in the missions' best interest to show off their schools, sisters feared criticism and resented intrusions.

While they disliked interaction, sisters also repeatedly complained of the lack of assistance they received from local French officials. In the 1890s, to undermine parents' influence over children, the mission hoped to make school mandatory for all children, at least to age fifteen. Of particular importance to the mission was the passing of legislation that would require parents in regions without schools to bring their children to the mission. In 1897, the administration passed a law requiring children within four kilometers of a school to attend. But one sister pointed out that the law did little to help the cause in the Marquesas, where "5 [children lived] in one valley, 6 in another, 15 on a neighboring island, etc. etc."[90] Even officials who seemed supportive of the mission, in the end, did little to help it. As late as 1900, a touring commandant who "seemed very content" with the school promised to fill the empty desks by mandating attendance to age fifteen, but he never did.[91]

Even when officials did become involved in truancy issues, sisters found their help to be ineffectual. Soeur Aldegonde went every month to the brigadier to report which students had left school without permission: "He always tells me: I have given an order to the gendarme and he told them, but they don't listen to anything; one responds: my wife is sick, [my daughter] will go when she gets better; another responds: I am going to prepare the *popoï* and next week I will send her back to school." To break the cycle of excuses, Aldegonde asked the official to fine the families of students who left school. The brigadier agreed that children at home learned from the "bad example" of their parents, but he said there was nothing to be done: forcing children into schools simply did not work. Exasperated, Soeur Aldegonde said her patience wore thin with these "nice words" that masked a "lack of good will."[92]

Sisters' frustration with the administration led them to dread official visits. For such events, the sisters at Atuona prepared their students to sing songs and recite passages to prove to the administration that they were fulfilling their most basic obligation to the regime: the teaching of French. A letter from the mid-1880s showed just how tense these visits could be for the sisters. During one visit, an admiral questioned some of the younger students in French. The girls luckily were able to respond, but, the sister admitted, it was not because they had studied the language: "As they are young they learn French quickly, more often by hearing us speak it than by studying it."[93] In fact, in the sisters' correspondence from the 1880s and 1890s, teaching French was infrequently discussed and never highlighted, as most lessons taught in school—from sewing to catechism—were conducted in the local Polynesian vernacular.

The language issue did become pressing after 1897 when the administrator of the Marquesas asked officials in Papeete to shut down the sisters' school in Taiohae due to expense and low attendance.[94] The following year, a visit from the new commandant of Taiohae inspired the sisters to have their students recite the Lord's Prayer in French. While certainly not the most republican of choices, on this occasion the prayer apparently pleased the visitor.[95] But when two administrators visited a few months later, they were less impressed and requested that the children speak entirely in French. Despite their presence on the island for nearly forty years, Soeur Aldegonde wrote that this would be "very, very difficult." The girls did learn to read, but to learn to speak French, she explained, "that's another thing." The administrators pushed, and after listening to a rehearsed song, they went from class to class testing individual students to read or speak in French. The officers "seemed happy enough," Aldegonde reported, "but still commented that they pronounced French poorly, and it was necessary to work on that."[96]

As for teaching a love of France, republican administrators had equal, if not greater, reason for skepticism. At best, the sisters personally showed little interest in France, making reference to it infrequently in their letters. They enjoyed news from Europe, but their very mission required them to accept the fact that they would likely never return home. In public, they refused—often with indignation and even disgust—to express their patriotism. In 1898, for example, in recognition of the *fête nationale* on 14 July, the bishop suggested that the *soeurs* teach their children a patriotic French song to be performed before the local administration. The exercise, the bishop said, "could do some good for the school," especially since the mission faced increasing competition from the local Protestant school. Aldegonde hesitated before refusing the suggestion. She told the bishop, "It is not our place, for us sisters," and left it at that.[97]

The following year, Aldegonde hoped to keep her pupils not just from singing in, but even from attending, any of the festivities on 14 July. But her plan was ultimately thwarted: having uncovered a plot by a number of students to sneak off to the event, she agreed to take them all, she reported, "despite the repugnance I endure in attending the *fête du 14 juillet*."[98] By trying to keep her students from the *fête nationale*, Aldegonde also aimed to deny them from seeing one of the few exhibitions of traditional dancing and singing. Since 1882, public gatherings—even dances—had been outlawed by the colonial regime and were allowed to take place only on 14 July and at other officially sanctioned events.[99] To the sisters, the patriotic holiday embodied the worst of both French and indigenous culture: the triumph of republicanism, on the one hand, and the celebration of traditional, non-Christian rituals, on the other.

Interaction with an increasingly visible French administration brought great frustration to the mission. As a bishop put it in 1900, "For two years, we have undergone a sort of persecution. If only it came from our Canacs! But no; it comes to us from those who should join us in civilizing them."[100] Such criticism of the administration, however, was unwarranted: officials had taken measures ostensibly designed to help the missions improve the moral and physical condition of the local population. In the mid-1890s, the administration outlawed first opium, then the local homebrew *jus-de-coco*; and it passed a law making school obligatory for students living near a schoolhouse.[101] The administration also sent doctors to the Marquesas to treat the ill and help slow the spread of disease. Even in this instance, missionaries found official assistance to be an annoyance. Soeur Aldegonde dreaded one doctor's visit, fearing he would discover that some of her students had leprosy and send them away.[102]

For the Soeurs de Saint Joseph de Cluny and the Catholic mission of the Marquesas as a whole, the colonial administration interfered both too much and not enough. Just as in France at the same time, officials did not leave it to the Catholic girls' schools to teach what and how they liked, choosing instead to monitor, albeit only occasionally until the late 1890s, curricula and results. Equally irksome to Catholic workers, officials failed to take measures that would limit the influence of Protestant schools and require all students to attend Catholic schools exclusively. When compared with many other missions in the empire in the 1890s—even the isolated ones in the central highlands of Vietnam—the sisters in Atuona had to suffer remarkably little colonial interference. Sentiments among officials and colonists were generally positive, regardless of criticisms of children's French accents. Missionaries complained official legislation should have done more to help the mission provide a moral education, combat disease, and overcome the social effects of alcohol abuse. Yet when the administration showed concern for students' health and progress, religious workers considered it a nuisance.

Republican Ideals and Catholic Realities

By 1900, the colonial administration had become aware that Catholic girls' education failed to promote core republican ideals. Just how different Catholic pedagogy was became apparent in 1903 when a government school inspector's report outlined republican goals in stark contrast to the education offered by Catholic schools, like that of the Soeurs de Saint Joseph de Cluny in the Marquesas. The inspector, André Salles, was a bureaucrat with a solemn respect for republican pedagogy. While missionaries saw teaching Catholicism to be their primary goal, Salles was enamored by the power of history, a "frankly laic and republican" subject.[103] In good positivist fashion, Salles believed that history was key to moral and civic reform, for it made "future citizens" (i.e., students) "hate error, intolerance, servitude, and honor loyalty, energy, devotion, science, progress, liberty, and feelings of social solidarity." It could also meet the challenge of spreading patriotism across the empire by showing the indigenous population "all that is great and generous in the history of contemporary France" by celebrating the "pacifying and civilizing role of France." "In a word," he concluded, "history must help the child to understand France and to love it."[104] Such motivations could not have differed more from those of Catholic missionaries.

If the administrator's hope was to teach a love of France through the simple beauty of its history, his methods closely paralleled religious missionaries' approach. As the historian Claude Langlois has pointed out, Third Republic educators consciously drew on Catholic tactics of seizing children early in order to "generate genuine revolutionary enthusiasm" that was to last their lifetimes.[105] To Salles, the republican instructor was a great missionary; the history of France was the catechism. Salles described a way of structuring history lessons that mirrored the story of the spread of Christianity. In place of the Crucifixion was the Revolution as the critical event in republican history. "The cult of great Frenchmen" provided saintlike heroes; their "bloody battles" and other "victorious acts" spread the word of the Revolution, in crusadelike fashion, to the world.

Salles's ideal colonial school would be adorned with imagery, icons, and texts that reinforced the idea of French grandeur. Every classroom was to exhibit a bust of Marianne, a French flag, and a copy of the Declaration of the Rights of Man. France was the holy land to which all geography lessons were to be linked. His suggested lesson on 1848 rang rhythmically with republican triptychs—"For Humanity . . . For Liberty . . . For Equality . . ."—designed to lull students into a trance of love and loyalty from which they would never wake.[106] In case there was question of the sanctity of it all, Salles told his teachers, "Don't shy away from a tear forming in your eye, or a sob cutting your voice each time you speak these sacred words: France—*Patrie*—Republic."[107]

Salles's curriculum represented an ideal republican education aimed at forming that oddest of colonial offspring: good indigenous subjects who were also revolution-loving republicans. But it was grossly out of touch with colonial realities. It did little to address the immediate challenges, such as disease and despair, facing Polynesian society at the turn of the century—a point Salles himself would come to admit. It was also a curriculum that religious missionaries, who remained deeply skeptical of the benefits of republicanism, could not and, indeed, *would not* teach. They had their own Trinity—tried and, in their minds, true.

The fact that colonial administrators believed teaching sisters to be the most effective means of reforming the immoral habits of indigenous children reveals much about how gender influenced republican approaches to civilizing the Polynesian population. Each colony in the empire presented unique challenges to republican reformers. In late nineteenth-century Indochina, security—the need to establish borders, build alliances, win indigenous allies, calm social discontentment—was a dominant theme. As a result, male missionaries with significant knowledge of and influence over Christian villages became a focus of the administration's (and critics') attention. By contrast, in Polynesia, where security was of little concern after the 1880s, and where worries over deviant morality and depopulation ruled the day, the protection of children and the formation of responsible, moral mothers became one of the guiding themes of official reform.

The administration relied, therefore, on those members of the colonial community with the greatest expertise in teaching and protecting children. Officials tried to pass legislation that would both improve the overall health of the society and enable the missions to teach more effectively. Though somewhat ad hoc, these measures conformed to a republican system of reform common in France: regulation of intoxicants, mandatory schooling, and the medical regulation of society was a cocktail of programs that allowed the Third Republic to monitor what the historian David Barnes calls the "morality and mortality" of the society.[108] But what remained clear to officials—as they toured schools where girls recited the Lord's Prayer at assembly—was that the education on offer in mission schools was overwhelmingly religious, and not one designed to win over students to the glories of republican France. As the goal was to form mothers who would perpetuate moral lessons, republican officials were willing to accept a dose of religion if it would save Polynesians from moral and physical ruin, especially since Catholic sisters were the only real candidates to work with young girls.

While republican officials across the empire expressed concern that male missionaries sought to solidify their own power before spreading French influence, the same accusation was rarely made about missionary sisters. To officials, missionary sisters in Polynesia were pleasingly reserved, committed, and silent. Sisters, however, did not see officials or the effects of colonialism in such benign terms. Envisioning their schools as sanctuaries from corrupting colonial influences, teaching sisters were critical of official policies, contemptuous of the administration, and disdainful of the colonial expansion that brought white men in close proximity to their girls. More than a love or a hatred of all things French, Catholic sisters instilled in their students a fear of French men of all kinds: merchants, marines, colonists, and officials. In missionary sisters' eyes, the very administrators who came to inspect their schools were symbols of moral debauchery that quite literally threatened the lives of their students. In adopting and expressing such views of French colonial society, sisters might have served their students' needs, but they certainly did not serve the empire.

Though teaching sisters were practical and inexpensive, officials' particular esteem for them became increasingly fraught with paradox. By the late 1890s, republicans at home were growing increasingly anxious about the influence the Church held over French women. Many republicans fretted over how the republic could survive if the nation's mothers took orders from Rome. With disease and low birthrates pushing entire archipelagos across Polynesia to the brink of extinction, colonial officials could little afford such anxieties about clerical influence—that is, until the politics of anticlericalism exploded in Tahiti after 1900. Then, radical officials and colonists insisted that missionaries were not the solution to islanders' moral and material demise, but the cause. In the span of a few short years, the very sisters who had worked in the remote corners of the colony became the ones easiest to blame for the death of a people. In remaining true to the qualities of the missionary sister—devout, patient, and immune to hardship—they refused to enter debates with secular officials over questions of patriotism, French influence, or civilization. Their silences would serve them no longer.

When Civilization Destroyed Paradise

*Thrice happy are they who, inhabiting some yet undiscovered island in the
midst of the ocean, have never been brought into contaminating contact
with the white man.*

—Herman Melville

In the summer of 1842, as France was establishing a colonial presence in
Polynesia, a young American sailor aboard a whaling ship arrived in Taiohae, the largest village on Nuku Hiva in the Marquesas Islands. Twenty-
three-year-old Herman Melville was not impressed by what he saw of
French intervention on the island. In Melville's semiautobiographical adventure novel *Typee*, the narrator lamented the incongruity of the belligerent
French warships floating beneath the lovely "green eminences of the shore
looking down so tranquilly upon them, as if rebuking the sternness of their
aspect." Equally out of place, wrote Melville, was the French desire to reform
and to civilize the islands—a project that he believed amounted to little more
than "a signal infraction of the rights of humanity."[1] In addition to overt acts
of violence—"in one of their efforts at reform they had slaughtered about a
hundred and fifty [Polynesians] . . . but let that pass"—Melville faulted the
logic of the civilizing process itself: "The French have ever plumed themselves upon being the most humane and polished of nations. A high degree
of refinement, however, does not seem to subdue our wicked propensities so
much after all; and were civilization itself to be estimated by some of its results, it would seem perhaps better for what we call the barbarous part of the
world to remain unchanged."[2]

Nearly fifty years later, another adventure-seeking author from the English-
speaking world picked up where Melville left off. When Robert Louis
Stevenson arrived in the South Pacific in 1888, he found Polynesian communities on the verge of extinction, despite—or perhaps because of—French
efforts to civilize them. Everywhere he visited, he was struck by how the

dead multiplied and the living despaired. The Scotsman, whose writings showed a relatively sophisticated knowledge of Polynesian societies, noted that of all the possible causes of this depopulation, none was more convincing than the malevolent impact of *change*. "The problem," he wrote, was thus: "Where there have been the fewest changes, important or unimportant, salutary or hurtful, there the race survives. Where there have been the most, important or unimportant, salutary or hurtful, there it perishes. Each change, however small, augments the sum of new conditions to which the race has to become inured." Stevenson concluded, "Experience begins to show us (at least in the Polynesian islands) that change of habit is bloodier than a bombardment."[3]

Stevenson's observation was no hyperbole: the world of 1888 had never known a war as devastating as a century of European contact with Pacific islanders. While commentators and historians have long debated exact population figures, the nineteenth century was, for Polynesia, an age of devastation of a magnitude comparable only to the conquest of the New World. The indigenous population of Tahiti, which was about 70,000 at the time of Captain Cook's visit in 1774, had tumbled to around 8,000 by Stevenson's time.[4] Death rates in more isolated islands were often even more dramatic. In the Marquesas Islands, the population at the end of the eighteenth century was estimated at about 78,000. By the decade of Melville's arrival, that number had fallen to below 20,000.[5] At the start of the twentieth century, Catholic missionaries reported the inhabitants of the archipelago to be 4,430.[6] One account from 1891 described how death had left many villages and valleys in the Marquesas literally empty.[7] In the remote Gambier Islands, the population plunged from an estimated 2,400 inhabitants in the 1830s to fewer than 400 by 1900.[8] Making such depopulation even more perplexing was the fact that Polynesia did not suffer any major epidemics.[9]

Observations about the deadliness of change had ominous implications for French colonial administrators. After all, at that very moment the colonial government was developing the economy, encouraging immigration, and promulgating laws—that is, intentionally orchestrating widespread change across Polynesia. The presence of Frenchmen also added new diseases, drugs, and desires to the mix. Officials, marines, and merchants helped spread venereal disease, alcohol, opium, and prostitution on the islands. The malevolent role of colonial exchange was not lost on French commentators. "It is impossible not to be struck," wrote one doctor who worked in the region, "by the disastrous effects brought upon the indigenous race by the establishment of the white race in these lands."[10] With depopulation in mind, a French traveler added that "civilization" presented the "barbaric races" not only with its benefits but also with its vices.[11] From the 1870s on, the colonial administration found itself in the awkward position of trying to counteract the malevolent by-products of its own programs. Stemming the tide of depopulation became the chief goal of the republican "civilizing mission" in Polynesia—even as many commentators believed French "civilization" itself to be among the chief killers.

The case of Polynesian depopulation offers a particularly revealing case study of how the civilizing mission took shape in the first decades of the Third Republic. Administrators made studying and ending the devastation of islanders the cornerstone of social reform in the possessions. They drew on current medical knowledge and theories of moral reform. French concerns about colonial control, as well as notions about race and gender, mediated the impetus to cure through civilization. But, perhaps more than anywhere else in the French empire, the civilizing mission in Polynesia was also deeply influenced—and even ultimately subverted—by the politics of religion. During the 1880s and 1890s, the republic's official program relied heavily on Catholic missionaries—especially on their girls' schools, which protected young children from sexual deviance and prepared them to be moral mothers. But when the missions proved ineffective at reforming Polynesian society, the potent force of anticlericalism drove officials to denounce religious workers—and by extension their very own civilizing program—as being the cause, not the cure, of islanders' ailments.

A Familiar Foe: Depopulation in France and the Pacific

Depopulation was so pressing a topic in late nineteenth-century France that one commentator observed it was impossible to pick up the newspaper without coming across an article on its causes, effects, and remedies.[12] Between 1870 and 1914, the rate of population growth in France fell precipitously. In the wake of the Franco-Prussian War, Germany grew at a healthy 58 percent, compared with the far less robust 10 percent increase in France. By the early 1890s, when French deaths outnumbered births, men and women from across the political spectrum warned that the demise of the nation was imminent.[13] Reformers pointed to the "terrifying trio" of syphilis, alcoholism, and tuberculosis as the chief cause of low birthrates.[14] Behind the clinical facade of this simple, if terrifying, trio were deep anxieties about not only the nation's biological susceptibility but also its moral "degeneration."

Campaigns to eliminate disease in France inspired an uncommon level of bipartisanship, as republican doctors joined parish priests to launch programs to stop alcoholism and reform immoral behavior.[15] Reformers took aim at the pervasive social problems of drunkenness, extramarital sex, prostitution, and suicide.[16] Put simply, in order to save the nation, reformers called on citizens to stop drinking and cavorting, and to start reproducing in a respectable manner. Sober and disease-free sex was eminently more patriotic than the drunken and licentious kind.

The issue of depopulation in the Pacific was deeply influenced by the French domestic experience. As in France, commentators in Polynesia—ranging from missionaries and navy commanders to doctors and administrators—pointed to the devastating effects of tuberculosis and syphilis that sailors, laborers, and colonists had brought to the region over the course of the nineteenth century. French opinion held that these diseases were particularly deadly in Polynesia because islanders weakened their immunity by drinking too much, having orgies, and eating one another. For many commentators, Polynesians were not the noble and erotic islanders of Enlightenment accounts but ignoble savages whose lives were plagued by alcoholism, violence, cannibalism, and deviant sexual practices, including prostitution and rape. As in France, colonial officials addressed the root causes of depopulation in decidedly gendered ways, looking to both current and future mothers as the key figures who could lead Polynesian society to safety.[17] Ensuring that girls could reach motherhood in a healthy and moral state was the linchpin of French civilizing efforts.

Many French voyagers, missionaries, doctors, and officials attempted to describe and explain the combination of biological and moral factors that brought about the demise of the Polynesians. While diseases such as tuberculosis and syphilis took lives, most commentators associated the deadliness of these maladies with the purely voluntary vices of the Polynesian.[18] An early version of what would become a familiar narrative of official correspondence was the 1880 report of the commandant of the French Pacific Naval Division.[19] While touring the Gambier and Marquesas archipelagos, the commandant found Polynesians with an appalling appetite for sex, drugs, and violence—moral degeneracy that caused biological devastation. With horror, he described "orgies" in which twelve-year-old girls "satisfied the passion of bands of maniacs [*forcenés*]." Such "diabolical scenes," he explained, were responsible for the islands' low birthrates, for they destroyed "the seeds of reproduction," leaving young Polynesian girls permanently unable to have children. In this conclusion, he concurred with a common belief that a licentious life led to infertility in women.[20] The commandant accounted for Polynesia's high mortality rates in similar fashion, conflating moral and biological factors. His report, for example, noted in rapid succession the cohabitation of boys and girls from the age of eight or ten, the quick spread of leprosy, and the disturbingly high murder rate on some islands.[21]

While the commandant made no effort to distinguish among fornication, disease, and murder, he—like other commentators—was certain that substance abuse made the effects of such ailments all the more severe. The French regime prohibited the sale of alcohol on many islands, but with little effect. The brewing of local *eau de vie*—an art brought to the region by whalers— continued to satisfy what one traveler called islanders' "immoderate passion for hard liquor." Many Polynesians also consumed kava, a local drink made from masticated root. Large quantities brought on a "heavy and stupefying drunkenness," causing skin to turn pale, eyes to burn, and limbs to shake.[22] In addition to rendering abusers debilitated, some doctors believed that kava killed the sex drive. "The kava drinker does not die prematurely," wrote one doctor, "but he has few or no children."[23] For similar reasons, officials also condemned the deleterious effects of smoking opium (produced locally on French farms), though the drug was far less common than *eau de vie* or kava. Few Frenchmen made direct links between the consumption of intoxicants and the death of communities. Rather, alcohol, kava, and opium accentuated islanders' already objectionable—and unhealthy—behavior, creating what the commandant called "a state of horrifying demoralization" on the islands.

In the 1880s, the defeat of the deadly cocktail of disease, immorality, and intoxicants came to be the ultimate test of French civilization. The determination to stave off depopulation stemmed from commentators' anxieties that France was responsible for the region's demise. The soul-searching took many forms. Some writers referred to how the "white race" seemed to bring depression and despair to the Polynesian.[24] Others—especially missionaries—pointed the finger specifically at the degenerate European riffraff that passed through the Pacific on whaling and cargo ships. And still other writers weighed the successes of European influence in stopping war, infanticide, and cannibalism against the imported blights of tuberculosis, venereal disease, and alcohol. Regardless of the specific rationale, Frenchmen wanted to make sure that the "progress" they brought could not be responsible for devastation.[25] As a result, civilizing these islands had ramifications not simply for the endangered and dying but for France as well. "The French flag flies on these islands," the commandant concluded in his 1880 report, "we owe it to *our* honor to make our protective and civilizing action felt."[26]

From 1880 to the First World War, colonial reforms controlled contagion not with medical science but by civilizing. And the best way to civilize these islands was to take children away from their parents and place them in boarding schools. In his 1880 report, the commandant considered adults to be helplessly corrupted; reform therefore had to strive to "prepare, in a word, new generations." Initially, officials had little hope that boarding schools would provide much of an education beyond the basics. Rather, as the commandant put it, the boarding school project was "simply about saving [children] during the first years from the debauchery and demoralization that devours them all, and that has led to truly appalling results here." The future portended only misery "if the children are not taken in hand . . . before they are plunged into debauchery."[27] Experts dispelled any concern that boarding schools would undermine the cohesiveness of the Polynesian family by pointing to local custom. Children were not raised by their own parents, but rather were put up for adoption—a practice that, according to one missionary writer, "destroyed the family" and left children without any parental authority.[28]

It is not surprising that reformers looked to the school as the most effective "civilizing" tool. As Eugen Weber has famously shown, by the 1880s, Frenchmen were experts in the business of reforming "savage" behavior, though not in the colonies. In France's rural provinces, this was the great era of republican public education, free and obligatory starting in 1882. As Frenchmen in Polynesia discussed the importance of schools, more than 30,000 were under construction or repair in France at a price of more than half a billion francs.[29] Republican public education taught children basic hygiene, instilled an appreciation of work, and introduced proper dress and schedules—all skills the "primitives" of the French countryside needed to know.[30] With such basics accomplished, education could then turn to loftier aspirations, such as imparting an understanding of Enlightenment values and the qualities necessary to be moral citizens of the republic.[31] Such objectives were perfectly suited to the needs of Polynesia. In addition to removing children from the destructive influence of their parents, boarding schools could teach agricultural skills, good work habits, the French language, and a love of France. If the school was at the heart of republican nation building in France, it was equally useful to empire building.[32]

Missionaries: The Imperfect Solution for Republicans

While officials' choice of schools as the centerpiece of reform was in keeping with the republic's civilizing ideology, their choice of schoolmasters definitely was not. In the 1880s and 1890s, the administration did not turn to republican teachers to fulfill the colonies' education needs but to their age-old foes, Catholic religious workers. Such a decision stood starkly at odds with trends in France. After all, as the historian Ralph Gibson so subtly phrased it, republicans and Catholics in the late nineteenth century truly "couldn't stand each other"—and competition over schooling stood as one of the main reasons.[33] In France, the republican impulse to educate was not entirely fueled by a need to unify the nation, but by anticlerical fervor as well. In many parts of rural France, Catholic instructors reigned—a fact that drove republicans in the 1880s to undertake a vigorous campaign to topple the clerical monopoly. Republicans attempted a full-throttled effort to displace religious education and to avoid the possibility of creating "two youths"—one raised by the Church, the other by the state, and each a stranger to the other.[34] Nonetheless, just as republicans in France were calling for the "separation of Church and school," administrators in Polynesia (and elsewhere across the French empire) were asking missionaries to play an important role in civilizing colonial subjects.[35]

From the outset, it was an awkward partnership, as the case of the Soeurs de Saint Joseph de Cluny in the Marquesas makes plain. And it increasingly drew fire from republican critics in France. Critics had long denounced the missions of Polynesia as independent theocracies that controlled—often violently—every aspect of local life.[36] The accusations had, in many instances, much validity. But critics were all the more enthusiastic in their attacks because the leading French missionary organization in the EFO was the Congregation of Sacrés Coeurs, or the Picpuciens, an organization with strong Assumptionist leanings.

Many Picpucien missionaries made no apology for their overtly political stances on issues or their disdain for all things republican. Echoing missionary claims common in the late nineteenth century, the Picpuciens' publication asserted, "Worldly things only concern us insofar as they interest our Master, Lord Jesus." But, in practice, it seems that very little did *not* interest their Master.[37] Among the topics the journal's editors considered of interest were the pope, the emperor of Russia, French ministers, Freemasons, Jews, the building of churches, seminarians, and politics more generally.

Where leaders and editors at the Oeuvre de la propagation de la foi made passing references to divine Providence rescuing the missions from hardship, the editors at the Sacrés Coeurs opted for a more aggressive political approach, often demonizing their opposition. Mirroring right-wing Catholic newspapers like *La Croix* and *La Libre Parole*, the organization's journal—the *Annales des Sacrés-Coeurs*—combined combative, nationalist political rhetoric with moral condemnation in a regular editorial called the "Religious Chronicle." "The Catholic Church," an 1895 editorial explained, "is the city of God on Earth, the immortal Spouse of Christ; we say that he who attacks it is perverse, he who hinders its liberty is a persecutor."[38] Defending Catholicism required more than setting the record straight, and the editors had no trouble going on the offensive. Among its strategies was even the fine art of personal attack. For example, in one piece critical of Félix Faure, the president of the republic, the editors found it relevant to point out that he had "shadows in his past; it's known that his wife is the daughter of a convict."[39]

During the Dreyfus affair, editorials aimed more broadly, exposing the journal's openly anti-Semitic, anti-Masonic, and antirepublican political philosophy.[40] These editorials reflected the view held by many on the far right that Freemasons and Jews wanted nothing less than "to dechristianize France" and destroy all the traditions that made France great.[41] The journal regularly accused Jews of conspiring against the nation ("Where are the country's finances," railed one editorial, "if not in Jewish coffers?"), and denounced Freemasonry for getting the devil involved in politics ("[Freemasonry] shows more clearly each day its Satanic character").[42] The journal's answer to how France could survive this affront can be easily gleaned from an 1897 headline to its regular "Religious Chronicle":

FRANCE'S MALAISE . . . —ITS MINISTERS, ITS MAGISTRATES. —ITS
UNIVERSITY. —THE JEWS. —THE DREYFUSARDS. —REMEDIES: RETURN
TO CHRISTIAN TRADITIONS.[43]

In spite of its initial political bravado, the *Annales des Sacrés-Coeurs* abandoned its "Religious Chronicle" in 1900—just as attacks on the missions in Polynesia mounted—draining the journal of the venom that once distinguished it from other missionary publications concerned with the apostolate. The journal remained politically combative, but the editors chose to address topics that more directly influenced the work of missionaries rather than provide a running commentary.[44] Though the editors of the publication offered no explanation, the change in format at the turn of the century coincided with the dissolution of the Assumptionists in France, as well as increased criticism of missionaries by colonial administrators and the Ministry of Colonies. Though the journal toned down its outrage, the right-wing nationalist press took up the cause, notably in 1903, when the reactionary *La Croix* defended the congregation against an attack from M. Dubief, the reporter on the foreign affairs budget in the Assembly, who accused its missionaries of terrorizing the inhabitants of the Gambier Islands.[45]

Throughout the 1880s and 1890s, regardless of their political leanings, Catholic missionaries remained favored by most colonial officials as the best resource for reforming local behavior and slowing depopulation. While the convenience of using Catholic missionaries—with their available manpower and financial support from Catholics in France—played an important role in dictating policy, administrators had good reason to expect positive results from the missions. Many commentators attributed the demographic stability of islands like Hawaii and Tonga to the work of both Protestant and Catholic missionaries.[46] On the French protectorate of Wallis, in the western Pacific, Catholic missionaries took credit for turning around a trend of depopulation. By the mid-1880s, according to the regional bishop, exposure to the doctrines of Catholicism and the sanctity of marriage had caused Wallis's population to grow after many years of waning.[47] In the South Pacific, the most severely depopulated archipelagos—the Marquesas and the Gambiers—were almost entirely Catholic.[48] While French officials were quick to condemn missionaries' abuse of power, their very influence over these islands made them logical candidates to fulfill the colony's civilizing needs. By the 1880s, the girls' schools run by the Soeurs de Saint Joseph de Cluny had proved their ability to draw students to school, where they received an education that included morality and hygiene—two key components in the campaign against depopulation—in an environment that protected them from immoral influences.

Catholic missionary work, especially in the Marquesas and Gambiers, also won approbation in the halls of government and columns of newspapers. In 1891, the unity of mission and republic was ceremoniously pronounced at the funeral of Mgr. Tepano Jaussen, the bishop of Tahiti. A crowd of Europeans and Polynesians filled the Papeete Cathedral to pay respects to this missionary who had spent decades developing the influence of Catholicism in the Pacific. François Cardella—one of the most prominent political figures in Tahiti—praised Tepano as the "last king of Tahiti" and a "true friend of France." In particular, Cardella extolled the missionary's work building schools, developing agricultural production, and "carefully preparing" the Gambiers for French annexation. "The government of the Republic," he announced, "had only to pick the fruit patriotically planted by the head of the Catholic mission."[49] The governor of the EFO then took the podium, commending the bishop's work for "France, Civilization, Science, and Humanity." The governor not only ignored long-standing differences between the missions and the state but also asserted that Jaussen's work stood as a *model* for the colony to emulate. In the governor's words, combining "Christian charity, ideas of Humanity, and feelings of Patriotism," the bishop inspired his successors to continue the "work of civilization" in Polynesia.[50]

Such optimistic assessments of the bishop notwithstanding, the 1890s did not bring to Polynesia the successes that either French officials or missionaries had hoped. Girls' schools, such as those run by the Soeurs de Saint Joseph de Cluny, in the Marquesas did not change local practices or drastically improve the health of the population. Teaching sisters increasingly complained that marriage failed to keep girls from infidelity or, in some cases, save them from prostitution.[51] The dead and dying were hard to ignore. "The population here is shrinking," complained one sister in 1900. "For some time, chest illness has made progress here among the *canacs*; some entire families die from this illness; two of our students this year are dead, and two others are probably going to die, at their homes luckily."[52] In 1901, in the wake of a dengue outbreak, flu spread among the sisters and children.[53] The mission rarely referred to the death of Marquesans in terms of the steady destruction of the population; one report, for example, spoke of the "strange reduction" caused by "wars, small pox, opium abuse and liquors." Death was just one more challenge to Catholicism that existed alongside anticlericalism and Protestantism.[54] But the sisters must have been aware of the severity of the problem: at their once thriving girls' school in Atuona, they saw enrollment slowly dwindle over the years, falling from 112 students in 1886 to ninety in 1899, and dropping under forty-five by the end of 1902.

Paul Gauguin, Witness to a Failed Mission

The 1890s witnessed the breakdown not only of the political partnership between the missions and the colonial administration but also of the colony's civilizing mission as a whole. One of the only Europeans in the Marquesas who was neither a missionary nor an administrator to leave an eyewitness account of the failures of colonial civilization was the painter Paul Gauguin. As a historical source, Gauguin's testimony is filled with pitfalls: he was extremely conscious of his image as an artist, and his notoriously anticolonial politics were certainly linked to his aesthetic vision and his avant-garde pretensions. Much of his written work was in the Exoticist tradition of writers such as Pierre Loti who saw colonial interaction in both aesthetic and political terms. Gauguin shunned sullying the Polynesian race with what Loti had called "our stupid colonial civilization."[55] He contrasted the "colonial snobbism" and "absurdities of civilization" brought by the French with the "primitive beauty" and "tradition" of Polynesia—an aesthetic sensibility that helped him win fame and profits from a European clientele hungry for paintings of exotic scenes.[56] Nonetheless, Gauguin spent nine of his last eleven years living in Tahiti and the Marquesas, and many of his observations correspond to other accounts of colonial life. While there, he was often an engaged member of colonial society, editing two newspapers filled with discussions of local politics, and writing letters to officials decrying the injustices of French policies.[57] He also left diaries and fictional pieces that provide sharp insights into colonial mentalities at the turn of the century.

Never shying from incendiary rhetoric, Gauguin was particularly fond of debunking the notion that French civilization cleansed or improved the lives of the local population. In a 1900 edition of one of his newspapers, *Les Guêpes*, for example, he directly linked the demise of the Polynesian population to the arrival of French colonialism: "The civilized hordes arrive and run up a flag; the fertile ground becomes arid, the rivers dry up; . . . They poison our land with their infected excrement . . . they sterilize the soil, deface and damage living matter. . . . Everything perishes."[58] His disdain did not stop at words: in 1903 he was caught encouraging islanders to stop paying taxes and to keep their children away from school. Administrators saw Gauguin's proclamations not as mere bravado but as an attack on "all established authority," be it missionary or official. The colonial government was particularly alarmed by how the painter defended indigenous "vices," such as his claim that drinking was, for the islanders, a "simple necessary distraction," and not a habit that would lead to their demise. Officials kept watch over Gauguin's activities, considering him a potential threat to the republic's projects for social reform.[59]

For Gauguin, it was the injustices of colonialism and the degeneracy of officials, not the immorality of the local population, that brought the greatest injury to the islands. In letters to the colonial administration, Gauguin complained that, at best, judges and gendarmes knew nothing whatsoever of the natives and used unreliable translators to gather inaccurate information. At worst, officials raped young girls and ruled by a brutally violent "reign of terror" over the population for personal gain.[60] He also claimed that it was the overtaxation of already impoverished communities—and not Polynesian salaciousness—that pushed girls into prostitution.[61] The prohibition on alcohol, in his opinion, did nothing but make islanders think more about drinking.[62]

The Catholic missions fared no better than the republic in the painter's estimation. Under Gauguin's stinging pen, the missions succeeded in little more than teaching their students to sing canticles and recite catechism "in incomprehensible French," and to dress in shoes and clothing that weakened their immunities and helped bring about "the extinction of the race."[63] At times, Gauguin fell to old-fashioned anticlerical rhetoric: he wrote of a bishop in love with a schoolgirl, of missionaries prone to sodomy, and of unclean, if virginal, teaching sisters.[64] But Gauguin also offered critiques of the fundamental cultural divide that separated missionaries from the Marquesans. In particular, he focused on the uselessness of introducing marriage—the desired culmination of a girl's Catholic education. Whether before the gendarme or the bishop, the marriage ceremony, in Gauguin's estimation, meant nothing to islanders. In the shadow of the chapel, he explained, newly married couples were likely to swap partners, "go deep into the underbrush," where, "before the Almighty," they committed the sins that the missionaries thundered against. Nonetheless, Gauguin concluded, the bishop remained satisfied with the missions' progress and assured himself, "We are beginning to civilize them."[65]

Gauguin used irony for effect, but the stories themselves did not stray far from missionaries' and officials' own accounts. What Gauguin added to these accounts was the claim that islanders' immorality was indeed conscious. As art historian Stephen Eisenman argues, such blatant disregard for French customs represented a form of Polynesian resistance to colonization that fit within a broader effort that included violence. Gauguin's writing suggested that Polynesians pursued the very practices that the French found most appalling—lasciviousness, infidelity, drunkenness, even prostitution—to express their unwillingness to submit to the Church, the colony, and the civilizing mission.[66] The painter reserved his greatest ire for those officials who brought "dishonor to the French Republic" by insisting on the successes of civilization and touting their "hypocritical esteem for Liberty, Equality, Fraternity under the French flag."[67] What Gauguin did not mention was that, in their private correspondence, many missionaries and officials shared his skepticism. Missionaries repeatedly expressed doubt about the depth of religious faith and the sanctity of Christian marriage. The administration was concerned by the difficulty it had policing its own officers in the gendarmerie and civilizing its own sailors, many of whom were prone to criminal behavior.[68] The effectiveness of the French effort to civilize the Polynesian "savages" was now in question, providing an issue that would fuel conflict between the Catholic missions and their most outspoken critics.

Protestant Challenges to the Catholic Missions

As the limits of France's civilizing reforms were becoming increasingly apparent, ominous clouds had started to gather over the Catholic missions in the South Pacific. Since the late 1830s, Catholic and Protestant missionaries had battled for souls in the Pacific. By the end of the century, in the French possessions, religious spheres of influence had become relatively cleanly delineated: Tahiti and the Society Islands (where the majority of the population lived) were solidly Protestant, while the Gambier, Tuamotu, and Marquesas Islands were almost entirely Catholic. Where the two groups did clash, however, was in Papeete, the center of government and colonial society. Neither

Catholics nor Protestants were above slandering the competition in their attempts to sway the administration to cede more authority, land, and funding to their missions. Such religious competition was intensified by fears on both sides that French domestic politics would spill over into the colony in the form of secularizing, antimissionary legislation.[69]

Competition between missionaries led to affairs, plots, intrigue, and general feelings of distrust. Protestants discussed curtailing their practice of sending regular reports to France for fear that the information they contained might fall, as one pastor put it, "into the hands of our adversaries."[70] The fear was not completely unreasonable; the Catholic Church in Papeete did have informants who kept tabs on members of the colonial administration and the political situation in the capital.[71] Missionaries on both sides gave gifts and made promises to officials and prominent islanders in the hopes of winning friends and followers. Priest and pastor occasionally bumped into each other at the bedside of a sick chief or other influential personage. Where personal interaction failed to win influence, there was always the printed word. One Catholic missionary was appalled by a Tahitian translation of *Pilgrim's Progress* he had procured from the Protestants. "The Protestant missionaries of Tahiti," he wrote to colleagues in Paris, "had added an engraving representing the pope at the bottom of a cave, devouring human victims that [Catholic] missionaries had brought to him! He had skulls, tibias, bones of all kinds at his feet, in front, behind, to the side, it was awful!"[72]

In 1899, the Conseil général, the most influential advisory board of colonists in Papeete, voted to exclude Catholic religious workers from its ranks. It was a clear signal of where the council would be heading under the direction of M. Viénot, who was also the president of the Protestant missionary organization in Tahiti. Thus empowered, Protestants in Tahiti challenged Catholic influence in brazen ways. That same year, for example, Protestants contested the annual Fête Dieu parade at Mataiea on Tahiti. Catholics insisted that the Protestants' legal justification—a law of 18 Germinal X that prohibited Catholic processions from leaving religious buildings in Protestant neighborhoods—was a stretch. But the acting governor of the EFO did not agree and he ordered that the procession remain on mission property.[73]

The episode revealed not just a new political climate in Papeete but the local Catholic missions' ineptitude at (or unwillingness to play) colonial politics. In the wake of the Fête Dieu decision, Mgr. Verdier, the apostolic vicar in Tahiti, set about listing reasons why his missions' rituals deserved the administration's respect and protection. In his notes, he vacillated between reason and anger: he claimed religious freedom, pointed out that Protestants in the area had traditionally participated in the procession, and denounced the order as "an abusive police act." At point number sixteen (of eighteen total arguments against the decision), the bishop finally made an assertion that might have resonated with colonial officials: "The missionaries spread French influence." This argument came in a revealing place, just after point fifteen: "the pope has a right to evangelize."[74] Even with anticlericalism mounting in France and Tahiti, the missionary could not bring himself to muster the sort of patriotic, civilizing rhetoric that missionaries in similar positions in other colonies were becoming adept at.

The pope's representative, or nuncio, in Paris, Mgr. Lorenzelli, showed more political savvy. Writing to the minister of foreign affairs on behalf of the Tahitian mission, he lamented the unfair treatment of the Catholics of Polynesia and demanded the same freedoms for them that Protestants enjoyed. Instead of mentioning the pope, he focused on the missions' patriotic achievements in the pursuit of civilization. "In Tahiti, a French country," he argued, "where the missionaries have civilized at the risk of their lives, and have annexed to France several islands once peopled by cannibals, these same missionaries must more than elsewhere enjoy their liberty."[75] The nuncio's request bounced around various ministries in Paris before ending up back in Papeete. The governor of the EFO explained to his superiors that the Catholics had exaggerated the unfairness of the ruling. The Fête Dieu procession was again denied.[76]

At the turn of the century, the Catholic missions found fewer and fewer allies. Missionaries in Polynesia started to worry that the polemics of the Dreyfus affair would spill over and end their evangelizing efforts in the Pacific. For Catholic workers, the ascendance of Protestant influence posed a palpable danger: a *soeur* in Papeete wrote of how "our great enemy" had taken control of the colony and was already plotting the ouster of teaching brothers and sisters from public schools under a project of laicization.[77] Mgr. Verdier started planning for the worst, asking the Holy See to allow his missionaries either to secularize to avoid expulsion from the island, or to relocate to the Cook Islands.[78] His concern was not completely unwarranted: in 1902, teaching sisters from the Soeurs de Saint Joseph de Cluny were expelled from their positions in public schools in Tahiti. With the press and the Conseil général against the Catholic missions, Verdier feared that the administration was sure to follow; all he could do, he reported to Rome, was wait for more unfavorable decrees to come forth.[79]

The Last Vestiges of Republican Support

The administration would turn on the mission, but not as quickly as the bishop might have anticipated. Even with the Dreyfus affair raging and conflicts over Catholicism intensifying in France, key republican officials in Polynesia still promoted the Catholic missions, at least in the outer archipelagos, as servants of civilization and as important tools in the effort to stem depopulation. In a speech delivered in November 1903, the governor of the EFO, Édouard Petit, called for a policy that supported the continuation of the work of the missions. Echoing many of his predecessors, Petit fingered disease, alcohol abuse, and moral degradation as the key causes of islanders' downfall. He held up boarding schools as one of the few ways of protecting children from the "sad examples of their parents." And he suggested requiring students—girls in particular—to stay in school until marriage. Petit proclaimed that to ignore the devastation that the "primitive races of Oceania" faced would reflect "an indifference that is not French." The governor outlined his plans without mentioning missionaries specifically, but anyone familiar with the Marquesas would have known that the only Frenchmen capable of implementing such programs were religious workers. Indeed, Petit's policies were welcomed by Catholic missionaries as a sign of official approbation. Unfortunately for them—and for the governor—Petit died unexpectedly just a few months later.[80]

Petit's speech was based largely on the findings of an unexpected source: the ardently republican school inspector André Salles. In 1903, Salles had toured the Marquesas Islands, a trip that left a "painful impression" on the bureaucrat. The report he filed with the minister of colonies uncannily mirrored the letter written by the commandant aboard the *Victorieuse* more than twenty years earlier. "The indigenous population," he wrote, "kills itself, is going to disappear; colonization is almost nil, of low quality; the Administration criticized, scoffed at, remains impotent and without authority." French influence was minimal: the little economic activity that existed on the island, he noted, was conducted by an American trading house, a German company, and two Chinese men. As for the Marquesans, the population, which five years earlier had been at 4,279, had declined to 3,317.[81]

Echoing Robert Louis Stevenson's observations, Salles attributed the depopulation to colonialism, stating that colonization "created a certain psychological state" in the islanders that diminished their resistance to disease. When he got to the specifics of causes, Salles reiterated what others had been saying for decades. He witnessed "orgies of alcohol" and "bestial customs" that left twelve-year-old girls "deflowered" and infertile for life. Putting aside his own fervent beliefs in the power of republican education, the school inspector determined that mission schools were the islands' only hope. Catholic boarding schools, he wrote, were the sole way to protect children and to teach them "to find horrible their parents' savagery." Such schools, he concluded, were necessary not only for "the Frenchization [*francisation*]" of the students but for their moral and material salvation as well. Aware of the atmosphere in Paris, he asked the minister of the colonies to accept the work of the Catholic missions rather than "sacrifice the population to a pure principle of *laïcité*."[82]

The Republican Attack on the Missions

But the atmosphere in Paris was indeed different. Evidence of a sea change in France's policy toward the missions could be found in the snappish marginalia scrawled on Salles's correspondence by the minister of the colonies. In red ink, the minister accused the school inspector of having "a slightly excessive interest in the Catholic mission." At the bottom of the final page, the word from Paris was clear: "It is neither the catholic missions, nor the protestant missions that can remedy evil. Neither one nor the other should play an administrative role. . . . Schools can be created outside the missions. We must push the government in this way, and give instructions in this sense."[83] The republic, which had relied on missionary work to fulfill its civilizing needs for more than three decades, was finished with the missions.

What followed over the next two years represented the single greatest change in the rhetoric and implementation of the civilizing mission in Polynesia since the arrival of French ships in the 1830s. The catalyst was not innovations in medical science or new ways of understanding local practices, but the politics of anticlericalism. Emboldened by their 1902 electoral victory, anticlerical radical republicans in Paris pressured the Ministry of Colonies (which had always been more critical of the missions than the Quai d'Orsay) to combat the influence of Catholic missions across the empire. The ministry responded by decreeing a policy of laicization, requiring the removal of crucifixes and other religious symbols from all public places, the removal of teaching and nursing sisters from their posts in government hospitals and schools, and the curtailing of all subventions paid to the missions. The ministry also launched a broader investigation of what further steps could be taken in each colony to weaken or even prohibit Catholic evangelizing.

In almost every French possession and protectorate, the ministry met some resistance. Administrators had little trouble taking down crucifixes and replacing religious nurses and teachers in government facilities. But officials in most parts of the empire deemed further limitations to be unwise: missions were inexpensive means of spreading French influence and fulfilling the "civilizing" mission promised by republican rhetoric. In most cases, the ministry ultimately respected the judgment of regional administrators. But in Tahiti a strongly anti-Catholic lobby had formed by 1904. This lobby, which included influential Protestant and Freemason colonists, as well as the newly appointed governor, fed off anticlerical rhetoric in France and sought the complete eradication of the Catholic missions and their schools in Polynesia. Anticlericals in Tahiti were so driven in their pursuit of the Catholic missions that they sacrificed the republic's own colonial ideology—its own civilizing mission—in the process.

The republican suppression of Catholic activities in France was exported with little difficulty to Polynesia despite the fact that the colony could ill afford to replace Catholic missionaries and *religieuses* with secular employees. In early 1904, Henri Cor, the governor of the EFO, officially laicized the colonial hospital in Papeete, but the enforcement of the decree, which entailed the expulsion of nurses from the Soeurs de Saint Joseph de Cluny, had to be postponed until nurses and laundresses could be found to take their places. At the same time, crucifixes were removed from public places, and the local administration started looking into building public schools in the Marquesas.[84] Within a few months, the administration's laïcisation program was in full swing, as the governor applied metropolitan laic laws to the outer Society Islands and removed teaching sisters from the public school in Rikitea in the Gambier Islands. As the governor put it in one letter, laicization was "*un fait accompli.*"[85]

At first, it did not seem that laïcisation in Polynesia would be substantially different from elsewhere in the empire, such as in Indochina. But within a few months, the administration in Papeete took a more aggressive approach to the missions. On 29 September, by administrative order, Catholic girls' schools in the Marquesas were shut down; in Atuona, Soeur Aldegonde recounted that the new lay instructor arrived by boat to deliver the news.[86] More serious still, the administration, rejecting the mission's claim of possessing a *personnalité civile*—an official legal status, which the mission had sought since the early 1880s—claimed all missionary property in the Marquesas belonged to the French state.[87] The mission in the Marquesas had six months to appeal the decision.[88] Mgr. Verdier in Tahiti recognized the mounting influence of local Freemasons on the colonial regime, fearing it would lead to the expulsion of all Catholic missionaries from the colony. "Nothing," he lamented, "is being spared to crush Catholicism in Tahiti."[89]

In justifying his action, Governor Cor simultaneously broke with twenty years of republican policy and unburdened the republic of any responsibility for the demise of the Polynesian population. The governor argued that, for decades, the Catholic missions in the Gambiers and Marquesas had *interfered* with the colonial administration's ability to deal with the paramount problems facing the local population, namely, alcoholism and tuberculosis. Instead of civilizing, he insisted, missionaries in the Marquesas pushed their followers "more and more to return to barbarity"; only by ending the Catholic regime could the republic lead islanders "back to more civilized customs."[90] In the Gambiers, Cor asserted that the missionaries accepted only students interested in their "narrow ideas of a militant Catholicism," and as a result "were never able to obtain . . . more than a fairly mediocre result in education." The governor's imagery evoked a colonial administration liberating local communities from the heavy shackles of the missions' "dominating influence." Rather than a central part of the nation's civilizing efforts, mission boarding schools, including those run by the Soeurs de Saint Joseph de Cluny, were a "kind of sequestration to which . . . the children of certain archipelagos had been submitted." Rather than help save the population by protecting children and forming future mothers, the missions had achieved only "the progressive reduction of the birthrate."[91]

The fervor of fin-de-siècle anticlericalism that gripped France transformed the link between Catholicism and depopulation in the distant Pacific into a salient political issue in the Chamber of Deputies in Paris. Six months after Governor Cor's reports denounced the Catholic missions, Député Dejeante, of Belleville, took the floor of the chamber and railed against what he termed the missionaries' "monstrous abuses" and "exploitation" of the Polynesians. According to Dejeante, the missions "stole, despoiled, and destroyed this peaceful population in a colony so rich and so fertile," and it was high time the government stepped in "to protect this population against the scandalous exploitation of which it is the victim." He described missionaries who traded land for promises of "a bit of paradise" and who shot any locals who challenged their authority. "Here's how it went," Dejeante explained to his audience, "in order to seize property, they paid nothing, and in order to protect it, they furnished bullets." Noises and shouts erupted from the right side of the chamber.[92]

Dejeante paid particular attention to the situation in the Marquesas. His speech made no mention of the drunken orgies, violence, or prostitution that had colored the pages of official reports for three decades, speaking only of the "so peaceful and so calm" Marquesans. The missions' boarding schools, he said, stole children from parents and worked pupils sometimes to death in prisonlike schools.[93] "It is not obligatory education," he accused, "it's obligatory internment, it's obligatory forced labor for indigenous children." In Dejeante's assessment, education and proselytization were directly linked to disease and death. He suggested that leprosy came to the Marquesas with the missionaries. Schools made matters worse, as mission teachers mixed healthy children with infected ones. "Tuberculosis," he added, "in the past almost unknown, has developed in terrifying proportions. The race is ruined, half the population of the archipelago has disappeared." The chamber was in an uproar, with exclamations and laughs to the right and center, and applause and calls of *"très bien!"* to the left: "There, gentlemen," Dejeante concluded, "are the results of forty years of theocracy."[94]

At that point, the minister of the colonies weighed in. Pointing out that Dejeante "had lightly dramatized the situation," the minister said that there was some truth to the allegations and that the administration was taking the necessary steps to improve the situation on the islands. These included the various reforms the governor had made to close the schools and develop a republican colony of civil administrators, doctors, and secular teachers. The radicals in the Chamber of Deputies, like the governor in Tahiti, seemed to ignore one essential fact: for more than twenty years, the work of the Catholic missions had been explicitly endorsed and, on occasion, championed by the republican colonial administration. If the missions had failed miserably at bringing "civilization" to Polynesia, then so too had the French republic. If the missions had brought only despotism, violence, and despair to the islanders, then so too had republican colonialism. By 1905, however, the polarization of French domestic politics had made such attention to details unnecessary. Instead, the colonial minister mouthed empty promises:

"The archipelago will again see, I am sure, the prosperity that it once knew."
In the Chamber of Deputies in Paris, half a world away from the islands of
Polynesia, the applause thundered.[95]

Damaged Missions, Dying Peoples

At the Paris *maison mère* of the Picpuciens, there was outrage at what missionaries deemed the "monstrous and absurd calumnies" spouted in the
Chamber of Deputies. One Picpucien likened the republicans' accusations to
those made to Augustine by fourth-century pagans.[96] Within the year, the
missionary organization had published a booklet refuting Dejeante's claims.
The Picpuciens both bluntly dismissed the deputy—some of Dejeante's
points, for example, "excited hilarity"—and provided a very serious, point-
by-point counterargument. Not surprisingly, the booklet turned back most of
the accusations onto the immorality of the local population and the destructive influence of "white colonists" (not including, of course, the missionaries). It cited kava, European alcohol, and young Polynesian girls' relations
with sailors as particularly harmful. The missions brought not disease, the
pamphlet insisted, "but civilization and faith." Thanks to the Catholic missionaries, "from the cannibals that they were, these people have become
sweet and hospitable."[97] In less public documents, however, missionaries on
the islands admitted that their followers remained weak in faith, belief, and
morality.[98]

Even in the face of bitter accusations against the missions, the Picpuciens
and other religious workers in Polynesia refused to defend their work with
the sort of flag-waving that French missionaries in other parts of the empire
resorted to when challenged. Instead of garnering political support for their
patriotic deeds, they survived at the mercy of the judicial system. A year after
Governor Cor tried to confiscate the missions' property, a French court ruled
that the missions had a right to their land. The missions' status as civil organizations remained an issue of much discussion throughout the period,
leaving them in a precarious legal position, open to future attacks.[99] The missions regrouped but never regained the influence they had enjoyed as part of
the official civilizing effort.

Teaching sisters in the Marquesas, for example, did what they could to continue the spiritual development of the children of the islands. They tended
their garden and visited the sick and elderly. But their position within the
mission was greatly diminished with the closing of their schools: forced to
work with the bishop and other male missionaries, the *soeurs* became cooks
and laundresses. They spent afternoons with some of their former students;
they started a choir and taught catechism to whomever would come.[100] But
they would never again play the central role in the republic's program to
protect girls from the alleged dangers of Polynesian society and to shape

moral mothers of the future. It is possible to wonder if they were not victims of their own silent servitude. Missionaries in the central highlands of Vietnam argued their way out of accusations of treason. Had the teaching sisters in the Marquesas been more forthright about their love of France and their support of republican colonialism, they would have been more likely to weather the assault on their work.

The depopulation issue in Polynesia offers a case study of French colonial ideology in crisis. In responding to the devastation, officials fought less with medicine than with moral reforms and programs to civilize. These programs were informed by French impressions of Polynesians as a sexual, violent, and bacchanalian race. But the civilizing mission cannot be understood simply in terms of republican responses to race and the exigencies of colonial control. The Polynesian case shows that an equal, perhaps greater, factor in shaping the contours of the civilizing mission was religious strife between Frenchmen. From the beginning, missionaries' preoccupation with conversion and their alleged craving for theocracy made them distrusted in the eyes of official France. The heated polemics of the Dreyfus affair and the religious laws of 1901–5 brought conflicts among missionaries, officials, and anticlerical colonists to a boiling point. The anticlerical impulse ultimately drove republican critics to attack the mission so blindly that they simultaneously condemned their own programs to save and "civilize" the local population. Unlike in Indochina, where high-ranking officials tended to defend the missions, in Tahiti, the most vocal critics of the missions included the governor of the EFO. Though these republicans apparently did not recognize it, their attacks were little more than eloquent autocritiques of their own failed policies.

The clearest indication that the campaign against the Catholic missions was more about politics and ideology than real sympathy for a dying people came in the wake of the imbroglio. Despite the missions' failures, republican reformers still determined that the best way to slow the destruction of the local population was to put children in schools. On more remote islands, a lack of government funds, mixed with Polynesians' general suspicion of the colonial regime, meant that these *écoles laïques* drew only a fraction of the students that the missions had.[101] The republican pedagogy pushed by Salles—designed to warm the hearts of Polynesian students with the glorious history of the French Revolution—did not fill classrooms with inspired pupils. Nor did laicization stem the depopulation of the Marquesas. Prostitution and alcoholism still bred despair. Tuberculosis and syphilis continued to kill. In the twenty years after the closing of the mission schools, the population of the Marquesas was cut in half, to just over 2,000.[102] In 1914, a French Protestant missionary traveling to the islands said what Robert Louis Stevenson and a host of officials had said decades earlier: "Everywhere civilization finds itself in contact with the so-called inferior races, it is *de rigeur* that they disappear rapidly." Civilization, which had decimated a part of the world

Europeans once considered paradise, offered no promises of regeneration. Nonetheless, the Frenchman concluded, a still greater effort to civilize was needed.[103] More than thirty years of failed policies pushed islanders in the South Seas precariously close to extinction but did little to shake the French faith in civilization.

IV

MADAGASCAR

6

1

In March 1897, the Société des missions évangéliques de Paris—the largest Protestant missionary organization in France—circulated instructions to five of its missionaries bound for the newly established colony of Madagascar.[1] In addition to standard orders to help open schools and to spread the gospel according to the traditions and methods of the organization, the instructions specifically addressed the issue of being French and Protestant in Madagascar. Under all circumstances, the instructions emphasized, the missionaries were to look and act as conspicuously *French* as possible, otherwise, these Protestants—Frenchmen, all—seriously risked being labeled *English*, anti-colonial, and treasonous by their own compatriots. For many Frenchmen, including some outwardly anticlerical administrators, to be French in Madagascar in 1897 was to be Catholic. So went a common saying in the colony: *"Qui dit Français dit catholique; qui dit protestant dit Anglais."* To say French was to say Catholic; to say Protestant was to say English. Nothing so clearly distinguished a Frenchmen from an Englishman, or signaled allegiance to the colonial regime, as religion.

Less than two years before the circulation of the Société's instructions, French forces had invaded Madagascar, an island in the Indian Ocean off the coast of southeastern Africa. After a ten-month campaign, the French took the capital of Antananarivo. In August 1896, Madagascar became a French colony, putting an end to decades of British involvement in Malagasy politics. But the arrival of a French colonial administration did not end the work of English Protestant missionaries, primarily from the London Missionary Society and the Society of Friends, though many officials suspected them of fostering anticolonial and anti-French sentiments in their more than 300,000 adherents. While colonial officials would soon document cases of English anticolonial meddling, they needed little convincing of the Protestants' malevolence. The founding of the colony came at the beginning of "three charged years" when war between France and Britain, sparked by tense imperial competition over Egypt and the Upper Nile, looked increasingly possible.[2] The race between French and British troops to the town of Fashoda, a river

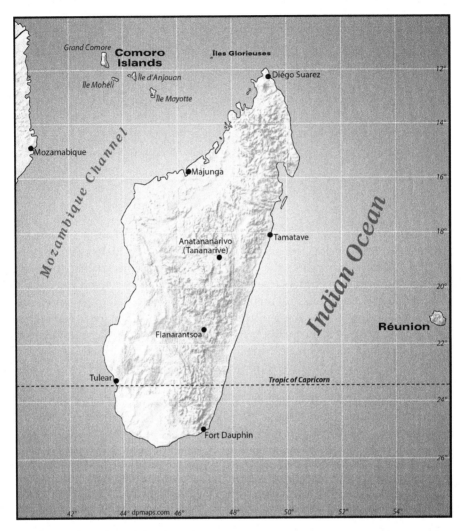

Map 6.1. Madagascar, c. 1914

port on the White Nile that Queen Victoria once described as "miserable and small," turned the French and British publics hostile toward each other and did nothing to endear English Protestant missionaries to officials in Madagascar.[3]

This diplomatic crisis made the French Protestants' position in Madagascar all the more complicated. They imagined their role to include defending the interests of Malagasy Protestants from both colonial officials and French Jesuits. To accomplish this, the Société des missions évangéliques sent its workers to the new colony in 1896 "not to replace" English Protestant missionaries (as it had done in other French colonies) but to facilitate the continuation of their work.[4] The presence of French Protestants, the Société hoped, would put an end to the suspicion and accusations that dogged English missionaries and that, consequently, threatened the future of Protestantism in the new possession. The already significant challenge of convincing French officials of the utility of English missionaries was made even more momentous by the particularly fervent anti-British prejudice felt by many French soldiers stationed in Madagascar at the turn of the century.

The central committee of the Société des missions évangéliques provided its missionaries with a veritable manual for how best to stay out of trouble and appear committed to the French colonial cause. Demanding discipline, the committee asked its missionaries to correspond frequently and exclusively with the Société, passing all communication with the government or the press, in either France or Madagascar, through the organization's directors. Missionaries were to pledge to the governor-general their "sincere cooperation with his efforts to assure peace and prosperity for the country under the flag of France." Missionaries were to be respectful and helpful to foreign Protestants but were instructed to "avoid everything that could give your mission the appearance of depending on a foreign association or leave in doubt your standing as good Frenchmen."[5]

Most important, French Protestants were to prove their commitment to the French administration's chief political and social mission in Madagascar at that time: "pacification."[6] The pacification of Madagascar was an official project that combined military force and the general goals of the republican civilizing mission. It quite literally was meant to bring civility to a countryside torn by civil unrest and violent rebellion. In 1897, Governor-General Joseph Gallieni, a seasoned, innovative colonial administrator whose policies dominated the first decade of French colonial rule in Madagascar, invoked the rhetoric of the civilizing mission when he wrote that, through pacification, France sought "the moral conquest of the country, by imposing our practices, our laws and above all our language."[7] The Société des missions évangéliques believed it was in an excellent position to help. By teaching French language and morals, it aimed "to introduce and make reign the union, the mutual affection, the habits of deference and support that have been the force of our most blessed missions, and without which no work would be able to prosper."[8]

French Protestant hopes were not to be realized. Despite their efforts, missionaries from the Société met hostility from their own compatriots, in both France and Madagascar. The period from 1896 to 1902, characterized by such religious strife it was dubbed *"les Troubles,"* witnessed some of the most vitriolic infighting known to the colonies. The two main combatants in this war of words, accusations, and deeds were French Protestant and Jesuit missionaries. Throughout, the colonial administration remained committed to religious neutrality, a policy that often incited more conflict than it settled. Religion would become the axis around which many central goals of colonialism would be defined. Before Gallieni proclaimed the pacification of the Malagasy population to be complete in the first years of the twentieth century, an array of Frenchmen, from missionaries to administrators, would hurl at one another accusations of terror, intimidation, and murder.

The treatment of French Protestants in Madagascar represents one of the most paradoxical twists in the story of how the religious politics, particularly during the Dreyfus affair, played out in the empire. During this era of "two Frances," Protestants were clearly on the side of anticlerical republicanism. Indeed, as the historian Philip Nord points out, many tenets of republican ideology can best be understood as "secularized" Protestantism.[9] Protestants held prominent civil and political positions during the Third Republic, and, among other reforms, they helped shape a new, secular education curriculum to provide a moral education based on faith in democratic symbols and ideals. The Société des missions évangéliques—though certainly a religious organization—was committed to these republican ideals while working in parts of French Africa and the Pacific. But, as the Société's 1897 instructions make apparent, the clear political divisions and alliances in metropolitan France did not hold true in the colony of Madagascar.

It was good, if unexpected, news for Catholic workers. Unlike Catholic missionaries in Indochina and Polynesia who met with increasing criticism from French colonists and administrators in the 1890s—mirroring political conflicts at home—the colonial government in Madagascar accepted and, in many instances, even cheered Catholic missionary involvement in the pacification of the country. The image of representatives of the Third Republic singing the praises of Jesuit missionaries could not have been more out of place in the fin de siècle: for many ruling republicans, the Jesuits embodied papist reactionary politics and were an obstacle to rational social reform. Nonetheless, officials in Madagascar remained even more suspicious of French Protestant missionaries, suggesting that many Frenchmen, including some traditionally anticlerical republicans, understood political and *cultural* links to exist between Catholicism and French identity—this in the very years when anticlericalism boiled over in French domestic politics. Catholicism abroad, as many missionaries and colonial officers put it, was France. While this formula was not true in every colony, it proved remarkably accurate in Madagascar. And Protestant dogma was one of the chief causes.

The Rise of Christianity in Madagascar

The religious conflict that gripped Madagascar in the late 1890s had roots set deeply in the history of the development of the state under the Merina ethnic group. When the French invaded Madagascar in 1895, the conquest put an end to a long history of ambivalent relations between the two countries. While French interests in the island stretched back to the seventeenth century, serious involvement in the country's affairs did not take shape until the second half of the nineteenth. At that time, Madagascar itself was the product of an internal colonialism: from the late 1700s, the Merina people of the island's central plateau (Imerina) started consolidating power over the island's twenty smaller groups, which were ethnically distinct but shared a common Malagasy language.[10] Under the leadership of the particularly powerful chief Andrianampoinimerina, the Merina developed a centralized government and grew wealthy from rice cultivation and trade (including slaves). In 1822, the king of the Merina, Radama I, named himself king of Madagascar.

Radama I's ascension to the Malagasy throne came in the wake of an Anglo-Malagasy treaty of friendship and cooperation, signed in 1817. According to the historian Phares Mutibwa, the British brokered the treaty less out of an interest directly in Madagascar—though they did demand the Merina government ban the slave trade—than in the hopes of undermining French expansion in the region.[11] The 1814 Treaty of Paris had turned the Ile de France (Mauritius) over to the British, who hoped to limit French influence around Madagascar to the small island possessions France retained— Réunion, Mayotte, Nossi Bé, and Sainte-Marie. A French claim to Madagascar, British officials feared, would allow a colonial and naval presence in the region that could hinder shipping to and from India around the Cape.

More significant for Madagascar, though the treaty of 1817 did not mention missionary work, the agreement encouraged Protestant missionaries from the Congregationalist London Missionary Society, known as the LMS, to venture to the island in 1818. With King Radama's support, the LMS mission started its work in Madagascar by opening a school in Antananarivo. The first school met limited success, as the missionaries did not speak Malagasy well. But they soon learned and began teaching in Malagasy, a move that required not only that they speak fluently but that they create a written form of the language as well. Their success was almost immediate: LMS schools reached more and more pupils and trained Malagasy teachers who opened additional schools in and around the capital. By 1824, LMS-inspired schools taught 2,000 children.[12] With the assistance of a number of their most talented students, the LMS set out to translate the Bible into Malagasy.[13]

The first baptisms did not come until the 1830s. A number of early converts were members of the ruling family, and many Merina elites grew wary of the spread of Christianity and European influences. The Merina welcomed the education and technical knowledge the LMS brought to the island, but many were unenthusiastic to see Christian beliefs replace traditional Malagasy practices. In the mid-1830s, when members of Queen Ranavalona I's own family and government wanted to convert, the monarch forbade it. She denied baptism for all members of the military and civil society and expelled all the missionaries from Imerina—a ban that stayed in place until her death in 1861.[14] This was a particularly tumultuous time in Malagasy history, as Ranavalona purged the country of Christians and others who rejected the primacy of Merina religious practices and symbols. Between 200,000 and 400,000 of a population of 1 million Malagasy lost their lives during these purges.[15] Despite the bloodshed, Christianity survived Ranavalona's reign and grew with renewed vigor when the ban was dropped after her death.

In the wake of the civil unrest, Christianity emerged as a key organizational factor of Merina politics, as many wealthy and powerful converts sought to take control of the country. In 1864, a particularly adept politician named Rainilaiarivony became prime minister and de facto leader of the country. Noticing the mounting political prowess of Merina converts, Rainilaiarivony decided the best way to avert a Christian coup was to have himself and his wife, reigning Queen Ranavalona II, baptized.[16] He then ordered all royal talismans—important indigenous religious symbols in Imerina—destroyed in an effort to undermine non-Christian political movements.[17] In his final move, he created a Palace Church—a Protestant congregation, but not under the control of European missionaries—which many prominent Merina political figures attended. The LMS looked to the countryside and devised plans to support and direct an elite group of indigenous teachers and evangelists to take Christianity to rural areas.[18]

The baptism of the queen motivated thousands of loyal subjects to follow her example. Congregations were formed around preexisting kinship groups, as Christianity became an important part of groups' political identities. Because conversion was a sign of political allegiance, many Malagasy were only nominally Christians, retaining their traditional practices and beliefs. New Protestant missionary organizations joined the LMS in the 1860s. The Friends' Foreign Mission Association, the Anglican Society for the Propagation of the Gospel, and the Norwegian Missionary Society divided territories in Imerina and Betsileoland so as to avoid direct competition. The numbers of churchgoers increased, with the LMS alone counting nearly 300,000 adherents by the 1880s. The numbers are somewhat misleading because many Christians were largely ignorant of Christian doctrine. As the historian Stephen Ellis points out, "To understand Malagasy Christianity it is more fruitful to regard religion as the Malagasy did, as the ritual form of the government of Imerina."[19]

For Rainilaiarivony, evangelization offered a means of solidifying political power. He worked closely with missionaries to build churches and schools across the country in order to expand literacy and impart technological know-how from Europe. In return, prominent members of these new congregations promised popular support for the monarchy. Through the powerful and wealthy Palace Church, the government also tried to modernize the country, publishing journals encouraging patriotism, trade, and political allegiance to the throne.

The close association between Protestant missionaries and the government made Catholic evangelization all the more challenging. A small number of French Jesuits arrived in the 1860s, but, from early on, they struggled to compete with the far more numerous and better-funded Protestants. A further strike against the Jesuits was that they were French; English missionaries did their best to convince the Malagasy government to avoid dealing with the French Catholics for fear of straining relations with London. But the very political nature of religion in Madagascar worked to the Jesuits' advantage. The Catholic mission became a harbor for unhappy political dissidents, especially in the countryside where people converted as a sign of their disdain for the centralized Merina administration.[20] While the Catholics never had the success of the LMS, by 1880 the Jesuits counted more than 50,000 adherents and had built an extensive system of stations, churches, leprosaria, factories, and schools run by the Frères des écoles chrétiennes and the Soeurs de Saint Joseph de Cluny. Despite the growth of Catholicism, throughout the second half of the nineteenth century, Jesuit missionaries, like their Protestant adversaries, lamented the halfheartedness of Malagasy Christianity.[21]

The Jesuits joined a choir of other Frenchmen unhappy with their treatment at the hands of the Malagasy government. From the 1860s, a small number of French traders and settlers in Madagascar complained that the government had refused to let them own property even though British subjects could. Landownership became an increasingly important issue in the 1870s, when Creole ranchers and traders from the neighboring French island of Réunion called on the government in Paris to pressure the Merina to allow them to live and work on the larger, richer island. The first Réunionnais deputy in the Chamber of Deputies, the persuasive, witty, and thoroughly abrasive François de Mahy, became temporary minister of the navy in 1883. Backed by vocal Réunionnais and Catholic lobbies, de Mahy used his office to push France into direct conflict with Madagascar. He stirred his colleagues' anger over British political maneuvers in Egypt the previous year, arguing that challenging British influence in Madagascar was an appropriate response. Much to the Malagasy government's dismay, the British backed down, unwilling to risk conflict with France. Nothing now stood in the way of French intervention.

The first French-Malagasy war—referred to by members of the LMS as the "de Mahy affair"—lasted from 1883 to 1885; the French never invaded the interior of the island, opting instead to bombard and blockade key ports. As the months passed, many French politicians lost sight of what their initial aims had been in Madagascar. The treaty that ended the war was welcomed by both sides, though its terms proved inconclusive and even confusing.[22] The French demanded an indemnity of 10 million francs and kept a foothold in Diégo Suarez, a port in the far north of the country considered key to future expeditions. More contentious was the wording of the 1885 treaty concerning France's future role in Malagasy politics. The queen refused to accept a treaty that designated Madagascar as a French protectorate. Rather than concede the point, French negotiators opted for phrasing that signified a protectorate without using the word. Though both sides signed, the Malagasy were left deeply suspicious of the French—and rightly so.[23] The treaty's vague language and unclear terms were the primary causes for the French invasion a decade later.

Britain removed itself from the uncomfortable position between the French and the Malagasy in 1890 when it signed a treaty acknowledging the French protectorate of Madagascar in return for French recognition of British interests in Zanzibar. The LMS and other British missionaries were left without the political support they had come to rely on, and divisions between "French" Catholics and "English" Protestants solidified in Madagascar. Catholic and secular newspapers in France denounced English missionaries as "political agents."[24] English missionaries in return claimed that all Catholics supported a French takeover of the island. Meanwhile, social and political unrest returned to Madagascar as the Merina government unsuccessfully tried to address economic troubles by raising taxes. Rainilaiarivony and Ranavalona II, greatly weakened by the 1883–85 war, continued to refuse to accept the French resident-general in Antananarivo as a representative of a French protectorate. In 1894, the French government—again pressured by de Mahy and the Réunionnais lobby—took advantage of the turmoil in Madagascar and voted to go to war.[25]

Invasion, Violence, and Social Instability

Hailed by politicians and the press as a glorious moment of colonial expansion, the invasion of Madagascar was at the same time a supreme example of a debacle.[26] A higher percentage of French combatants died in the ten-month conquest of Madagascar than in the trenches of the First World War.[27] The deadly foe in the 1895 campaign was not the machine gun or mustard gas but rather malaria and dysentery. French troops and colonial conscripts ascending to Madagascar's highland capital of Antananarivo encountered little serious resistance from their Malagasy adversaries. But the island's climate proved to be a formidable—and often fatal—obstacle. The campaign took nearly 6,000 soldiers' lives on the French side, roughly a third of the men mobilized.[28] Of these, fewer than twenty were killed in combat.[29] Nearly two-thirds of all deaths resulted from malaria, the rest from typhoid, dysentery, and tuberculosis.[30] The conquest of Madagascar ended in both victory and disaster: France reasserted its protectorate over an unruly indigenous regime, a political "success" paid for with more French lives than in any modern colonial war to date. And the struggle for control of the island had just begun.

For more than five years after the invasion, Madagascar remained in the grips of social and political unrest. The fall of Antananarivo immediately gave rise to a number of rebellions in the countryside. In November 1895, the largest and best known of these revolts, the *menalamba*, or "red shawls" up-rising, saw local elders and notables bent on defeating the French and pun-ishing the Merina elites responsible for the country's defeat. Uprisings like the *menalamba*, though shaped by local politics and social circumstances, were overwhelmingly anti-European and anti-Christian. Through violence, they sought to purge Madagascar of the corruption introduced by foreigners and to return to traditional practices and beliefs.[31]

Though no uprisings ever seriously threatened French rule, insurgents' acts of violence did succeed in terrorizing European residents. The first vic-tim of the *menalamba* uprising, for example, was an English missionary family. William and Lucy Johnson refused to flee with their baby daughter in November 1895 despite warnings from members of their own Quaker congregation. Rebels came to their house the morning of 22 November and, after demanding money from William, stabbed him to death, threw his body from an upstairs window, and mutilated it. After deciding that Lucy Johnson and her child represented future European generations in Mada-gascar, the rebels killed them as well.[32] The murders brought cries of out-rage from the European community in Madagascar, as well as from Europe. The Johnsons would not be the last European missionaries to meet such a death, attesting to the importance of Christianity in the politics of Madagascar.[33]

Catholics were not sheltered from the violence. The letters of Bishop Jean-Baptiste Cazet, the head of the Jesuit mission and apostolic prefect of Mada-gascar, chronicled the fear and uncertainty felt by many in the European community in the wake of the invasion. Even before the end of the French military campaign or the beginning of the *menalamba* uprising, Cazet pre-dicted that when the Hovas (the term the French commonly used to refer to the Merina) saw "that all is lost," they would turn their hatred of France into all sorts of excesses. "God knows it!"[34] By the summer of 1896, his predic-tions seemed to have come true: bandits had brazenly taken to robbing and attacking in broad daylight, even on the outskirts of the French-controlled capital. Travel without armed guards became dangerous, and some roads were completely impassable.[35] "The situation," wrote Cazet,

> is bad; there is no place safe for isolated Europeans. Also, we have
> recalled to Tananarive all the Fathers who do not have French soldiers
> in their principal residence. And everything is paralyzed, commerce,
> colonization, missions. Further, the rebels want to attack the Capital
> at night and massacre all the Europeans; this project has been known a
> long time; and the final moment approaches. Do they dare to try to
> execute it? I hope not. Pray for us.[36]

In June, Cazet got word that one of his missionaries, Père Jacques Berthieu, had been captured and killed by rebels.[37] A newspaper article carried an eyewitness account of the missionary's demise. It reported that the insurgents stripped Berthieu naked, cut off his nose and ears, put out his eyes with a red-hot stick, and submitted him "to a horrible mutilation." With his intestines dangling from his torso, the *fahavalo*, or insurgents, tied Berthieu to a post and lined up to take turns stabbing him with their spears.[38] The insurgents finally forced the priest's own servant to render the final blow. The body was never found. "The Reverend Father Berthieu is dead," Cazet wrote, "victim of his charity."[39]

To counter such terrifying acts, French troops responded with violence. In 1895, French authorities avenged the murder of the Johnson family by burning rebel villages and decapitating suspected leaders.[40] One of Père Berthieu's suspected murderers was captured and sentenced to life in irons. "Why not death?" Cazet asked angrily, expressing how many Frenchmen felt about punishing insurgents. "He is guilty, or he is not."[41] Cazet got his wish, according to a later account, for a number of Berthieu's murderers were eventually shot or exiled to Réunion.[42] More than two years later, after the initial disorder of the conquest had abated somewhat, administrators still sought harsh retribution for thievery and violence. In one case, an official asked permission "to have shot in the field" any *suspected* chiefs of a band of cattle thieves. The official added that the chiefs were assumed to have "contributed" to the murder of two Frenchmen—a fact by no means proven, or even heard, in court. Justification for the summary executions was simple, if not fair: the two murdered Frenchmen, said the official, had been treated "with the worst cruelty."[43]

In a letter indicative of French misunderstandings of Malagasy attitudes, Cazet wrote of a conversation he had with "an intelligent Malagasy" involved in current affairs. The priest asked, " 'How do you explain that the rebels expose themselves to a certain death, to the confiscation of their goods, to the misery of their families sooner than give themselves up?' He responded to me: 'They love so much the independence of their country, and they hope so much that they'll recover it some day, that they are not afraid to die for this motive. . . . ' " But Cazet, who had worked in Madagascar longer than most Frenchmen (he arrived in the early 1860s with the first Jesuits), seemed unwilling to accept this line of reasoning alone. Instead, he pointed to the way in which the Malagasy had fallen back to worshiping their *sampy*, or talismans, and carrying other "superstitious objects" with them into battle. The gruesome accounts of the deaths of the Johnsons, Père Berthieu, and other Europeans only redoubled French determination. The occupation of Madagascar did not strip the Malagasy of their freedom, many Frenchmen believed; it saved them from regressing into paganism and the primitive beliefs and behavior of the past.[44]

In September 1896, Governor-General Gallieni arrived in Madagascar with the goal of pacifying the violent turmoil in the countryside. The first and perhaps most easily accomplished facet of his plan was to bring the island under formal control by setting up regional stations around the country where military and administrative operations would be staged. This colonial administration would eventually be combined with his famous *politique des races* that replaced Merina regional administrators outside of Imerina with officials of the local dominant ethnicity. The hope was both to minimize the conflict between ethnic groups—primarily between those peoples who resented the decades of Merina domination—and to weaken Merina power more generally, as it represented the chief adversary of French colonial rule.[45] As a quick blow to Merina legitimacy, the French administration shot or exiled a number of prominent political leaders, including the queen, who was packed off to Réunion.

Gallieni's second and more ambitious goal was to persuade the people of Madagascar to welcome French control. A key step was to undermine the "English influence" on the island that Gallieni considered to be a "corollary" to Merina power and a direct challenge to French control. The administration particularly scrutinized the actions of English missionaries. Once English and Merina power was neutralized, the administration would undertake the difficult job of calming and winning over the Malagasy to French habits and customs. The administration relied heavily on the work of the Jesuit missionaries and French Catholic teaching brothers and sisters who knew the terrain, language, and cultures of Madagascar perhaps better than any Frenchmen.

Religious Liberty and the English Protestants

Within a month of his arrival in Madagascar, Gallieni knew that religion would pose a great problem to the pacification of the island. In October 1896, he reported to the Ministry of Colonies in Paris that "incessant conflicts" between Protestants and Catholics weighed heavily on the administration and involved not only local Protestant and Catholic communities but European pastors, priests, and other missionaries as well. Gallieni learned quickly just how petty missionary bickering could be. On the occasion of the execution of Malagasy Minister of the Interior Rainandriamampandry, whom the colonial regime had convicted of treason, Gallieni gave permission to both the curé of the Antananarivo cathedral and a local French pastor to be with the condemned man during his last hours. But the mix of priest and pastor had unfortunate consequences, and the two started quarreling almost at once. Gallieni was deeply disturbed by the image of two religious men fighting during "the final minutes of a condemned man."[46]

Nonetheless, Gallieni stuck steadfastly to a policy of neutrality and religious liberty. "I have taken an absolutely independent attitude" regarding religion, he reported shortly after his arrival in Antananarivo. With administrative backing from Paris, he "made known" his formal policy of religious neutrality, "not wanting to favor the one [religion] to the detriment of the other." Should the pastors and priests want the neutrality to continue, missionaries needed fulfill only two obligations: they had to use French as the language of instruction in religious schools, and all European religious workers were barred from ever making pronouncements "of a political character" from their pulpits. Should ministers trespass from their spiritual role into questions of government, Gallieni warned that he would not hesitate to resort to "severe repression" of the offending parties and their congregations.[47]

Despite the official position of neutrality, French officials—Gallieni included—remained suspicious of English subjects living in Madagascar, especially Protestant missionaries. In correspondence and reports, officials closely associated Merina insurgents with English missionaries. Proof enough was the fact that many rebels suspiciously spared the lives of British colonists and missionaries even during the most destructive uprisings. Though their conclusion was flawed, French authorities assumed all British subjects who survived attacks to be involved in their planning.[48] In February 1897, for example, a British missionary couple named Peill survived an attack in the town of Ambohimanga, even though the *fahavalo* destroyed every other house in town. What raised the suspicions of the local French official was that *fahavalo* usually targeted *vahaza*, or whites.[49] With little proof of wrongdoing, officials considered expelling the Peills but feared that they would protest their expulsion as an infraction of the *liberté du culte*. For such missionaries, Gallieni decided on "a discreet but tight surveillance."[50]

A more serious confrontation came with Pastor W. J. Edmonds of the London Missionary Society. Relying on inconsistent testimonies, officials believed Edmonds was using his pulpit in the town of Antsaramanga to spread anti-French sentiments. Officials suspected Edmonds of spreading rumors about French plans to persecute Protestantism and about a pending English invasion of the island.[51] When French authorities tried to investigate, some witnesses changed their accounts of Edmonds's statements out of fear of recriminations. The English missions, Gallieni reported,

> recently spread in Imerina the rumor that the French were grappling
> with diplomatic difficulties in the Orient and that a rupture with
> England was imminent. Three English ships had arrived, they said, in
> front of Mananjary, the port of which they blocked, and where they were
> going to land troops which, joined with those of the rebel chiefs, would
> not hesitate to drive out the French. These ridiculous fables spread on
> purpose found credence with the Malagasy, and sufficed to intimidate
> the witnesses who had dared testify against the English.[52]

The directors of the LMS in London found the French assertions to be completely without merit.[53] But that did not put an end to French investigations. Another report spoke of "an ardent anti-French campaign" under-taken by the LMS around the town of Fianarantsoa, a province the French believed would remain calm. In April 1897, secret societies allegedly "composed of active agents of the English Mission," and under the leadership of two LMS missionaries, vowed to tolerate no longer the "schemes of the French in Madagascar." The campaign, the author of the report feared, would result in "a veritable uprising. The English agents disperse money profusely in order to help make successful their anti-French campaign." The report combined a deep fear of violent resistance to French colonialism with the language of nationalistic competition: Malagasy resentment was matched only by the English sense of entitlement in all questions imperial. "*Bref,*" the official concluded, "the arrogance of the English is becoming intolerable."[54]

The alleged "maneuvers" of the LMS were dangerous to French authorities for a number of reasons. In addition to having hundreds of thousands of adherents, the Protestant missions had a legion of Malagasy pastors working in their midst. Even though the colonial administration warned the English to steer clear of political issues, French officials still feared that the LMS used Malagasy pastors as intermediaries "to constantly arouse difficulties."[55] Rumors of the fall of the French played well in the countryside, where the population remained convinced that an eventual "return to English power" was certain.[56]

The clash with English Protestants was not simply a colonial affair but potentially had international consequences. In London, in the spring of 1897, George Cousins, the acting foreign secretary of the LMS, deemed the claims against Edmonds "absurd and groundless" and questioned how any officials of a "civilized Government" could believe them.[57] At the same time, the English vice-consul in Antananarivo met with Gallieni to discuss the treatment of the Peills and Edmonds at the hands of colonial officials. The LMS mission in Madagascar was the organization's largest single operation; it took necessary steps to defend its turf. Fearing that private meetings with officials would not work, the LMS tried to persuade the British public that French oppression in Madagascar was a harbinger of treatment to come in other regions of the world where Protestant missions flourished.

It was not long before the story of French oppression became an important news item in Europe. Reuters ran an article reporting that "French subaltern bureaucrats" colluded with Jesuit missionaries to undermine the work of British Protestantism—a form of "terrorism" that made their work "almost impossible" in certain districts.[58] In no time, members of the British Parliament demanded better treatment of the "Protestant natives of Madagascar" as well as British missionaries.[59] To avoid controversy with Britain, Gallieni opted to relocate, rather than exile, British missionaries accused of wrongdoing.

The Administration, the Military, and the Jesuits

As in other parts of the French empire, the administration in Madagascar viewed the Catholic mission with a certain ambivalence. Opinion was notably divided between republican-appointed colonial administrators in Paris and Antananarivo and the many military commanders who took up the day-to-day oversight of regional affairs in small posts across the new colony. High-level officials tended to be wary in their support of the Jesuits, though they rarely doubted Catholic missionaries' commitment to the colonizing effort. Gallieni, despite a career in the French military, was no different. His personal opinion of Catholic missionaries tended toward anticlericalism, as he suspected them of serving their spiritual aims, not those of the state.[60] Nonetheless, his policies steadfastly remained neutral, and his public statements regularly showed optimism that the Catholic missions would serve the colonial cause. In all cases, French officials were far better disposed to Catholic religious workers than to the "English agents" of the LMS and other foreign missions.

By contrast with administrators, French military commandants were much more vociferous in their support of Catholic missionaries. From the beginning of the conquest, Catholic missionaries worked as chaplains among the invading Expeditionary Corps, and the relationship between French soldier and priest was typically one of camaraderie and respect. In addition to believing that missionary assistance was imperative to winning the country over to French power, the military had a long tradition of affinity for the Catholic Church in France. In the late nineteenth century, French soldiers and priests believed they had much in common: they were typically from rural areas or small towns, rooted their virtues in the French soil, imagined their vocations as tied to great old traditions, and distrusted urban technocrats and republicans.[61] In the colonies, this translated into a relationship between cross and sword of mutual respect and shared visions of French moral and political imperatives abroad.

Missionaries and soldiers in Madagascar forged friendships from the first days of the conquest. In early 1896, Père Denjoy celebrated Easter with soldiers and generals who welcomed him "affectionately." The week's ceremonies wedded military and religious metaphors. According to Denjoy, two generals took the occasion to speak at mass: one spoke of soldiers needing to be always ready before God; the second quoted Joan of Arc. The soldiers sang songs to ask for Mary's protection in victory; one officer referred to the conquest as a continuation of the Crusades. While Denjoy's report of his Easter festivities underlined the involvement of the entire corps, he did express preference for the officers and soldiers over the "doctors, majors, and administrative officials," who, of course, were more likely to be republican and—so the missionary assumed—less enthusiastic about religious festivities.[62]

Officers were particularly eager to see Catholic missionary schools open around military posts. In early 1897, the Jesuit mission made a list of letters and requests written by military officials expressing preference for French Catholic schools over existing Protestant ones. One captain complained that the Protestant school near his post on the route from Tamatave to the capital was run by two schoolmasters, neither of whom knew French. In addition to the benefits of teaching French, officers believed the Catholic mission won the population over to French rule. A lieutenant colonel in the town of Ambato was pleased to hear that local inhabitants wanted to transform their Protestant temple into a Catholic church. "You know that the French are Catholic," he wrote, "Catholics are the friends of the French, and, for that, the people of Ambato are completely among our friends." Another officer showed his approval of missionaries across the empire, noting that "in Tonkin as in Madagascar," they were the best means of spreading "our authority."[63]

That high-level republican officials entertained similar hopes for the Catholic missions is nothing short of remarkable. After all, these missionaries were not just Catholics, they were *Jesuits*. Throughout the nineteenth century, the Jesuits had experienced difficulty getting along with any French regime, let alone republican ones. Their order was kicked out of France at least three times over the course of the century, most recently in 1880, when republicans denounced it as an obstacle to modernization and a tool of papal power. Republicans dissolved the Jesuit congregation at the height of the secularization crisis in French education. Jules Ferry and other politicians, hoping to replace Catholic schools with state-run ones, saw the Jesuits as one of the greatest challenges to republican-inspired secularization.[64] Despite the rekindling of republican-Catholic animosities in 1890s France, in Madagascar the republic looked to Jesuits as potential allies. Though many colonial administrators remained concerned that Jesuit meddling in colonial affairs and local politics would further complicate colonization, most believed the Jesuits to be a source of valuable assistance on the distant island.

Luckily for the Jesuits, Mgr. Cazet was politically savvy; he quickly acted to alleviate official anxieties by stressing repeatedly that his missionaries did not get involved in political issues. This served missionaries well, as it conformed to Gallieni's admonition to priests and pastors to refrain from political banter. In early 1897, Cazet sent a circular to all his missionaries, imploring them to continue their work during the difficult times with patience and goodwill for all, and insisting that they avoid political debate. Cazet invoked the words of Saint Ignatius: "The least good done with calm and edification seems to me preferable to the greatest things accomplished through trouble and scandal."[65] Should the good saint not be inspiration enough, Cazet reminded them of Gallieni's promise to respect religious liberty and the freedom of education as long as missionaries avoided intrigue.

Gallieni—obviously one of Cazet's intended readers—responded enthusi-
astically. Using the exact language of Cazet's circular, Gallieni agreed that
"the sentiment of patience, goodwill, and caution which animates the Fathers of the mission will overcome all the difficulties" facing it. Cazet's willingness to work with Gallieni brought out an uncommon level of approbation
from the general: "The work of patriotism that you have pursued for long
years in Madagascar has already given results from which the colony has
profited," he wrote. In the governor-general's mind, there was no doubting
Catholic allegiance: "I join you," he told Cazet, "and your devoted missionaries in order to realize the eminently French program you have outlined."[66]
By assisting in education and moral reforms—a boon to Gallieni's program
of pacification—the Jesuits proved not only their allegiance to colonial rule
but also their patriotism. Gallieni's response led Cazet to suspect that the
general was "very favorable to us," though he had to appear neutral in public. Gallieni's prudence, Cazet surmised, was an attempt to avoid "violent attacks" and accusations that "he is in the Jesuits' hands."[67]

With pacification in full swing, the Catholic mission took the opportunity
to persuade colonial officials in both Antananarivo and Paris of its usefulness. The Ministry of Colonies was initially open to Jesuit collaboration.
Even before Gallieni's arrival, the minister noted that "the services rendered
by the [Jesuit] missionaries to our cause in Madagascar and the losses that
they still suffer today by representing in the eyes of the rebel populations the
French idea can only merit our benevolence."[68] The Jesuits, while thankful
for the minister's warm words, hoped the administration would show its appreciation in cash and, in mid-1897, they asked the government to increase
the mission's subvention.

Public demonstrations of patriotism did not come naturally to the Jesuits.
But the mission's propaganda machine was well oiled and adapted readily.
Paul Camboué, the Jesuit who administered the Madagascar mission from
Paris, took the lead. In a letter to the colonial minister, he emphasized that it
was Catholic schools that had paved the way for French colonization: "It is
from these schools, where our language was taught long before the annexation of the island to France, that came the majority of indigenous interpreters
and employees of our Residents, of our military, and of our colonists."[69] Camboué was a man of action as well as rhetoric: he demonstrated the Jesuit contribution to colonialism by teaching classes in Malagasy in Paris. A flyer said
the course was designed "for all those who have French influence in Madagascar at heart and propose to work for a truly civilizing colonization."[70]

While the administration associated the Jesuits with French influence on
the island, the politics of neutrality, as well as concern that the Jesuits would
become too powerful, moderated official support. The administration not
only failed to increase the official subvention for the mission in 1897 but also
started to look for ways to dilute Jesuit power over the Catholic population.[71]
The new colonial minister, André Lebon, concerned about potential Jesuit

"abuses," aimed to bring in priests from another missionary congregation, the Pères du Saint Esprit, in an effort to break the Jesuit monopoly.[72] Officials also praised the teaching brothers from the Frères des écoles chrétiennes, who were "highly appreciated by the indigenous population" and served the "French cause" by teaching French. Most impressive to Hippolyte Laroche, resident-general before Gallieni's arrival, was that the *frères* seemed content with teaching French and were not preoccupied with the low number of converts they won in the process. Laroche suggested giving the *frères* a subsidy separate from the 20,000 francs paid to the Jesuits and used for purposes other than teaching French.[73] Upon his arrival, Gallieni concurred with Laroche that it was important for the Frères to be independent of the Jesuits.

Gallieni's position on the Jesuits remained most ambiguous. Two days after he wrote his letter to Cazet congratulating him on his commitment to remain out of politics and to help the French cause, Gallieni expressed reservations about the Jesuits' "too marked influence" over the indigenous population. The Jesuits, Gallieni continued, "do not hold themselves, in effect, solely to things of a spiritual order; they profit from all occasions to interfere in the affairs of Government and politics." If the administration did not "take guard" then the Jesuits could cause "grave difficulties."[74] Despite his concerns, Gallieni, like most high-level administrators, pressed the administration in Paris to help develop Catholic missionary work in Madagascar by continuing to subsidize missionary travel to and from the colony.[75] Administrators hoped to dilute the Jesuit presence with missionaries from other orders, but none suggested removing the Jesuits altogether. And laïcisation, especially of the schools, was well beyond the budget and manpower of a colony still in the grips of violence.[76] Thus Catholic missionaries remained, for the time being, central to the plan of pacification and civilization.

Discouraging the French Protestant Alternative

Considering the number of Malagasy adherents to LMS and other foreign Protestant churches, as well as the initial concern officials showed for Jesuits working in Madagascar, it would seem logical that the administration would have welcomed French Protestant missionaries to the new colony. French Protestants could replace the dreaded "English agents" of the LMS while also balancing Jesuit influence by offering an alternative "French" religion to Catholicism. Unlike their British coreligionists, French Protestant missionaries could teach French, help in Gallieni's "moral conquest" of the country, and spread much-needed French influence. And French Protestants played a prominent role in national republican politics. But such was not the case.

From the early 1890s, when a French invasion of Madagascar appeared a fait accompli, organizers at the Société des missions évangéliques began investigating the possibility of sending workers to the island. Facing strong opposition from the beginning, the Société had to define its role in Madagascar carefully. Noting that the island was home to "great and powerful" missions from both England and Norway, an 1892 circular to the Société's auxiliary committee stressed that the French mission's chief undertaking would be to mediate between French officials and Malagasy Protestants. A member of the Société was to remain in Antananarivo to "represent our Protestantism" before the resident-general of France. In addition, the mission would send French teachers to the protectorate to help develop a French-language program in Protestant schools.[77]

The directors of the English and Norwegian Protestant efforts in Madagascar were some of the first to decline the French offer to help mediate between Malagasy Protestants and French officials. In 1892, the LMS's foreign secretary Wardlaw Thompson replied to an offer from Pastor Boegner, head of the Société des missions évangéliques, to provide missionaries to teach French in Protestant schools in Madagascar, deeming it "unacceptable." Thompson's main concern was that the Malagasy would consider the Protestants too pro-French if their schools started offering the language, producing "great irritation" among their followers. Though he confessed that "the days of the London Missionary Society in Madagascar are numbered," Thompson did not see the members of the LMS willing to work with the Frenchmen despite the likelihood that France would colonize the island. Correspondence from Thompson reveals how national pride shaped the English policy: he clearly did not like the idea of a *French* occupation of the island—Protestant or not. "I fear I am too much of an Englishman," he wrote, "not to feel a deep sense of injury and resentment at the prospect of such a change."[78]

A year later, the Société got no more encouragement from the Norwegian mission. Rev. Dahle, a Norwegian, expressed his appreciation for the offer to step in and act as mediator between the Protestants of Madagascar and the French administration, but, he added, "we do not feel quite sure as to the advisability of the prospected step." Dahle assumed that in addition to helping mediate, the French Protestants would want "some field of labour" of their own that "might prove rather difficult. . . . The districts accessible to missionary work are pretty well occupied." The only districts left open to spread the gospel were ones he deemed too dangerous or unhealthy: "It therefore appears to us that you would have difficulty in finding a district where you could work without stepping into ground partially tilled already. And if you found such a district, it would more likely be too far off to enable your missionaries to intervene effectually for the other Protestant missionaries, which is your chief aim." Dahle concluded by saying that the LMS might need more help than the Norwegian mission, since the English were widely suspected of having political aims in the country—"quite a groundless suspicion." "As for us Norwegians," he added, "we have been subject to no such suspicion, as the French authorities in Madagascar know perfectly well that our country has no colonial interests . . . to fight for."[79]

English and Norwegian missionaries in Madagascar had concerns that a partnership with French Protestant missionaries might make them look too *French* in the eyes of the Malagasy. But a number of vocal French interests suggested that a French Protestant presence in the possession was tantamount to an act of treason. On 16 May 1893, the question of Madagascar arose in the Chamber of Deputies when François de Mahy, perennial deputy from Réunion, asked the foreign minister for an update on the island. De Mahy's chief concern was continued English influence on the island despite the French protectorate.[80] De Mahy explained this influence in religious terms: the "Hova" government, he noted, subscribed to "the English religion" and was controlled by the English missions. But, de Mahy added, pro-English sentiments were not confined to the English missionaries. In rather mysterious and vague terms, de Mahy warned his colleagues of a "politico-religious school" operated by Protestants in France that hoped Britain would prevail in Madagascar and plotted "the complete expulsion of France" from the island. "But that would be treason!" exclaimed one shocked deputy.[81] De Mahy continued unfazed:

> We have in France a vast organization that casts its web over our entire country: I mean *la France coloniale* as well as the metropole. This organization is the French Société des Missions Évangéliques, it's the international evangelic alliance, it's the British and Foreign Bible Society, which has its seat, its *maison mère*, on the shores of the Thames, and in France in branches composed of half English, half very honorable French coreligionists.

M. le Comte Armand, the minister of foreign affairs, swayed by de Mahy's allegations, retorted that they might be honorable, "but not patriots!"

De Mahy continued, "You say 'not patriots!' Allow me to follow you on this terrain," and, in defending the French Protestants' patriotism, he proceeded to condemn them of treason: "I believe in their patriotism; but it is a patriotism *sui generis* (*Laughter.*) which differs from yours and mine; they are convinced that it is good for France not to have colonies . . . they fear for us the embarrassment of riches and think that the poorer our country is, the less it will excite envy. (*New laughter.*)" In de Mahy's caricature, Protestant missionaries believed France to be "a degenerate race"; as a result, they supported English expansion to the detriment of France and worked to proselytize—with the help of English missionaries—in France as well as in the empire. De Mahy accomplished the unimaginable when he linked Catholics and *libres penseurs* as true Frenchmen who needed to fight a common adversary committed to sectarianism. De Mahy was so convincing he garnered applause and cries of alarm from all corners of the house.[82]

To no one's surprise, de Mahy was strongly pro-Catholic and no stranger to lambasting French Protestants (he once accused them of helping the Germans annex Alsace). But de Mahy's main goal in exposing the alleged Protestant conspiracy was to whip up support for a Madagascar military campaign. His speech in the chamber was aimed more at producing concern about the dangers of English influence than at criticizing French Protestants. Either way, his words were devastating for the Société. De Mahy's reception that day in the chamber—best described by the laughter, applause, and cries of "*très bien!*" recorded in the official transcript—reveals how many politicians saw French Protestants as a threat to France's colonial aspirations. By linking French and English Protestants, de Mahy even brought the left wing in line; as "one member to the left" yelled from his seat, foreign missions (which includes French Protestants) were "more dangerous" than homegrown Catholic ones.[83] Left-wing traditions of anticlericalism notwithstanding, in May 1893 there was near consensus in the Chamber of Deputies that France, be it Catholic or "free-thinking," needed to beware of Protestants, be they English or French.

Between English and Catholic

The directors of the Société des missions évangèliques de Paris were appalled. Little more than a week after de Mahy's performance, the Société sent out a mass mailing to dozens of *députés* denying the existence of any sort of "Protestants' International" designed to submit the world to English domination. No link existed between the three organizations that de Mahy claimed worked together to undermine France—the Société, the British Bible Society, and the Alliance évangélique. French Protestants had even addressed this question in a public séance in 1887 when a number of speakers outlined the facts that proved the "imaginary nature" of de Mahy's alleged "Protestant league."[84]

The letter signaled an important step in the development of the Protestant mission's strategy in two important regards. First, the mission addressed its patriotism directly. "As for the Société des Missions," the letter insisted, "its patriotism is above all suspicion." The fact that the mission had served already in a number of colonies and was founded and run by patriots of all sorts, including admirals, counts, barons, and senators, was proof enough. In addition to patriotism, liberty was a prominent theme throughout the letter: in all questions colonial, the Société said that Protestants were not "antinational" and did not differ from other French, all of whom were allowed a "freedom of opinion." The Société also defended the Alliance évangélique against de Mahy's attack. The alliance was a "pure affirmation of the moral unity of Protestantism" that only entered politics, the directors noted, "to protest against violations of religious liberty."[85] Liberty and patriotism—two main ingredients in the republican recipe for empire—would become mainstays of French Protestant rhetoric in the years of "the Troubles"; liberty gave Protestants the right to work freely and patriotically in Madagascar.

With the letters mailed, the directors of the Société turned to research. In June 1893, they interviewed two experts on Madagscar, Alfred Grandidier of the Institut sur Madagascar and Charles Le Myre de Vilers, *député* and former resident-general of Madagascar. Neither gave encouraging responses. In Grandidier's opinion, the Merina were neither pro-French nor pro-English; rather, they sought independence and believed England to be more likely to help them achieve it. Echoing the admonitions of English and Norwegian Protestants, he warned that introducing French Protestant missionaries was a bad idea, not because they were Protestant but because they were French. And should the French Protestants seek to work with foreign Protestants on the island, they would be condemned as pro-English by the French administration. "In short," the author of the Société's report wrote, "there is no room according to M. Grandidier for a French Protestant mission between the French Catholic mission and the English Protestant mission.[86]

Were Grandidier's advice not frank enough, Le Myre de Vilers, an ardent supporter of Catholic missionaries, was brutal. "You have *nothing to do* in Madagascar," he said, "neither from the Protestant point of view, nor the French. From the French point of view, you will do bad, you will be an obstacle, a hindrance; from the Protestant point of view, you won't do any good. I do not hesitate to clearly discourage you from any intervention. The government does not want it, it asks nothing of you, refrain."[87] The interviewer from the Société pushed the issue, asking if there was not room between "France and Catholicism" on one side, and "Protestantism and English influence" on the other. Le Myre de Vilers answered by moving well beyond the questions of Madagascar. He said that, for centuries, it had been a fact that "abroad, France is Catholicism, and that Protestantism, across the seas, is England. Everywhere it is thus, and nowhere more so than in Madagascar." Even if prudent, he warned, the Protestants would be entangled in a fight between French and English and would ultimately be deemed traitors to France. Such would be one more division in the country for the administration to worry about.[88]

The negative responses the Société received from de Mahy, Grandidier, and Le Myre de Vilers proved invaluable in their own way, providing the mission with future lines of attack and allowing it to set up its defenses. For nearly two years, internal correspondence and other publications from the Société carefully plotted how the mission would describe its work in Madagascar. One document outlined points to make to the foreign ministry: these included the fact that the mission's primary task was spreading the gospel, that it did not receive any money or have any affiliation with English missions, and that its work cultivated the "sphere of French influence."[89] A letter from the head of a French Protestant organization suggested that the delegation to Madagascar show itself to be at once "Christian and patriotic," since French Protestantism had been so "unjustly misunderstood."[90]

In November 1895, the Société's position on Madagascar went public when an anonymous "subscriber" published a piece in *Le Temps* calling for French Protestant missionaries to seek work in the recently invaded country. While it is uncertain whether the author was a member of the Société or simply an ardent admirer, the piece clearly and persuasively described the benefits of having French Protestants in Madagascar. Chief among the author's concerns was the presence of foreign missions there. With a French colonial presence now on the island, the situation had quickly changed: "In effect, it is now about doing the work of pacification, but also of civilization, that is to say, of moralization, of education among these peoples who believe only in the prestige of force." Invoking the language of republican colonialism, the author continued that "after having conquered [the Malagasy], we must . . . make of these adversaries of yesterday the adoptive children of the mother country, knowing laws and loving them, persuaded that the indissoluble link of moral life and of all political life is the cult of justice and truth."[91]

The *Le Temps* article presented the French Protestants just as the Société itself wanted: as fitting neatly between English Protestantism and French Catholicism, and as being promoters of the republican colonial agenda. To keep French Protestants from Madagascar, the argument went, was tantamount to abandoning the Malagasy—especially the dominant Merina population—to English influence. Only French Protestants could both aid in the pacification and help bring to the Malagasy the *liberté de conscience* that republican colonialism promised. Echoing the goals of the civilizing mission, the article encouraged the French people to call on the patriotism of the Protestants to go to the colony in order "to raise the young generations, to clarify their convictions, to introduce them to the French ideas, to make them love France." The Merina, the article concluded, would then understand that "the French want to work for the social and religious progress of their country and the liberating truth of these words would be felt: 'Everywhere the flag of France is planted, a great people precede it, and a great idea follows.' "[92]

Protestants Off to War

Whether or not "a great idea" followed the French into Madagascar, a great deal of trouble certainly did not lag far behind the French Protestant mission. Despite all the warnings to avoid Madagascar, in early 1896, the Société sent a delegation to the island to investigate the installation of missionaries. The thirty-six-page report, written by the two Protestant delegates, Henri Lauga and Frédéric-Hermann Kruger, reiterated and underscored many of the arguments made over the previous few years as to the usefulness of a French

Protestant presence to both the Malagasy and the colony. But Lauga and Kruger made two new and ultimately inadvisable contributions: they attempted to defend the integrity of the English missionaries in Madagascar, and they swiftly and harshly denounced the intrigues, plots, and criminality of the Jesuit mission there. According to the two delegates, the Jesuits not only manipulated French officials and abused the indigenous population but also politicized religious identity by making commonplace the formula *"Qui dit Français dit catholique; qui dit protestant dit Anglais."* Overcoming this common association would be of paramount importance if the French Protestants were to succeed.[93]

Despite the obstacles, the Société remained hopeful after reading the report; and by summer of 1896 a missionary named Benjamin Escande was permanently in country. He arrived when Resident-General Laroche, a Protestant, was still in office. Though short-lived, Laroche's tenure promised an easy transition for the French Protestants. (Indeed, Mgr. Cazet worried that the arrival of the Protestant missionaries, coupled with the presence of Laroche and his group of "Protestant bureaucrats," could spell trouble for the Jesuits.)[94] But the arrival of Gallieni in October 1896 signaled a turn for the worse. It was not that Gallieni was outwardly hostile to the Protestants; in fact, Gallieni had showed himself cordial to both the French and foreign missionaries. But with the departure of Laroche, Escande reported in a letter to Paris, the Jesuits seemed empowered, profiting from the new state of affairs to transform Madagascar into "the France of Louis XIV"—a reference to the violent religious persecution of the Huguenots.[95]

Escande viewed the situation in Madagascar in martial terms, quickly embracing Lauga and Kruger's assessment of Catholic missionaries. The violent attacks of the *fahavalos*, the uprisings that left both Malagasy and Europeans dead, the brigandage—these were secondary concerns. The French Protestants' true enemies were the Jesuits. After having been in Madagascar just a few months, Escande became convinced that the future seemed dark: "Today, war is declared," he reported; the Jesuits had the advantage, using lies and calumny as their weapons, and benefiting from the protection of French troops who threatened Malagasies with death should they be implicated with "the English." What Escande wanted, like any good general heading off to war, was troops. "We need lots of men. We need pastors, we need missionaries, we need teachers." Escande wrote the line "send us an army"; then he thought better of it and crossed it out.[96]

The Catholics, for their part, were ready for trouble. Despite Escande's certainty that the Jesuits held a significant advantage in this battle, Mgr. Cazet feared only one thing as much as the fast-approaching "bands of pillagers": the arrival of French Protestants.[97] When Cazet first heard news of the Protestants' planned arrival in Madagascar, his immediate reaction had long been foreseen by Le Myre de Vilers and others: the apparent partnership between the English and French missions struck Cazet as "completely antipatriotic!"[98] "To the great astonishment of all, foreigners and indigenous, the French Protestant ministers have made a common course with the English independents." For their part, he added, the Malagasy considered the French Protestants to be English. "And some think [this is the way] to win the English to the French cause. *Quelle utopie!*"[99] The Protestants would only cause difficulty for the colony, even if they were to replace the English, he warned—"heresy is a source of disunion." Practicing his rhetoric in a letter to his *maison mère*, Cazet concluded, "One fact is certain: who in the group have shown themselves faithful to France? The Catholics."[100]

With the language of conflict in place, Protestant and Catholic missionaries needed only a pretext to start quarreling in earnest. Two laws gave them an issue to fight over. The first, which took effect during Resident-General Laroche's tenure, allowed students the right to change schools. Since the early 1880s, the Malagasy throne had prohibited children from switching schools in an attempt to stabilize religious affiliations and the political bases linked to them. Under the new French law, children and their parents could decide which school to attend; if they grew unhappy with one, they could switch to the other. Gallieni's policy of neutrality, implemented in March 1897, which gave the Malagasy population the freedom of religion, provided a liberty with ramifications similar to the school law. Under this law, the administration took possession of all churches in the country and allowed local populations to choose whether they would be Protestant or Catholic. Should a previously Protestant village, for example, decide to become Catholic, the village's church properties would be turned over to the Catholic mission.

As religion in Madagascar had for decades been closely linked to politics, the colonizing of the island by France drove thousands of Malagasies to abandon their Protestant roots and convert to Catholicism. The shift did not represent great changes in opinion about Christian doctrine. Most missionaries agreed that Malagasy Christianity was not particularly deep-seated. Catholics regularly complained that the local population was more prone to Protestantism because the LMS and other organizations allowed them to keep some of their traditions and beliefs intact, especially the *sampy*, or talismans. One Jesuit observer noted that the local populations viewed religion as yet another corvée, or obligation to the new rulers, and possessed no real conviction for Christianity whatsoever. Such an admission, however, did not keep this priest from attributing the turn toward Catholicism after the arrival of the French to anything but divine grace.[101]

Catholic missionaries certainly reaped the benefits of French colonialism. With the Malagasy now free to choose both school and church, a massive social, political, and religious shift took place. By Christmas 1896, Cazet reported the Catholic churches and schools were "overflowing" with new adherents. Before the war, the Catholics had fewer than 30,000 followers, but in the two months after the arrival of Gallieni, the number rose to more than

65,000. By January, in the district around Fianarantsoa alone, the Catholic mission had acquired 124 new posts and more than 25,000 new students. Whole villages converted to Catholicism in the space of a day. Protestant temples were converted into Catholic churches. "The English," Cazet reported, "are furious."[102]

In the bishop's opinion, the movement to Catholicism was "very much favored by the heads of military posts." One captain wrote to the Jesuit that the Catholic school in his region had 300 students; "send other professors and we will immediately have 900; Hurry! without [professors] the English who came the other day will cut the grass from under our feet."[103] The Catholics suddenly faced disturbing financial and personnel shortages. By February, one priest—alone and in poor physical health—found himself in charge of sixty-four posts and 8,000 students.[104] Gallieni offered no specific help, though Cazet was encouraged by rumors that the general was working to "promptly accelerate the thaw of Protestantism"—a plan he figured could only help the Catholic mission. Beyond Gallieni, Cazet saw the military as a whole turn against Protestantism, "convinced, proof in hand, that it was the enemy of France."[105]

A Colonial Ancien Régime

The Reverend Benjamin Escande was in many ways the perfect choice to head the first French Protestant mission in the colony. A tireless pastor with a combative personality, Escande did not believe in half measures. Shortly after his arrival in Madagascar, he had adopted the language of republican anticlericalism to fight Jesuit intrigue. Like radicals and Freemasons in Indochina and Polynesia, Escande accused the Third Republic of having completely failed in its civilizing goals by relying on the violent trickery of the Jesuits. Escande and his Protestant compatriots leveled their accusations in historical terms, the significance of which would not have been lost on colonial officials: rather than export the ideals of the French Revolution to Madagascar—liberty, equality, the promise of progress—France and its Jesuit servants had re-created the ancien régime there.

In addition to distributing Bibles and anticlerical publications across the countryside, the Protestants' main task was to appeal to, and sometimes confront, the administration directly.[106] Exhibit A in Escande's case against the Jesuits was their rampant corruption and use of intimidation. The flow of many Malagasy to Catholicism, he insisted, was anything but natural. Rather, the "movement" was motivated by a conspiracy of military officers and Jesuit missionaries (those Old Regime pillars) who relied on violence and intimidation to achieve their goals. By December 1896, Escande had become convinced that Gallieni had turned definitively against all Protestants. But the real problem for the Protestants rested not with Gallieni but with the dozens of commanders of posts, "all, or nearly all" of whom showed themselves to be in the Jesuit camp. Escande reported a case in which one commander had allowed five Protestants to be imprisoned for failing to become Catholic. Other local officials ordered all children under their jurisdiction to attend Catholic school.

Letters from Escande helped form the basis for an 1897 report published by the Société on "the religious troubles in Madagascar" that cataloged dozens of cases of manipulation, intimidation, condemnation, and even murder perpetrated by Jesuit priests and their collaborators, including French officials.[107] In one example, from the eastern edge of the Merina highlands, the report detailed how a Jesuit named Gardes and the regional commandant, Lieutenant-Colonel Borbal-Combret, had convinced the local population that all Protestants were enemies of France. On one occasion, the priest asked a local indigenous leader if it was true that he was Protestant. When the man answered in the affirmative, the priest had the man beaten until bloodied. The punishment not only left the man scarred; it convinced him to convert to Catholicism. The incident, the report asserted, was not isolated: with the help of the post sergeant, Gardes threatened the local schoolteacher with the same fate unless he converted; the following day, the teacher reportedly brought 150 students to the priest to join the Catholic school.[108]

On other occasions, Père Gardes proved more daring. He and a crowd of his followers tried to storm a Protestant church during Sunday services. He brazenly entered a Protestant school and, on the spot, persuaded 100 students to come to the Catholic school. He threatened to order local soldiers to haul away an indigenous pastor who refused to convert. Instead of facing this humiliation, the pastor left his village. In addition to intimidation, the Protestants said that Gardes also tried to play on Malagasy political allegiances. One Sunday he entered a Protestant church and announced, "I am French! Those who want to be French may follow me." Much to the Jesuit's dismay, an evangelist named Rainisoa responded, "And I too am French. You are a white Frenchmen, I am a Malagasy Frenchmen." Such a retort took extraordinary courage, the report noted. Gardes did not back down, turning to Borbal-Combret for support. The local commandant reportedly told villagers that "the only way to please France was to embrace Catholicism."[109]

While the vast bulk of the accusations made by the Protestants concerned priests and officials threatening or intimidating local Protestants, a few were far more serious, including even murder. In these cases, priests or officers were not directly implicated; rather, Protestants claimed the Catholics employed Malagasy intermediaries to carry out the violence. In April 1897, for example, two indigenous pastors, with a number of their followers, were shot at the gates of their villages. The pastors had been Christians for twenty years and were widely respected. No one knew who committed the crime, the Protestant report noted, but it suggested the involvement of a Malagasy governor who wanted everyone under his control to be Catholic.

One of Escande's reports implicated the Jesuits much more directly. According to him, one Malagasy governor had met with the Catholic bishop to discuss how best to destroy Protestantism in the region around Ambatomanga. After the meeting, the governor made a series of false accusations against local Protestant leaders and pastors and had them all shot. He then warned a Protestant schoolmaster that should he fail to convert, he would meet the same end. Within a matter of months, Escande wrote, a region that had been almost entirely Protestant converted to Catholicism.[110] Escande notified the governor-general of these outrages, but to no avail. On the one occasion that the government did launch an investigation, it determined that Escande's accusations were without merit, prompting the accused commander to file his own report on Escande. The French Protestant's "militant evangelists," the commandant claimed, "serve, under the pretext of religious tolerance, the hereditary hatred of the English against our colonial extension."[111]

The Protestant claims against the Jesuit mission were not simply a topic of internal reports at the Société des missions évangéliques; they soon made their way into print in both Madagascar and France. The Société's *Journal des Missions Évangéliques* regularly published letters from the colony depicting Jesuit abuses. In 1897, it ran letters from the Norwegian Protestant missionary Reverend Engh describing episodes similar to those reported by Escande. Engh wrote of Jesuit-organized bands of twenty to forty individuals who entered houses and abused residents. Those few who had "the courage to resist," wrote Engh, "tremble for their lives and wonder what will happen to their children." On one occasion, a Catholic priest announced publicly in a Protestant village that he would shoot, shackle, or confiscate the property of anyone who failed to become Catholic.[112] The French administration chose not to intervene, the Norwegian continued, out of fear of how the priest would react. But Engh also hinted at the "predicament" faced by administrators trying to investigate the conflict: "When we make one accusation, our adversaries invent ten false ones; when we produce two or three reliable witnesses, they depose twenty false ones. What can the government do, in such cases?"[113]

Mainstream newspapers in France, England, and Norway, not to mention publications in Madagascar, criticized the mistreatment of Protestants in the colony. Most articles, like a series that appeared in the Protestant publication *La Voix de la Montagne*, attacked the Jesuits for resorting to the cruelest methods—"from lies and calumny . . . to punches and poison"—to spread their domination.[114] Most played on fears that clericalism risked pulling the republic back into the mire of the Old Regime. One piece, for example, warned that the pope wanted "universal domination." The *ralliement* was a papal plot to extinguish the values dearest to republicanism; for "when the Church reigns," the article warned, "it is over slaves."[115] Turning to Madagascar, the article argued that Jesuits cared only for their own successes.

"Their order, that is their *patrie*," the article concluded, resorting to a common antimissionary adage, "the spirit of domination, that is their religion."[116]

Despite the mountain of documented cases of abuses compiled by French, English, and Norwegian Protestants, despite the aggressive articles that criticized official inaction, and despite the persuasive argument that the colony looked more like the France of Louis XIV than that of Jules Ferry, the colonial administration refused to get involved. In his first year in office, Gallieni expressed exasperation at the incessant bickering among religious workers, but he launched few serious investigations. When officials did look into affairs, they took as much notice of Protestant abuses as they did of Jesuit ones.

Until at least the summer of 1897, the administration had its hands full accomplishing its military objectives. Investigating internecine rivalries between French missionaries was a low priority, particularly when the vast bulk of accusations were made by Protestants whom many regional commandants associated with Merina and English influence. The lack of official interference was also a by-product of the administration's commitment to neutrality. In late 1896, for example, a Jesuit complained to Resident Alby in Antsirabe that an indigenous Protestant preacher had caused damage to Catholic property. The local priest made a report and demanded an investigation. Mgr. Cazet even went so far as to write to Gallieni about the "acts of persecution" historically committed by such "little tyrants."[117] But the resident did little to settle the case; a short investigation found that there was no proof of the priest's accusations and that further meddling might cause more serious strife between Catholics and Protestants. "I believe for my part," Alby wrote to Gallieni, "that moderation and patience are better means of calming such difficulties" than resorting to legal processes "absolutely unknown to the indigenous population."[118]

An abundance of administrative "patience," however, did not mean that there was not a certain amount of truth in the Protestants' accusations. Were the Jesuits murderers? Did they beat and abuse local inhabitants who failed to convert? The polemics of the moment made documentation unreliable. The fact that so many reports were filed from different regions by different European sources—Norwegians as well as French Protestants—strongly suggests that French Catholic missionaries and officials did actively encourage, and might have threatened, Malagasy to convert. As long as it did not cause social turmoil, the administration welcomed the Malagasy exodus from Protestantism to Catholicism as a sign of weakening support for the English and Merina. On a very few occasions, the administration did punish its officials for excesses. Gallieni ultimately removed Lieutenant-Colonel Borbal-Combret from his post for being essentially too pro-Catholic and for believing "false" accusations made against Protestants under his command.[119] Considering the political nature of religion in Madagascar, some Malagasy Catholics likely worked independently of missionaries to influence or even intimidate competitors or adversaries. But Protestants could certainly have used similar methods. Only when Europeans were the victims of violence or intimidation did the administration become more aggressive in its search for resolution.

One such opportunity came in May 1897, when Escande and another French pastor were murdered while touring Protestant establishments outside of Antananarivo.[120] The initial investigation into the murders determined that the crime had no political significance whatsoever but was committed by a band of brigands who had come to the local market day to steal taxes being collected by indigenous officials.[121] The investigation revealed the names of about fifteen assailants and considered the local population to be complicit in the affair for failing to warn the pastors of the attack. As retribution, the commandant proposed the complete destruction of the village where the murders occured (thirty-six houses, 150 inhabitants), the suppression of the local market, a fine of 10,000 francs on the district, and a criminal trial of suspects who, he was sure, would "sooner or later" be arrested.[122] The criminal tribunal swiftly condemned a number of indigenous found guilty of "complicity," sentencing six to death, and seven more to between two and twenty years in irons.[123]

The murder of the two pastors did not attract much attention in the non-Protestant French community. One administrator mentioned to Gallieni the "regrettable murder" of the two, but then called them "victims of their zeal and imprudence," suggesting they were partly responsible for their own deaths.[124] Gallieni concurred, noting that, had the pastors taken the most elementary precautions, they would never have been attacked. He faulted them for refusing the administrative assistance available to all French travelers, including letters of introduction, military protection, and advice about carrying arms. Far from a eulogy, Gallieni's report on Escande's death accused the missionary of hindering the French cause "by showing solidarity . . . with the members of the English mission."[125] In Mgr. Cazet's correspondence, the news of Escande's passing was relegated to a postscript. "One of [the murdered] is the famous Escande who wrote everything against us," he penned. "God did not want him to go on corroborating the lies of the famous Lauga."[126] Ironically, the only figure troubled by the murders was the pro-Catholic deputy de Mahy; he wrote a letter to the colonial minister warning that the Protestants would use the murders to criticize Gallieni's handling of religious affairs. His prediction proved accurate.[127]

Escande's death became a rallying point for Protestants. A few months after the murder, Gallieni received a letter from Escande's brother arguing that the missionary had been much hated by the Jesuits and was "the victim of an odious plot" against him—a position supported by the Société des missions évangéliques.[128] Gallieni turned the letter over to Commandant Schaeffer, who had conducted the initial investigation. Schaeffer rejected the claim of Escande's brother, stating that the "odious plot" existed only in his "overexcited imagination." Then he attacked the Protestant pastor for having appeared to be a "friend of the English" and warned Gallieni against allowing "a religious sect to use the two cadavers as arms of war against the adverse party."[129]

Schaeffer's response to the "odious murder plot" hypothesis reflected a broader shift in official attitudes toward dealing with the Protestant mission after mid-1897. Protestant missionaries continued to be embroiled in affairs that attracted the administration's attention. These cases differed little from earlier episodes allegedly involving Jesuits. One pastor, for example, was investigated for entering a Catholic church and yelling that "these men in black robes" knew only how to abuse the Malagasy. The local commandant decided to report the incident, as he did not think it coincided with Gallieni's ideal of proper behavior. Indeed, Gallieni wrote to Edmond Meyer, the new head of the Protestant mission, to point out that this sort of behavior "augments the difficulties of my task and compromises the success of the work of pacification."[130]

Gallieni also grew increasingly agitated by disputes over church property, considering them to be "certainly the most serious cause of religious troubles" in Madagascar. Because of the general shift from Protestantism to Catholicism in the early months of French rule, the majority of complaints came from Protestant pastors who often claimed foul play or legal technicalities in disputing the changing of ownership. Administrators particularly resented Protestant missionaries who brought forth claims as it often stirred up problems in otherwise tranquil regions.[131] In 1901, the administration decided to end the skirmishes and threw out the 27 March 1897 law, ruling that local populations would no longer be able to change their religious affiliations on demand.[132] While the measure minimized the amount of trouble Malagasies could cause, it did little to slow the Société's attack on either the Jesuits or the colonial administration.

In Defense of 1789

Starting in 1897, French Protestants renewed their efforts to defend their right to religious freedom in Madagascar by alluding not simply to the promises of republican colonialism but to the French revolutionary ideals of 1789. One of the first such publications came from the Société des missions évangéliques itself. At the height of *les Troubles*, the Société published *La Liberté religieuse à Madagascar*, a report based on the findings of Lauga and Kruger, the first delegation to the colony. Aimed at Protestants, as well as members of parliament and the press, the publication echoed many of the standard Protestant complaints.[133] With a healthy dose of republican rhetoric, the pamphlet had a more politically and historically sophisticated tone than the accusatory reports of Escande.

In the pamphlet, Lauga and Kruger condemned the Jesuits for perpetuating the formula *"Qui dit Français dit catholique; qui dit protestant dit Anglais"* because it reflected a mentality redolent of the seventeenth century, not the nineteenth.[134] "By exploiting passions unworthy of our century of liberty, of tolerance," *La Liberté* argued, the Jesuits had deprived Madagascar and France of "extremely precious progress." Here, the two authors took a page from anticlerical Freemasons: the Jesuits of Madagascar dreamed of making "a new Paraguay in which the immortal principles of 1789, that is the principles of justice and liberty, are substituted by the mortal principles of the *Syllabus*."[135] The Paraguay claim served the Protestants well in their effort to defuse the *"qui dit Français dit catholique"* myth. Far from patriots, they argued, Jesuits were traitors hiding beneath a "dishonest veil of patriotism" while actually working "for the profit of Rome."[136]

Lauga and Kruger's pamphlet presented a historical critique of Jesuits that distanced the Catholics from France, and placed the French Protestant mission squarely within the republican tradition. First, they protested that the Jesuits threatened the very "spirit and conscience of our liberal and republican France." To allow the state of Jesuit terror to continue, the two Protestants argued, would have signified that "religious liberty, that glorious conquest of the France of 1789," was but a "false lesson hiding the most shameful tyranny, that of consciences."[137] The argument effectively turned the *"qui dit Français"* formula on its head; according to Lauga and Kruger, to be true to its republican foundations, France had to protect the Protestants against the intimidation of the Jesuits. Such protection would ensure freedom of conscience not only for the French missionaries but also for their Malagasy adherents, now "French" in their own right. After all, the Protestants wrote, "it is the duty of our France to assure to all its subjects, whomever they be, the rights of man that it so well captures in its beautiful motto: *Liberté—Egalité—Fraternité*."[138] What else was the republican civilizing mission for?

Not all the defenses of the Protestant mission came from the Société. In *Madagascar et le Protestantisme français* (1897), Protestant commentator John Viénot also drew on republican history and the idea of *liberté* to break down the Jesuits' patriotic formula. In this booklet that quickly went through three editions, Viénot wrote a stinging indictment of the state of affairs in Madagascar. Stating that "liberal France will not accept [Jesuit behavior] without protestation," Viénot examined the historical veracity of the common "colonial principle" that "abroad, Catholicism is France."[139] He admitted that in the past, the dictum made sense when there was *"une foi, une loi, un roi,"* or "one faith, one law, one king"—again, referring to the monarchical past. But, "since then, the Revolution occurred; it proclaimed liberty of conscience, and from this great principle, henceforth unassailable, came the absolute neutrality of the State in religious matters. The modern State can no longer, *without being guilty of veritable treason*, champion one religion or one philosophy, neither abroad nor in France."[140] For Viénot, as for Lauga and Kruger, France abroad was not being true to the values of the Revolution—in fact, it was treasonous to support the Jesuits' cause in Madagascar.

Viénot's booklet concluded by linking Protestantism to another key tenet of French republican civilization: economic prosperity. He claimed that economists everywhere had noted that the "Protestant principle" was "an element of civilization of the first order." Catholicism, with its "logical rigor," weighed heavily on societies; Protestantism, by contrast, allowed for "free expansion." Now, he argued, the two religions were at war in Madagascar: "Will you let the Jesuitical principle triumph there, or do you want to work for the development of a colony that can become admirable and productive by favoring . . . the extension of the Protestant mission?"[141] Moving well beyond the *"qui dit Français"* formula, Viénot argued that the republican goal of civilizing—of developing the political, social, and economic potential of France's colony—was best served not by so-called French Catholics but by Protestants.

The following year, Mme. Escande, wife of the slain pastor, entered the chorus of Protestant protests by publishing both a book and an article in the *Journal des Missions Évangéliques*. Each publication tried to show how Madagascar had become, as she put it, "the touchstone of French Protestant patriotism."[142] Her article, in particular, built on the Protestants' new strategy of championing republican myth and ritual by recounting how the Protestants of Madagascar celebrated the "patriotic and religious cult" of the *14 juillet*.[143] On that special day in 1898, the students of the Protestant schools came together. After the singing of "The Marseillaise," the ceremony included a religious service and a patriotic lecture given by a pastor on the Revolution of 1789 and its impact on French Protestantism. The event, she noted, offered an opportunity to prove to the indigenous population that the Jesuits had lied when they had said that there were no Protestants in France. The Malagasies saw the Protestants celebrating the *14 juillet*, while the Jesuits, Escande was quick to point out, ignored it. "I very much hope," she concluded, "that it no longer will be said that we are not good Frenchmen or good patriots."[144]

Mme. Escande's article may well have been a response to an administrative inquiry made the previous year. In September 1897, Gallieni had received a report that a Protestant missionary who stood accused of publicly criticizing Jesuits had refused to teach his students "The Marseillaise." At that time, the head of the Protestant mission had told Gallieni that nonreligious songs were prohibited in their churches.[145] But in her article, Escande set out to dispel this notion. On the *14 juillet*, she led the students in song for her guests' benefit: "After the singing of the 'Marseillaise,' I presented our children to the Resident and expressed to him our vows in favor of the *mère-patrie*, the government of the Republic, and his person." They sang another song, "Le Drapeau de la France," and then exited. For Mme. Escande, the songs were more than music; they expressed the ideals that Protestants worked for—the triumph of French Revolutionary ideals in Madagascar. Her achievement also tried to rise above religious discord. The Malagasies that day, she wrote, were full of joy; they had given up the old national festival and had "fully adopted the *14 juillet* as their own holiday."[146] The Protestants had made their adherents love France.

In response to the Protestant campaign to break down the reactionary simplicity of *"qui dit Français,"* the Jesuits reasserted the old formula again and again. In 1897, Cazet published a letter in the *Missions Catholiques* in which he wrote that France seemed to have finally come to accept that "Catholics and Frenchmen are all one in Madagascar."[147] The same year, the Jesuit Père J. Brucker published a pamphlet responding to Lauga and Kruger that usurped the Protestants' title *La Liberté religieuse à Madagascar.* Brucker's pamphlet reiterated many of the old Jesuit standbys about the close ties between the French Protestants and their English colleagues, but with one original twist: he claimed that the English Protestants lured their French coreligionists to Madagascar in the hopes of inciting "a war" with the Jesuits.[148]

The bulk of Brucker's pamphlet was dedicated to establishing as historical truth that the French mission in Madagascar had always been the Catholic mission. Instead of the Protestant call to liberty and justice, those ideals of 1789, the Catholic author's theme of choice was sacrifice. The Jesuits, he argued, had long "suffered" at the hands of the English missions, which had "used and abused" their authority over the Malagasy government to hurt the French and the Catholics of the country. The English and Norwegians "forced" the Jesuits' followers to convert. But the Jesuits survived "the English religion" to be free to represent their church in the new colony.[149] Brucker closed with an appeal to the French Protestants: he did not wish to deny them the right to evangelize, but he refused to accept an enterprise directed "against France as well as Catholicism." They could not attack the Jesuits, for Catholic missionaries had made France honored and loved in Madagascar, had won many friends to the colonial cause, and rendered greater the future of the colony.[150]

In all these publications, *les Troubles* came to mirror domestic debates in fin de siècle France and were intensified by the heated imperial competition between France and Britain. These publications also show that the debates and conflicts in the colony were about more than simply proselytization, church buildings, and schools: they essentially set out to define the meaning of France and French patriotism abroad. The Protestant belief in justice and liberty and the Catholic concern with sacrifice, commitment, and tradition were colonial expressions of debates taking place in metropolitan France. Was France defined by its traditions, its history of kings and saints, its institutions like the military and the Catholic Church? Or was it the product of Enlightenment values, the Revolution, and the Rights of Man?

Civil War Abroad

In 1899, Gallieni announced that the "spirit of hostility" between Protestants and Catholics that had had such grave consequences for "the French cause" in Madagascar had started to wane.[151] There would be plenty of religious turmoil in the colony in the years that followed, including continued strife between Catholics and Protestants and debates over laicization—especially the replacement of missionary nurses and teachers with government employees. Officials in Madagascar congratulated themselves, believing that the policy of neutrality had finally carried the day, bringing *les Troubles* to an end. For French Protestants, however, the vigorous campaign to prove their commitment to the ideals of the Revolution and republic did not succeed in deflecting official suspicion at the turn of the century. There was still a need—as there had been in 1897 when the Société's instructions encouraged its missionaries to appear as French as possible—to prove their "ardent love of the *patrie*."[152]

If *les Troubles* were, as many of the Frenchmen thought, a war of words and deeds, then the Catholic mission was the side to emerge the least damaged. In trying to navigate the no-man's-land between the Jesuits and the English missions, French Protestants experienced a serious shortage of funds by 1900. Financial difficulties forced the French Protestants to return their schools to the English Protestants. The move raised eyebrows. In 1901, General Pannequin, acting as interim governor-general, saw the returning of schools to the English as a sign that French Protestants had never been committed to teaching French or providing professional training; rather, he believed they had always shown themselves primarily devoted to "religious education." Disappointed, Pannequin wrote to the colonial minister that he was equally disturbed that the French Protestants continued to talk about "our brothers from London" and "our English brothers." Should the colony wish that French be taught and that the LMS be kept in check, Pannequin advised opening more secular schools funded and run by the state.[153]

By contrast, Pannequin gave a glowing review of the Catholic missions, especially the Frères des écoles chrétiennes. The Frères were "a precious auxiliary" for the government. "Without doubt their method of teaching reserves a large part to religious education," he wrote, "but the Frères take equal care to give the students truly French instruction." Pannequin was so pleased with the "very satisfying results" that he took money from the local budget to open another school in Ambositra run by three *frères*. The French Protestants were incensed. But Pannequin held firm: the Protestants, after all, had little say in the matter, having abandoned their schools to the English. The general, who expressed an opinion held by many military officials, congratulated Catholic workers across the island for spreading civilization and assisting in the colonizing process. Catholic workers, he concluded, had helped "render our domination durable and profound."[154]

Against the backdrop of the previous five years of acrimony, Pannequin's report read like a scorecard. According to the general, the French Protestants disappointed the administration, lost territory to the English, and refused to fulfill one of Gallieni's central requests of all missions, to teach the local population to speak French. They were more concerned with spreading a love of God than with spreading a love of France; indeed, their attitudes toward France were questionable because they seemed to prefer the company of their brothers, the English. The Catholics, on the other hand, were useful to the colony, as they taught, civilized, and won their adherents over to French domination. Even their meddling with administrative business was little cause for concern. Their work was, to quote Pannequin, *truly French*. Though the general did not say it, his opinion gave merit to the oft-quoted phrase *"qui dit Français dit catholique, qui dit protestant dit Anglais."*

The continued difficulties and suspicion that the French Protestant mission endured in Madagascar are remarkable when compared with events in France at this time. The widely held Protestant conviction that France was built on the revolutionary values of liberty, equality, and justice—and not on the corrupt traditions and retrograde institutions of the ancien régime—directly corresponded to the dominant republican ideology at the turn of the century, especially during the Dreyfus affair. In France, radical republicans equipped with these same ideals were on the verge of taking power in 1901, under the leadership of Émile Combes, the most notorious in a line of anticlerical prime ministers. The 1901 Law on Associations enabled radicals to close down dozens of Catholic organizations in France. On the diplomatic front, the Fashoda crisis had come to an end, and the Dreyfusard republicans in power were eager to strengthen ties with Britain.[155] Yet in that very same year an official report from the chief administrator of the Third Republic in Madagascar questioned Protestant allegiance to France and hailed Catholic missionaries for helping to make French rule "durable and profound."

"Abroad," Le Myre de Vilers had asserted, "Catholicism is France." The campaigns of vocal anticlerical radicals and Freemasons in Indochina, Polynesia, and elsewhere in the 1890s and 1900s made certain that, for many Frenchmen at home and overseas, France was *anything but* Catholicism. But in the case of Madagascar, Le Myre de Vilers's phrase evoked a certain truth. Nowhere in the French colonial world was religion, and especially Christianity, more closely linked to indigenous politics than in Madagascar. To the Malagasy peoples, religion was, to return to Stephen Ellis's adage, the ritual form of government. Decades before the French invasion, the Merina government had enjoyed political and religious ties with Britain and its Protestant missionaries. To be a religious dissident in Malagasy society was to be Catholic; the natural correlation in the political realm was to be pro-French. For Malagasy politics and society, the opposition of French Catholicism and English Protestantism was deeply entrenched.

The arrival of French Protestant missionaries in 1896 complicated these distinctions; but their presence was never enough to dispel the truism of *"qui dit Français."* The French Protestants' defense of foreign missionaries—especially the dreaded "English agents"—seemed only to reconfirm their willingness to destabilized French colonial control. Their tirades against Jesuit violence—while, at times, undoubtedly justified—fell all too easily into place. In attacking the Catholics, who for decades had been the most substantial representatives of France on the island, the French Protestants perpetuated the appearance of their own treachery.

Nonetheless, the alliance of colonial officials and Jesuits was no match made in heaven. Many officials sided with Catholic missionaries in spite of their anticlerical instincts. Gallieni, who was personally no supporter of Catholic missionaries, remained neutral on the religious question because it was expedient to the tasks of quelling rebellion and establishing power. In Madagascar what tipped the balance in favor of the Jesuits was the large percentage of military officials on the island in the years of the "pacification." The military, which traditionally identified with the Catholic Church, warmly greeted an alliance with Jesuit missionaries knowledgeable of the mores and language of the new possession. French soldiers, often Anglophobic, would also have been particularly suspicious of the seemingly pro-English French Protestants in these years when imperial competition between the two nations came to a head. Considering the long-standing connection between religion and politics in Madagascar, French officials—republicans and military alike—saw conversion to Catholicism as a clear measure of how willing the Malagasy were to shed their ties to England and accept French rule.

Officials' fear of Protestantism in Madagascar, however, can be pushed beyond concerns over English plotting. From the moment of their arrival in 1896, French Protestant missionaries invoked the language of revolutionary republicanism. Rather than dispel official suspicion of an alliance with their English coreligionists, French Protestant rhetoric made matters worse. After the fall of the Merina, officials not only considered the English to be anti-French but also suspected them of promoting Malagasy independence. At the turn of the century, the administration became increasingly concerned about French Protestant missionaries' relationships with their parishioners. The colonial regime closely monitored the Protestants' accounts of their interaction with their congregations. In one report, Gallieni worried that French Protestants considered themselves the "natural protectors of the indigenous"—that is, defenders of indigenous society against what the Protestants called the "economic exploitation" by the "whites."[156]

Unlike Catholics, Protestants fostered the careers of indigenous pastors. Powerful and prestigious, these pastors challenged the racial balance of power—both between different ethnic groups and between the Malagasy and the French. In both cases, officials worried that the French Protestants were trying to undermine or circumvent the system of colonial control that

Figure 6.1.   Indigenous Protestant preachers and deacons. In the eyes of French officials, they were the feared auxiliaries of the London Missionary Society. (Reproduced from London Missionary Society/Council for World Mission Archives.)

the pacification had accomplished. Working for a more equitable political and economic balance between the Malagasy and the government was—in the eyes of officials—tantamount to sabotage. While the Protestants' adoration of liberty and justice put them on the side of the republican government in France, the same rhetoric was potentially subversive when taught to the indigenous population of the republican colony. Beneath the banner of "liberty, equality, and fraternity" that republicans carried to the empire was a host of exceptions and restrictions written in very fine print.[157]

By favoring the Catholic mission, republican officials again revealed the extent to which they were willing to sacrifice their own ideals of civilization. Gallieni transformed the colonial civilizing mission to coincide with the larger project of pacification, a melding of military operations with projects to conquer the Malagasy morally, socially, and politically. In defending their position in the colony, French Protestants presented a far more *republican* vision of civilization than the administration could accept. Protestant writers called on France to bring *liberté* not simply to French missionaries but to the Malagasy as well. Using metaphors straight out of the Revolution—not to mention many French republican schoolbooks—religious freedom in Madagascar was about freeing the people from tyranny.

Inherent to this freedom was a need for true justice, which included treating all French subjects—whether from France or the colonial world—equally.

In their wish to solidify their rule, officials exchanged their own ideals for the simple language of nationalism—and no one spoke it more fluently (if perhaps disingenuously) than Mgr. Cazet and the Catholics of Madagascar. A love of France uncomplicated by relations with English coreligionists was, in the wake of the Madagascar campaign, more valuable to colonial officials than even the most deep-seated republican beliefs. The price—and not the dividend—of colonialism in Madagascar was French republican civilization.

Finally, *les Troubles* in Madagascar suggest that, despite the anticlerical crusade in metropolitan France, Catholicism was still a defining feature of French national identity. Evidence of this can be found both in France and in the colony. In 1893, François de Mahy had little difficulty convincing the staunchly republican Chamber of Deputies of the existence of a far-fetched Protestant plot to weaken the French empire. And in Madagascar, colonial officials continually associated Catholic missionary work with "truly French" ideas, hopes, and beliefs—a connection that evoked more than it explained. While the familiar slogan did not ring true in all the colonies, in the first years of French rule in Madagascar, Catholicism was France.

The towering challenges of colonialism did not always minimize political and religious conflicts among French interests. In the face of violent opposition and a daunting task of establishing a presence in the country—that is, at the very moment when the French most needed harmony among their own—French Protestants and Jesuits had no qualms about denouncing one another in the most vicious manner. Such was not always the case: in Indochina, for example, struggles between missionaries and anticlerical Freemason colonists flourished most in the 1890s, *after* French colonial rule had achieved a certain degree of stability and organized opposition had been greatly (if temporarily) weakened. The prevalence of "violence" and "terror" as words of denunciation in Madagascar, coupled with the importance of "liberty" and "justice" in debates between Protestants and Jesuits, hints that Frenchmen found it easier to turn on one another than to face the ethical pitfalls of conquest. Pacification may have defeated Malagasy rebellions, but it did little to quell the disagreements of those who triumphed.

How British Protestants Helped
Save French Catholicism

It is well you should remember that all these persecutions are winked at, if not encouraged, by the French authorities, notwithstanding their professed "Liberté, Egalité, et Fraternité." This arises from their hatred of English Protestantism and English missionaries, or perhaps I might say their hatred of England and all that is English.
—The Reverend B. Briggs, Antananarivo, 1897

From the beginning of the French invasion of Madagascar, workers from the London Missionary Society complained about the anti-English and specifically anti-LMS atmosphere that became a part of their everyday lives. Conversations and correspondence with officials filled British Protestants with emotions running from frustration to dread. One missionary in Ambohimandrosa complained that the local French resident had repeatedly told him that the LMS was "hated by France" and that the organization should hand over its work to Norwegians (who, in the French official mind, had no imperial intentions).[1] Even the ardently neutral Governor-General Gallieni gave LMS workers the impression that he considered them "disaffected and disloyal" to colonial rule.[2] "We have been working for our Master," wrote one missionary, "but we have been loyally serving Caesar too, and unfortunately for us Caesar can recognize no loyalty in an English protestant missionary."[3] It was clear from the start that the administration's preference was that the LMS pack up and go home—and this was a sentiment slow to fade.

Just months after the French arrived, with the countryside unsettled and a French-British imperial rivalry nearing a crisis, it seemed very possible that the LMS's white evangelists would be forced out of the new colony. Letter after letter from missionaries documented their uncertainty, anxiety, and sorrow. For Pastor J. Richardson, the turn of events brought about by colonization was so devastating that he asked to be reassigned to another country, finding it impossible to continue if the government ordered him to work under the direction of French Protestants. He had nothing against his French coreligionists, he insisted, but he simply could not bring himself to hand over all he had worked to build. In early 1897, he signed his letter of resignation to his superiors in London "with profound regret at having to leave my life's work."[4]

Truth be told, many LMS missionaries were, if not enemies, then certainly staunch critics of the French "pacification" effort. Many were no doubt patriots who saw the French as national adversaries, not allies, and were moved by reports of diplomatic tensions escalating between the two imperial powers over Egypt. For more immediate reasons, like Protestants of all nationalities in Madagascar, they were horrified by the administration's refusal to deal with what one Englishman termed the "rascality" of "unscrupulous Jesuit priests."[5] LMS missionaries complained to their superiors, supporters, and government about the meddling of the Catholic missions, especially the Jesuit tactic of intimidating indigenous Protestants. Corroborating the claims of Benjamin Escande and other French Protestants, LMS workers reported instances of Jesuit terror that ranged from the manipulative to the brutal. One LMS pastor described Catholics who baptized groups of children en masse and then told parents that any child who returned to Protestantism would become a leper.[6] Another letter noted that "the Natives have experienced the power of the arm of France, and they still tremble with fear at the uplifting of that arm"; the Jesuits had left communities "panic stricken." Unfortunately, this report lamented, the "evil" had paid off, driving Protestants to Catholicism out of fear. "The devil himself," the author concluded, "not infrequently scores a victory."[7]

The LMS's odium for all methods Jesuit devolved into resentment toward the French colonial government. The French failure to deal with the Jesuits and bring stability to the countryside convinced the English that the French lacked the necessary experience as colonizers—a belief that also corresponded to British criticisms of France's actions elsewhere in Africa.[8] "There can be little doubt," wrote one missionary shortly after the invasion, "that the French Protectorate is a dreadful fiasco at the present time."[9] Even worse than administrative ineptitude, the double standard applied to Englishmen caused deep frustration. Catholic priests could lie or deceive without fear of official retribution, complained one LMS pastor in a letter to London, "whereas the Protestant missionary is accused of saying things which only a madman would have the foolishness to say, and what is worse such statements are believed by many of the Anglophobist [sic] officers."[10] Whether incompetence or national rivalry fueled French antagonisms, English missionaries felt they understood the government's aim. "One thing is clear," penned an LMS worker named C. Jukes, "the French intend getting rid of us at no distant date, and the Directors have better be prepared, for the time may come sooner than expected."[11]

The Reverend Jukes was partially right. The time did come when it looked like the French would "get rid" of the LMS, but it was later than one might have expected. The conflict between Protestants and Catholics that erupted in the wake of the French invasion faded within a few years. Reflecting on the previous decade, an LMS report from 1900 noted hopefully that the "persecution" of British Protestants by the Jesuits and French officials was a thing of the past. The following year, another report from the island welcomed the "changed attitude of the authorities" toward LMS missionaries; both publicly and privately, officials had finally given them "full liberty" to work.[12] With the Jesuits in check and French administrative authority established, it seemed that Gallieni's promise of neutrality had finally come to fruition.

In the early 1900s, the climate in Madagascar changed, though for missionaries of the LMS, it was not for the better. The battles with the Jesuits had calmed, and the culture war in France over the separation of Church and state had started to cool. Having recalled their troops from Fashoda in 1898, the French had backed down on British influence in Egypt. The two imperial foes had set out to rebuild relations, finalizing in 1904 a set of agreements known as the Entente Cordiale on a host of colonial and diplomatic issues.

Nonetheless, British missionaries' problems with the colonial administration in Madagascar were just beginning. In late 1905, the arrival of the new governor-general, Victor Augagneur, brought a renewal of official efforts to end missionary influence on the island. Although Augagneur was blunt and boastful about his anticlericalism and his dislike of missions, his methods at undermining their influence were crafty. Relying largely on laws established during Gallieni's time, Augagneur invoked the administration's discretionary power in new and—for the missions—debilitating ways. While Gallieni emphasized neutrality, most of his regulations dealing with the missions, no matter how clearly stated on paper, required the governor-general's final consent. Augagneur wielded this consent like an ax, refusing to allow missions to develop even the most basic projects. He denied requests to build new or even repair existing churches and prohibited even the tiniest of religious gatherings in private homes. New regulations of his own fashioning indirectly helped break the missions' hold on education.

The LMS, more than any other missionary organization working in the colony (including French Catholics, who remained surprisingly quiet throughout), protested Augagneur's handiwork. It denounced his policies in the same terms that French colonizers had described many retrograde indigenous political systems: they were arbitrary, irrational, and not grounded in law. The policies certainly did not, in British opinion, befit any power that pretended to be civilized. The LMS's campaign to end the disadvantageous regulation of their evangelizing efforts pushed the missionary issue to the center of the international diplomatic stage. Three decades of bickering between critics and proponents of the Catholic missions in France had failed to settle the question of missionary rights in the empire. Instead, it was diplomats and lawmakers from across the Channel—defending the rights of British citizens to work in French possessions—who forced officials in Paris to decide, once and for all, whether anticlericalism was an article for export.

"Protestantism—There Is the Danger!"

In the first years of the twentieth century, with the tumult of "pacification" behind them, all missionaries had reason to believe that the colonial government would ease its regulation of evangelizing. The violent rebellions witnessed in the wake of the French invasion had become far less frequent. The regime enjoyed a measure of administrative stability and control over much of the countryside. Governor-General Gallieni, both in public and in private, acknowledged the contribution of missionary schools—Protestant as well as Catholic. Even British Protestant missionaries responded to the government's goodwill in kind. Rather than fight orders that all missionary teachers speak French, the Englishmen took to studying the language. A sign of their acceptance of a new colonial order, a photo from 1900 of an LMS classroom in Antananarivo shows "*Vive la République*" painted in large letters on the wall above the students' desks. The LMS, however, still defied the strict secularism of republican pedagogy by painting another slogan on the wall: "*Rien sans dieu*"—nothing without God.[13]

The government continued its legislative hold on religious life. In June 1901, for example, Gallieni decreed that no new religious building could be opened without the governor-general's approval. He added, however, that, after a proper inquiry, authorization would be given. The same decision also restated an 1897 rule that deemed all church property to be the property of the colony, and that no religious rituals could take place outside of a church. A masterpiece of mixed messages, the 1901 *arrêté* was of unclear significance to many missionaries, especially since Gallieni claimed privately that it was simply a measure of public security not meant to limit evangelizing. Should his word not suffice, Gallieni put it in writing, reasserting his commitment to religious neutrality and stating that all requests to build new churches should be granted.[14] Missionaries, it seemed, were at absolute liberty to do what they pleased, as long as they got government permission first.

While the administration's exact motivation for making new laws remained unclear, the new decrees came on the heels of the 1901 Law on Associations. This law, which shut down dozens of unauthorized religious organizations in France, was not directly applied to the colonies. Abroad, religious organizations were not required to attain special authorization to operate. But the law still caused considerable concern for many French missionaries, especially the unauthorized and always controversial Jesuits in Madagascar. When Bishop Jean-Baptiste Cazet worried aloud in his correspondence "Where will the hatred of religion stop?" he clearly was wondering

Figure 7.1. Assembly of students and teachers in the London Missionary Society high school, Antananarivo. (Reproduced from London Missionary Society/Council for World Mission Archives.)

if anticlerical laws would spill outside the borders of France.[15] With the 1901 law looming, Gallieni took the opportunity to pull the noose of missionary regulation a little tighter. Concern on the part of the Catholic missions was palpable; in the wake of the Law on Associations, Catholic missionaries maintained a low profile, avoiding all interaction with the administration whenever possible. Even future decrees that limited the Catholic missions' ability to open schools met more often with shaking heads and knitted brows than with written complaints or public statements of outrage. Having gained a tremendous number of new Catholics in the years following the French invasion, the Catholic missions laid low.

British Protestants were in a different position. The Law on Associations was not a threat to British Protestants, but Gallieni's new regulations were. Always sensitive to issues of neutrality, many at the LMS feared that Gallieni's decisions would leave important religious policies to the whims of local French officials or Malagasy administration. They, after all, would conduct the initial inquiries to determine whether a request to build a church would win the governor-general's authorization. Missionaries viewed the governor-general's promise that all requests would end in approval with skepticism. At best, the system meant delays and uncertainties in building; at worst, officials hostile to either evangelization or British interlopers (a distinct possibility, according to LMS representatives) could deem a request unnecessary, essentially rejecting it outright. Limitations on religious meetings put what the LMS considered to be undue restrictions on "native" converts' ability to hold private prayer meetings and officiate at ceremonies such as funerals, weddings, and births. While Gallieni claimed that the government would stay true to religious neutrality, the LMS saw it differently: the first years of colonialism had placed missionary work firmly under what some called "the absolute rule" of local officials.[16]

The LMS's fears were not misplaced. By 1906, the installation of Governor-General Augagneur had ushered in a new era of heated relations between the missions and the colonial government. Augagneur faced a tremendous challenge replacing Gallieni, whose strong leadership style had won him fame as the "king without a crown" of France's newest colony. But the new governor-general assumed his position with unflagging confidence. Augagneur was a doctor by training, a deputy from the Rhône, an ardent Freemason, an outspoken anticleric, and the first socialist governor in the French empire. His appointment to the post of governor-general came just a few days after the December 1905 passage of the law separating Church and state in France, and part of his agenda was to reassess the place of religion in the colony. As historian Jérôme Braquet points out, Augagneur would have liked nothing better than to steer the people of Madagascar away from the missions and toward atheism.[17]

Augagneur did nothing to hide his dislike of missionaries, particularly English Protestant ones. He often explained his attitudes toward missionaries in terms of simple colonial policy: in his opinion, no one—neither missionary nor any other individual—should have stood between the indigenous population and the colonial regime. In newspaper interviews, Augagneur readily showed himself to be bombastic and ideological. In a 1907 article tellingly entitled "Le Protestantisme, voilà le danger!" the newspaper *Le Matin* quoted him as saying, "For my part, I have always considered Gambetta's famous phrase: 'Anticlericalism is not an item for export,' as a solemn and monumental blunder." He continued that, since being in Madagascar, he had not been anticlerical in a "radical" way; rather, he had been—and wanted always to be—"a frankly laic governor." He was determined, he added, to treat English Protestants and French Catholics as if they were no different from merchants of cotton or purveyors of whiskey.[18]

Augagneur liked to think that an important distinction between his and other anticlerical officials' attitudes was his disdain for Protestants. In the governor-general's opinion, supporters of laicization often embraced Protestants' anticlericalism and even worked to replace Catholics with Protestant missionaries in the empire. Knowing his anticlerical leanings, Protestant workers in Madagascar initially welcomed him, believing his regime would show none of the preference for Catholic missionaries of his predecessors. But when

Augagneur did not favor Protestant workers, he recounted, they considered the "equality of treatment as a persecution." Despite his vehement denials, his distrust of Protestants in the empire was clearly linked to their predominantly British nationality. He was quick to point out that of the 210 Protestant missionaries in Madagascar, only 31 were French (the rest were British, Norwegian, or American); "all these Anglo-Saxon Protestants," he said, had contempt for the "immoral and irreligious Latins" from France. The governor-general found it unthinkable to allow such Protestants to teach the indigenous, for they would form in them "a mentality forever incomprehensible to our own."[19]

Even more worrisome to Augagneur than Anglo-Saxon contempt for Latin decadence were indigenous pastors who, already powerful, represented what the governor-general candidly called "a danger for French authority."[20] In 1908, a British representative of the Friends' Foreign Mission Association in Madagascar met with Augagneur and made a record of their conversation.[21] Augagneur's blunt responses to the missionary's questions reveal how the governor-general's approach to religious matters lacked Gallieni's characteristic diplomacy. Augagneur did not hesitate to finger "native pastors" as posing the greatest trouble to the colony; committed to what he called a "passive rebellion," these pastors encouraged congregations to refuse to pay taxes and generally undermined French influence. At this stage in the conversation, the missionary interjected, insisting that Christians made the best subjects. Augagneur reportedly retorted:

> Oh, as for that, there is no difference between them. The heathen tribes are as loyal as the Christians. But the difference lies in the fact that here in the central parts [of Madagascar] there are bodies of natives whose intelligence has been developed, and who are imbued with ideas tending towards resistance to our rule. Now I am determined to limit this sort of thing. For instance, *I would never allow churches to be formed amongst the Sakalava, under native pastors!* Europeans—ah!! that is quite different. I do not use the word *Frenchmen*, for I am not a nationalist in that sense of the word. A *European* pastor I do not object to. They have the European mind and way of looking at things. But Natives! that is altogether different![22]

When the missionary tried to convince Augagneur that he was mistaken in his views, the governor-general said he had "heaps of reports" to back him up. Many of these reports were penned by the very military officers who had questioned Protestant allegiance to the French during the troublesome years of the pacification. One 1907 report from the commandant in Fort Dauphin, for example, said that indigenous Protestant preachers "served foreigners" and, as a result, showed themselves to be "little devoted to the French cause." Echoing the formula "*qui dit Français dit catholique*," the commandant added that the indigenous population in his region associated the *vazaha* (whites) with the English, and the English with being "enemies of the French."[23] Augagneur may or may not have been a "nationalist" when it came to dealing with missionaries (though his actions certainly made the claim seem disingenuous). But for many of his officers across the colony, old rivalries died hard.

Subtle Forms of Persecution

If Protestant missionaries remained uncertain whether Augagneur disliked them or the idea of indigenous preachers more, they agreed on one thing: within a year of his arrival, the governor-general's measures had significantly undermined their work. In November 1906, by *arrêté*, Augagneur revised the colony's policy on missionary education in a number of ways that, in the words of one Norwegian missionary, ruined nearly every mission school.[24] First, Augagneur decreed that no building erected to fulfill a religious function could be used as a school. For the hundreds of church schools built in small villages and rural areas across the colony, the ruling spelled disaster. Initially constructed so local pastors could offer services on Sunday and teach school during the week, many churches were now ordered to construct separate buildings for spiritual and intellectual pursuits. Since the decree was issued in the wet season (when construction was difficult) and allowed only two months for compliance, most church schools had little choice but to shut their doors. The LMS complained that some local administrators took the opportunity to shut down church schools entirely, allowing them to function neither as churches nor as schools. The new rules were a "crushing blow."[25]

Augagneur's regulations did not stop there. He required all missionaries who ran private schools to be certified as morally upstanding. Non-Frenchmen had to prove their fluency in the French language. The *arrêté* regulated a minimum distance of six kilometers between schools, effectively closing any religious school located near an official one. With a few strokes of a pen, Augagneur closed, according to a number of estimates, about half of the Protestant schools in Madagascar. Some districts were devastated: one lost 20 of 23 mission schools; another, 27 of 33. The number of students in Protestant schools in one region dropped from more than 1,000 to 155.[26] Overall, French Protestant schools lost well over half of their 15,000 students between 1906 and 1907.[27]

For schools that weathered this onslaught of regulations, Augagneur further undermined them by decreeing that only students who had spent four years in official schools could win government jobs. A 1908 report on the LMS's Boys' High School at Ambatonakanga, in Antananarivo, outlined how Augagneur's policies had "made it impossible to retain the large number of scholars" the school enjoyed in the years prior to 1905. In addition to being banned from government jobs, mission students were also barred from sitting any official examinations, such as the entrance exams to medical or administrative schools. The law stripped mission schools of their best students, leaving only those with, in the words of one French Protestant, "no precise goals" in life.[28] The only official examination left open to mission students was for a teacher's certificate, but even this avenue was hindered by official intervention. In the years preceding 1905, 65 to 70 percent of the pupils at the Boys' High School who took the teaching exam passed it. Since Augagneur's arrival, each year had brought a higher percentage of failures, until 1908, when every student failed—a fate experienced by students from nearly all the mission schools on the island. With little hope of competing with official schools, the LMS considered retooling some of its most successful schools to prepare students for manual labor or work in commerce.[29] Many missionaries firmly believed their schools offered a superior education to official schools, but they had to admit that, by limiting the prospects of church school graduates, Augagneur had made the Protestants a far less attractive option.

What infuriated Protestants even more was that the government did not have enough schools to compensate for the students the churches lost. Many complained that Augagneur sacrificed a central tenet of republican civilizing ideology—education—in order to pursue his campaign against missionaries. The criticism had merit. Like Governor-General Klobukowski in Indochina, Augagneur pushed to expand the building of official schools while isolating the missions. But unlike his compatriot in Hanoi, Augagneur did not simply leave the mission schools alone; he actively worked to close their doors. With the closing of so many religious schools, by early 1909, the nearly 500 official schools had surpassed the 353 religious schools on the island. But, overall, it was a net loss, as the countryside had been stripped of more than a hundred private secondary schools and a thousand nursery schools.[30] If the number of schools, religious as well as secular, was the measure of French civilization in Madagascar, Augagneur's new rules represented a significant step back. For the governor-general, however, religious education was no sign of progress.

In addition to undermining missions' influence over schools, Augagneur's decrees rewrote the rules regulating public meetings. Under Gallieni, up to twenty-five indigenous men could hold meetings without government authorization. But, shortly after arriving, Augagneur prohibited all unauthorized gatherings, including religious meetings in private homes. New rules defined what constituted a "meeting" with razor-sharp precision. Families could hold prayers or practice rituals alone, but as soon as two neighbors joined them, the gathering became, by definition, a public meeting. Enforcement was left to the discretion of local administrators. In some officials' reading of the decree, if an indigenous preacher in a rural area helped teach an illiterate farmer to read, then it could constitute an unauthorized public religious meeting.[31]

In the years that followed Augagneur's *arrêtés*, complaints poured into the London headquarters of the LMS from Protestant evangelists working in Madagascar. Missionaries and indigenous Protestants alike reported a new atmosphere of spying, intimidation, and retribution. With indigenous and French officials suspicious of all Protestant activities, missionaries were left without any way of confronting their persecutors. In early 1908, Rev. J. C. Thorne told his superiors in London that he had decided against filing a complaint with the administration for fear that it "might bring trouble on the natives who had given us information."[32] A letter from an evangelist named James Sharman offered details of what "trouble" meant. One "native tutor" was reprimanded by French officials for saying, in a sermon on the Resurrection, "that the Kingdom of God would yet overcome all obstacles and conquer the whole world." Another preacher was told not to read certain passages of Isaiah. Cases such as these resulted in accusations that the indigenous pastors involved were fomenting rebellion. "There is thus," concluded Sharman, "a regular system of espionage going on."[33] Indigenous pastors were not the only ones spied on. Another LMS worker reported that a "native soldier in plain clothes" had attended his religious meetings in order to report the group's activities to the authorities. He concluded: "No wonder the people are afraid!"[34]

LMS missionaries compiled lists of "hindrances" that Protestants experienced at the hands of French officials. These included delays teachers faced in getting authorization for their schools, orders to cease building schools and churches already under construction before Augagneur's decrees were announced, and statements of "opposition and discouragement," as well as "indirect attacks" made by officials.[35] One pastor deemed the system of authorizing church building and repair to be a "farce" open to the random abuse of the officials involved.[36] In a response to a request to build a church serving a particularly remote rural area, Augagneur wrote that the populations in question were "situated at less than two hours' walk from villages already possessing religious edifices."[37] A four-hour round trip walk to Sunday services, the governor-general apparently believed, was short enough.

The spirit of conflict with the Protestant missions that Augagneur fostered in Madagascar was slow to fade. By 1911, with his replacement, Governor-General Picquié, in office, Augagneur's policies had solidified into accepted practice. Despite early hope that the colony's new chief would usher in an era of amicable relations, the LMS soon realized it would continue to suffer what one of its missionaries labeled "the most subtle forms of persecution" in the history of the Malagasy mission. These desperate words came in the wake of new government investigations that threatened to close every organization—from Bible societies to Sunday School unions—linked to the Protestant churches. "If this is the law by which we are to be governed," warned one LMS missionary, "then our work is doomed." The missionary continued: "We ask for no favours, but simply religious liberty, such as is enjoyed in France, and granted by all other civilized nations to their colonies."[38] If France would not give this liberty willingly, then the Protestant missions would have to rely on higher authorities.

The Uses of Diplomacy

In Augagneur's era, colonial governors-general answered to the colonial minister. But shortly after he arrived, and for nearly a decade to come, Augagneur's policies generated considerable concern at the Quai d'Orsay, the foreign ministry. Augagneur, like many of his superiors in Paris, believed that colonial policy was not an issue open to international discussion; rather, as an extension of France abroad, the empire was a place of purely domestic concern. Foreign powers had no more right to critique colonial policy than France's metropolitan laws. Nonetheless, a number of foreign governments took issue with the rules in Madagascar on the basis that their nationals did not receive the same treatment in the colony as they would in France. The republic's foggy vision of where missionaries fit in the empire became an issue that foreign diplomats increasingly wanted clarified.

In June 1907, Henry White, the United States' ambassador in Paris, wrote to the French foreign minister at the Quai d'Orsay to express his concern about the mistreatment of the United Norwegian Lutheran Church of America's mission at the hands of the colonial government of Madagascar. Ambassador White's letter reiterated complaints made by representatives of the mission that Augagneur's policies had blocked the mission from purchasing property in the colony and building churches in rural areas. White admitted to not knowing all the details but asserted that, if true, the policy was "certainly contrary to the spirit, if not the terms" of the Treaty of 1853 that allowed American subjects to own property in France, as well as Frenchmen to own property in the United States. This treaty, White assumed, extended to the French possessions, "as the law of other civilized nations permits in like circumstances."[39] The foreign minister passed the letter on to the colonial minister asking for information. The latter curtly responded that the Lutherans had not asked to buy property, but rather had requested a concession of land. This concession was denied, the colonial minister continued, as were the requests to build new churches, because the inhabitants of the region in question were clearly hostile to "religious ideas"—they had torched a church in 1904—and would have looked askance at new religious buildings. The minister added, however, that he would ask Augagneur for a report, if necessary. In the margin, next to this offer, someone at the Quai d'Orsay—likely the minister himself—penciled a simple "*Oui.*"[40]

Governor-General Augagneur's report was slow in coming. He was busy traveling in France, granting interviews to newspapers, including *Le Matin*, which ran "Le Protestantisme—Voilà le danger!" that same summer. The trip was made in large part to defend his hostile approach to the Madagascar missions, which had drawn criticism in France even among some of Augagneur's staunchest allies. In addition to granting interviews, he gave a speech to the Freemasons of the Grand Orient de France and met with radical politicians. Though generally not friends of religious proselytization, these allies were both confused by Augagneur's attack on Protestants, who were commonly seen as supporters of laïcité in France, and concerned that his harsh policies were turning many Protestant Malagasies against colonial rule. Augagneur's visit was, nonetheless, a success, convincing many of his dubious friends at the lodge and in government of the successes of his policies.[41]

The publicity his visit created could not have been welcomed at the Quai d'Orsay, where French diplomats were still concerned about sustaining good relations with Britain. Within a month of the publication of Le Matin's interview, the French embassy in London forwarded a report generated by the Foreign Office in London expressing concern that the various British missions working in Madagascar were not "tolerated" as in the days of Gallieni but were increasingly dealt with in what the British government deemed "an unfriendly spirit." The Foreign Office's report outlined the litany of complaints by British missionaries—restrictions on building and maintaining churches, restrictions on religious meetings, restrictions on job opportunities for church-school students—all of which exposed the colonial government's bias against the missions. By closing mission schools, the Foreign Office suggested, the colony was endangering itself; unable to replace Protestant schools with official ones, the French authorities threatened to push the "extremely superstitious" population back to "barbarism." The report ended with the expectation that the French would deal with the situation "in a spirit of equity and justice."[42]

The concerns of the British government garnered no quick response from the Quai d'Orsay. Months passed, and the French ambassador in London wrote again, warning his colleagues of the growing impatience of Sir Edward Grey, the current British foreign secretary who had been a key undersecretary during the Fashoda crisis. Grey found himself in an embarrassing position, unable to respond to members of Parliament concerned over the fate of British missionaries under Augagneur. In a meeting with the French ambassador, Grey explained that all the missions wanted was to be treated as they had been under Gallieni—a perfectly reasonable request in the foreign secretary's mind. The Englishman pointed out that the missions were very powerful in Britain, and their treatment could easily become a political issue in Parliament. "This could become," the French ambassador ominously closed his note to Paris, "a very serious affair."[43]

Very serious or not, the machinations of diplomacy cranked along at a glacial pace. For the next three years, letters and reports continued to come in from the French embassies in Britain and Norway with attached complaints about the treatment of Protestant missionaries in Madagascar. While the diplomats at the Quai d'Orsay had to deal with Britain, they had little control over the policies implemented in Madgascar. They passed the accusations on to the Ministry of Colonies, which repeatedly defended its governor-general's policies. While Protestant missionaries took issue with the arbitrary nature of colonial rule, the French officials defended their policies, portraying

Augagneur as a reasonable and consistent administrator. Ministerial correspondence made liberal use of qualifiers. The colonial regime allowed churches to be repaired—*usually*. It granted liberty to groups wanting to hold religious meetings—*normally*. Other reports and letters nitpicked. For example, as for the claim that the governor-general's attack on the missions had cost the colony half of its schools, one report retorted that the allegation "plays on the word 'school,'" admitting that the exact number of closures was unknown. This sort of wordplay did little to dismiss the Protestants' accusations. But the colonial minister was firm about one thing: under Augagneur, France had never pursued what he termed a *"politique d'hostilité."*[44]

After an unsuccessful campaign in 1911 to win reforms, British missionaries stepped up pressure on their government in 1912. If diplomatic communications—particularly in the hands of British diplomats—were typically studies in understated outrage and passive aggression, then exchanges between French and British officials were surprisingly blunt. By 1912, the Protestants had stopped lodging complaints and had started making demands. The LMS presented the British government with a list of concessions to win: liberty for any Malagasies who wanted to hold prayer meetings in their private homes; the ability to build churches and mission houses in villages lacking such facilities; and the right to form church organizations in accordance with the principles of the denominations, not according to the whims of the colonial government.

Like the missionaries, Sir Edward Grey was losing patience. He instructed his ambassador in Paris to "impress on [minister of foreign affairs] Monsieur Poincaré the very real importance which His Majesty's Government attaches to the demands of the missionaries." Gone were the days when Grey mentioned the sway of the missionary lobby in Parliament. Now he flatly pointed out that the mistreatment of the missionaries of Madagascar had caused a "formidable agitation in the United Kingdom," which would reflect "unfavourably on Franco-British relations, should the French government fail to give satisfaction to the grievances of the Missionaries."[45] In an era when the two nations were aiming to build stronger diplomatic relations, Grey's words were very stern indeed.

The Separation of Missions and State

In the summer of 1912, when the LMS maneuvered to gain its government's support for its demands against the French administration, its leaders debated the best way to frame their complaints. The leaders of the LMS were careful to strike just the right political tone and to formulate the precise legal argument. To accomplish this feat, they hired a barrister, met with representatives of the Foreign Office, and requested advice from their French Protestant colleagues at the Société des missions évangèliques, who were equally incensed by the treatment of Protestants in Madagascar. As the French government was currently working on a new draft decree to settle religious issues in Madagascar, the time had come for the LMS to assert its rights. French Protestants counseled the LMS against making the issue one of discrimination against and mistreatment of non-French missions. Instead, the French suggested the LMS push its demands purely in terms of the religious liberty owed to all British subjects under existing laws and treaties.[46] But positing its complaints without implicating or even mentioning French missionaries was impossible for the LMS to do. LMS representatives, as well as diplomats in London, discussed the possibility of insisting that the French government extend the 1905 separation of Church and state in France to all its possessions. Such an extension of the 1905 law, they hoped, would give legal definition to the missions' position vis-à-vis the colonial government. If it was the law of the land in France, they asked, should it not be in the empire as well?

The LMS expected, however, that the request would meet with significant resistance. First, the separation of 1905 was closely linked to the 1901 Law on Associations that gave legal status to organizations—religious and otherwise—to exist independently in France. To demand the 1905 separation in Madagascar would, therefore, place pressure on the colonial government to recognize free associations, including indigenous ones. As the French Protestants explained, the colonial administration held "that the natives are not ripe to associate together freely, and that if they were authorised to do so it would result in very serious political difficulties."[47] Demanding the application of the 1901 law also risked appearing like an attack on French Catholics, particularly the Jesuits, who were not an authorized association in France at the time, and who would face dissolution if the law were applied to the colony. Again, the LMS's French colleagues warned that the French public would not support any law that gave religious liberty to British, Norwegian, and American Protestants while denying a significant number of French Catholics the right to evangelize. With French society still recovering from the tumultuous years of the Dreyfus affair, representatives from the Société warned that the times were "not favorable to religious persecutions" in France. The British Protestants' demands could not threaten to undermine the work of their Catholic adversaries without appearing to be a petty attempt to win converts.[48]

As a result, British Protestants debated insisting on the promulgation of the 1905 separation of Church and state without mentioning the 1901 law.[49] But some significant legal details got in their way. First, the 1905 separation law presumed that Church and state were linked, which was not the case in Madagascar where the colonial administration had always taken a position of neutrality. The law also had a specific provision stating that it would not be applied to France's colonies without consideration of social conditions in individual possessions. The British Foreign Office, therefore, suggested seeking the application of only the second part of the law, which regulated the conditions of forming religious associations and the policing of religious activities. While such partial application might have seemed a stretch, the British found an important precedent. The law had already been similarly adapted to Algeria. "Obviously," it was decided at a meeting between LMS and Foreign Office representatives, "if it is possible to extend to the Musselmans of Algeria the right of forming religious Associations it must be more possible to give that right to the Christian Malagasy."[50]

For the British Protestants, the law of 1905 embodied the formula of liberties that missionaries sought. Under the 1905 law, most religious issues would require notification of—rather than authorization from—the administration.[51] Such a law in Madagascar, the British believed, would offer "complete liberty" to form religious associations and hold public meetings. The colonial government would be allowed to regulate associations, making sure they paid taxes, followed the law, and respected public order. Because the French Parliament had already passed this law at home, the British saw no reason it should not be persuaded to apply the law to Madagascar. The Foreign Office and the LMS felt confident: "This places the Missions at once in a very solid position."[52] By calling for the application of the 1905 law but not the 1901 law, the British also appeared interested in winning liberty without weakening the French Catholic missions. In fact, debate over religious liberty had brought an uncommon amount of conciliation in this colony once traumatized by *les Troubles*. G. L. King, the Anglican bishop of Madagascar, even met with the Catholic bishop in Antananarivo to discuss what measures could be taken to influence the details of the decree being drafted by the Ministry of Colonies.[53]

The question remaining was how to make the British Protestants' wishes known. On this subject the LMS's barrister, Thomas Barclay, advised patience. He suggested it would be "highly impolitic and even useless" to make demands on the French government before the draft decree appeared in the *Journal Officiel*. Any interference, he told the LMS, in issues that the French considered domestic political affairs would be met with resentment.[54] A couple of weeks later, however, Barclay wrote to the French colonial minister asking to see the draft decree being worked on. Unfortunately for him, Barclay proved himself right: French officials were peeved at the request. The French minister of foreign affairs replied that he did not feel compelled to respond to the requests of "un 'barrister' "; Barclay could read the draft when it was printed in the *Journal Officiel* like everyone else.[55]

Barclay was not the only one curious about the draft decree: Norwegian representatives had made the same request. For the first time in years, officials at the Quai d'Orsay started to show concern. M. Le Myre de Vilers, the longtime political adviser on Madagascar and no friend of Protestant missions (this is the man, after all, who said that, abroad, Catholicism was France), warned the minister of foreign affairs of "certain difficulties" in applying laws that restricted the LMS's liberty in the colony.[56] Officials within the Quai d'Orsay concurred. Most troubling was the realization that the British could demand liberty based on a declaration of 1890 whereby the French government had pledged to assure "religious tolerance" including liberty for all religions and religious education. The same declaration promised that English subjects would enjoy the rights they had on the island before it became a colony, including the right to own property and open churches where they pleased. The Quai d'Orsay communicated this information to the Ministry of Colonies with the request that the decree be passed through them before being signed by the president of the republic.[57]

Less than a week after the request was made, the colonial ministry sent a copy of the draft decree to the Quai d'Orsay. Officials there pored over the decree with concern not shown since the "pacification" of the colony. Noting that the decree could be "unfavorable to relations between France and Great Britain," the Quai d'Orsay directly addressed the three concerns repeatedly mentioned by the LMS: the questions of church property, the building and maintenance of churches, and religious meetings in private homes.[58] The decree then went back again to the Ministry of Colonies for further revisions. Colonial legislation might not have been a topic for international debate, but complaints from France's Protestant neighbors had finally spurred the Quai d'Orsay into action.

Expressing a desire to show "very great prudence" in all dealings with Britain on the missionary issue, officials at the Quai d'Orsay worked closely with British representatives to make sure the final decree would conform to the Protestants' exact concerns. Negotiations, which even included meetings with "le barrister" Barclay and Bishop King, produced a decree passed on 11 March 1913. The new decree amended the legislation that had made all religious buildings in Madagascar the property of the state; all churches built with English funding or from subscriptions would remain mission property. Augagneur's "religious perimeters" were made smaller, allowing for more churches to be built in rural regions. In May 1913, the colonial minister wrote to the Quai d'Orsay to close the matter. Reflecting the extent to which international relations shaped colonial policy, the minister stated that the decree had been written "for religious peace, and for good Franco-English relations in Madagascar."[59] The desire to keep the Entente Cordiale strong ruled the day.

But few regulations, no matter how widely negotiated, can meet everyone's expectations, and the decree of 11 March 1913 was no exception. Conceding that the decree was "liberal in essence," one LMS publication complained that it still failed to put an end to the "arbitrary regime" that controlled religious issues in Madagascar. While the decree promised many of the freedoms afforded by the 1905 Separation of Church and state, it left in place the key provision that religious liberty would remain subordinate to the concerns of public order. For some LMS missionaries, this caveat left the regulation of religious life unacceptably open to the administration's discretion. For missionaries hungry for absolute liberty, even the rules that seem fairly reasonable—such as one stating that no more than five churches could be built in an eight-kilometer radius without official permission—were deemed a form of "oppression."[60] But less than a year and a half later, the First World War gave the French and British new reasons for entente. Their alliance against Germany in war, according to one missionary who spent five decades in Madagascar, finally brought about "a more pleasant feeling" between the two.[61]

Through Foreign Eyes

Ironically, the real beneficiaries of the success that the LMS and other British Protestant organizations achieved in Madagascar might have been French Catholic missionaries. In the years after 1905, critics of Catholic missionaries, such as radicals, Freemasons, and the supporters of the Mission laïque, also called on the government to "separate" from the missions in the empire. The LMS's careful examination of the question, however, showed the many pitfalls of a colonial application of the law. The controversy over Augagneur's policies in Madagascar revealed that the separation most anticlericals called for possessed more rhetorical than legal power. The separation of missions and state in the colony, if enacted along the lines of 1905 metropolitan law, could have left the missions and indigenous Christians more stable, rather than less. Few critics who made the demand apparently gave serious thought to what its application in the colonies would entail. The 1901 Law on Associations could have been used to shut down unrecognized organizations, such as the Jesuits. But even French Protestant missionaries—avid critics of Jesuit abuses—realized that such a move was politically untenable if it were not also applied to foreign missionaries.

Debates over the application of 1905-inspired legislation were shaped not only by diplomatic concerns but by racial ones as well. Unless tailored like the 1913 Madagascar decree to a specific colonial context, the 1905 separation would have enabled indigenous populations to form associations. LMS missionaries wanted for themselves as well as their indigenous preachers absolute freedom to teach, preach, and hold meetings. In a colony where the French administration was concerned about keeping public order and solidifying its own authority, and where religion had long been tied to political power, religious freedom was deemed potentially explosive. The fear that religious organizations would become centers of indigenous political activity exposed yet another paradox at the heart of republican colonialism. Many a colonial administrator promised to douse the "arbitrary rule" of retrograde indigenous political systems with the waters of rational republicanism. But in practice, French officials regularly traded their ideals of the French Revolution for law and order. Rational republicanism was still the goal—but a republicanism dictated by an authoritarian French regime.

Ironically, republican colonial ideology in Madagascar corresponded well to the Catholic missions' hierarchy, where indigenous priests remained under the leadership of French missionaries. While Augagneur himself certainly did not champion Catholicism, his criticism time and again was leveled specifically at Protestants: "Protestantism," he told *Le Siècle* in 1907, "is menacing for the future of our colonies." The comment was revealing in its silences: "Christianity" or "religion," apparently, was not the problem, though as a Freemason anticleric, the governor-general obviously had little use for Christian dogma. When applied to the colony, however, Augagneur's anticlericalism acquired a slightly different hue. It was no longer purely about attacking a source of antimodern superstition; rather, now, anticlericalism also provided a salve for quelling colonial unrest and potential rebellion. Augagneur made clear that it was indigenous Protestant pastors, with their sway over large congregations and their language of spiritual liberation, who most threatened the colonial balance of power.[62]

Even though many Catholics in France reacted to the passage of the 1905 separation of Church and state with horror, the spirit of the law stood to solidify the position of Catholic missions in the empire. Catholics in France opposed the separation for two major reasons. For them, the law was painful proof of the ascension of anticlericalism in French national politics. After a decade of heated conflict over Dreyfus, the law embodied radicals' hostility to Catholicism and symbolized the political triumph of their secular values. The law also had damaging practical ramifications, not least of which was that it undermined the Roman hierarchy and the centrality of the Vatican. Under the terms of the separation, the state considered Church property to belong to individual French religious associations, which no longer had any legal connection to the Vatican.

But in the empire, where Church and state had never been linked, the 1905 law had far less symbolic sting. Across the empire, and Madagascar was no exception, the French administration had already curtailed subventions to missions, had removed religious workers from schools and hospitals, and taken down crucifixes from public spaces in its policy of laicization. The application of aspects of the 1905 law gave legal legitimacy to missions by officially recognizing them and by delineating their relationship with the colonial state. In the case of Madagascar, the administration clarified missionary ownership of properties and officially accepted missionaries as representatives of the members of their congregations—two issues that had been constant concerns for Catholic workers elsewhere in the empire, such as Indochina and Polynesia.

When critics of Catholic evangelizing called for separation, what they really had in mind was a system of authorization that would enable colonial governments to shut down missionary organizations entirely. But when foreign missionaries—especially British Protestants, behind the LMS's lead—demanded rights in the French empire, they exposed the paradoxes of French policies and attitudes toward Catholicism. LMS requests for liberty pushed officials at the Quai d'Orsay to see their missionary policy through foreign eyes, and to encourage their colleagues at the Ministry of Colonies to do the same. Diplomats from Britain, Norway, and the United States pressured the French government to offer Protestants the liberty enjoyed by all religious workers, as many diplomats pointed out, in "civilized countries." If treaties and diplomacy forced France to grant foreign Protestants religious freedom in Madagascar, were officials in Paris really willing to deny the same freedom to their own Catholic religious workers? While colonial rule was far more secure than in the years following the invasion, spreading French influence continued to be a central goal. In the competitive imperial atmosphere of the early twentieth century, undermining French Catholics while protecting British Protestants was politically impossible and practically unfeasible. By pushing to end the arbitrary rule of religion in this corner of the French empire, LMS missionaries and their coreligionists did the Jesuits and other French Catholic missionaries—unwittingly, no doubt—a great service.

V

FROM THE EMPIRE
TO THE *MÈRE-PATRIE*

Martyrs, Patriots, Frenchmen

From the 1880s to the First World War, France's colonizing and civilizing goals were the subject of intense debate and conflict in the colonies. As the cases of Indochina, Tahiti and the Marquesas, and Madagascar reveal, no topic was more contentious than the place of religious missionaries in the republican empire. Faced with an onslaught from a host of critics, Catholic workers—from missionaries in the field to regional bishops—emphasized the services they provided colonial rule and retooled their daily work to coincide, at least rhetorically, with republican civilizing ideals. In public ceremonies, private meetings, publications, and correspondence, missionaries repeatedly asserted, often with patriotic flourishes, their determination to serve France. By simultaneously playing down their spiritual designs and stressing how their local influence, schools, and ostensibly humanitarian programs benefited France's colonizing and civilizing needs, religious workers in disparate regions defended their right to evangelize.

Missionaries abroad did not work alone. Just as colonial bishops took to local stages to pronounce their missions' commitment to France, the Oeuvre de la propagation de la foi, the country's leading missionary organization, took to the national stage with new vigor in the attempt to redefine the movement's contribution to the empire. An early example of this new effort to engage in national discussions about empire came in May 1894 at the Colonial Exposition in Lyon. The exposition was an opportunity for an array of procolonial groups to celebrate the French commitment to improve the moral and material lives of the inhabitants of the nation's foreign possessions.[1] While the event was overwhelmingly republican, the leaders of the Oeuvre eagerly participated by hosting an Exposition of Missions where visitors could learn of Catholic projects around the globe. The exhibit made a strong political argument that missionaries had contributed as much to civilization and progress as any secular force in French history. According to the program, missionaries were "the first, well before trade, well before colonization, well before the flags of European nations, [to] penetrate the most savage countries in order to bring, with a more elevated morality, calmer practices and a superior well-being." Evangelizing was a "peaceful conquest" whereby missionaries established "French influence, of which they have always been the most precious auxiliaries."[2] The Exposition of Missions, much like the correspondence of many bishops with colonial officials, left religious workers' spiritual preoccupations—such as spreading the word, converting pagans, and teaching catechism—largely unmentioned.

The Lyon exposition is but one example of the multifaceted effort the French missionary movement launched to reshape the public perception of its contribution to colonialism. Directors of the Oeuvre de la propagation de la foi were well aware of the conflicts unfolding in France's colonies; by the early 1890s, missionary commitment to the republic had already come under scrutiny in Indochina, New Caledonia, across Polynesia, Madagascar, and elsewhere. Following the lead of the Oeuvre, and drawing on the latest innovations in mass media technology, missionary organizations in France set out to show the public that the civilizing of the empire was incomplete without the moral edification and spiritual transformation that only Christianity could offer.

Though closely tied to the effort to defend evangelization in the empire, the domestic campaign to redefine missionary work had far broader implications. Aimed both at drawing support and at addressing calls to apply domestic anticlerical legislation to the colonies, the revamping of missionary rhetoric at home simultaneously challenged hundreds of thousands of the movement's supporters to see the empire in a new light. For much of the nineteenth century, the missionary was a lone figure wholly committed to spreading the love of God. By the start of the First World War, however, the redefinition of the movement would push supporters to consider religious evangelizing as an eminently patriotic vocation committed to spreading civilization as much as God's word. As a result, non-Christians of the empire would no longer simply be lacking in salvation; they would increasingly be portrayed as uncivilized and racially inferior. Largely ignored by historians of French colonialism, the publications in which missionary organizations described their nation's moral obligations to the empire offer a window into how a significant portion of Frenchmen understood colonialism.

A New Kind of Publication for a New Kind of Missionary

Starting in the late 1880s, missionary organizations in France entered the politicized fray of public opinion in a number of new ways. Events such as the 1894 Exposition in Lyon, as well as missionary exhibits and museums, allowed religious organizations to promote their work in a way that would continue to attract donors and recruits, and to emphasize the important contribution missionaries made to French colonialism in order to deflect criticism. Leading organizations like the Oeuvre de la propagation de la foi also explored these themes in the medium they knew best: publishing. Missionary presses produced a host of new kinds of journals, almanacs, atlases, and history books—all designed to entertain and educate their supporters and to prove to a wider public the value of missionary work.

While new missionary publications covered many traditionally Catholic subjects, they also sought to make the missionary into a French national icon. Publications were often overtly patriotic, suggesting that the missionary was not only a soldier of God but also a hero of France. Like missionaries of old, the men (and less often women) described in these publications were committed to humanitarian and philanthropic projects, such as education, medical assistance, and care for children and the elderly. A new list of goals was also laid out, melding the apostolic vocation with the republican colonial project of the civilizing mission. Article after article made clear that moral, political, and economic development could be accomplished in colonial societies only when coupled with Catholic proselytization, catechism, and baptism.

The series of new publications launched by the Oeuvre in the late 1880s aimed at a wider, more popular audience than some of its older publications. New annuals resembled the journal *Missions Catholiques*, which was originally founded to supplement the reports and letters from missionaries in the field published in the bimonthly *Annales de la Propagation de la Foi*. Unlike the *Annales*, the biweekly *Missions Catholiques* was richly illustrated on larger, tabloid paper. From its inception, it shared the look and format of popular magazines like *A Travers le Monde* and *L'Illustration* that reprinted serial narratives from European travelers around the globe. Though sales of the *Missions Catholiques* barely covered the expense of its production, the Oeuvre's Paris council considered it an impressive and important emblem of the missionary project.[3] In the early 1900s, the council said that the *Missions Catholiques* "occupies, now, a choice place among the great *revues* concerned with colonial, geographic, ethnographic, and other issues. By its illustrations, further, it has nothing to envy of the best travel journals."[4] The fact that the journal was distinguished by its exclusive religious focus went unmentioned.

The directors of the Oeuvre used *Missions Catholiques* to advertise the publication of a range of new annuals, such as the *Almanach des Missions*, the *Album des Missions*, and the small and large *Almanachs de l'Oeuvre de la Propagation de la Foi*.[5] The goal of these new publications was, like the journals, to report the spreading of the gospel by Catholic missionaries outside of France and to raise money for further proselytizing projects.[6] The new almanacs were clearly designed with a younger, less religious, and, in some instances, more female audience in mind. Boasting that the *Almanach des Missions* had sold 50,000 copies in one of its first years, a notice in the *Missions Catholiques* described the publication as popular with clubs, with families, and in schools, "everywhere, in a word, where people are interested in the spreading of faith and civilization."[7]

Whereas the *Annales* and *Missions Catholiques* were international journals, published in a number of languages, these annuals were made for a specifically French audience. A short fund-raising announcement called "Let's Love the Missions" in the 1885 *Almanach des Missions* foretold more intense appeals to readers' combined patriotism and religion.[8] Considering the long missionary tradition of ignoring national differences, when the announcement posed the question "Reader, who are you?" the answer was uncharacteristically specific: "French and Catholic." The ad endeavored to link these two identities. First, it explained, "You must have at heart the interests of your Mother the Church," the most important of which was spreading the faith. But, the notice also argued, Catholicism was intricately entwined with French history, including French crusaders who defended the Holy Lands from "the domination of infidels." A final point melded the missionary project, religion, and the nation together. The ad assured readers that prayer not only helped spread God's "divine reign" but also would bring "the blessings of Heaven to your *patrie*." If the connection were not clear enough, across the bottom of the page, a final banner read: "For the Church and France, let's love the missions."[9]

The *Almanach des Missions* also embraced, like many nonreligious journals dealing with the colonies and travel, all that was exotic, adventuresome, and bizarre about the world of the missionary, in an attempt to reach beyond a strictly religious readership. The cover of the tabloid-sized *Almanach des Missions* set the tone for the pages within. An image of four non-European men decorated the front page, each figure's ethnicity codified in his dress.[10] The four peered out from dense, dark foliage at a glowing image of an approaching ship with a brilliant cross and the figure of Mary floating in the sky above, casting light across the horizon. The leaders of the Oeuvre's Paris council understood the importance of a publication's cover; in a later debate they noted how a cover is a means "to draw attention, excite the curiosity, and incite to open the booklet, to browse through, and finally to read" the publication.[11] The *Almanach*'s cover promised that the pages within explored myriad places on every inhabitable continent. And an advertisement in *Missions Catholiques* made this diversity a chief selling point, emphasizing that the *Almanach* passed from India to Australia to Arabia, where, following some Egyptian pilgrims, readers could penetrate "the holy land of Islam" and explore the "secrets" of Medina and Mecca. "After Mohamed, Buddha!" it further enticed. "We are at Kandy (island of Ceylon)."[12] The possibilities in the book's covers were endless.

Starting in 1886, the first few pages of each *Almanach* contained information that served the curious and, most likely, the young. Printed here were lists of facts that would be useful to Catholics, such as a chart mapping the hierarchy of the Catholic Church and a list of the year's religious holidays. Other pages presented historical facts: one table calculated the age of the world and the passage of time according to various yardsticks, such as the time elapsed since the founding of Rome, the birth of Christ, and the first Olympiad; another listed the exact moments of seasonal changes, eclipses, and tide movements. A calendar finished off this first section, and, in the case of 1886, illustrations of Maoris as well as "diverse kinds of *coiffures*" from New Caledonia adorned each month.

This section was followed by a wide range of stories, reports, reviews, poems, pictures, and cartoons that made up the bulk of the book. The inaugural edition of the *Almanach des Missions* presented pieces on religious topics such as "The Apostolate in 1884: Its Joys, Its Sorrows," a short piece titled "His Eminence Cardinal Lavigerie," and a recap of the five martyrs of Tonkinese Laos. It also included studies written by missionaries, but not about evangelization per se: Père Augouard, founder of the mission at Stanley Pool, wrote an article on the Congo, another priest covered civilization in Zanguebar, and a third dealt with the "morals and superstitions" of the Bélep tribe in New Caledonia. Other articles—no doubt aimed at the less zealous reader— had nothing whatsoever to do with Catholic missionaries. These articles reveled in the exotic and even grotesque character of the non-European world. One described an opium den, another the life of "Suéma, or the little African slave buried alive."[13] The *Almanach* even printed a translation of Henry M. Stanley's *New York Herald* account of finding the British Protestant missionary Livingstone, complete with the famed line, "Le Docteur Livingstone, je présume."[14]

The trend of exploiting all that was sensational in the non-European world—especially articles on morally and physically repugnant subject matter—came to distinguish these publications from regular missionary journals. An article in the 1887 *Almanach*, for example, examined in horrific detail Chinese torture.[15] Though written by a missionary, the topic had little to do with proselytization. The author ran down a list of methods of torture as diverse as beating, slapping, decapitation, "la question" (foot or hand torture), and strangulation. Drawings accompanied the text, and colorful prose made the article all the more dreadful, if intriguing.[16] The author paid special attention to the *koua*, or death by a thousand cuts. The reader learned how the executioner chose from many knives specially designed to cut certain parts of the body, as well as the finer points of scalping.[17]

Cannibalism was another topic that made its way into these new publications. A story from the French Congo in the *Petit Almanach de la Propagation de la Foi* told the "terrible story of Bandzinga," a slave who was slaughtered and eaten by "Cannibal Peoples." Père Augouard gave a detailed explanation of the butchering process—"one gathers the blood; here is a right leg, a left arm"—and which members of society preferred which cuts of meat, such as the old women who particularly enjoyed young people's flesh. The article was decorated with sketches of a cannibal from distant Fiji and of a man-eating warrior from central Africa.[18] Subjects such as torture or cannibalism were occasionally explored in the pages of traditional missionary journals, but most commonly in terms of Christianity's power to reform immoral behavior. In the pages of the *almanachs*, by contrast, articles seemed primarily designed to fascinate, horrify, and appall. References to the moralizing powers of evangelizing often were left unstated.

Lessons for the Catholic Family

Despite forays into the sensational and gruesome, all these new publications were essentially pedagogical. In 1890, an advertisement described the *Almanach des Missions* and the *Almanach de l'Oeuvre* as "especially aimed at children in school and catechism." In these years when free, compulsory education taught students across France the traditions of a national republican culture, the Oeuvre's publications increasingly tried to balance the state's laic messages with religious ones. The almanacs did not reject the patriotism regularly taught in schools; rather, they augmented it by asserting the glory that Catholicism could bring to the nation.

While at school, Eugen Weber tells us, students learned that their first duty was to fight for France.[19] But the *Alamanach des Missions* suggested that children could win glory by becoming soldiers of a different sort. In a poem called "I Want to Be a Missionary," for example, a young boy realized—from reading accounts of missionaries' lives—that God needed apostles to spread his word. After learning of the evil done by the "villain angel" Satan, the child told his mother:

> Well, if, in order to save the world,
> The good Lord tells us: Depart!
> Mother, we must answer him. . . .
> I want to be a missionary . . .

Knowing that her son had correctly understood God's wish, the mother responded through tears, "Oui, mon enfant."[20] Not all the stories in these new publications possessed such contrived Christian messages; but there was no doubt that these annuals, in one way or another, offered stories, as one ad put it, "to fortify the soul by witnessing the great devotion of our missionaries."[21]

The relationship of mother and child in "I Want to Be a Missionary" is indicative of how publications targeted the home as the center of moral and religious learning where future missionaries would be formed. Some publications, such as the *Petit Almanach*, printed stories dealing with French family issues among reports from distant lands. The *Petit Almanach*'s articles regularly explored spiritual trials and growth, and focused on gendered subjects such as marriage and children. Among the standard missionary reports were poems relating to children's religious development, such as "Let the Small Children Come to Me" and "The Child's Prayer."[22] Themes relevant to French families could also be found in stories from abroad. A piece entitled

"Paul Rakoto, a Malagasy Story," recounted the experiences of a shepherd boy who found Christianity and who thus could "serve as a model for our dear children of Europe."[23] Finally, the odd line of wisdom filled in empty corners of some pages, with sayings like "Dirty boys never become clean men."[24] In these ways, the *Petit Almanach* reached beyond the immediate concerns of the missions, guiding French mothers in the religious upbringing of their children.

Not all the stories aimed at women were specifically related to child rearing and evangelization. In the 1899 *Petit Almanach*, a story called "La Relique" explored the life of Marceline, a woman so distraught she considered suicide. Hers was "a life of Hell with her husband who drank and beat her, failed to give her money, and left her to run the household with the little she made herself."[25] One evening, Marceline decided to build a fire to asphyxiate herself, but as she dug through the newspaper she would use to start the fire, she came across a pair of baby boots—the pair her deceased child had learned to walk in. Memories filled her head of how happy their family had been then, when her husband did not drink, and when they attended mass. She feared that if she killed herself she would go to a place where she could never again remember that happiness. Just then, her husband returned and they embraced: "She forgot all the resentment," the story continued, "she no longer recalled that her shoulders were blue from punches received. . . . And they cried together." The couple built a fire to make dinner; the husband had been paid that day yet had decided not to go to the cabaret that night, or ever again. The closing image detailed their lives a year later. With their new baby, they again attended Sunday mass.[26]

The variety of articles in these new annuals—ranging from the exotic and perverse to the quaint and saccharine—suggests that the editors and leaders of the Oeuvre de la propagation de la foi consciously targeted a diverse audience but always had the interests of the family in mind. It is possible to imagine a family, each member with his or her own missionary publication. Father studied the *Album des Missions Catholiques*, which appeared annually in massive 600-page tomes, richly illustrated with etchings, maps, and photos. The sheer size of the *Album* made it seem more like a museum than a book.[27] Mother read the short articles in the *Petit Almanach*, which inspired her as a wife and mother. Even the book's tiny size had a delicate, feminine appearance when compared with the bulk of the *Album*. Finally, the children, with the *Almanach des Missions* in hand, squirmed through articles about ghastly rites and were captivated by stories of missionary heroics. And each publications had messages that further defined these demographic variations. The *Album des Missions* stressed, like missionary journals, the importance of financial support of the missions abroad. The *Petit Almanach* stressed the need to develop children's sense of Catholic spirituality, notably through prayer and mass. And the message of the *Almanach des Missions* was that missionaries were heroes, pushing wide the boundaries of God's empire, encountering strange cultures, and helping to eradicate un-Christian behavior.

Songs and Poems of Patriotism

The editors of the Oeuvre's publications further fostered the communal and family-oriented nature of their almanacs by regularly printing songs, including lyrics and sheet music. For agricultural workers in the fields and shop owners in town, singing was a popular diversion in a world with limited options for entertainment. Musical shows at urban *cafés-concerts* attracted diverse bourgeois audiences throughout the century.[28] In 1872, in the wake of the Prussian defeat, singing became an integral part of the republican school curriculum. Third Republican politicians and educators believed music to be an effective way of both promoting literacy and forming citizens through teaching patriotic tunes.[29] The most common genre of patriotic song taught in fin-de-siècle French schools was the military anthem—exemplified by the likes of "The Marseillaise" and "Le Régiment de Sambre et Meuse." Anthems celebrated, as the historian Regina Sweeney has written, "ideals such as patriotism, martyrdom for one's country, and liberty"—all things dear to republican hearts.[30]

In the late 1880s, with similar ends in mind, missionary publications started printing the music and lyrics of inspirational songs about the apostolic life. Like the Third Republic's school songs, the Oeuvre de la propagation de la foi's publications often highlighted the more martial tunes from the missionary repertoire. It is a little hard to imagine many families or church groups gathered around the piano to sing "The Martyr's Desire," which included refrains of the line "My blood, my blood, my blood!"[31] But, in fact, the Oeuvre expected just that. Publishing the sheet music of the "Chant pour le départ des missionnaires" (a song whose very title echoed the hugely popular, secular patriotic tune "Chant du départ"), the editors of the *Almanach* encouraged readers to enjoy "this hymn glowing with holy enthusiasm" *in their homes*.[32] Traditional missionary songs echoed many of the themes common to secular ones, such as the soldier leaving for battle, willing to give his life for his cause, and ultimately seeking glory, but they typically had nothing whatsoever to do with France since they often dated from a period when missionaries shunned all national affiliations. But in the context of the rest of the *Almanach*'s content, which included stories of how missionaries worked for the benefit of French colonialism and the glory of the nation, their lyrics took on new significance. Words such as *victoire*, *gloire, empire*, and *mourrir* that once described missionaries' strictly spiritual pursuits now seemed interchangeable with sentiments and ideals described in martial, patriotic songs. Notions of sacrifice blurred. Allegiance to *patrie* and God intermingled.

The *Almanach des Missions* accentuated this process of blurring distinctions by asking artists to write overtly patriotic tunes about missionaries. One such song was by the Breton singer Théodore Botrel, famous as much for his ballads about the lives of fishermen and peasants as for his fervent conservative nationalism.[33] One of the most successful *café-concert* singers of his day, Botrel was, according to the *Almanach*, a master of that "popular and so French" genre who had elevated his craft "to the sublime."[34] Botrel's song, "The Missionary," told a story similar to other missionary melodies. "Far, far from his family," Botrel's apostle was "Happy to find / Some soul to save." The song did not shy from the violence associated with the work, noting that "if he is taken by Infidels," the missionary "suffers it all, without murmuring." Even the "cruelest tortures" could not make the missionary apostatize.

Where Botrel's song did depart from traditional missionary hymns was in its portrayal of missionaries as heroes of the French nation. The lone priest was no longer simply a servant of the Church, as he was in traditional tunes.[35] Now, Botrel sang:

In the name of France, his Mother,
I send a *Salut!* to the Soldier
Whose only weapon is Prayer,
Whose slogan is a *Sursum Corda*,
> Who has but one cry:
> Long live Jesus Christ!
>> *Refrain:*
> Let's salute the Apostle who prays
> Fights and suffers and dies if need be
> For the Church and for the *Patrie*,
> For the Cross and for the Flag![36]

Traditional songs like "The Martyr's Desire" portrayed a world in which spiritual salvation was the missionary's only concern from birth until his arrival in heaven, the celestial *patrie*. The last stanza of this tune, by contrast, planted the missionary firmly in France, the mother who gave him life, and for whom he ultimately worked and died "if need be."

In addition to recasting the priorities of the missionary, the song inscribed the missionary as a figure of the popular cultural imagination. In a reprinted letter to the *Almanach*, Botrel underscored this point: "In the popular feel of my most popular song, I sang of this Hero, popular par excellence in the entire world."[37] By incorporating missionaries into the popular cultural imagination—for example, as a subject to be sung about at home—songs like Botrel's made the missionary more familiar yet still heroic. No longer was the missionary to be held on a sacred pedestal; now he emerged as a man of the soil—in Botrel's terms, of the French *pays*.

The *Almanach*'s new missionary was an amalgamation of nationalist imagery—God, sacrifice, the soil—typical of the conservative right in French politics. But the editors of the *Almanach* adorned Botrel's sheet music with a medley of symbols that softened the political tone of his lyrics: coats of arms with crosses and a crown floated in front of a French tricolored flag bound to a staff engraved with "RF" for République Française.[38] In this drawing, there was something for everyone, from monarchists to republicans. This decorative motif appeared again the following year, this time providing the background for the poem "Les Grands français" by Joseph Serre. This time the motif had a smaller crown and a shield with fleurs-de-lis, a bright cross in the center of the image, and a backdrop of the republic's flag. Serre's poem fit well with the decorative flourishes, waxing about "bloody heroes of our history" and the "sweet bloody heroes—lion-lambs" of Christ. Serre literally mixed the victories of missionaries with those of France; his soldiers of God even carried the flag of the republic to "horizons, everywhere, splendid and tricolored" by the white of deserts, the blue of sky, and the red of missionary blood.[39] The evangelist who left his home to spread Catholicism now sailed into a sunset blazing with the glory of the republic's red, white, and blue.

It was no accident that this reinvention of the missionary—as Frenchman and cultural icon—came in a song published in 1901, the year of the electoral victories of the anticlerical politician Émile Combes, at the height of the Dreyfus affair and debate over the role of the Church in French society. In the pages of the *Almanach*, the missionary movement campaigned for its own salvation, insisting that evangelizing was a patriotic endeavor that helped France as well as Catholicism, and that the missionary suffered for the nation as well as God. With a range of subjects to broaden its audience beyond merely the religiously zealous, popular missionary publications began a long rhetorical battle, one that portrayed the missionary as not only a religious force but also a colonial facilitator.

Servants of French Colonialism

From the first publication of the *Almanach des Missions*, the editors highlighted the benefits that missions brought to France's colonial efforts around the globe. In the early editions of the 1880s, stories explored the myriad ways by which missions helped colonial administrators and military officers abroad. In 1885, for example, the first edition of the *Almanach des Missions* published a story that departed from how most missionaries defined their roles in lands recently open to proselytism. The story, recounted in a letter by a Père Lutz, told of a showdown in the West African village of Rio-Pongo that captured the emerging dynamic of missionary-colonial relations in the expanding empire.

The tale began on the morning of 22 November 1884 at the mission where Lutz taught catechism and tended to the sick and old. The narrative appeared to follow the daily work of a missionary in the field, but soon a new role awaited Père Lutz. A regional king, Benoît Katty, had arrived in Rio-Pongo that morning, bent on forcing the departure of a local man working as a translator for the French. With a force of fifty *krouba* soldiers, Benoît Katty sent word to Monsieur Bour, the local French commandant, that the translator was to depart the French ranks immediately or face a punishment of death. Bour met the threat with defiance, promptly arresting the king's messenger. Infuriated at this snub, Benoît Katty excited his men to attack the post and take the prisoner by force. The king's soldiers outnumbered the French force of thirteen men; "the *noirs*," the missionary pointed out, "would thus overrun them with ease."[40]

Père Lutz soon emerged as the sole man capable of averting bloodshed. Acting as negotiator, he spoke with both Bour and Benoît Katty, convincing the latter that an attack would cost him dearly: "A warship will not hesitate to arrive, and then not only will they take back the 6,000 francs you receive from France, you will certainly be shot."[41] But less than an hour passed before Lutz heard shots fired near the French post. The *krouba* soldiers, whose opportunity to pillage had been dashed by the brokered peace, returned when the king had gone and provoked the French soldiers. The French fired at two *krouba*, killing one and wounding the other. The *krouba* retreated, regrouped, and charged the post a second time, spears drawn and rifles blazing. This time, an unarmed Père Lutz appeared on the battlefield, crying, "Listen to me, remain calm until Benoît returns; he will tell you what you have to do." The *krouba* obeyed, knowing—said Lutz—that the missionary was an esteemed friend of the king.[42]

Lutz also wove an important religious subplot into his story. Amid the turmoil, Lutz returned to the injured *krouba*, to whom death would come at any moment. Lutz asked him several questions, and finding the *krouba* "well disposed" to becoming a Christian, the missionary baptized the dying man. His religious duty done, Lutz hurried back to the diplomacy, finding the king desperate for the missionary's help with the uncontrollable *krouba*. The news of the fallen *krouba* had spread through the country, and warriors were coming from all over, ready to avenge the death of their comrade. After much talk, Lutz appeased the warriors, allowing the king to lead them away from the French post. Calm was restored at Rio-Pongo.

But Lutz's role as negotiator did not end there. A number of political issues remained undecided, most notably the compensation the French would make for taking the life of a *krouba*. Four days after the violence, Benoît called on the missionary to discuss the matter, explaining that his chiefs were demanding justice.[43] Hoping that Lutz could explain the situation to the chiefs, Benoît invited the missionary to preside over a meeting. Upon entering the meeting, Benoît and his brother rose in honor of the priest and allowed him to sit between the two leaders. After considerable debate, Lutz convinced the chiefs to take the matter before the lieutenant governor, which they did, and ultimately made an agreement with the French authorities.[44]

Lutz pointed out that the commandant lauded him for his "peaceful counsel" and "courageous intervention," which helped avoid what "would have been a veritable butchery." Lutz had "avoided bloodshed and powerfully contributed to the breakup" of the *krouba* bands. The lieutenant governor of Senegal, M. Bayol, later toured Lutz's mission and assured his support and protection. But for Lutz the best news to come out of the event was the unexpected recovery of the dying *krouba* soldier whom he had baptized in the midst of drama. Despite his serious injuries, Lutz noted, the soldier was "saved." Another missionary discussed religion with the *krouba*, attracting other pagans to the hut to listen, some of whom eventually asked to be baptized. "Such was my role during these troubling days," Lutz reflected. "How did I have the courage to accomplish it and the grace to lead it all to a good ending? Saint Joseph only knows; for it is he who did everything."[45] Whether it was divine inspiration or just good negotiating, Lutz's part in the showdown at Rio-Pongo signaled a shift in the portrayal of missionary activity. For decades, journals such as the *Annales* and *Missions Catholiques* printed accounts of missionary battles to win converts without interest in national or colonial politics. But with accounts like Lutz's, these goals began to change: now, in addition to the souls of the world's non-Christians, the missionary saved French colonizers' necks.

Just as missionaries increasingly underscored their role as facilitators to French colonial expansion, so, too, did they invoke the metaphor of colonization to characterize evangelizing. For example, joining the story of Rio-Pongo in the first *Almanach des Missions* was an article that described missionaries' preaching, caring for the sick, and teaching virtue everywhere they lived in the language of the day. "Go to Africa, to America, to the lost islands of Oceania," it said, "everywhere you will find *the same method of colonization*."[46] Colonization became a process that required both republican administrators *and* Catholic missionaries to achieve the nation's goal. An 1890 article in the *Almanach* described the acquisition of Tahiti in such terms: France conquered the island with its "valiant soldiers" and "civilized" the islanders with its "heroic missionaries."[47]

By the 1890s, especially during the *ralliement*, reports even in the *Annales de la Propagation de la Foi*—by far the most traditional publication in the Oeuvre's arsenal—increasingly equated accomplishments of the missions with those of colonial France. In 1892, for example, the editors wrote that the newly opened cathedral in Antananarivo, Madagascar, was an homage to "the glory of the Church and France"; a similar tone was used to describe the inauguration of the cathedral in another colonial city, Noumea, New Caledonia.[48] A news item from 1893 noted that everywhere the French Pères du Saint-Esprit went in West Africa, they carried "the teaching of Christ and the love of France."[49] The timing of this new rhetoric was not coincidental: with the pope's call to French Catholics to join the republic, and with many resisting or refusing to do so, the Oeuvre made clear its intention to work with France in the colonies.

Ribbing Republicans

While the object of the new missionary publications was to redefine evangelizing as compatible with a republican colonial framework, the almanacs were not without their critiques. Oeuvre publications often used humor and cartoons to question the effectiveness of laic (often coded as Freemason) civilizing projects. Humor allowed a certain leeway in leveling criticisms. Some cartoons portrayed radicals and colonial officials as little more than buffoons. Whether these were biting commentaries or all in good fun was left to the reader to decide.

One of the first pieces to blend humorous text and imagery, "Let's Civilize!" appeared in the *Almanach* in 1887 and established themes that would be found elsewhere in missionary publications for the next three decades.[50] This satirical piece—a play rendered as cartoon—dropped the reader in on a meeting held by the society " 'For the Expansion of Strictly Laic Civilization' Founded in Order to Fight Religious Missions." Mixing political jabs with silliness, and masking invective with laughter, the play told of how a meeting at the "Lodge of the Fraternal Kiss" aimed to make Africans into "strictly laic peoples."[51] From its opening lines, "Let's Civilize!" mocked, with absurd dialogue and ridiculous situations, a version of the republican civilizing mission. But by casting an international group of Freemasons—the delegates of this fictional society included the likes of M. Grandgousset, Sir John Bullson, William Yankee, and the German doctor Sweinspells—the play made clear its target was not the French government. Nonetheless, the jump from Freemasons to republicans was not a great one, since some 40 percent of civil ministers in the Third Republic were affiliated with Freemasonry between 1877 and 1914.[52]

In "Let's Civilize!" a Dr. Cascavelle introduced an African case study, a young man named "Libre-Pensée," whom the association set out to civilize on the spot.[53] Clarifying his commitment to a strictly secular civilization, the good doctor stated that it was important that the African man not "tire himself by dreaming of a Supreme Being," nor "fall into prayer," nor "torment himself with metaphysical aspirations." After much deliberation, the lodge agreed on a number of crucial stipulations, including that the African should carry an umbrella and wear shoes, a hat, and pants. But disagreement reigned. The proceedings got out of hand, as other delegates fought to amend this wardrobe: a Brit insisted that the African have opium in his pocket, while an Italian suggested pasta, and a delegate from Marseilles offered soap. Others objected. The debate over how best to civilize Libre-Pensée turned to pandemonium.

With the lodge president unable to control the outbursts from all corners, the meeting lost all sense of decorum until it was silenced when a member of the gallery tossed an egg at the president. Wiping his face with a handkerchief, the president said, "Citizens . . . we are here to civilize a people; we will not withdraw because of a rotten egg!. . . . Citizens, I am proud to suffer for civilization and progress, this egg [makes this] the most beautiful day of my life! (*Prolonged applause*.)"[54] The meeting went on. Delegates considered the prohibition of the use of money—"the vile metal"—in the colonies, opting instead to trade with rifles, gunpowder, and "above all *l'eau-de-vie*, which one can call quite rightly the rational drink" of the nineteenth century. As they voted to make the diffusion of spirits obligatory, Libre-Pensée indulged himself with a tall bottle until, drunk and tired, he hurled the empty bottle and sent the crowd running. He stripped off his new wardrobe while delegates cried "Save yourselves!" In the end, though Libre-Pensée was left tipsy and still in his traditional garb, the Freemasons held to the belief, despite their apparent defeat, that "laic pants suffice to form a man."[55]

Though "Let's Civilize!" built on the innocent cartoon gags of the age of new imperialism, its message was not without its political barbs. Freemason attacks on missionary activities in the colonies were commonplace—a fact that lent "Let's Civilize!" an unmistakable flavor of counterattack. Despite its overt silliness, the cartoon skewered Freemasons as internationalists, immoral, misguided, and cowardly. "Let's Civilize!" did not directly cast religious missionaries as at odds with, or even alternatives to, these staunchly "laic" citizens. But with stories of severe missionary hardship filling the surrounding pages, a reader of "Let's Civilize!" would have been hard put not to see the irony in the lodge president's "suffering" an egg in the face. While its humor ranged from slapstick to cutting, the message was serious. The play established a theme that missionary journals would revisit throughout the period: a strictly republican civilizing mission, poisoned by ineffectual measures and economic interests, could only end in failure. With Libre-Pensée, the African subject of the Freemasons' civilizing mission, as a clear example, this humorous story argued that staunchly secular policies would result in the unenviable ends of drunkenness, indolence, and savagery.

Other cartoons had little to do with the missionary movement itself but rather poked fun at colonial encounters generally. Like "Let's Civilize!" they appeared to make no direct criticism of republicanism, relying instead on unfortunate miscommunications between Europeans and "natives." But beneath the colonizer's oblivion lurked the missions' assertion that the welfare of the uncivilized should not be entrusted to the inept. One cartoon, for example, skewered the colonizer's concern about whether indigenous populations preferred British or French rule. An aptly dressed cartoon colonizer put the question to an absurdly caricatured "native," whose clownlike hairdo, polka-dot pants, and umbrella made him appear like a circus freak. "Me no know," the savage replied. "Me no eaten Frenchman yet!"[56] Another cartoon had a colonial official presenting a local chief with a medal. "Valliant chief," the European pronounced, "to compensate you for your bravery, I present to you the cross, of which my government thinks you worthy . . . and which I am proud to be able to pin on your chest." As the European pinned the

Figure 8.1.   –"Ah well! You, who are from this country,
do you like Frenchmen or Englishmen better?"
–"Me no know. Me no eaten Frenchman yet."
From "Récréation," *Petit Almanach de la Propagation de
la Foi* (1900). (Reproduced with permission from the
Oeuvres pontificales missionnaires—Coopération
missionnaire, Lyon.)

medal, the grossly caricatured native jumped and screamed in agony, for like
all stereotypical "savages" he wore no shirt, only a feathered skirt.[57] This cartoon subverted the common military theme that pervaded official colonial
imagery, recalling photos and etchings from the colonies in which officers
called indigenous soldiers to attention.[58]

    Both of these cartoons reflected popular European beliefs that beyond the
boundaries of Europe were lands inhabited by half-clad cannibals.[59] While
the images undoubtedly played to Frenchmen's sense of racial superiority,
the uncivilized ways of the cartoon "natives" were not the butt of the jokes.
Rather, the cartoons relied on the incongruous attitudes and actions of the

colonizers. Taken by themselves, these cartoons posed little serious criticism of the French colonial project—in fact, many nonmissionary publications and popular newspapers shared a similar sense of humor. Only when placed side by side with stories of missionary successes at converting unseemly behavior did the innocence of these cartoons begin to pale.

In 1891, the *Almanach des Missions* published a two-page cartoon conceived by Père Alexandre Le Roy called "The Introduction of Civilization in Africa." Le Roy made use of humorous juxtapositions of the cultural practices of Europeans and Africans in twelve separate but related images.[60] The influence of republican colonizers shaped every picture, though no actual French officials were depicted. Instead, the cartoon followed a young African man, showing the ways in which republican "civilization" had reshaped his life. In the first image, dressed in little more than a loincloth, the young man tried on a shoe, placing "one foot in civilization." Another had the figure struggling with an ill-fitting dinner coat, with a caption reading "a black suit for visiting *Moushu le Gouvernu*." In other scenes, the African battled ratty umbrellas, monstrous top hats, and immense *pantalons*.

Though it resembled countless other colonial gags, Le Roy's cartoon was a biting commentary when considered from the perspective of the republican *mission civilisatrice* in Africa. It systematically ridiculed colonial education, military training, and other "civilizing" projects. For example, in an image subtitled "breaking in," the French colonial presence made its only appearance, here in the shape of a boot kicking the African's backside. The African showed a "taste for things of the mind" with a copy of *Le Figaro* in hand; but he revealed his illiteracy by holding the paper upside down. Instead of reading, he satiated his "taste" by licking the ink from the page. Le Roy also lambasted the example set by colonists with Africans in their employ. In two images, Le Roy's cartoon houseboy drank "a small cup of vermouth while *he* has *his* siesta" and kicked back in a comfortable chair "like *him*," smoking a cigar and drinking alcohol like the master of the house. Again, even while *he*—the colonist—remained absent, his debauched practices poisoned the locals around him. Le Roy's final image had a group of young Africans gathered around a European missionary. Here, in this ordered place contrasting with the caricature of the republican's civilizing project, the reader finds that "a bit of catechism is still what succeeds the best."

More than a decade later, cartoons critical of the republican civilizing mission continued to re-create similar scenarios. "The Disciple," in the 1903 *Almanach*, was composed of four poorly drawn caricatures that told the moral of republican education. In the cartoon, a republican colonist, dressed in pith helmet and appropriate garb, taught a stereotypical native, in loincloth and jewelry and toting a spear, about the true meaning of civilization. The colonist started his lesson in predictable fashion: "Above all, no prejudice. Neither god, nor the devil. . . . Understand?" The African grunted affirmatively, "*Hé!*" The colonist equated hell with having nothing to eat, and heaven with a good piece of meat, and then described "a truly civilized person" as someone who wore a hat, pants, a jacket. "*Compris*?" the Frenchman again asked. A fast-learning disciple, the African undressed the colonist and donned his clothes, then threw the colonist into a pot of stew for dinner. "*Compris!*" the African answered, with a ghoulish grin.[61]

Cartoons provided in shorthand the crux of the missionary movement's argument against a purely republican vision of civilization. At the heart of this critique was the belief that republican methods of reform were superficial at best. To dress and look like a Frenchman only masked a deeper moral and intellectual backwardness. A truly civilized individual needed more than a top hat and tails. The repeated use of these visual types—the republican as defined by hat, suit, shoes, and umbrella—also suggests a broader critique of French bourgeois society as a whole. Though the dressing of indigenous populations was certainly a component of republican colonization, never were local peoples expected to wear, as missionary cartoons suggested, the uniform of the bourgeoisie.[62] Missionary cartoonists and satirists may well have chosen these images to appeal to their readership's sensibilities; many of the Oeuvre's readership came from rural France, which itself was undergoing a cultural transformation at the hands of republican colonizers. The arrival of bourgeois colonizers with different fashions and cultural prejudices was likely a recognizable—and distasteful—image to certain readers of the Oeuvre's publications.

Further, French colonizers, according to these cartoons, not only failed to help reform cultural practices in indigenous societies but also provided new vices to be overcome. Alcohol was the worst of these. *L'eau de vie* caused indolence, death, and violence and led to other, unspeakable acts. The introduction of alcohol, as well as money that could be used to buy alcohol, was a point of contention between missionaries and colonialists in many parts of the empire. In Polynesia, for example, where concern about drink was particularly serious, missionaries regularly cited alcohol as a source of immorality and even depopulation. But so too did republicans. In fact, alcoholism was a preoccupation of Third Republic France. Republican politicians, novelists, and scientists all associated alcoholic consumption with a host of anxieties linked to domestic and colonial fears: race degeneration, violence, and irrationality.[63] Like workers in France, indigenous drinkers were likely to quit their jobs, to neglect their families, to waste the little money they had, or even to rebel.[64] But the language of these cartoons, which essentialized characteristics in order to give clarity and meaning, did not allow for such vagaries: missionaries supported abstinence and a rejection of spirits; French colonists did not. Thus, the republican civilizer not only failed to improve the lot of the "native" but threatened to worsen it.

With claim to the French "civilizing mission" at stake, the use of dehumanizing racial stereotypes became a key ingredient of the missionary movement's rhetoric. To prove the importance of missionaries in "civilizing" non-European societies, missionary journals increasingly portrayed potential converts as idiotic. The message was that savage and barbaric habits could not be corrected easily; rather, it required the patience, experience, and godly guidance offered by missionaries. As with all racist humor, the more extreme the stereotype, the more effective the punch line. The same held true in the political message of the cartoon: the more hapless, repugnant, and irredeemable the indigenous caricature appeared, the more necessary was the mission's work. In these years when France was torn apart by anti-Semitism and anticlericalism, the mission repeatedly avoided the divisive language of domestic politics. Instead, in search of unity and conciliation, it adopted a racially charged language of French supremacy.

The Catholic "Civilizing Mission"

As chapter 1 showed, the term "civilization" was of secondary importance to the Catholic missionary movement from its regeneration in the 1820s until at least the mid-1880s. For decades, civilization was little more than a positive by-product of the religious, spiritual, and moral awakening that missionaries brought to neophyte communities. Overwhelmingly, missionaries were committed to one goal: winning souls. Conversion was an essential precondition of (and, frankly, more important than) spreading civilization, a concept many missionaries associated with staunchly laic (read: sinful) republicans. As an almanac put it in 1885, by living among a group of people and teaching them the "Christian life," the missionary "engendered in them civilization." Only after conversion could missionaries teach their followers the benefits of modernity, such as farming techniques and industry. This was the same process, as missionaries often noted, that had made old Europe "the foyer of civilization."[65]

With the deepening divisions of the Dreyfus affair, and with left-wing radicals calling to ban missionary work in the colonies, the Oeuvre's publications increasingly pushed the concept of civilization as their own. This vision of civilization made room for the missionary agenda of old: conversion and the acquisition of a "Christian" mode of behavior were necessary preconditions of civilization. But civilization allowed missionary editors to outline their objectives in terms that closely mirrored republican colonial rhetoric. Articles, for example, hailed new missions as opportunities to spread *civilization*—not Christianity—to previously isolated regions. One such case was the White Fathers' mission to Timbuktu in the mid-1890s. The *Annales* and *Missions Catholiques* both covered the event, with editorial comments rich with imagery of conquest. Cardinal Lavigerie took on the role of a general who dreamed of someday planting the cross in this place legendary for its remoteness. According to an article in the *Annales*, the opening of the mission in "the mysterious city" ultimately sounded "the hour of deliverance and civilization"—*not*, as one might expect to find in a missionary journal, the hour of conversion to Christianity.[66]

Once the movement embraced civilization as a metaphor of evangelization, it then portrayed missionary work as inextricable from the republican civilizing mission. The missions and official France became partners in a great civilizing project. In 1895, the *Annales*'s "Coup d'oeil" spoke of how a North African hospital opened by France and run by the White Sisters "attests to the marvelous power that the double action of the cross and the sword exercises for civilization."[67] Stories of French administrators assisting missions further unified the religious and the colonial. There was continuing coverage, for example, of the help that the French minister in Peking had lent French missionaries in gaining reparations from the Chinese government.[68] Another piece reported with pride the president of the republic's acknowledgment of the achievements of missionaries abroad.[69]

Visits by French soldiers to Catholic churches abroad were another common news item that brought Catholicism and colonialism closer. One report told of the service held at Antananarivo Cathedral for the French soldiers who had fallen in the battle to take Madagascar. Crowds gathered to see the spectacle of Frenchmen packing the flag-strewn church: "Once again . . . *Catholic* and *French* signify as always one and the same thing."[70] Another recounted how a ceremony at a church in France put the 1895 expedition to Madagascar "under the protection of the great saint" Vincent de Paul "of whom the Church and France are equally proud."[71]

The rhetorical blend of Christianity, civilization, and patriotism in the pages of the *Annales* became all the more potent after 1901. The editions following that year's electoral success of anticlerical radicals suggest that the Oeuvre's strategy in adopting their new rhetoric paralleled efforts by missionaries in Indochina, Madagascar, and other colonies. With the passing of anticlerical legislation that closed religious associations in France, the *Annales* began publishing articles that emphasized missionaries' patriotism and commitment to civilization, as well as highlighted the practical benefits of missionaries in the colonies. Articles commonly described missionary work as spreading French influence around the globe. The bishop of Peking, Mgr. Favier, wrote one such article, noting how the missionary "makes France loved by all Chinese without distinction." France was always in the missionary's thoughts, he went on, and even his religion passed through "the French prism."[72] A letter from a missionary in Dahomey noted that the mission in Benin had already taught a number of students to speak French and sing patriotic songs like "Salut au drapeau de la France!" It concluded by saying that missionaries "are certainly the best and the most useful pioneers of civilization and French influence."[73]

In 1903, the *Annales* published the first of a number of articles underscoring the important scientific developments made by missionaries. The piece, which covered missionary contributions to geography, natural history, archaeology, meteorology, and linguistics, demonstrated the services the mission rendered "even to material civilization." Nothing could be "more opportune or more timely," the article continued, than missionary contributions to science, considering that the "patriotism of the apostolate" was currently under question and attack.[74] Four years later, the secretary general of the central council of the Oeuvre published a series of more detailed articles in the *Annales* on the same subject, carefully noting the praise secular organizations like the Société de géographie de Paris had for missionaries on all continents of the globe.[75] This emphasis on the practical benefits of missionary work—scientific advances and the spreading of French "influence" abroad—added another facet to the religious civilizing mission, blurring still further the rhetoric of evangelization and colonialism in the 1890s and early 1900s.

Perhaps the clearest delineation of the missions' new relationship to colonialism came in an article entitled "What Missionaries Do in Africa," which appeared in 1911. In a detailed description of the Catholic civilizing process, Père Cayzac of the Congregation de Saint-Esprit addressed those critics who believed missionaries inhibited the "march of progress and of modern civilization." Central to the civilizing mission, he argued, must be a process that transformed the very ideas that informed savage behavior in the first place. None was more effective than conversion, "that is," Cayzac wrote, "a revolution, a complete change in the ideas . . . that hold the savage in barbarity, and [that] bar the road to all moral, social, humanitarian, and even material progress." In preparing an individual for baptism, the priest explained, "one prepares his soul to receive the germs of progress and civilization."[76]

Though baptism was a necessary step toward civilization, Cayzac's article touched on issues of interest to republican civilizers in Africa. In defending the efficacy of Christian civilization, for example, he noted how the reform of marriage practices among certain African groups would improve the plight of women. "One exaggerates nothing," he noted, "when one compares the African woman to a beast of burden"; in Africa, "to buy" and "to marry" are expressed "by one and the same verb." By introducing Christian marriage rituals, missionaries could end this "slavery." Such Christian reform figured centrally in Cayzac's general argument:

> The missionary has no other ambition than that of establishing the greatest number of Christian households; for it is only by the Christian family that the black race will one day be able to be civilized. And seeing that, of all the whites, the missionary is the *only one* to occupy himself with the creation of these Christian households, it seems to me to demonstrate: first, that missionaries do the work of civilization, and second, that missionaries *alone* do it sincerely![77]

Cayzac's article in many ways represented the culmination of twenty-five years of retooling the missionary project. By addressing republican goals, such as ending slavery and spreading civilization, Cayzac also redefined and justified the importance of missionaries' function in French colonialism. The new missionary was not the same warrior he had been thirty years earlier. The homeless soldier of God was now a faithful and proud servant of France. The missionary, once concerned solely with the cosmic battle between God and Satan, now contributed to much-debated programs to educate and reform populations in a way that served both missionary ends and colonial concerns. The only step left was to prove that French missionaries had *always* been committed to imperial expansion. To do that, they needed to rewrite history.

New Chapters in the Missionary Past

New missionary publications launched in the late 1880s were consciously historical. Articles placed the history of the Catholic mission not simply within the context of the Bible and the rise of Christianity but within the triumph of the modern French nation as well. In making this effort, missionary publications took up a national pastime. From the French Revolution forward, Frenchmen defined and defended their nation through history. Michelet, Lamartine, and Taine are only a few examples of writers who tried to explain the political and moral identity of the nation—its obligations, motivations, and aspirations—in historical writing. Historical interpretation often revealed more about the historian's politics than the actual past events explored. As Robert Gildea has argued, Adolph Thiers's nostalgia for Louis XVI and Louis Blanc's rehabilitation of Robespierre were less contributions to historical debates than commentaries on contemporary politics and moral arguments.[78] Many history books accomplished on paper what the Panthéon in Paris achieved in stone: they cast new national heroes—republican writers, politicians, and savants—whose lives in the past gave shape to the nation's present and future.[79]

Missionary publications positioned their workers, past and present, within the context of republican colonial and national politics. Starting around 1900, the Oeuvre de la propagation de la foi and other missionary organizations supported the publication of detailed histories that revisited the lives of distant missionary figures. New histories rewrote past missionary deeds, often making Catholic workers appear entirely devoted to and conscious servants of France. Missionary history was by no means a new genre: organizations traditionally produced their own histories that chronicled the founding, growth, and works of their missions. But these works typically explored only spiritual questions, paying special attention to the sacrifices of missionaries, the successes of proselytization, and martyrdom. In the divisive climate of fin-de-siècle France, a new type of missionary history emerged that would both celebrate organizations' religious triumphs and emphasize religious workers' contributions to French empire.

Two books in particular attempted to place the history of French missions within the context of colonial expansion. The first was the publication in 1901–3 of the massive, six-tome history *Les Missions catholiques au XIXe siècle* under the direction of a Jesuit, Jean-Baptiste Piolet. The second was the more compact, more manageable one-volume history *Héros trop oubliés de notre épopée coloniale* (or *Forgotten Heroes of Our Colonial Epic*), written by Valérien Groffier in 1905.[80] Both works, in somewhat different ways, presented missionary history as French colonial history and wrote missionaries into a narrative of national sacrifice motivated by patriotism.

Piolet's exhaustive collection presented chapters on every corner of the globe, written by dozens of missionary historians and ethnographers. Piolet's own expertise was in Madagascar, about which he had been writing since the 1890s, though not everyone in the missionary community was convinced of his literary talents, including the Jesuit bishop in Antananarivo, Jean-Baptiste Cazet. "There is in this work much that is good," Cazet commented, having read one of Piolet's works. "But to those who know the men and things of Madagascar," he continued, there were "such regrettable things: inexactitudes, falsehoods" in Piolet's pages.[81] Regardless, in France, Piolet won numerous awards and endless praise from the missionary community and beyond.[82] In the late 1890s, he was invited to give lectures on Madagascar at the Sorbonne, and he published a number of texts on French possessions in the Indian Ocean.[83]

With a layout similar to the Oeuvre de la propagation de la foi's journal *Missions Catholiques*, Piolet's project included photos, maps, and engravings from around the world. The work focused on ethnographic material, in the spirit of the *Lettres édifiantes* of the Jesuits of old, which had chronicled every aspect of non-Christian societies to ease future proselytization. In the age of colonialism, however, ethnographic and geographic studies by missionaries took on new significance. In addition to providing information useful to proselytization, works such as Piolet's also provided colonial administrators and officers valuable data concerning the rituals, morals, and landscapes of colonized populations. Missionaries made full use of this in defending their political claims. For example, they had for a number of years publicized the value of their maps to colonial expansion. In 1900, the Oeuvre encouraged the editor of *Missions Catholiques* to organize a geographic exhibition at the Universal Exposition in Paris.[84] The missionary community showed maps from around the world, drawing considerable attention and winning one priest a silver medal for his efforts organizing the show.[85]

In addition to ethnographic and scientific data, the studies in Piolet's collection recorded the history of Catholic proselytization and the current state of Catholic missions. Stories of martyrs, descriptions of hardships overcome, and lists of churches and chapels were interspersed with commentaries that situated each mission within the past and present of French colonialism. For example, Père Louis Chatelet authored the section on New

Caledonia in the wake of missionary-Freemason conflict in the colony.[86] Residue of the conflict was apparent on every page of Chatelet's history. He reminded his readers that when the first French colonists arrived on the island in 1855, they were welcomed ashore by missionaries, and that, in 1869, when the free colonists of Païta decided to build a sugar refinery, they turned to missionaries for guidance.[87]

With the history of the colony thus stated, Chatelet then directly rejected claims of missionary wrongdoing by arguing that the accusers—"self-described defenders of republican theories" who were supported by a "complaisant press"—did not enjoy the support of the majority of the colonial population. The mission, he claimed, played both a key spiritual and an economic role. First, he noted that most Europeans in the urban centers of New Caledonia were happy to have priests: "The proof that colonists don't see in the missionary an adversary is that all the European centers which don't have a priest in residence have asked to have monthly or bimonthly religious services, and are happy to receive the priest." Were that not reason enough to support the mission in this era of *mise-en-valeur*, Chatelet quoted the president of the Union agricole calédonienne as saying that the mission always helped to the fullest extent with agricultural development for the benefit of the colony. "*Voilà la vérité.*"[88]

Other entries followed suit—from Algeria to the Marquesas, from Guyana to Madagascar. Piolet's collection wove regional ethnographies and histories with the contemporary political concerns of a missionary project under attack. Entry after entry provided material to support the assertion that Catholic missions and their followers were friends of France and assets to colonization. Piolet's work melded anthropological, historical, and scientific interest in the colonies with stirring commentaries on France's moral and political relationship to the outside world. This weaving of colonial with domestic concerns explained Piolet's title for the series as a whole: *La France du dehors*— suggesting the making of France abroad as well as the making of France *from* the outside.

France's Culture of Proselytization

The entries in the massive compendium were linked by the collection's conclusion, written by Ferdinand Brunetière. The choice of Brunetière was a significant statement in itself. An influential literary critic, erstwhile professor at the École normale, editor of the *Revue des Deux Mondes*, and member of the Académie française, Brunetière converted to Catholicism in 1895 after a trip to Rome. He explained his conversion in philosophical terms, remaining strongly committed to that most republican of intellectual traditions, positivism. His political allegiances were complex. He revered Ernest Renan, who was honored with a statue in Tréguier in 1903 at a ceremony hosted by the radical anticlerical prime minister Émile Combes. Yet he was also a conservative and anti-Dreyfusard. Brunetière's "Conclusion" in Piolet's book therefore reflected the missionary movement's desire to address political and cultural issues in a language true to both republicanism and the sanctity of Catholicism. For Brunetière, what linked religion and republicanism was civilization; Piolet's work proved that France could not spread civilization—even republican ideals of civilization—without the help of Catholicism.

Brunetière began his conclusion by asking whether Piolet's work was a monument to the glory of God or to the glory of France. "But is it necessary to decide," he wondered. Missionaries, he claimed, had never distinguished "French" from "Catholic" in their own minds. And so it was true the world round: "Catholicism is France, and France is Catholicism."[89] This formulation did little more than reiterate the most basic premises of missionary rhetoric of the time. But Brunetière's argument took an innovative turn that raised it above the missionary din and that indirectly challenged the concept of a republican civilizing mission. Rather than suggest that missionaries were valuable to colonialism, he defined their main occupation as an essentially French characteristic. Missionary organizations, including the Oeuvre de la propagation de la foi, were "exclusively French projects," according to Brunetière; "French not only for being born and developed in France, but French for being marked by an expressly French character; French for being animated by an ardor for proselytism that one could compare to that of our great writers of all kinds; French for remaining, even abroad, centers of French culture and action." In Brunetière's view, proselytism—not necessarily evangelization but simply the desire to spread ideas and cultural sensibilities— was a national trait of *religieux* and laypeople alike. More than other nations, he claimed, Frenchmen wanted to mold ideas and opinion. When abroad, he noted, the Englishman took England with him and the German was notoriously adept at adaptation. But the Frenchman, Brunetière insisted, wanted to change the world around him.[90]

Brunetière's argument defended French Catholic missionaries while providing a justification of French colonial expansion. In contrast to the Englishman and German, "the Frenchman converts the *indigène* to the genius of our race," he wrote, "he fills him with his qualities and his flaws, he endeavors to make him a 'man,' an equal, a 'brother of his kind.'" It was a selfless task for the French, Brunetière continued, for they cared neither for making money nor for exercising their power over "a so-called 'inferior' humanity." Rather, the Frenchman wanted "to spread his ideas" in order to rejuvenate the soul of Asians and "the infantile soul" of Africans. Adeptly, Brunetière brought this line of reasoning, which so clearly elaborated the republican colonial project, back to the issue of missionaries. The Frenchman, he continued, "preaches, he teaches, he persuades. His most ardent ambition is to change hearts. And, precisely, because this is also the ambition of Catholicism, that's why, when we say 'France is Catholicism', and 'Catholicism is France' . . . we want above all to say that between the genius of France and that of Catholicism, there are relations, harmony, intimate and providential 'affinities.' "[91]

In addition to linking the missionary's and the colonialist's desire to spread the genius of the French race across the globe, Brunetière denounced Freemasonry and the anticlericalism of the radical left, and attacked the strictly laic vision of the civilizing mission. What kept the world from "falling back into barbarity," he argued, was not "progress of mathematics or chemistry"; rather, "it is active virtues, 'the sacrifice of man for man' and this abnegation of self which Christianity made the law of human conduct. *'Love thy neighbor as thyself.'* " Some societies, he conceded, were more developed than others—noting that the Chinese, for instance, had lagged behind Europe by closing their borders to outside influence. But all societies were open to Christian teaching and therefore could be helped by the work of missionaries. The true work of the missionary, he reflected, was to teach across the world what it meant to be human. For when civilizations crumbled away, the essence of "man" remained—and this, according to Brunetière, did "not vary with the degree of facial angle, the obliqueness of the eyes, or the color of the skin."[92]

In teaching the essential qualities of all human beings, Brunetière's missionaries developed societies to a state that looked remarkably republican. For example, he argued that missionaries freed converts from customs and superstitions that "imprisoned their natural liberty. They give their catechists knowledge of their dignity. They put them in a state of knowing themselves, conducting themselves, and governing themselves." He added that missionaries "deliver the 'oppressed,' they free the 'imprisoned.' "[93] Such liberational language was central to the republican civilizing mission. In describing missionaries in these terms, Brunetière refused to see them as simply serving the glory of god; instead, by accepting the potential of all races missionaries developed a fraternity among people.[94] "It is thus for the progress of civilization that our missionaries work," he wrote, brushing aside a long tradition of considering civilization of secondary importance.[95] He drew a picture of missionary civilization that could not be more French or more republican. Brunetière's missionaries worked for three ideals that he found in no ways at odds with Christianity: liberty, equality, and fraternity.

Brunetière's conclusion framed Piolet's opus as a massive history of the French desire to spread civilization. If Frenchmen were defined by their need to spread the benefits of their culture—to proselytize—then no one was more French than missionaries. Brunetière even questioned whether progress, or at least "any progress that is a gain for humanity," was possible without Christianity. Piolet's collection portrayed the missionaries' world, including the French colonial world, as a "peaceful empire" where, according to Brunetière, "the arts of the West follow them"; as a result of missionary work, he added, communal life was improved, familial relations were consolidated, and slavery disappeared. For Brunetière and the missionary movement as a whole, proselytizing was at the core of French identity, of what France and Frenchmen stood for morally in the world. Scattered in distant corners of the globe, missionaries constantly "constructed" France "*du dehors*"—from outside.[96]

Remembering Forgotten Heroes

In May 1905, two years after the final publication of Piolet's series, the leaders of the Oeuvre in Lyon and Paris agreed to support the production of a history of the missionary contribution to French colonial expansion.[97] The Paris council designated Mgr. Morel, director of *Missions Catholiques*, to act as intermediary in order, as the council put it, "to assure the success of the publication for the greatest good of the association."[98] When Morel returned seven months later to present a copy of the final book—Valérien Groffier's *Héros trop oubliés de notre épopée coloniale*—the council was unanimous in "admiring its beautiful execution."[99] Groffier's book, which went through a number of reprints until the late 1920s, addressed debates in the empire and France over the work of missionaries. Even more than Piolet's collection, Groffier's book focused on individual heroes—ranging from Pigneau de Béhaine to Cardinal Lavigerie—to produce a collective portrait of God's martyrs and servants who deserved a place both in heaven and in France's pantheon of great national heroes.

Groffier wrote *Héros trop oubliés* at a critical moment for the missionary movement. The Oeuvre first encouraged the work in the wake of the passing of the law of 5 July 1904 that withdrew the right of religious congregations to teach in France. When the bill had passed the Chamber a few months earlier, a provision was added exempting the application of the bill to congregations teaching in the colonies. But how long this exemption would remain in place was anyone's guess. Missionary organizations had real reason for continued concern: the anticlerical wave was still rising, and radical politicians were pushing for the final blow, the separation of Church and state, which was passed in December 1905. While congregations in France organized themselves to counter the law's domestic repercussions, foreign missions faced the task of justifying their importance to the colonial cause, fearing that the same spirit of anticlericalism would cripple their efforts.

In announcing the publication of the book, the *Annales* made reference to the political crisis of the hour in its usual circumscribed manner: "Ten years ago the glory of the missionary was not contested," the announcement began; "men of good faith" in parliament and the press recognized "the great service" missionaries rendered "to their *patrie* and to civilization." Now approbation had fallen to silence. Revealing their goal of writing missionaries into national history, editors at the *Annales* complained that a recent, well-written book on French colonialism had completely ignored Cardinal Lavigerie in its discussion of Algeria and Tunisia and had failed to mention the contributions of missionaries in New Caledonia, "where everyone knows of the patriotic role of the Marists." They searched the book's pages on French Indochina, but Mgr. Pigneau de Béhaine was nowhere to be found. Groffier's book, the announcement concluded, would correct these grave inadequacies.[100]

The Oeuvre's selection of Groffier was significant, for his career bridged religious and secular interests. His professional affiliations included acting as secretary of both the journal *Missions Catholiques* and the Geographical Society of Lyon. He was also a professor of economic and colonial geography at the École supérieure de commerce de Lyon, a recipient of the Chavalier de Saint Grégoire le Grand, and an officer of the Académie française. Groffier's background made him well suited to assert the patriotism of missionaries. In his expert opinion, they were "charged to perpetuate the most pure traditions of a very Christian nation, its charity, its faith, its generous inspiration"; by serving religion and humanity, he argued, they "serve and honor France." Groffier's life to some extent mirrored his subjects': the goal of his study, he explained, was to show how missionaries reconciled their "patriotic obligations with the obligations of their sacred ministry."[101]

Groffier's book was in many ways the culmination of the rewriting of the missionary past. Rather than offer new insights into the nature of the missionaries' relations with colonial administrators, or their feelings of nationalism, he restated existing formulations with rhetorical flourishes. Nor did he provide new philosophical arguments in the fashion of Brunetière. In fact, in his epilogue, Groffier borrowed freely—often word for word—whole passages from Brunetière's conclusion. The passages he chose to plagiarize are telling in their own way: Groffier especially appreciated Brunetière's assertions that French missionaries were "French for being animated by an ardor for proselytism," as well as the idea that missionaries "constructed" France abroad.[102] Groffier reiterated the ideas of countless other missionary commentators both in France and abroad, such as Launay, Louvet, Mossard, Cazet, and Chatelet: missionaries honored the French race by spreading in the colonies the influence of France; their converts were "clients" and lovers of France; and in making Christians, missionaries also made Frenchmen.[103]

What was unique to Groffier's history was how tightly it intertwined missionary and French colonial history. Whereas Piolet's collection balanced ethnographic and geographic reports with historical and political analysis in an attempt to justify missionary work, Groffier literally rewrote colonial history, attributing to missionaries as much, and often more, credit in the expansion of empire as soldiers, officers, and administrators. Missionary pamphlets, books, and speeches in the 1890s and early 1900s regularly bragged about the important role missionaries played in the history of colonialism, but Groffier made far bolder assertions. He wrote, for example, that

Mother Javouhey—the founder of the Soeurs de Saint Joseph de Cluny—
"will incontestably remain the most remarkable figure in the history of French
colonization in the nineteenth century." Regarding Madagascar, Groffier declared that the history of the island would never be separated from the memory of Saint Vincent de Paul, who first sent missionaries there.[104] With such
hyperbole, Groffier aimed to place missionary work at the center of French
colonial history.

Groffier evoked the inseparable relationship between French missionary
and colonial history with repeated visual and textual images. The first image
to appear in the text foretold formulations to come. The frontispiece entitled
"The Missionary on Apostolic Excursion" portrayed a missionary in a boat
drifting from shore. In the background, a group of people gathered around a
single mission building nestled among the palms. A pole rose above the tree-
tops, hoisting the tricolor flag of France. A frame bordered the whole scene,
decorated with a bamboo pole and a larger flag, this one tattered, symbolizing the hardship of missionaries' lives and their undying commitment to the
patrie.

Like this image, Groffier's narrative wrapped his religious missionaries
in patriotic regalia. The book started with Algeria, itself a symbolic choice.
France's most important overseas possession, Algeria was not a colony but an
integral part of France and thus embodied the central theme of Groffier's
book—that possessions abroad were inextricable from the nation as a whole.
The taking of Algiers by French troops offered further proof of the linking of
France's history of religious and colonial proselytization: "The very day of the
taking of Algiers," Groffier wrote, "Marshall de Bourmont planted the cross,
symbol of redemption and of Christian faith, on the highest summit of this
capital. A very French gesture, that is, very noble, very courageous, very ex-
pressive, very true to our purest national traditions." Immediately, Groffier
added, the missionaries arrived "to consecrate, to translate in acts and living
works this eloquent reaffirmation of the old *Gesta Dei per Francos*" in the new
possession.[105] By linking the army to missionary work, and missionaries to
the memory of the Crusades—*Gesta Dei per Francos* was the cry of French crusaders, and the title of Guibert de Nogent's twelfth-century account of the
First Crusade—Groffier unearthed the historical origins of Brunetière's claim
that proselytization was an inherently French cultural trait.[106] Despite its clear
Christian message, such a retelling of the Algerian conquest did not deviate
from republican ideas at the time. Even contemporary republican historians
cited the Crusades as the origin of French foreign policy, a kind of medieval
French colonialism that had its own version of a civilizing mission.[107]

What followed in Algeria was, according to Groffier, a history that wove together apostles and generals, bishops and diplomats. The author interspersed
throughout the chapter images of towns, churches, Algerians, farms, army officials, and portraits of missionaries. The logical end point of the chapter was
"the great Frenchman" Archbishop Lavigerie. The allusion emphasized the

book's commitment to *ralliement*: Lavigerie's 1890 "toast," which encouraged Catholics to engage with the republic, would have been fresh in the minds of Groffier's readers. In the figure of Lavigerie, Groffier's desired links between France and colony, between missionary and patriot-hero, were complete.[108]

Such links were not lost on the book's readers. The bishop of Autun, for example, described Groffier's heroes as carrying "across the entire world the flag of France wrapped around the Cross," proving once again "that 'piety is useful to all.' "[109] Just as the raising of the statue of Pigneau de Béhaine, bishop of Adran, in front of the Saigon cathedral had allowed the missions of Indochina to redefine their place in local history, Groffier's book recast Catholic missionaries as heroes of both religion and colonialism. The book's patriotic Christian heroes were meant to complement, not challenge, the republic's own pantheon of secular saints. In a climate of political division where glorifying domestic Catholic heroes was controversial, Groffier's book, and the French missionary community more generally, looked to the empire with its tales of martyrs and converts to reconfigure the past in a way that would embrace both religious and secular national aspirations.

Missionaries and a New Image of Empire

The overtly patriotic missionary publications like the almanacs, albums, and histories that were produced with increasing frequency after the mid-1880s had no equivalents earlier in the century. There had been no need for them. French regimes before the Third Republic did not pose any real ideological challenge to evangelization. In such a climate, missionaries were able to win the support of a variety of French Catholics by doing what they did best: embracing and celebrating the deeply spiritual roots of the apostolic life. Looking to scripture and centuries-old traditions, missionaries for much of the century rejected the petty matters of worldly politics in order to join the legions of religious soldiers who battled the forces of Satan and spread the light of Catholicism in the world. But in the 1880s, with the expansion of republican colonialism and the simultaneous rise of anticlericalism in metropolitan politics, French missionaries found it increasingly necessary not only to appeal to their supporters' faith but also to engage and defuse their critics' accusations. As the role of missionary work in a republican empire became the subject of heated conflict, missionary organizations decided that their best defense was to address their accusers and assert their commitment to the nation.

The new publications set out to accomplish in France what newspaper articles, meetings, correspondence, and pronouncements did in Saigon, Papeete, Antananarivo, and elsewhere in the empire: to prove that Catholic missions were patriotic outposts essential to the fulfillment of France's civilizing goals in its colonies. These publications were, with very few exceptions, neither overtly antirepublican nor counterrevolutionary; instead, like missionaries abroad, the Oeuvre and other organizations regularly adopted the language and imagery of *ralliement*, blurring the lines between their religious goals and the colonial aspirations of republican France. The close similarities between the metropolitan and colonial campaigns to defend the missions reveal the extent to which ideas and information constantly bridged the distances separating France from its overseas empire: the concerns and responses of religious workers flowed ceaselessly along channels that led from missionaries and bishops abroad to organizations in France like the Oeuvre de la propagation de la foi, and back again. From this intricate network, a coherent strategy for undermining hostile criticism of missionary work emerged and took shape.

But while missionary efforts in the colonies were aimed primarily at appealing to colonial governments in order to minimize the damage wrought by their foes' attacks, the impact of the metropolitan process of redefining the movement's goals had much broader implications for how many French men and women viewed both colonialism and the populations that inhabited their empire. To protect themselves from radical anticlerical threats to outlaw evangelization, missionary organizations that had long emphasized their international flavor started to nationalize. They redefined past glories to be no longer simply chapters in a never-ending chronicle of the battle between God and Satan. Now, missionary histories were rewritten to show Catholic workers as key figures in the story of French national greatness and the triumphs of republican colonialism. The readiness and speed with which missionaries reconfigured their venerated spiritual traditions are evidence of the power of the modern nation-state—especially through the experience of colonialism—to demand patriotic conformity from all quarters of the population, even traditionally nonnational organizations like Catholic missionary orders. Within a few fleeting years, Catholic missionaries found it impossible to see their work in purely spiritual terms. The politics of religion in fin-de-siècle France required missionaries to work for their *patrie* on earth or else risk giving up their service to their God in heaven.

The striking revision of missionary motivations not only suggests a shift in the way that many Catholic workers viewed their vocation but also shows that, for hundreds of thousands of French men and women who supported evangelizing, colonialism emerged as a topic of great interest late in the century. Like older journals, the new, overtly patriotic missionary publications that appeared in the wake of colonial expansion were essentially fund-raising tools. The annual *comptes-rendus* of the Oeuvre de la propagation de la foi reveal that the effort to place missionary work within the context of colonialism won the movement broader support from the public.[110] Despite the onslaught of anticlerical critics and the divisiveness of the Dreyfus affair, the 1890s represented the apex of support for French missionary work abroad. From 1887 to 1900, the Oeuvre consistently raised about 4 million francs per year in France—the most in its history. Perhaps more telling, during the same period, the readership of the Oeuvre's *Annales* steadily increased. Since the number of *Annales* published corresponded to the number of subscribers to the Oeuvre, the wave of new publications that focused directly on missionary experiences in the empire coincided with a growth in the Oeuvre's base. The greatest show of support came in 1903, in the midst of Émile Combes's government and the supposed triumph of anticlerical politics.

The effects of the 1901, 1904, and 1905 religious laws are marked on the revenue the Oeuvre generated in France but not significantly on its membership. From 1901 to 1906, the amount of money raised in France declined steadily to around 3 million francs, where it would remain until the First World War. Considering the disastrous impact the Law on Associations had on countless religious congregations across France, the support base of the Oeuvre's fund-raising system, such a drop was predictable. By contrast, French readership of the *Annales*—the clearest indication of membership to the organization—did not slump dramatically. This was not a movement in drastic decline: missionaries enjoyed even greater French support in the early 1900s than in the late 1880s. They survived both the Dreyfus affair and the triumph of anticlerical republicanism. And the arrival of republican colonizers in lands once inhabited only by Catholic missionaries—places like Indochina, Madagascar, and Polynesia—attracted a larger audience curious about the apostolic life in the nation's empire.

Because the directors of the Oeuvre believed their publications to be key mouthpieces, they must have been convinced that highlighting Catholicism's gifts to French colonialism would pay off. The number of subscribers held steady, even if individuals did not donate the funds they had before 1901. And missionary recruits—another audience of the Oeuvre's publications—kept coming, likely motivated increasingly by the transparent connection between a love of God and country. As Yannick Essertel notes, the recruitment of religious workers weathered the era of Dreyfus and the ensuing religious conflict, dropping off only after 1907. Even then, the golden age of missionary ordination that began in the 1850s did not truly come to an end until the devastating impact of the First World War.[111] The Oeuvre's success must be attributed to its directors' ability to gauge public concerns, interests, and desires and to use the latest technology to address them.

The Oeuvre's readership offers a rare chance to consider what appealed to a remarkably large group of French men and women—by the Oeuvre's math, more than 1.5 million—in the age of new imperialism. The continued popularity of the missionary movement in France during the politically contentious Dreyfus years suggests the existence of a large segment of the public that historians have ignored. Histories of fin-de-siècle France overwhelmingly focus on the staunch antagonisms between the reactionary right and the radical left, between nationalist Catholicism and rationalist republicanism, and between anti-Semitism and anticlericalism. The missionary movement, however, did not fit into such a neat series of opposites. In contrast to the polemics of national political life, missionary organizations had a complexity all their own: their patriotic publications could dehumanize indigenous people, but, unlike reactionary journals of the era, they were rarely anti-Semitic; they condemned Freemasonry and radicalism but embraced colonial expansion, and they promoted aspects of republican colonialism with the express hope that it would serve evangelization. The onslaught of anticlerical criticism of religious work paradoxically brought the missionary movement into colonial politics by creating important historical and practical links between evangelizing and colonizing.

The impingement of the colonial civilizing mission on the Catholic apostolic tradition also had significant consequences for how French men, women, and children understood non-Christian populations in the world. Throughout much of the nineteenth century, missionary publications focused almost exclusively on evangelization. Readers of journals such as the *Annales de la Propagation de la Foi* and the *Missions Catholiques* found stories of souls saved and pagans redeemed through Christian teachings. While many of these accounts were pejorative, often filled with behavior deemed immoral and un-Christian, the overwhelming message was of the reformative powers of the Catholic faith. Faith, not "civilization," would improve the lot of the nonbeliever. But the civilizing rhetoric of republican colonialism that increasingly became a part of Catholic accounts in the decades after the 1880s added stronger cultural and racial distinctions to missionary views of non-Christians.

Patriotism transformed the most fundamental motivation for evangelizing. Winning converts was no longer simply a victory for God; it also proved the vitality of the nation. This shift to associate conversion with nationalism was not lost on contemporary Catholics, some of whom found the break with tradition deeply disturbing. In 1919, Pope Benedict XV, in his encyclical *Maximum Illud*, deemed the transformation of missionary practices "deplorable." With France clearly in mind, Benedict XV highlighted "certain publications on the subject of Missions, which have appeared in the last few years," that had shown themselves less concerned with the triumph of the kingdom of God than with "the influence of the writer's own country." For the pope, in addition to stripping missionaries of their "dignity," such a desire to serve the nation as well as heaven could only alienate "the heathen."[112] By 1919, however, "for God and *patrie*" had effectively become the mantra of French missionaries hoping both to avoid accusations of treason and to benefit from the security and stability brought by colonial regimes.

Patriotic missionary publications, with their caricatured savages and sensational stories of immoral souls, offered a new image of non-Christians as people in need of both the word of Christ and the policies, technology, and education that only French colonization could offer. Throughout the nineteenth century, the portraits of "heathens, pagans, and heretics" in the pages of missionary publications no doubt fed culturally and scientifically racist notions prevalent in French society. But the far more pejorative representations of France's colonial populations evident in the patriotic missionary literature of the 1890s and later left little to the imagination. Differences between missionary and potential convert, which were long predicated on the alterable issue of faith, became ineluctably fixed along cultural and racial lines. In this way, by adopting civilization as a central concern, missionary organizations abandoned the belief that Christianity could save the world's non-Christians. By linking their work more closely to secular notions of civilizing, missionaries ceased to see non-Christian peoples simply as "pagans" in need of saving and, instead, represented them increasingly as the "inferior races" of Jules Ferry's famous equation of the republican civilizing mission.

The infusion of missionary literature with pejorative representations of indigenous populations did not stop at the debasement of non-Christians. The immutable category of race transformed—no doubt unintentionally—the power of Christian conversion itself. Once the primary goal of the wandering apostle, conversion increasingly became represented as only a first step in the transformation of colonial societies; it was an integral but incomplete stage of a process that necessarily included schooling and improved hygiene, the reform of morals and social habits, and programs of economic and political development. The linking of religious salvation to more secular projects of civilizing meant that, as French men and women grew more convinced of racial differences and skeptical of the possibilities of culturally assimilating indigenous populations, the transformative potential of religious conversion was likewise called into question. Patriotic missionary publications' incessant calls to civilize the world's converts, coupled with their dehumanizing representations of non-Christians, not only rendered indigenous populations into savages but also threatened to undermine French men and women's faith in the ominpotence of their own God—a fact that worried Benedict XV. By reorienting the goals of the movement, patriotic missionary publications thus argued what many secularists had been saying for years: the good Lord above could not alone guarantee a "savage" salvation. For that kind of miracle, one needed to bask in the glory of France.

Conclusion: Finding France Abroad

All things come into being by the conflict of opposites.
—Heraclitus

For well over a century, scholars, politicians, and social critics of all stripes have struggled to describe imperialism, debating economic theories, political models, diplomatic concerns, and subaltern sensibilities, leaving few pieces of colonial life unturned. Critiques of imperialism have fed revolutions and filled history books but have achieved, perhaps predictably, little consensus. While plenty of uncertainties about the nature of empires have emerged, one point is hard to dismiss. Beneath the shipping lanes, military posts, and mountains of reports, underpinning the laws and bureaucracies, modern empires have been built soundly on faith—be it religious, secular, or a combination of both. In the late nineteenth century, imperialists saw themselves as conquerors, innovators, scientists, patriots, moralists, reformers, and planners. Even if the more refined of these characterizations have subsequently given way to images less pretty—opportunists, oppressors, torturers—the same truth holds: French colonizers appeared eminently sure of themselves. Little tied Tahitians to Berbers or the Fang to the Bahnar other than France's profound faith in its own greatness. While political will and superior technology were essential to winning colonies, it was overweening confidence and zeal that, in the minds of Frenchmen, melded disparate tracts of land and transformed populations into something concrete, meaningful, even glorious—into an empire.

The question remains whether the French men, women, and children who supported the empire all had faith in the same gods. During the crucial period of expansion from the 1880s to the First World War, they clearly did not. The significant presence of Catholic missionaries evangelizing in the empire reveals that France's colonial expansion often caused as much division as unity. Committed to spreading Christian teachings, combating the malevolent reach of Satan, and expanding the Church's hierarchy across the globe, Catholic missionaries were profoundly wary of officials and colonists armed with liberal, secular ideals, who seemed to pose a great threat to evangelization. Although most officials tried to live by the notion that republican anticlericalism was not for export, they could only do so much to keep radical politicians, Freemason colonists, Protestant missionaries, and their own outspoken administrators from taking aim at the alleged corruption and abuses of Catholic workers.

Missionaries responded to attacks with vigor, though most often not in the way that might have been expected. Instead of lashing back at the dangers and debauchery of republicanism as many reactionary conservatives did, missionaries—from workers on isolated islands to massive organizations in France—sought to prove how evangelizing could serve colonialism. By reveling in the rhetoric of imperialism, with its promises of civilizing savages and remaking the world in a distinctly French image, republican officials and Catholic missionaries smoothed over the great differences of traditions, ideals, and goals that separated them. But the divisive nature of colonialism, with its concerns over budgets and disagreements about policies, meant that, in practice, missionaries and officials more often agreed to ignore each other than arrive at any real consensus.

The central contention of this book has been that the discord over the role of religion in the young republican empire exposes unexplored themes that are crucial to understanding French political and cultural history between 1880 and 1914. First, the histories of colonial conflict in Indochina, Polynesia, and Madagascar show that colonial ideology was anything but programmatic. Rather than the implementation of prescribed republican projects, French colonialism took shape according to the exigencies of limited colonial manpower and budgets, as well as fears over indigenous unrest and establishing effective rule—all concerns that intersected with the deep uncertainties about the presence of Catholic missionaries. Decisions regarding colonial policies were not made by bureaucrats in Paris but were shaped by vibrant political cultures in the colonies that produced rich discussions and heated arguments between Frenchmen deeply divided over *what France stood for* in the world. Competing concerns about race and gender were central to discussions of French colonial objectives, but these categories themselves were skewed and distorted when disagreement hinged on religious discord. Even central tenets of republican ideology, such as the civilizing mission, were debated in the context of establishing, sustaining, and justifying colonial rule.

Critics of Catholic missions regularly played the role of catalyst in motivating changes in both religious and republican work in the empire. Both at home and abroad, Freemasons, Protestant missionaries, low-ranking administrators, outspoken commentators, and radical politicians forced Catholic missionaries to assert their allegiance to France and place their missions within the context of the colonial effort. Missionaries expressed their patriotism and their commitment to France often in the very terms defined by their staunchest republican critics. But, crucially, they in turn *adapted* the language of republican colonialism by asserting that there could be no civilizing mission without Catholicism. This effort to reconfigure "civilization" undermines the widely held view that the civilizing mission was a fundamentally secular ideology either in practice or in representation. For the legions who supported organizations like the Oeuvre de la propagation de la foi, France's colonial ideology—both the rhetoric of the empire's goals and the policies designed to implement them—was defined by conversion to Catholicism as well as to French culture, by the reading of the Bible as well as the study of science, by the learning of catechism as well as the French language.

The onslaught of the missions also acted to motivate both Parisian and local officials to implement the republic's promised civilizing mission in a way that suited their political ideals. By settling disputes and responding to the political climate in France, colonial regimes reconfigured many key colonial projects, including their policies regarding security, economic development, education, hygiene, and the extension of the rule of law and basic political rights. Anticlerical campaigns in the colonies pressured colonial administrators to increase funds for official schools and other programs, and to laicize hospitals and public spaces. In this way, criticism of missionaries pushed the government to adopt a more proactive—and, as a result, more republican—civilizing program.

But while critics of the missions brought pressure on administrators to laicize certain aspects of the empire, their attacks did not spell the end of the missions. In most circumstances, the official policy remained—with the temporary exception of Polynesia—to tolerate evangelization and the contribution that religious workers made to the civilizing mission, especially schools, orphanages, and hospitals. Despite scandals and brushes with disapproving officials, missionary work had much to gain from colonial rule. The increased physical protection of missionaries, combined with the impression that they were a part of the new political order, led to a flurry of conversions in Indochina and Madagascar. Baptisms fed new schools, churches, and mission complexes. The suspension of government subventions was a small price to pay for such blessed progress. The result was an empire where republican laïcité reigned, but so too did the hierarchy of the Catholic Church. Such an image of empire throws into question the usefulness of the notion that colonialism was an essentially modern project, aimed at spreading Enlightenment-inspired, capitalist, "bourgeois" values around the globe. While many officials and merchants no doubt packed such values in their trunks before setting off to sea, the tens of thousands of French religious workers who spanned the globe in the same era came armed with very different and often antithetical ideas.

The cases of Indochina, Polynesia, and Madagascar also reveal that indigenous leaders and communities played a significant role in the political culture of the early decades of republican colonialism. In the course of this study, ethnic minority leaders, indigenous Freemasons, protonationalist rebels, native preachers, and others have made demands, voiced complaints, or leveled criticisms against both missionaries and representatives of the government. Added to these were less specific, though no less eloquent, demonstrations of disapproval by colonial populations—parents refusing to send their children to mission schools in Polynesia, the thousands of Malagasy who bounced between Catholicism and Protestantism, the anticolonial Save the King movement in Vietnam—that pushed French men and women to question their motivations, goals, and plans. While the focus of this study has been on how the French defined, shaped, and justified their empire, the story of the divergent methods of missionaries and republicans demonstrates that indigenous populations did not face a unified colonial presence but one fraught with inconsistencies, conflict, and contradictions. By negotiating and exploiting these contradictions, indigenous populations avoided, challenged, and defied French authority—both religious and official. But French divisions had a less sanguine effect, as well. They often created social frictions along the very lines that divided French men and women, pitting indigenous Catholics against non-Christians or Protestants, often leading villages to split and neighbors to turn on one another with resentment and violence.

In their effort to minimize the differences between them, missionaries and officials ultimately had to abandon some of their most cherished ideals. Put simply, the politics of discord led missionaries to leave behind centuries-old traditions of being homeless warriors of God who served no king or nation. With the arrival of colonial administrations, missionaries began to redefine their allegiances to include France and its imperial goals. By 1900, they had embraced "civilization" as one of their chief pursuits, even though some twenty years earlier, Catholic workers had believed it to be an infidel's poor substitute for salvation. But championing the *mère-patrie* and spreading civilization beat facing anticlerical legislation that could shut down the missions entirely. The two instances where the missions most insistently redefined their goals—Indochina and Madagascar—were the very cases where Catholics avoided serious sanction. In Tahiti and the Marquesas, by contrast, where missionary sisters remained silent and where male missionaries refused to bow to republicanism, Catholic evangelizing faced the fierce hand of the law. Serving Caesar, especially when Caesar represented a political regime as anticlerical as the Third Republic, was distasteful to many missionaries across the empire. But, in general, even missionaries who chided the immorality of secular officialdom soon saw it as a potential, if often unwitting, ally in saving souls.

Republicans, for their part, benefited from missionary knowledge of local languages, culture, and politics. Mission schools, hospitals, and orphanages were far cheaper and more successful than official ones could hope of being. In weighing costs and values, officials chose to err on the side of the financial, not the ideological. By allowing missionaries to continue to evangelize, colonial administrations tacitly accepted that a significant component of the rational, scientific, and secular civilizing ideology would in practice entail catechism, conversion, and the Church hierarchy. It is not surprising that some of the most vocal critics of the missions—particularly Freemasons—started to lose faith in the liberal potential of colonialism just as the missions and the government found accord.

In addition to making necessary a reassessment of the "republican" civilizing mission, the story of Catholic missionaries reveals the centrality of the empire to many Frenchmen's definition of patriotism and duty at the fin de siècle. Historians of French colonialism regularly face the task of having to justify the importance of their scholarship to skeptical colleagues who question the significance of the empire in the lives of average Frenchmen. The fact that the missionary movement has rarely made its way into histories of modern France suggests that historians might not be looking hard enough for evidence of populist interest in the empire. As one of the largest associations in nineteenth-century France, the Oeuvre de la propagation de la foi alone is evidence of a massive interest from many sectors of French society in the nation's interaction with the outside world, including the empire. The political divisiveness over missionary work in the colonies—conflicts that ranged from clashes of egos in rural Madagascar to debates in the National Assembly—testifies to the variety of men and women who believed that French moral, cultural, and political legitimacy hinged on the nation's accomplishments abroad.

The discussions that took place both in the empire and in France are striking not simply for their richness and intensity. Equally notable is how they turned to fundamental questions of French history and morals. Contrasting traditions, such as the image of the Old Regime, France's place as the "eldest daughter of the Church," the meaning of the Enlightenment, the significance of 1789, and the power of *liberté* and *égalité* were the subjects of speeches, articles, and pamphlets across the empire. The men and women who engaged in battles over these concepts showed their concern not only about the nation's colonial policies but also about preserving the nation's moral integrity, its ideals, and its history. Freemasons and Catholics, divided on so many issues, both repeatedly insisted that the resolution of the missionary question would decide what France stood for in the world. To these men and women, the empire did not represent France; the empire defined France. Commentators as different as de Lanessan, Le Myre de Vilers, Brunetière, and Mgr. Mossard agreed that France's greatness was to be determined by what it accomplished abroad.

The controversy over missionaries also casts light on politics and society in metropolitan France. Key issues that were definitive of politics in France—such as those raised by the Dreyfus affair or the religious laws of 1901–5—not only were relevant in the colonies but in fact were shaped by events and debates across the empire. The historiography of modern France, itself concerned overwhelmingly with metropolitan society, focuses often on what seems to be the irreconcilable differences of *les deux France*: republican versus Catholic, secular versus religious, left versus right. But the uneasy entente eventually reached in the empire warns against such dichotomies. As the case of missionaries abroad and their popular support at home shows, a considerable portion of the French population was tolerant—even proud—of both Catholicism and the republic. The challenges of colonial expansion from the 1880s to 1914 signal not the solidity but the *malleability* of Catholic and republican ideologies. The experience of colonialism forced French men and women to redefine their nation's moral goals and objectives in a way that overcame the most important political and cultural divisions in France—divisions that had plagued French society since 1789.

Finally, exploring the turbulent relations between religion and republicanism brings into focus both the colonial past and its legacies. While the chauvinism of the "civilizing mission" has been tempered by the aspirations of international aid and development, France still claims a political and moral duty to assist its former colonies. Today, French troops in countries in Central and West Africa are occasionally deployed for peacekeeping, not "pacification." French companies and government programs sponsor economic development in former colonies—as in times of old—for mutual gain. Groups like Doctors without Borders work to improve health and hygiene. The Alliance française still teaches French. Motivations are now described as humanitarian but are no less manifestations of French culture and power. While French memory of the nation's colonial past certainly remains conflicted, politicians and commentators continue to champion partnerships with the former empire as evidence of a still-vital republican commitment to the ideals of the Enlightenment and 1789.

But it is equally important to remember that decades after colonial officials have left the empire, Christianity continues to thrive. French missionary organizations still train and support religious workers abroad. Despite having a troublesome relationship with socialism, Catholicism still has a surprisingly sizable following in Vietnam—about 7 percent of the population (the largest religion, Buddhism, is practiced by only about 9 percent). More than half of Malagasy today are Christian, and divisions between Protestants and Catholics are still a source of political rivalry. Relationships in the archipelagoes of Polynesia are still influenced by one's attendance at a Protestant chapel or a Catholic church. Across the former colonial world, the most imposing structures—be it in the Old Quarter of Hanoi, or in the port of Papeete—are often the spires of century-old French churches. Today, in many regions of the world once under the French flag, Catholicism has often endured and even flourished where liberal, republican ideals have faded and where French has become an archaic tongue. Considering how deeply religion shapes people's lives and defines their communities, the most profound legacy of French republican imperialism may well be, ironically, Christianity.

Appendix

Comptes-Rendus of the Oeuvre de la Propagation de la Foi

Year	Francs raised in France	Total Francs Worldwide	Publications in French/Breton	Total Publications
1887	4,073,250.80	6,462,276.04	166,700/6,350	257,500
1888	4,079,944.31	6,362,142.22	167,000/6,350	259,950
1889	4,013,905.84	6,541,918.56	167,000/6,500	261,200
1890	4,310,862.10	7,072,811.55	168,000/6,500	265,700
1891	4,085,474.74	6,694,457.86	170,000/6,500	272,900
1892	3,913,560.66	6,621,674.23	170,000/6,500	271,400
1893	4,122,304.61	6,599,622.55	171,000/6,500	269,000
1894	3,895,834.85	6,820,164.43	171,000/6,485	269,550
1895	4,136,825.74	6,587,049.49	171,000/6,485	269,550
1896	3,921,696.96	6,332,686.87	172,000/6,485	274,610
1897	4,167,664.88	6,772,879.52	174,000/6,485	278,810
1898	4,077,085.59	6,700,921.35	174,000/6,485	282,310
1899	4,009,990.84	6,820,273.93	176,000/5,225	290,680
1900	4,068,407.95	6,848,700.86	176,500/5,225	292,680
1901	3,956,183.12	6,728,666.94	177,500/5,225	296,000
1902	3,859,697.91	6,598,044.65	178,000/5,225	298,000
1903	3,508,358.54	6,237,105.00	178,000/5,225	320,260
1904	3,510,043.24	6,760,085.37	177,000/5,225	320,660
1905	3,294,996.82	6,497,697.01	176,000/5,225	320,860
1906	3,075,315.35	6,403,958.64	175,000/5,225	318,860
1907	3,123,463.40	6,644,397.72	174,000/5,225	320,110

(continued)

Comptes-Rendus of the Oeuvre de la Propagation de la Foi (*continued*)

Year	Francs raised in France	Total Francs Worldwide	Publications in French/Breton	Total Publications
1908	3,082,131.86	6,402,586.74	174,000/5,225	320,710
1909	3,153,442.57	6,711,461.84	174,000/5,225	326,210
1910	3,041,280.97	6,986,678.05	174,000/5,225	326,210
1911	3,025,788.89	7,274,226.59	174,000/5,225	336,210
1912	3,106,830.95	8,051,575.55	174,000/5,225	343,770
1913	2,950,959.35	8,114,983.07	Not given	Not given

Note: Publication figures indicate the number *Annales de la Propagation de la Foi* published six times per year. The *Compte-rendu* of the previous year appeared annually in the *Annales*. Figures were not provided from 1914 through the duration of the war.

Notes

Archive Abbreviations

AAP	Archives de l'Archidiocèse de Papeete, Tahiti
AEEP	Archives de l'Église évangélique de la Polynésie française, Papeete, Tahiti
AJ	Archives Jésuites, Vanves, France
AN	Archives nationales de France (CARAN), Paris
AOPF	Archives de l'Oeuvre de la propagation de la foi, at the Centre national de documentation et d'archives missionnaires, Lyon
APM	Archives des Pères Maristes, Rome
ASME	Archives de la Société des missions étrangères de Paris
ASSC	Archives des Soeurs de Saint Joseph de Cluny, Paris
ATPF	Archives territoriales de la Polynésie française, Papeete, Tahiti
CAOM	Centre des archives d'outre mer, Aix-en-Provence
CPGE	Archives of the Congregatio Pro Gentium Evangelizatione, Rome
GOF	Archives du Grand orient de France, Paris
LMS	London Missionary Society Archives, Council for World Missions, at the School of Oriental and African Studies, University of London
MAE	Archives du Ministère des affaires-étrangères (Quai d'Orsay), Paris
SMEP	Archives de la Société des missions évangélique de Paris (Département évangélique français d'action apostolique), Paris
TTLT	Trung Tam Luu Tru Quoc Gia—1 (National Archives of Viet Nam, No. 1), Hanoi

Introduction

1. Centre des archives d'outre mer (CAOM): Madagascar, Gouverneur Gallieni (M/GG): 6(4) D 6: Julia to M. l'Administrateur en Chef du Betsiléo à Fianarantsoa, No. 14, 25 Nov 1899.
2. Julia seemed not to notice that the man's comment criticized the colonial government as much as the missions. CAOM: M/GG: 6(4) D 6: Julia to M.

269

l'Administrateur en Chef du Betsiléo, No. 23, Ambalavao, 13 Dec 1899, and No. 26, 14 Dec 1899.

3. CAOM: M/GG: 6(4) D 6: Julia to M. l'Administrateur en Chef du Betsiléo, 14 Dec 1899.

4. CAOM: M/GG: 6(4) D 6: L'Administrateur en Chef de la Province de Fianarantsoa to Gallieni, Fianarantsoa, 22 Dec 1899.

5. CAOM: M/GG: 6(4) D 6: Télégramme Officiel, No. 5692B, 23 Dec 1899; and Delmont to Julia, Ambalavao, 6 Apr 1900.

6. Throughout this book, words like "civilization" and "civilizing mission"—as well as "civilized," "savage," "immoral," "pagan," and similar terms—should be read as if enclosed in quotation marks. These terms should be understood in their proper historical sense, as ideas invested with the meanings of their nineteenth-century and early twentieth-century context.

7. Valérien Groffier, *Héros trop oubliés de notre épopée coloniale* (n.p., 1905), vi.

8. As Claude Nicolet points out, republican ideas predated the Revolution and existed throughout the nineteenth century regardless of regime. Nicolet, *L'Idée républicaine en France* (Paris: Gallimard, 1982), 9–11.

9. Owen Chadwick, *The Secularization of the European Mind in the Nineteenth Century* (Cambridge: Cambridge University Press, 1975), 107.

10. Robert Gildea, *The Past in French History* (New Haven, CT: Yale University Press, 1994), 13–61.

11. Reproduced in Claude Langlois, "Catholics and Seculars," in Pierre Nora, ed., *Realms of Memory, vol. 1, Conflicts and Divisions*, trans. Arthur Goldhammer (New York: Columbia University Press, 1992), 119.

12. Victor Hugo, quoted in Gildea, *The Past in French History*, 216.

13. Chadwick, *The Secularization of the European Mind*, 118.

14. Maurice Agulhon, *The French Republic, 1879–1992*, trans. Antonia Nevill (Oxford: Blackwell, 1995), 26.

15. James McMillan, " 'Priest Hits Girl': On the Front Line in the 'War of Two Frances,' " in Christopher Clark and Wolfram Kaiser, eds., *Culture Wars: Secular-Catholic Conflict in Nineteenth-Century Europe* (Cambridge: Cambridge University Press, 2003), 77–79.

16. Ralph Gibson, *A Social History of French Catholicism, 1789–1914* (New York: Routledge, 1989), 128.

17. Pierre Chevalier, *La Séparation de l'Église et de l'école: Jules Ferry et Léon XIII* (Paris: Fayard, 1981).

18. Gildea, *The Past in French History*, 218.

19. From Tocqueville, "L'Emancipation," quoted in Tzvetan Todorov, *On Human Diversity: Nationalism, Racism, and Exoticism in French Thought*, trans. Catherine Porter (Cambridge, MA: Harvard University Press, 1993), 195.

20. Gordon Wright, *France in Modern Times*, 5th ed. (New York: Norton, 1995), 292.

21. Gambetta, quoted in Robert Tombs, *France, 1814–1914* (London: Longman, 1996), 202.

22. Paul Leroy-Beaulieu, *De la colonisation chez les peuples modernes* (Paris: Librairie Guillaumin et Cie, 1886), xiv.

23. Stuart Michael Persell, *The French Colonial Lobby 1889–1938* (Stanford, CA: Hoover Institute Press, 1983), 7.

24. Charles-Robert Ageron, "Jules Ferry et la colonisation," in François Furet, ed., *Jules Ferry fondateur de le République* (Paris: Éditions de l'EHESS, 1985), 197.

25. Leroy-Beaulieu, *De la colonisation*, xv (in the introduction to the 1874 edition). On Leroy-Beaulieu's writing on imperialism, see Dan Warshaw, *Paul Leroy-Beaulieu and Established Liberalism in France* (DeKalb: Northern Illinois University Press, 1991), 78–105.

26. Raoul Girardet, *L'Idée coloniale en France de 1871 à 1962* (Paris: La Table Ronde, 1972), 82.

27. Persell, *The French Colonial Lobby*, 10–13.

28. Ferry, quoted in Denise Bouche, *Histoire de la colonisation française, vol. 2, flux et reflux (1815–1962)* (Paris: Fayard, 1991), 55.

29. On Ferry's colonial stance, see Ageron, "Jules Ferry et la colonisation," 191–206.

30. See Alice Conklin, *A Mission to Civilize: The Republican Idea of Empire in France and West Africa, 1895–1930* (Stanford, CA: Stanford University Press, 1997), 248–49.

31. Tocqueville, quoted in Todorov, *On Human Diversity*, 195.

32. The concept of *civilisation* dates from the 1760s. Lucien Febvre, "Civilisation: Évolution d'un mot et d'un groupe d'idées," in *Pour une histoire à part entière* (Paris: École Pratique des Hautes Études, 1962), 481–528. Quoting Mirabeau, Norbert Elias argues that, from its inception, civilization was indelibly linked to reform, as it provided an increasingly decadent society "the form and the substance of virtue." Elias, *The Civilizing Process: The History of Manners and State Formation and Civilization*, trans. Edmund Jephcott (Oxford: Blackwell, 1994), 32.

33. Eugen Weber, *Peasants into Frenchmen: The Modernization of Rural France, 1870–1914* (Stanford, CA: Stanford University Press, 1976), 486.

34. On the spread of revolutionary values in colonial or international contexts, see Christopher L. Miller, "Unfinished Business: Colonialism in Sub-Saharan Africa and the Ideals of the French Revolution," in Joseph Klaits and Michael H. Haltzel, eds., *The Global Ramifications of the French Revolution* (New York: Woodrow Wilson International Center, 1994), 105–126. On the importance of revolutionary values to French Jews abroad, see Aron Rodrigue, *French Jews, Turkish Jews: The* Alliance Israélite Universelle *and the Politics of Jewish Schooling in Turkey, 1860–1925* (Bloomington: Indiana University Press, 1990), chap. 1. In the colonies, citizenship was not granted to indigenous populations as easily as it was to French peasants in France. On race and citizenship, see Owen White, *Children of the Empire: Miscegenation and Colonial Society in French West Africa* (Oxford: Oxford University Press, 1999), esp. chap. 5; Jean Elisabeth Pedersen, " 'Special Customs': Paternity Suits and Citizenship in France and the Colonies, 1870–1912," and Alice Conklin, "Redefining 'Frenchness': Citizenship, Race Regeneration, and Imperial Motherhood in France and West Africa, 1914–1940," both in Julia Clancy-Smith and Frances Gouda, eds., *Domesticating the Empire: Race, Gender, and Family Life in French and Dutch Colonialism* (Charlottesville: University Press of Virginia, 1998), 43–64, 65–83.

35. Reference to the republican "civilizing mission" can be found in nearly every book on French colonialism during the Third Republic. Works on the history of the concept of civilization include R. A. Lochore, *History of the Idea of Civilization in France (1830–1870)* (Bonn: Ludwig Rohrscheid, 1935); Hubert Deschamps, *Les Méthodes et les doctrines colonials de la France du XVIe siècle à nos jours* (Paris: A. Colin, 1953); Raymond Betts, *Assimilation and Association in French Colonial Theory, 1890–1914* (New York: Columbia University Press, 1960); Martin D. Lewis, "One Hundred Million Frenchmen: The Assimilationist Theory in French Colonial Policy," *Comparative Studies in Society and History* 4, no. 2 (1962): 129–53; Girardet, *L'Idée coloniale*; Charles-Robert Ageron, *France coloniale ou parti colonial?* (Paris: Presses Universitaires de France, 1978); Thomas G. August, *The Selling of the Empire: British and French Imperialist Propaganda, 1890–1940* (Westport, CT: Greenwood Press, 1985); Alice Bullard, *Exile to Paradise: Savagery and Civilization in Paris and the South Pacific* (Stanford, CA: Stanford University Press, 2000); and Jennifer Pitts, *A Turn to Empire: The Rise of Liberalism in Britain and France* (Princeton, NJ: Princeton University Press, 2005), 167–85. Despite the numbers of books mentioning the civilizing mission, very few works have examined it in detail. Notable exceptions are Denise Bouche, "L'Enseignement dans les territoires français de l'Afrique occidentale de 1817 à 1920: Mission civilisatrice ou formation d'une elite?" 2 vols. (Thèse, l'Université de Paris I, 1974); Mathew Burrows, "'Mission Civilisatrice': French Cultural Policy in the Middle East, 1860–1914," *Historical Journal* 29, no. 1 (1986): 109–35; and Conklin, *A Mission to Civilize*.

36. Betts, *Assimilation and Association*; on how local administrators implemented the civilizing mission in West Africa, see Conklin, *A Mission to Civilize*.

37. Groffier, *Héros trop oubliés*, vi. As a point of comparison, the French colonial administrative service in all of Africa including Madagascar—by far France's largest collection of possessions in total area—did not number more than 4,000 from its inception in 1867 until 1960. William Cohen, *Rulers of Empire: The French Colonial Service in Africa* (Stanford, CA: Hoover Institute Press, 1971), xiii.

38. Le R. P. Deniau, *Conférence sur les missions d'Océanie* (Chartres: Imprimerie Marcel Laffray, 1900), 5.

39. Patrick Tuck, *French Catholic Missionaries and the Politics of Imperialism in Vietnam, 1857–1914: A Documentary Survey* (Liverpool: Liverpool University Press, 1987), 28.

40. John Laffey, "Roots of French Imperialism in the Nineteenth Century: The Case of Lyon," *French Historical Studies* 6 (1969): 80.

41. In the case of Vietnam, Nola Cooke has pointed out that missionaries have been treated as merely a "footnote" to the colonial story—an observation that could be extended to the empire as a whole. Cooke, "Early Nineteenth-Century Vietnamese Catholics and Others in the Pages of the *Annales de la Propagation de la Foi*," *Journal of Southeast Asian Studies* 35 (June 2004): 261. There are a few important exceptions: Tuck, *French Catholic Missionaries*; Joseph-Roger de Benoist, *Église et pouvoir colonial au Soudan français: Les relations entre l'administrateurs et les missionnaires catholiques dans la Boucle du Niger de 1885 à 1945* (Paris: Karthala, 1987); Patrice Morlat, ed., *La Question religieuse dans l'empire colonial français* (Paris: Les Indes Savantes, 2003); Matt K. Matsuda, *Empire of Love: Histories of France and the Pacific* (New York:

Oxford University Press, 2005); Elizabeth Thompson, "Neither Conspiracy Nor Hypocrisy: The Jesuits and the French Mandate in Syria and Lebanon," in Eleanor H. Tejirian and Reeva Spector Simon, eds., *Altruism and Imperialism: Western Cultural and Religious Missions in the Middle East* (New York: Middle East Institute, Columbia University, 2002), 66–87; Owen White, "The Decivilizing Mission: Auguste Dupuis-Yakouba and French Timbuktu," *French Historical Studies* 27, no. 3 (Summer 2004): 541–68. Though a history of science, Lewis Pyenson's *Civilizing Mission: Exact Sciences and French Overseas Expansion, 1830–1940* (Baltimore: Johns Hopkins University Press, 1993) does examine the contributions of Jesuit science to the empire. While important works, none of these explore in detail how religious missionaries shaped French colonial politics or ideology.

42. For a critique of the notion of colonial modernity, see Frederick Cooper, *Colonialism in Question: Theory, Knowledge, History* (Berkeley: University of California Press, 2005), 113–52.

43. On the discourse of imperial writing and its impact on European imperial ideology, see Edward Said, *Orientalism* (New York: Vintage, 1978), and *Culture and Imperialism* (New York: Vintage, 1993); Patrick Brantlinger, "Victorians and Africans: The Genealogy of the Myth of the Dark Continent," in Henry Louis Gates Jr., ed., *"Race," Writing, and Difference* (Chicago: University of Chicago Press, 1985), 185–222; Mary Louise Pratt, *Imperial Eyes: Travel Writing and Transculturation* (New York: Routledge, 1992), esp. pt. 3, "Imperial Stylistics, 1860–1980"; David Spurr, *The Rhetoric of Empire: Colonial Discourse in Journalism, Travel Writing, and Imperial Administration* (Durham, NC: Duke University Press, 1993); and Anne McClintock, *Imperial Leather: Race, Gender, and Sexuality in the Colonial Contest* (New York: Routledge, 1995). For a critique of the application of "cultural imperialism" to missionary work, see Ryan Dunch, "Beyond Cultural Imperialism: Cultural Theory, Christian Missions, and Global Modernity," *History and Theory* 41 (October 2002): 302–7.

44. In her survey of nineteenth- and twentieth-century colonialism, for example, Denise Bouche describes the role of missionaries in French history as an "extremely delicate question," since so much written on missionary work in colonialism is by partisans. Many colonial historians concur; however, very few dedicate more than a passing reference to the role of missionaries. In addition to Bouche, *Histoire de la colonisation française*, 217, see, for example, Robert Aldrich, *Greater France: A History of French Overseas Expansion* (New York: St. Martin's Press, 1996); Christopher M. Andrew and A. S. Kanya-Forstner, *France Overseas: The Great War and the Climax of French Imperial Expansion* (London: Thames and Hudson, 1981); Catherine Coquery-Vidrovitch, *L'Afrique noire de 1800 à nos jours* (Paris: Presses Universitaires de France, 1964); Girardet, *L'Idée coloniale*; Pierre Guillen, *L'Expansion, 1881–1898* (Paris: Imprimerie Nationale, 1985); Yves Monnier, *L'Afrique dans l'imaginaire français (fin du XIXe–début du XXe siècle)* (Paris: L'Harmattan, 1999).

45. See Claude Prudhomme, ed., *Une appropriation du monde: Mission et missions XIXe–XXe siècles* (Lyon: Éditions Publisud, 2004).

46. While the focus of this book is on French ideas, politics, and identities, divisions among Frenchmen along religious lines are also crucial for scholars who study indigenous responses to colonial rule.

47. See Paul Rabinow, *French Modern: Norms and Forms of the Social Environment* (Chicago: University of Chicago Press, 1989); Gwendolyn Wright, *The Politics of Design in French Colonial Urbanism* (Chicago: University of Chicago Press, 1991); a critique of the "laboratories of modernity" model is offered by Peter Zinoman, *The Colonial Bastille: A History of Imprisonment in Vietnam, 1862–1940* (Berkeley: University of California Press, 2001).

48. Guillen, *L'Expansion*, 35–36.

49. Ibid.

50. See Girardet, *L'Idée coloniale*, chap. 3.

51. Even after 1894, with the creation of the Colonial Ministry, the Quai d'Orsay remained involved in making colonial policy, especially regarding religious missions due to the potential for diplomatic tensions with the Vatican.

52. Thompson, "Neither Conspiracy Nor Hypocrisy," 66–67.

53. Guillen, *L'Expansion*, 39–40.

54. Patrick Cabanel, "Introduction" in Patrick Cabanel and Jean-Dominique Durand, eds., *Le Grand exil des congrégations religieuses françaises, 1901–1914* (Paris: Éditions du Cerf, 2005), 11–12; on the impact of the 1901–1905 laws on missionary orders abroad, see Claude Prudhomme, "Les Congrégations missionnaires face aux lois anticongréganistes: Un régime de faveur?" in Cabanel and Durand, *Le Grand exil*, 310–16.

55. The secondary material on Catholic revival and republican politics is sizable; however, none addresses the impact of missionary work. Influential books that lack a colonial dimension include John McManners, *Church and State in France, 1870–1914* (London: SPCK, 1972); Maurice Larkin, *Church and State after the Dreyfus Affair: The Separation Issue in France* (New York: Harper and Row, 1974); René Rémond, *L'Anticléricalisme en France de 1815 à nos jours*, 2nd ed. (Brussels: Éditions Complexe, 1985); Émile Poulat, *Liberté, laïcité: La Guerre des deux France et le principe de la modernité* (Paris: Cerf-Cujas, 1987); Ralph Gibson, *A Social History of French Catholicism, 1789–1914* (London: Routledge, 1989); Frank Tallett and Nicholas Atkins, eds., *Religion, Society, and Politics in France since 1789* (London: Hambledon, 1991).

56. On politics and the OPF, see Richard Drevet, "L'Oeuvre de la Propagation de la foi, de l'encyclique *Probe Nostis* (1840) à *Sancta Dei Civitas* (1880)," Mémoire de maîtrise sous la direction de Claude Prudhomme, Université Lumière, Lyon II, 1997.

57. See, for example, the language used in *Annales* 57 (1885): 344; and 58 (1886): 1.

58. See, for example, William B. Cohen, *The French Encounter with Africans: White Response to Blacks, 1530–1880* (Bloomington: Indiana University Press, 1980); and William H. Schneider, *An Empire for the Masses: The French Popular Image of Africa, 1870–1900* (Westport, CT: Greenwood Press, 1982). Volumes of essays concerned with colonial culture that almost entirely ignore missionaries include Tony Chafer and Amanda Sackur, eds., *Promoting the Colonial Idea: Propaganda and Visions of Empire in France* (Palgrave: Houndmills, 2002); Martin Evans, ed., *Empire and Culture: The French Experience, 1830–1940* (London: Palgrave Macmillan, 2004); Pascal Blanchard and Sadrine Lemaire, eds., *Culture coloniale: La France conquise par son empire, 1871–1931* (Paris: Éditions Autrement, 2003);

Blanchard and Lemaire, eds., *Culture impériale: Les colonies au coeur de la république* (Paris: Éditions Autrement, 2004).

59. On the limits of the *union sacrée*, see James McMillan, "French Catholics: *Rumeurs Infâmes* and the *Union Sacrée*, 1914–1918," in Frans Coetzee and Marilyn Shevin-Coetzee, eds., *Authority, Identity and the Social History of the Great War* (Providence, RI: Berghahn Books, 1995), 113–31. McMillan's argument addresses Jean-Jacques Becker, *The Great War and the French People*, trans. A. Pomerans (Leamington Spa: Berg, 1986).

60. Ageron argues that in the 1920s and 1930s a new "humanitarian" conception of colonization emerged that effectively melded missionary work and the civilizing impulses of republican colonizers. The following chapters will argue that this phenomenon was the culmination of the redefinition of missionary work within the civilizing mission that started in the 1880s. Ageron, *France coloniale*, 36–41.

61. See Annette Becker, *La Guerre et la foi, de la mort à la mémoire 1914–1930* (Paris: Armand Colin, 1994); and Philip Nord, "Catholic Culture in Interwar France," *French Politics, Culture, and Society* 21, no. 3 (Fall 2003): 1–20.

62. Weber, *Peasants into Frenchmen*; see also Maurice Agulhon, *La République au village* (Paris: Plon, 1970); Michael Burns, *Rural Society and French Politics: Boulangism and the Dreyfus Affair, 1886–1900* (Princeton, NJ: Princeton University Press, 1984); Georges Duby, ed., *Histoire de la France rurale, vol. 4, 1914 à nos jours* (Paris: Seuil, 1976); Caroline Ford, *Creating the Nation in Provincial France: Religion and Political Identity in Brittany* (Princeton, NJ: Princeton University Press, 1993); Nancy Fitch, "Mass Culture, Mass Parliamentary Politics, and Modern Anti-Semitism: The Dreyfus Affair in Rural France," *American Historical Review* 97 (February 1992): 55–95; Robert Gildea, *Education in Provincial France, 1800–1914* (Oxford: Clarendon Press, 1983); James Lehning, *Peasant and French: Cultural Contact in Rural France during the Nineteenth Century* (Cambridge: Cambridge University Press, 1995); Annie Moulin, *Peasantry and Society in France since 1789* (Cambridge: Cambridge University Press, 1991); Charles Tilly, "Did the Cake of Custom Break?" in John Merriman, ed., *Consciousness and Class Experience in Nineteenth-Century Europe* (New York: Holmes and Meier, 1979).

63. See Peter Sahlins, *Boundaries: The Making of France in the Pyrenees* (Berkeley: University of California Press, 1989); Herman Lebovics, *True France: The Wars over Cultural Identity, 1900–1945* (Ithaca, NY: Cornell University Press, 1992); and Conklin, *A Mission to Civilize*.

64. On the significance of missionary work at an earlier time, see Sue Peabody, " 'A Dangerous Zeal': Catholic Missions to Slaves in the French Antilles, 1635–1800," *French Historical Studies* 25 (Winter 2002): 53–90; and Peabody, " 'A Nation Born to Slavery': Missionaries and Racial Discourse in Seventeenth-Century Antilles," *Journal of Social History* 38, no. 1 (Fall 2004): 113–26.

65. Until the 1860s, Catholics in Algeria worked almost exclusively among the white population. This changed in the late 1860s, under Archbishop Lavigerie, when missionaries increasingly tried to convert Muslim orphans and to use the Kabyle myth to justify evangelizing. Christopher Harrison, *France and Islam in West Africa, 1860–1960* (Cambridge: Cambridge University Press, 1988), 18; Karima

Direche-Slimani, *Chrétiens de Kabylie, 1873–1954: Une action missionnaire dans l'Algérie coloniale* (Paris: Éditions Bouchene, 2004), esp. 33–37; and Patricia Lorcin, *Imperial Identities: Stereotyping, Prejudice, and Race in Colonial Algeria* (London: I.B. Tauris, 1999), 173–81.

66. Benoist, *Église et pouvoir colonial*, 68–110.

Chapter 1

1. "R. P. Guillemé, Missionnaire à Kibanga (Haut Congo), au T. R. P. Deguerry, Supérieure Général de la Société des missionnaires d'Afrique (d'Alger)," *Annales de la Propagation de la Foi* 60 (1888): 231.
2. Ibid., 233.
3. Ibid., 231.
4. An interesting comparison to Guillemé is George Orwell, "Shooting an Elephant," in *A Collection of Essays by George Orwell* (New York: Harbrace Paperback, 1946), 148–55.
5. *Annales* 60:235–36.
6. Ibid., 238, 236.
7. For a disturbing portrait of the destructive technology used in the European exploration of Africa, see Adam Hochschild, *King Leopold's Ghost: A Story of Greed, Terror, and Heroism in Colonial Africa* (New York: Mariner Books, 1999), chap. 6.
8. For an excellent historiographical overview of the tendency to see Protestant missionaries as servants of wider British colonial goals, see Andrew Porter, *Religion versus Empire? British Protestant Missionaries and Overseas Expansion, 1700–1914* (Manchester: Manchester University Press, 2005), 1–11.
9. Adrien Launay, *Histoire générale de la Société des missions-étrangères*, vol. 1 (Paris, 1894), 1.
10. For a detailed account of the economic, political, and military history of early New France, see Marcel Trudel, *The Beginnings of New France, 1524–1663*, trans. Patricia Claxton (Toronto: McClelland and Stewart, 1973).
11. W. J. Eccles, *The Canadian Frontier, 1534–1760* (New York: Holt, Rinehart, and Winston, 1969), 45.
12. On the lives of religious workers in seventeenth-century Canada, see Natalie Zemon Davis, *Women on the Margins: Three Seventeenth-Century Lives* (Cambridge, MA: Harvard University Press, 1995), chap. 2 on the life of Marie de l'Incarnation; René Latourelle's two books, *Pierre-Joseph-Marie Chaumonot* (Quebec: Editions Bellarmin, 1998), and *Jean de Brébeuf* (Quebec: Editions Bellarmin, 1999); and Allan Greer, *Mohawk Saint: Catherine Tekakwitha and the Jesuits* (Oxford: Oxford University Press, 2004).
13. James T. Moore, *Indian and Jesuit: A Seventeenth-Century Encounter* (Chicago: Loyola University Press, 1982), 11; and Allan Greer, ed., *The Jesuit Relations: Natives and Missionaries in Seventeenth-Century North America* (Boston: Bedford/St. Martin's, 2000), 14–16.
14. Eccles, *The Canadian Frontier*, 45–46.
15. Ibid., 42.

16. The designation of the age is Georges Goyau's. *La France missionnaire dans les cinq parties du monde*, vol. 1 (Paris: Plon, 1948), 127–54.

17. Davis, *Women on the Margins*, 107.

18. See Jérôme Lalemant, "How Father Isaac Jogues Was Taken by the Iroquois, and What He Suffered on His First Entrance into Their Country," in Greer, *The Jesuit Relations*, 157–71.

19. Peter C. Phan, *Mission and Catechesis: Alexandre de Rhodes and Inculturation in Seventeenth-Century Vietnam* (Maryknoll, NY: Orbis Books, 1998), 46.

20. Mgr. S. Delacroix, ed., *Histoire universelle des missions catholiques*, vol. 2 (Paris: Librairie Grund, 1957), 63–65, 142.

21. On missionary rivalries in this period, as well as the creation of apostolic vicars, see Stephen Neill, *A History of Christian Missions*, 2nd ed. (London: Penguin, 1986), chap. 6.

22. Launay, *Histoire générale*, 1:97.

23. *Monita ad missionarios: Instructions aux missionnaires*, first edited by François Pallu in 1665. Reissued as *Monita ad missionarios: Instructions aux missionnaires de la S. Congrégation de la Propagande* (Paris: Archives des Missions Étrangères, 2000). See also Launay, *Histoire générale*, 1:97–110.

24. *Monita ad Missionarios*, 21–23.

25. Ibid., 58.

26. Ibid., 43–47.

27. Ralph Gibson, *A Social History of French Catholicism, 1789–1914* (London: Routledge, 1989), 90.

28. Margaret Lavinia Anderson, "The Divisions of the Pope: The Catholic Revival and Europe's Transition to Democracy," in Austen Ivereigh, ed., *The Politics of Religion in an Age of Revival: Studies in Nineteenth-Century Europe and Latin America* (London: Institute of Latin American Studies, 2000), 24.

29. Delacroix, *Histoire universelle*, 3:27, 45–47.

30. Richard Drevet, "Le Financement des missions catholiques au XIXe siècle, entre autonomie laïque et centralité romaine: L'Oeuvre de la propagation de la foi (1822–1922)," *Chrétiens et Sociétés, XVIe–XXe Siècles* (Bulletin du Centre Latreille, Lyon), no. 9 (2002): 86–87.

31. Yannick Essertel, *L'Aventure missionnaire lyonnaise, 1815–1962* (Paris: Les Éditions de Cerf, 2001), 27.

32. Launay, *Histoire générale*, 2:508. Nola Cooke also shows that Missions étrangères officials borrowed the system from British Protestants. Cooke, "Early Nineteenth-Century Vietnamese Catholics," 263.

33. See Raymond Jonas, *France and the Cult of the Sacred Heart: An Epic Tale for Modern Times* (Berkeley: University of California Press, 2000), 207–11.

34. *Annales* 77:14–15.

35. On the origins of this status, see René Rémond, "La Fille ainée de l'Eglise," in Pierre Nora, ed., *Les Lieux de mémoire. III: Les France, 3. De l'Archive à l'emblème* (Paris: Gallimard, 1992), 540–81.

36. Essertel, *L'Aventure missionnaire*, 15.

37. Sheryl Kroen, *Theatre and Politics: The Crisis of Legitimacy in Restoration France, 1815–1830* (Berkeley: University of California Press, 2000), 8.

38. Ibid., 76–108; Drevet, "Le Financement des missions catholiques," 87.
39. L'Abbé Augustin Aubry, ed., *Aux séminairistes: Conseils pratiques tirés des oeuvres du P. J. B. Aubry (1844–1882)*, 3rd ed. (Paris: Pierre Téqui, 1929), 2.
40. Cooke, "Early Nineteenth-Century Vietnamese Catholics," 263–65.
41. On missionary efforts to rehabilitate slaves in the early nineteenth century, see Troy Feay, "Mission to Moralize: Slaves, Africans, and Missionaries in the French Colonies, 1815–52" (Ph.D. diss., University of Notre Dame, 2003).
42. "L'Oeuvre de la propagation de la foi. Son organisation et son administration," *Annales* 77 (1905): 13–14.
43. In fact, as Richard Drevet shows, relations between the Oeuvre and the Congregation in Rome were often competitive and rocky. Drevet, "Le Financement des missions catholiques," 94–97.
44. Delacroix, *Histoire universelle*, 3:52–54.
45. Ibid., 71.
46. Paul Lesourd, *Histoire générale de l'oeuvre pontificale de la Sainte-Enfance depuis un siècle* (Paris: Imprimerie Les Presses Continentales, 1947), 7.
47. Lesourd, *Histoire générale*, 35, 64, 66–67.
48. Delacroix, *Histoire universelle*, 3:85–86.
49. This first-year figure, from 1823, comes from "Une intéressante statistique," *Petit Almanach de l'Oeuvre de la Propagation de la Foi* (Paris and Lyon, 1889), 24. In 1884, the total amount raised was 6,832,518.27 francs, of which 4,645,702.12 were raised in France. See the *comptes-rendus* in *Annales* 57 (1885): 330.
50. Essertel, *L'Aventure missionnaire*, 98.
51. Pierre Guillen, *L'Expansion, 1881–1898* (Paris: Imprimerie nationale, 1985), 38–39.
52. Delacroix, *Histoire universelle*, 3:66.
53. *Annales* 77, 9.
54. According to the annual *comptes-rendus*, the number of Breton editions published each year increased steadily until 1893, when 6,500 copies of each issue were published. By 1912, this number dropped to 5,225. See the annual *comptes-rendus* of the *Annales* 57 (1885) through 85 (1913).
55. The formula of distribution is described in *Annales* 77:16; the calculations are based on annual numbers of publications reported in the *Annales* multiplied by ten.
56. *Le Petit Journal* had what was at the time an unprecedented circulation of 582,000 in 1880. Theodore Zeldin, *France, 1848–1945* (Oxford: Clarendon Press, 1977), 527.
57. Guillen, *L'Expansion*, 106.
58. This collection of images is taken from *Missions Catholiques* 35 (1903): 10, 40, 49, 50, 102, 114, 174–75, 223, 239, 244–45, 308, 313, 575, 609. A similar combination of images could be found in any single tome from the 1880s to 1914.
59. *Annales* 58 (1886): 1.
60. *Annales* 58:9–10, 1; *Annales* 64 (1892): 9, 10.
61. *Annales* 58:1.
62. "The evangelical version of Protestantism," David Bebbington has written, "was created by the Enlightenment." *Evangelicalism in Modern Britain: A History from the 1730s to the 1980s* (London: Routledge, 1989), 74. For an overview of the historiography on Protestants and the Enlightenment, see Brian Stanley, ed., *Christian Missions and the Enlightenment* (Grand Rapids, MI: Eerdmans, 2001), 1–21.

63. Essertel, *L'Aventure missionnaire*, 40.

64. "Le Missionnaire," in the *Almanach des Missions* (Paris, 1885), 6–7.

65. *Annales* 60:238, 236.

66. M. L'Abbé F. Marnas, *Paiens et Catholiques en extrême-orient; Allocution prononcée à Marseilles pour la fête patronale de la propagation de la foi, le 3 décembre 1891* (Lyon: Imprimerie Emmanuel Vitte, 1891), 12.

67. On the biological and cultural dimensions of French conceptions of race, see Sue Peabody and Tyler Stovall, eds., *The Color of Liberty: Histories of Race in France* (Durham, NC: Duke University Press, 2003), 1–7.

68. Marnas, *Paiens et Catholiques*, 26.

69. Weber, *Peasants into Frenchmen*, 364–65.

70. Archives de la Société des missions étrangères (ASME): 787: Guerlach to L'abbé Cauvigny, 29 Jan 1893, p. 13.

71. *Allocution prononcée dans l'église paroissiale de Ferrières-en-Gatinas à l'occasion des adieux de six missionnaires partant pour l'extrême-orient (le 19 Aout 1888)* (n.p.), 7–8.

72. Dubois in Paul Lesourd, *L'Oeuvre civilisatrice et scientifique des missionnaires catholiques dans les colonies françaises* (Paris: Desclée de Brouwer, 1931), 26.

73. Jean Pirotte, *Périodiques missionnaires belges d'expression française: Reflets de cinquante années d'évolution d'une mentalité, 1889–1940* (Louvain: Publications Universitaires de Louvain, 1973), 98–99. Pirotte's scientific study of missionary journals focuses on Belgian journals but generally holds true to French publications as well.

74. *Allocution prononcée dans l'église paroissiale de Ferrières-en-Gatinas*, 13.

75. *Annales* 64:8.

76. *Annales* 65:12.

77. Essertel, *L'Aventure missionnaire*, 44–45.

78. "Le Missionnaire," 7.

79. Dubois quoted in Lesourd, *L'Oeuvre civilisatrice*, 26.

80. Aubry, *Aux séminairistes*, 141–42.

81. Essertel, *L'Aventure missionnaire*, 114.

82. Jean-Baptiste Aubry, *Le Radicalisme du sacrifice: Meditation*, 7th ed. (Paris: P. Téqui, 1903), 18, 36.

83. Augustin Aubry, *Jean-Baptiste Aubry, docteur en théologie, ancien directeur de grand Séminaire, missionnaire au Kouy-Tchéou (Chine): Le professeur—le théologien—le missionnaire* (Lille: Société de St-Augustin, 1888), vi.

84. Aubry, *Aux séminairistes*, 51–52.

85. "Chant pour le départ des missionnaires du Séminaire des missions-étrangères de Paris," words by "M. ***" and music by Charles Gounod, as reprinted in *Almanach des Missions* (Lyon: Imprimerie Générale, 1887), 12–13.

86. On sacrifice in war rhetoric, see George Mosse, *Fallen Soldiers: Reshaping the Memory of the World Wars* (New York: Oxford University Press, 1990), 62–65.

87. In the Middle Ages, religious men rejected allegiance to their cities or states, choosing instead to be representatives only of God. See Ernst H. Kantorowicz's classic article "*Pro Patria Mori* in Medieval Thought," *American Historical Review* 56 (1951): 472–92. Kantorowicz attributes this particular view of the *patrie* to Saint Augustine ("*Pro Patria Mori*," 475).

88. *Allocution prononcée dans l'église paroissiale de Ferrières-en-Gatinas*, 3–4, 11.

89. François Renault, *Cardinal Lavigerie: Churchman, Prophet, and Missionary*, trans. John O'Donohue (London: Athlone Press, 1994), 129–35.

90. On the exhibit in the Salle des Martyrs at the Société des missions étrangères de Paris, see Robert Aldrich, *Vestiges of the Colonial Empire in France: Monuments, Museums, and Colonial Memories* (London: Palgrave Macmillan, 2004), 185–87.

91. Essertel, *L'Aventure missionnaire*, 114.

92. On the life expectancy of Lyonnais missionaries, see ibid., 161–78.

93. Père Retord, Evêque d'Acanthe, "Le Désir du Martyre," in *Le Messager du Coeur de Jésus: Bulletin Mensuel de l'Apostolat de la Prière* 72 (December 1897): 702–3.

94. Mgr. A. S. Neyrat, a member of central council of the Oeuvre, put the poem to music. "Le Désire du Martyre," *Almanach des Missions* (1889), no page number.

95. Ibid., emphasis added.

96. The French claimed that military intervention in these regions defended French interests in Cochinchina in the south of Vietnam, where they had been a colonial presence since the 1860s. For details on European intervention prior to, and including this period, see Truong Buu Lam, *Patterns of Vietnamese Response to Foreign Intervention: 1858–1900* (New Haven, CT: Yale Southeast Asia Studies, 1967), 3–29; and David Marr, *Vietnamese Anticolonialism, 1885–1925* (Berkeley: University of California Press, 1971), 45–47.

97. Jean Chesneaux, *Contribution à l'histoire de la nation vietnamienne* (Paris, 1955), 427.

98. "Common Letter," *Compte-Rendu* (31 Dec 1885) de la Société des missions étrangères (Paris: Imp. de l'Oeuvre de Saint-Paul, L. Philipona, 1885), 1–2.

99. The violence between Christians and Buddhists was so fierce that it was remembered in Vietnamese politics nearly a century later. Marr, *Vietnamese Anticolonialism*, 54.

100. ASME: 817A: Événements de l'Indochine; articles des journaux (1885), 3. Letter from Mgr. Colombert, Saigon, 29 Aug 1885. The letter appeared originally in *Missions Catholiques* but also ran in an unidentified newspaper article saved in a bound book of clippings in the archives' collection. The page numbers refer to this bound book.

101. "Les Missionnaires en Chine," *L'Avenir du Tonkin* (16 Oct 1886): 3.

102. On martyrdom in the late Middle Ages, see Brad Gregory, *Salvation at Stake: Christian Martyrdom in Early Modern Europe* (Cambridge, MA: Harvard University Press, 1999), 30–62.

103. *Compte-Rendu* (1885): 219.

104. Ibid., 224.

105. Ibid., 246.

106. Ibid., 236.

107. Ibid., 3.

108. *Missions Catholiques* 18 (1886): 38.

109. "A la suite des missionnaires," *Almanach des Missions*, 2e Année (Lyon: Imprimerie Catholique, 1886), 26.

110. *Compte-Rendu* (1885): 241.

111. Ibid., 242.

112. "La Persécution au Tong-King. Lettre de Mgr. Puginier . . . à MM les directeurs de l'Oeuvre de la propagation de la foi. Hâ-nôi, 22 Mai 1885," *Missions Catholiques* 17 (1885): 325, 459.
113. *Missions Catholiques* 17:325.
114. *Missions Catholiques* 17:506.
115. Ibid.
116. Gregory, *Salvation at Stake*, 8.
117. "A nos bienfaiteurs," *Annales* 57 (1885): 344.
118. Owen Chadwick, *The Secularization of the European Mind in the Nineteenth Century* (Cambridge: Cambridge University Press, 1975).
119. Hugh McLeod, *Secularization in Western Europe, 1848–1914* (New York: St. Martin's Press, 2000), 147–48.
120. Susan Thorne, *Congregational Missions and the Making of an Imperial Culture in Nineteenth-Century England* (Stanford, CA: Stanford University Press, 1999), 56; and Catherine Hall, *Civilizing Subjects: Metropole and Colony in the English Imagination, 1830–1867* (Chicago: University of Chicago Press, 2002), 12. An excellent overview of studies of British missionaries is Anna Johnston, *Missionary Writing and Empire, 1800–1860* (Cambridge: Cambridge University Press, 2003), 13–37.
121. Peter van der Veer, in his "Introduction" to his edited collection, *Conversion to Modernities: The Globalization of Christianity* (New York: Routledge: 1996), 9.
122. See Jean Comaroff and John Comaroff, *Of Revelation and Revolution: Christianity, Colonialism, and Consciousness in South Africa*, vol. 1 (Chicago: University of Chicago Press, 1991).
123. Brian Stanley, *The Bible and the Flag: Protestant Missions and British Imperialism in the Nineteenth and Twentieth Centuries* (Leicester: Apollos, 1990); and Johnston, *Missionary Writing and Empire*, 15, 22.
124. The most influential discussion of class, race, and gender in colonial studies is Ann Laura Stoler and Frederick Cooper, "Between Metropole and Colony: Rethinking a Research Agenda," in their edited volume *Tensions of Empire: Colonial Cultures in a Bourgeois World* (Berkeley: University of California Press, 1997), 1–58.
125. Agulhon, *The French Republic 1879–1992*, trans. Antonia Nevill (Oxford: Blackwell, 1995), 26.
126. See Thomas Kselman, *Miracles and Prophecies in Nineteenth-Century France* (New Brunswick, NJ: Rutgers University Press, 1983).
127. Ruth Harris, *Lourdes: Body and Spirit in a Secular Age* (New York: Viking, 1999), 289.
128. Kselman, *Miracles and Prophecies*, 196.

Chapter 2

1. Indochina was not a formal colonial entity until 1887; it was composed of the regions of modern-day Vietnam (Tonkin, Annam, and Cochinchina), Laos (after 1893), and Cambodia. For simplicity's sake, I will refer to the regions of Tonkin, Annam, and Cochinchina collectively as Vietnam, and to the inhabitants of those regions as Vietnamese, except in the case of ethnic minorities.

2. Stephen Roberts, *History of French Colonial Policy (1870–1925)*, vol. 2 (London: P. S. King and Son, 1929), 421.
3. See Jules Ferry's introduction to his book *Le Tonkin et la mère patrie* (Paris: Havard, 1890).
4. CAOM: Indochine, Gouverneur-Général (Indo/GG): 11624: Report, Puginier to M. le Général de Division, Commandant en chef, le Corps expéditionnaire du Tonkin, Hanoi, 27 Mar 1884.
5. See, in particular, Jean Michaud, "French Missionary Expansion in Colonial Upper Tonkin," *Journal of Southeast Asian Studies* 35, no. 2 (June 2004): 287–310; others who portray the missions as uncomplicated collaborators in colonial expansion include Vo Duc Hanh, *La Place du catholicisme dans les relations entre la France et le Viêt Nam de 1851 à 1871* (Leiden: Brill, 1969); Nicole-Dominique Lê, *Les Missions-étrangères et la pénétration française au Viet-Nam* (Paris: Mouton, 1975); Cao Huy Thuan, *Les Missionnaires et la politique coloniale française au Vietnam (1857–1914)* (New Haven, CT: Yale Southeast Asian Studies, 1990); and Oscar Salemink, *The Ethnography of Vietnam's Central Highlanders: A Historical Contextualization, 1850–1900* (London: Routledge Curzon, 2003), chap. 2.
6. See, for example, Nicola Cooper, *France in Indochina: Colonial Encounters* (New York: Berg, 2001), 12.
7. There were just over 17,000 Catholics in Cambodia. "Tableau générale de l'état des missions et des résultats obtenus en 1888," *Compte-rendu de la Société des Missions Étrangères* (Paris: Imprimerie de l'oeuvre de Saint Paul, 1888).
8. The history of the Missions étrangères in Vietnam obviously long predated this. See Jean Guennou, *Missions étrangères de Paris* (Paris: Fayard, 1986); and Alain Forest, *Les Missionnaires français au Tonkin et au Siam*, 3 vols. (Paris: L'Harmattan, 1998).
9. The bishop's name was originally spelled "Pigneaux," but in the late nineteenth century, missionary biographers dropped the "x." Because this chapter largely discusses how Pigneau was remembered, the nineteenth-century spelling is used. On Pigneau, history, and memory, see J. P. Daughton, "Recasting Pigneau de Béhaine: French Missionaries and the Politics of Colonial History," in Nhung Tuyet Tran and Anthony Reid, eds., *Vietnam: Borderless Histories* (Madison: University of Wisconsin Press, 2006).
10. See Mark W. McLeod, *The Vietnamese Response to French Invasion, 1862–1874* (New York: Praeger, 1991), chap. 6.
11. Tuck, *French Catholic Missionaries and the Politics of Imperialism in Vietnam, 1857–1914. A Documentary Survey* (Liverpool: Liverpool University Press, 1987), 166.
12. ASME: 817A, 2. The archive does not indicate what newspaper this letter came from, but a number like it were published in various newspapers sympathetic to the missionary cause. It was also common for newspapers to publish letters and articles from other newspapers with similar political views. Romanet du Caillaud's letter responded to the violence of 1884 in Thanh Hoa province and 1885 in Binh Dinh.
13. ASME: 817A, 12.
14. ASME: 817A, 3. In what is an example of the awkward alliances wrought by French imperialism, in making his point, Drumont cited Gabriel Charmes's

book *La Politique extérieure et coloniale*. Charmes, who wrote for a number of leading republican journals like the *Revue des deux Mondes* and the *Journal des Débats*, insisted that France would fall to the rank of a secondary power if it remained indifferent to the "great battle . . . for the world." Raoul Girardet, *L'Idée coloniale en France de 1871 à 1962* (Paris: La Table Ronde, 1972), 57–58.

15. ASME: 817A, 3.
16. Ibid.
17. "Les Missionnaires en Chine" started in *L'Avenir du Tonkin*, 3e année, 2e série, no. 18 (16 Oct 1886), 3.
18. "Les Missionnaires en Chine," *L'Avenir du Tonkin*, no. 20 (30 Oct 1886), 2.
19. "Les Missionnaires en Chine," *L'Avenir du Tonkin*, no. 21 (6 Nov 1886), 5.
20. "Le Protectorat des Missions Catholiques en Chine," *Courrier d'Haiphong*, 1e année, no. 12 (28 Oct 1886), 1.
21. Excerpted from Simon's book *Cité chinoise* in *L'Avenir du Tonkin*, no. 21 (6 Nov 1886), 5.
22. A "Tableau général de l'état des Missions et des résultats" was published in the back of every annual volume of the *Compte-rendu de la Société des Missions Étrangères*.
23. "Lettre de Mgr Mossard sur l'education donnée par la mission de Cochinchine" (Saigon: Imprimerie de la Mission, 1903), 2.
24. The official statements are reproduced in ASME: 757: "Memoire de S. G. Mgr. Mossard sur les écoles de la mission de Cochinchine" (Saigon: Imprimerie de la Mission, 1902), 2–3.
25. Tuck, *French Catholic Missionaries*, 206–8.
26. CAOM: Indochina, Résident-Supérieur du Tonkin (Indo/RST): 28861: Mgr. Puginier, "Réflexions et Renseignements," Hanoi, 6 and 11 Apr 1888.
27. CAOM: Indo/RST: 28861: Mgr. Puginier, "Réflexions et Renseignements," Hanoi, 6 Apr 1888.
28. Ibid.
29. ASME: 757: Folder 1901: Doc. 87: Compte-Rendu, 1900–1901 from the Vicariat Apostolique de Cochinchine Occidentale, Saigon, 1 Oct 1901.
30. CAOM: Indo/GG: 22555: M. le Résident-Supèrieur au Cambodge to M. le Governeur-Général de l'Indochina, Hanoi, No. 25, Phnôm-Penh, 15 May 1891.
31. CAOM: Indo/GG: 22555: Dr. Hanh to the Résident-Supèrieur au Cambodge, Phnom Penh, 24 May 1891.
32. CAOM: Indo/GG: 9234: Hector to M. le Gouverneur Général de l'Indo-Chine, Saigon, No. 614. Hué, 21 Aug 1889; another case in 1896 resulted in a similar exchange of letters. See CAOM: Indo/GG: 9800: Difficultés survenues entre MM Duranton et Guillet et la mission du Tonkin méridional.
33. ASME: 759: Cochinchine Occidentale, 1888–1898: vol. 2; Folder 1890: Doc. 367: Compte-Rendu, 1 Sept 1890.
34. The first missionaries to try to evangelize in the highlands were captured in 1842 and sentenced to death by Vietnamese mandarins. M. l'abbé P. Dourisboure, *Les Sauvages Ba-Hnars, souvenir d'un missionnaire* (Paris: Lecoffre, 1875), 3. In 1852, the vicariate of East Cochinchina established a mission at Kon Trang. See Tuck, *French Catholic Missionaries*, 237–40.

35. A number of studies of the region reflect this usage. Dourisboure, *Les Sauvages Ba-Hnars*; le Marquis Barthélémy, *Au Pays moï* (Paris: Chez Plon, 1904); Henri Maître, *Les Jungles moï* (Paris: Émile Larose, 1912); and for usage in French administrative documents and newspaper articles, see those collected in Jean Marquet, "Un Aventurier du XIXe siècle: Marie Ier, Roi des Sédangs (1888–1890)," *Bulletin des Amis du Vieux Hué* 14, no. 1 (Jan. 1927): 107–28.

36. Of particular value, in early 1893, Guerlach wrote a 204-page letter to a friend, a curé outside of Paris (ASME: 787).

37. Ibid., p. 40.

38. Ibid., pp. 41–43.

39. Ibid., pp. 44–46.

40. His role of the common "father" to a large family of Sedang "sons" also mirrored French official attitudes vis-à-vis the Indochinese population. For example, French announcements to the Vietnamese population commonly referred to the local population in familial terms. At the declaration of the First World War, French officials described the Vietnamese as the "preferred children" in the colonial family. See, for example, Trung Tam Luu Tru Quoc Gia 1, Hanoi (National Archives of Vietnam, No. 1) (TTLT): RST: 20,324: Proclamation au peuple annamite a.s. de la déclaration de la Grande Guerre, 1914.

41. ASME: 787, p. 36, emphasis in the original.

42. ASME: 787, p. 38. In the manuscript, an editor has deleted these lines with a blue pen; as much of the letter was later published in *Missions Catholiques*, the editor was likely a superior at the Missions étrangères who wanted to clear out contentious material.

43. Ibid., pp. 61, 64.

44. Ibid., p. 120; the anti-Masonic rant has been marked for deletion.

45. Ibid., 787, pp. 157, 164.

46. David Marr, *Vietnamese Anticolonialism, 1885–1925* (Berkeley: University of California Press, 1971), 47.

47. Ibid., 54–55.

48. A useful discussion of the "Siamese Question" and its relation to Mayréna is in Hickey, *Kingdom in the Morning Mist-Mayréna in the Highlands of Vietnam* (Philadelphia: University of Pennsylvania Press, 1988), chap. 4.

49. A more detailed account of the mission's involvement in the Mayréna affair can be found in J. P. Daughton, "Kings of the Mountains: Mayréna, Missionaries, and French Colonial Divisions in 1880s Indochina," *Itinerario: European Journal of Overseas History* 25, nos. 3, 4 (2001): 185–217.

50. CAOM: Indo/GG: 11890: Dossier Mayréna (8): Traité avec Pim.

51. Mayréna's letters at times were nearly incomprehensible. See, for example, the rambling notes in CAOM: Indo/GG: 11890: Mayréna to M. le Gouverneur-Général. Kon-Jeri-Krong, 25 July 1888.

52. Marquet, "Un Aventurier du XIXe siècle," 39.

53. Mayréna's army never received the uniforms because the king never paid for them. CAOM: Indo/GG: 11894: Dossier Mayréna (12): Liébard to Guerlach, Haiphong, 23 Jan 1889.

54. Maurice Soulié claims that older Parisians in boulevard cafés still reminisced about Mayréna's exploits in the 1920s. Soulié, *Marie I, Roi des Sédangs 1888–1890* (Paris: Marpon et cie., 1927), 5. Mayréna's legend lived on in Indochina for decades, as well. In the 1920s, three studies of him appeared, and as late as 1967, Mayréna's antics even made their way into André Malraux's *Antimémoires*. Gerald Hickey provides a useful essay on printed sources dealing with the king of the Sedangs in *Kingdom in the Morning Mist*, xxi–xxix.
55. Marquet, "Un Aventurier du XIXe siècle," 101–5.
56. CAOM: Indo/GG: 11897: Dossier Mayréna (15): Consulat de France à Singapore to M. le Gouverneur-Général de l'Indochine, No. 145, Singapore, 24 Nov 1890.
57. Marquet, "Un aventurier du XIXe siècle," 9.
58. In 1887, a French administrator investigated Mayréna's home on suspicion of arms trafficking, found and impounded a number of weapons, but never—for reasons that remain unclear—brought charges against him. Marquet, "Un Aventurier du XIXe siècle," 18–19.
59. See, for example, CAOM: Indo/GG: 11883: M. le Directeur de l'Intérieur, Cochinchine Française, to M. le Gouverneur-Général, No. 19. Saigon (reçu), 15 June 1885.
60. CAOM: Indo/GG: 11890: Cabinet Lieutenant-Gouverneur de Cochinchine Française to M. le Gouverneur-Général de l'Indochine, No. 9. Saigon, 7 Jan 1888.
61. The letter of 24 March 1888 is reproduced in Marquet, "Un aventurier du XIXe siècle," 25.
62. For protection, Mayréna brought along twenty-one rifles, four revolvers, and 2,500 cartridges—an arsenal he thought rather too light for conquest. Marquet, "Un Aventurier du XIXe siècle," 25–26.
63. Ibid., 30.
64. The task of securing treaties had not been asked of Mayréna by the French government; he simply signed agreements that would later require official ratification by the French government. See the letter from Governor-General Richaud to Émile Jamais, undersecretary for the colonies, Hanoi, 14 Dec 1888, reprinted in Tuck, *French Catholic Missionaries*, 241–42.
65. Lemire in 1888, in Marquet, "Un Aventurier du XIXe siècle," 111. Both Navelle, who traveled in the region in 1884, and Père Vialleton, the superior of the mission at Kontum, discussed the benefits of such alliances.
66. Marquet, "Un Aventurier du XIXe siècle," 34.
67. ASME: 751: Cochinchine Orientale: vol. 2 (1887–1900): Folder 1889: Doc. 110: Marie I to Mgr. Van Camelbeke, No. 939. Paris, 9 Mar 1889.
68. CAOM: Indo/GG: 11890: Mayréna to M. le Gouverneur-Général, 15 May 1888; Mayréna to M. le Gouverneur-Général, Kon-Jeri-Krong, 25 June 1888.
69. Hickey, *Kingdom in the Morning Mist*, 93.
70. "Lettres de l'Annam," *Le Temps*, 28 Aug 1888.
71. CAOM: Indo/GG: 11892: Dossier Mayréna (10): M. le Résident de France à Qui Nhon to M. le Gouverneur de l'Indo-Chine, Saigon, No. 865, Qui Nhon, 20 Sept 1888.
72. Marquet, "Un Aventurier du XIXe siècle," 46.

73. On Lemire's life, see *Index bibliographique français* I, 642: 179–84.

74. Letter from Lemire to Mayréna, No. 728, Qui Nhon, 15 April 1888, reprinted in Marquet, "Un Aventurier du XIXe siècle," 27–29.

75. Marcel Ner rejects Marquet's claim that Lemire was blinded by anticlericalism; see Ner, review of Marquet and Soulié in *Bulletin de l'École Françaised' Extrêm Orient* 27 (1927): 329–30.

76. Marquet, "Un Aventurier du XIXe siècle," 70–71.

77. "Lettres de l'Annam," *Le Temps*, 28 Aug 1888.

78. ASME: 751: vol. 2: Folder 1889: Doc. 113: Guerlach to Pean, Kon-Jori-Krong, 9 Apr 1889.

79. Rheinart to Van Camelbeke, Hue, 27 Nov 1888, reprinted in Tuck, *French Catholic Missionaries*, 242.

80. Richaud to Jamais, Hanoi, 14 Dec 1888, reprinted in Tuck, *French Catholic Missionaries*, 241–42.

81. Mayréna in his letter to the editor, *Courrier d'Haiphong*, 8 Oct 1888, reprinted in Marquet, "Un Aventurier du XIXe siècle," 49.

82. CAOM: Indo/GG: 11894: Extract of Van Camelbeke letter, Qui Nhon, 25 Dec 1888.

83. CAOM: Indo/GG: 11894: Extract of Van Camelbeke letter, Qui Nhon, 5 Dec 1888.

84. Van Camelbeke to Rheinart, 1 Dec 1888, reprinted in Marquet, "Un Aventurier du XIXe siècle," 72.

85. CAOM: Indo/GG: 11894: "Notes secrètes et privées sur la question de Mayréna et les Sédangs," Hanoi, 29 Dec 1888.

86. "Chez les Sédangs," *Courrier d'Haiphong*, 27 Dec 1888, reprinted in Marquet, "Un aventurier du XIXe siècle," 62–63.

87. Marquet, "Un Aventurier du XIXe siècle," 69.

88. Ibid.

89. "Chez les Sédangs," *Courrier d'Haiphong*, 3 Jan 1889, reprinted in Marquet, "Un Aventurier du XIXe siècle," 66–67.

90. Marquet, "Un Aventurier du XIXe siècle," 69.

91. CAOM: Indo/GG: 11894: Guerlach to Rheinart. Hanoi, 28 Dec 1888.

92. Marquet, "Un Aventurier du XIXe siècle," 69.

93. CAOM: Indo/GG: 11894: Report from the Vice-Résident de France à Qui Nhon to M. le Résident-Général, Hue, Qui Nhon, 6 May 1889.

94. Ibid.

95. Ibid.

96. ASME: 751: vol. 2: Folder 1889: Doc. 115: Guerlach to "Bien cher et Vénéré Père." Kron-Jori-Krong, 21 June 1889.

97. Van Camelbeke, quoted in Ner, review, 332.

98. ASME: 751: vol. 2: Folder 1889: Doc. 115.

99. ASME: 785: Vie du Père Jean Baptiste Pierre Marie Guerlach, 1858–1912, par l'abbé Cauvigny, 25 June 1913 to 12 Sept 1914, Notebook I: 6. According to another biography, Guerlach was an ambulance worker in 1870; see (no author), *Le Père Guerlach, provicaire apostolique, supérieur de la mission de Kontum (sauvages Bahnars) (1858–1912)* (Quinhon: Imprimerie de Quinhon, 1912), 2.

100. ASME: 786: Guerlach to his parents, 15 Dec 1874.

101. ASME: 787: pp. 200–201; the emphasis is Guerlach's.

102. ASME: 787: p. 200.
103. ASME: 751: vol. 2: Folder 1888: Doc. 109: Résident-Général en Annam et au Tonkin to Van Camelbeke. No. 86G. Hanoi, 27 Dec 1888.
104. Rheinart to Guerlach, reprinted in J.-B. Guerlach, *"L'Oeuvre Néfaste": Les Missionnaires en Indo-Chine* (Saigon: Imprimerie Commerciale, 1906), 147–48.
105. ASME: 751: vol. 2: Folder 1888: Doc. 109.
106. Tuck, *French Catholic Missionaries*, 245–46.

Chapter 3

1. TTLT: Résident-Supérieur du Tonkin (RST): 20,241: Proclamation, M. le Résident Général de la République française en Annam et au Tonkin. 8 Apr 1886.
2. For periodization of French rule, see Truong Buu Lam, *Colonialism Experienced: Vietnamese Writings on Colonialism, 1900–1931* (Ann Arbor: University of Michigan Press, 2000), 1–2.
3. Philippe Devillers, *Français et Annamites: Partenaires ou ennemis 1856–1902* (Paris: Editions Denoel, 1998), 428.
4. Tertullian, quoted in Maurice Agulhon, *The French Republic, 1879–1992*, trans. Antonia Nevill (Oxford: Blackwell, 1993), 56.
5. René Rémond, *The Right Wing in France, from 1815 to de Gaulle*, trans. James M. Laux (Philadelphia: University of Pennsylvania Press, 1966), 208–12; and see Maurice Larkin, *Church and State after the Dreyfus Affair: The Separation Issue in France* (London: Macmillan, 1974), 37.
6. This was especially true during the ministries of Charles Dupuy, Alexandre Ribot, and Jules Méline (1894 to 1898). As Maurice Larkin notes, "The Catholic Ralliés had some thirty to forty seats in the Chamber of Deputies which, when added to the two-hundred and fifty odd moderate republicans, gave these governments a comfortable majority against the radicals and Socialists, as well as marginalizing still further the fifty or so members of the dissident Right." Larkin, *Religion, Politics and Preferment in France since 1890: La Belle Epoque and Its Legacy* (Cambridge: Cambridge University Press, 1995), 7.
7. For a complete discussion of Dreyfus's influence on religious politics, see Larkin, *Church and State after the Dreyfus Affair*.
8. Melchoir de Vogué, quoted in John McManners, *Church and State in France, 1870–1914* (London: SPCK, 1972), 131.
9. McManners, *Church and State*, 132–33.
10. "Les Congrégations Religieuses," par le F∴ Ch-M. Limousin, in *L'Acacia: Révue mensuelle d'études M∴*, rédigée exclusivement par des FF∴MM∴. 1 (1903): 159.
11. Pierre Chevalier, *Histoire de la Franc-maçonnerie française, vol. 3: La Maçonnerie: Église de la république (1877–1944)* (Paris: Fayard, 1975), 19–21.
12. On Masonic goals in France, see Avner Halpern, *The Democratisation of France, 1840–1901: Sociabilité, Freemasonry and Radicalism* (Atlanta: Minerva Press, 1999), 285 and passim.
13. Archives du Grand orient de France, Paris (GOF): BR 1176: *La Question coloniale et la Franc-Maçonnerie* (Angers: Imprimerie A. Poitevin et V. Scipion, 1885), 4–5, 14.

14. Ibid., 18.

15. On Masons in West Africa, for example, see Owen White, "Networking: Freemasons and the Colonial State in French West Africa, 1895–1914," *French History* 14, no. 1 (2005): 91–111.

16. E. L. G van Raveschot, *La Franc-maçonnerie au Tonkin et les agissements des missionnaires en extrême-orient* (Paris: E. Comprègne, 1906), 11–18.

17. Jacques Dalloz, *Francs-maçons d'Indochine, 1886–1975* (Paris: Editions Maçonniques de France, 2002), 33.

18. Ibid., 37.

19. Tuck, *French Catholic Missionaries and the Politics of Imperialism in Vietnam, 1857–1914: A Documentary Survey* (Liverpool: Liverpool University Press, 1987), 249.

20. Tuck reproduces two letters from Mgr. Depierre in ibid., 252–53.

21. GOF: BR 1246, *L'Amenité*, letters from L∴ La Fraternité Tonkinoise, O∴ de Hanoi, 8 Juillet 1887.

22. GOF: BR 1246, *L'Amenité*, Réponse par le F∴ Victor Cauchin d'après les conclusions du F∴ Félix Faure, A∴N∴E∴S∴L∴A∴ DU G∴O∴D∴F, ∴ de L'Aménité, Or∴ du Havre, le 19 Octobre 1887 (E∴V∴).

23. Georges Piermé, Délégué de Cochinchine au Comité exécutif du Parti Radical et Radical-Socialiste, in his introduction to van Raveschot, *La Franc-maçonnerie*, 9.

24. The Freemason "Jamais," quoted in "Nicolas" (Le Franc-maçon), *Le Role des missionnaires religieux en Extrême-Orient (Conférence faite à la Tenue du 21 Février 1893)* (Paris: Imprimerie Alexandre Pichon, 1893), 10.

25. ASME: 757: Doc. 105, Mossard, Compte Rendu 1903, Saigon, 30 Sept 1903.

26. Van Raveschot, *La Franc-maçonnerie au Tonkin*, 32.

27. CAOM: Indo/GGI: 9801: M. E. Le Tonnelier de Breteuil to M. le Gov.-Gen. de l'Indochine. Tourane, 9 June 1896.

28. Pâris, quoted in Tuck, *French Catholic Missionaries*, 254.

29. Camille Pâris and Alfred Barsanti, *Les Missionnaires d'Asie. Oeuvre néfaste des Congrégations. Le Protectorat des chrétiens* (Paris: Imprimerie "Le Papier," 1905), 37–39; Pâris wrote the section on Indochina.

30. Armand Séville, "La Question sociale et la politique coloniale," in *L'Acacia: Révue Mensuelle d'Études M∴*, 4e volume (1904): 185.

31. GOF: BR 622: L∴ La Fraternité tonkinoise, *Du role des missions catholiques* (Hanoi: Imprimerie Librairie J-E Crebessac, 1900), 6–7.

32. J. L. de Lanessan, *Les Missions et leur protectorat* (Paris: Librairies Félix Alcan et Guillaumin Réunies, 1907), 69.

33. Pâris and Barsanti, *Les Missionnaires d'Asie*, 61.

34. De Lanessan, *Les Missions et leur protectorat*, 70.

35. Pâris and Barsanti, *Les Missionnaires d'Asie*, 53.

36. On these trends in French colonial thought, see Raymond Betts, *Assimilation and Association, in French Colonial Theory, 1890–1914* (New York: Columbia University Press, 1960), 106–32.

37. Van Raveschot, *La Franc-maçonnerie*, 26; Pâris and Barsanti, *Les Missionnaires d'Asie*, 37–38.

38. L∴ La Fraternité tonkinoise, *Du role des missions catholiques*, 3.

39. As recently as 1887, a Masonic congress determined this to be true. Halpern, *The Democratisation of France*, 285.

40. L∴ La Fraternité tonkinoise, *Du role des missions catholiques*, 5.

41. Pâris and Barsanti, *Les Missionnaires d'Asie*, 43–44.

42. Ibid., 68–70.

43. Van Raveschot, *La Franc-maçonnerie*, 26.

44. Séville, "La Question sociale," 185–86.

45. Pâris and Barsanti, *Les Missionnaires d'Asie*, 10–11.

46. Camille Pâris, *Reponse à "L'oeuvre néfaste" du Père Guerlach* (Haiphong: Editions du Courrier d'Haiphong, 1906), 7.

47. See, for example, Tran Tu Binh, *The Red Earth: A Vietnamese Memoir of Life on a Colonial Rubber Plantation*, trans. John Spragens Jr. (Athens: Ohio University Center for International Studies, 1985).

48. L∴ La Fraternité tonkinoise, *Du role des missions catholiques*, 10–11, emphasis in the original.

49. Pâris and Barsanti, *Les Missionnaires d'Asie*, 64.

50. ASME: 759: Folder 1898: Doc. 472: L'Evêque de Saigon to M. Le Président du Conseil Colonial de la Cochinchine, Saigon, 25 Aug 1898.

51. Devillers, *Français et Annamites*, 464–65.

52. De Lanessan, *Les Missions et leur protectorat*, 68.

53. GOF: BR 622: L∴ La Fraternité tonkinoise, *Du role des missions catholiques*, 10.

54. Pâris and Barsanti, *Les Missionnaires d'Asie*, 35–36, emphasis in the original.

55. Piermé, introduction to van Raveschot, *La Franc-Maçonnerie*, 6–7; "congaïes" is a transliteration of "con gai," or "girl" in Vietnamese, but it also commonly meant a Vietnamese mistress. "Boy" was borrowed from the English, meaning houseboy. But in this case, the author suggests a clear sexual connotation.

56. Séville, "La Question sociale," 184.

57. Piermé, introduction to van Raveschot, *La Franc-maçonnerie*, 7.

58. De Lanessan, *Les Missions et leur protectorat*, 212.

59. GOF: BR 622: L∴ La Fraternité tonkinoise, *Du role des missions catholiques*, 11.

60. De Lanessan, *Les Missions et leur protectorat*, 213, 216.

61. M. François Nicol, *La Politique coloniale française. Rapport présenté par M. F. Nicol (Sécretaire général du Comité républicaine aux Colonies françaises, Membre de la Délégation permanente des Sociétés Française de la Paix) au VIIe Congrès National de la Paix, à Clermont-Ferrand—1911* (Clermont-Ferrand: G. Mont-Louism, 1911), 2.

62. ASME: 757: Mossard, "A Monsieur C., Réponse à Monsieur X," p. 10. This document, which took the form of a letter, addressed a variety of common criticisms leveled against the missions and outlined possible responses to each.

63. ASME: 757: Doc. 87: Mossard, Compte-Rendu 1900–1901, Saigon, 1 Oct 1901.

64. Joseph Chanel, "Voyage chez les Moï du Bassin du Bla. Leurs moeurs et leurs coutumes," *Bulletin de Géographie Historique et Descriptive* (Année 1897): 305. The *Bulletin* was published in Paris under the Ministère de l'Instruction Publique et des Beaux-Arts.

65. Ibid., 338–39.

66. Ibid., 340.

67. ASME: 757: vol. 2: 1902: Doc. 95: Compte-rendu, Vicariat Apostolique de Cochinchine Occidentale, Saigon, 5 Oct 1902.

68. Adrien Launay, *Histoire ancienne et moderne de l'Annam, Tong-King et Cochinchine depuis l'année 2,700 avant l'ère chrétienne jusqu'à nos jours* (Paris: Challamel Ainé, 1884), 189.

69. Louis-Eugène Louvet, *Mgr. D'Adran, notice biographique* (Saigon: Imprimerie de la Mission, 1896), "Préface," n.p.

70. Ibid.

71. Ibid.

72. Ibid.

73. Dépierre, in Louvet, *Mgr. D'Adran, notice biographique*, ii.

74. Ibid., vii.

75. Ibid.

76. Letter from Mossard reprinted in Louis-Eugène Louvet, *Mgr. D'Adran, missionnaire et patriote* (Paris: Delhomme et Briguet, 1900), i–ii.

77. Louvet, *Mgr. D'Adran, missionnaire et patriote*, 156.

78. Ibid., 111.

79. Louvet, *Mgr. D'Adran, notice biographique*, "Préface," n.p.

80. Louvet, *Mgr. D'Adran, missionnaire et patriote*.

81. Robert Gildea, *The Past in French History* (New Haven, CT: Yale University Press, 1994), 38.

82. See Maurice Agulhon, *Marianne au pouvoir, l'imagerie et la symbolique républicaines de 1880 à 1914* (Paris: Flammarion, 1989).

83. Mona Ozouf, "The Pantheon: The Ecole Normale of the Dead," in Pierre Nora, ed., *Realms of Memory: The Construction of the French Past, vol. 3, Symbols*, trans. Arthur Goldhammer (New York: Columbia University Press, 1998), 326.

84. Nord, *The Republican Moment: Struggles for Democracy in Nineteenth-Century France* (Cambridge, MA: Harvard University Press, 1995), 191.

85. "Discours de S. G. Mgr. Mossard . . . prononcé à l'inauguration de la statue de Mgr Pigneau de Béhaine, le 10 mars 1902," *Annales de la Société des Missions-Etrangères* (1902): 155.

86. Ibid., 156.

87. Ibid.

88. Ibid.

89. ASME: 757: vol. 2: Doc. 100: *Mémoire de S. G. Mossard sur les écoles de la Mission de Cochinchine* (Saigon: Imprimerie de la Mission, 1902), 4–5.

90. Ibid., 12, 13.

91. Mossard's writings were read aloud during the debates over the Leygues Amendment in 1904. See Tuck, *French Catholic Missionaries*, 261–63.

92. Freemason critics happily cited this affair; Diep's comments were quoted at length in Pâris and Barsanti, *Les Missionnaires d'Asie*, 66–67.

93. *Lettre de Mgr. Mossard*, 14–15.

94. TTLT: RST: 56,941: M. le Gouverneur-Général de l'Indo-Chine to M. le Résident Supérieur au Tonkin. No. 422, Hanoi, 11 Apr 1903. Marcou's "Note" is an attachment to this letter.

95. TTLT: RST: 56,941: "Note relative aux peuplades Muong des Provinces de Thanh-Hoa et Hoa-Binh," Confidentielle, no page numbers, no date (1903).
96. Ibid.
97. Ibid.
98. Ibid.
99. Père J.-B. Guerlach, *"L'Oeuvre néfaste": Les Missionnaires en Indo-Chine* (Saigon: Imprimerie Commerciale, 1906), 4; Camille Pâris replied to this in the pamphlet *Réponse à "L'oeuvre néfaste"du Père Guerlach* (Haiphong: Éditions du Courrier d'Haiphong, 1906).
100. CAOM: Indo/GGI: 15806: Père Artif to M. Klobukowski, Saigon, 3 Oct 1908.
101. By the 1890s, for example, the colonial administration had outlawed a wide range of political crimes, as distinct from criminal ones, suggesting concern over growing anticolonial activities. See Peter Zinoman, *The Colonial Bastille: A History of Imprisonment in Vietnam, 1862–1940* (Berkeley: University of California Press, 2001), 108–9.
102. CAOM: Indo/GGI: 7719: Gaston Doumerge, Ministère des Colonies, to M. le Gouverneur-Général de l'Indochine, No. 161, Paris, 12 Dec 1903.
103. Tuck, *French Catholic Missionaries*, 276.
104. Ibid., 274–75. Tuck also provides an excellent discussion of the impact of the religious laws of 1901–5, pp. 255–58.
105. CAOM: Indo/GGI: 7719: M. le Gouverneur-Général de l'Indo-Chine to M. le Ministre des Colonies, No, 1578, Saigon, 3 July 1903.
106. Acting Resident Superior of Annam M. Moulié to Governor-General Beau, Hué, 18 Mar 1905, reprinted in Tuck, *French Catholic Missionaries*, 278, emphasis added.
107. *Le Temps*, 16 June 1908, clipping in Archives du Ministère des affaires-étrangères (Quai d'Orsay) (MAE): Correspondance politique et commerciale, Indochine (CPC/Indo): NS 1: Administration et Défense de l'Indochine, 1897–1917, doc. pp. 114–15.
108. TTLT: GGI: F.03: 147: Report, "L'Indochine de 1908 à 1911. Program d'action. Suite au rapprt du 15 Avril 1911. Le Gouverneur-Général de l'Indochine à M. MESSIMY, Ministre des Colonies, Paris," 2–3.
109. See Marr, *Vietnamese Anticolonialism*, 1885–1925 (Berkeley: University of California Press, 1971), 98–119.
110. MAE: CPC/Indo: NS 1: Rapport au Ministre des Colonies, 22 Oct 1908, pp. 126–27.
111. CAOM: Indo/GGI: 15806: M. le Gouverneur-Général de l'Indo-Chine to M. le Ministre des Colonies, No. 2566, Saigon, 4 Oct 1908.
112. Tuck, *French Catholic Missionaries*, 289.
113. TTLT: S.17: 74,514: Domergue to M. le Résident-Supérieur, 20 May 1908.
114. TTLT: S.17/S.60: 74,526: Bonnal to M. le Directeur des affaires civiles et politiques au Tonkin, No. 287, 18 Jan 1885.
115. TTLT: S.17: 74,514: Minute to the Résident de Hung Yen, No. 293, 27 May 1908.
116. "Conférence de M. Klobukowski," *Bulletin de la Mission Laïque Française* 7, no. 4 (July 1910): 85. The director of the Mission laïque, A. Aulard, in a Freemason

periodical in 1907, condemned the missions for teaching Latin instead of French, and for serving the pope instead of France. A. Aulard and O. Pontet, "La Mission laïque française," *L'Acacia* 1 (1907): 184–85.

117. TTLT: RST: 39,111: M. le Ministre des Colonies to M. le Gouverneur-Général de l'Indochine, No. 497, Paris, 26 Dec 1896.

118. TTLT: RST: R 02: 73,401: "Procès-Verbal de la Seance du 11 Avril 1906," in the booklet *Conseil de perfectionnement de l'enseignement indigène* (Hanoi: L. Gallois, 1906), 13.

119. TTLT: RST: 38,363: "Rapport sur le Service de l'Enseignement au Tonkin. Hanoi, 21 Juillet 1909," Par M. Péralle, Chef du Service de l'Enseignement, no page numbers.

120. "Extrait du rapport du secrétaire général pour l'année 1906–1907," *Mission Laïque Française* (Paris, 1908), 4.

121. MAE: CPC/Indo: NS 1: clipping, Aulard, "La Mission laïque et les jeunes anna-mites," *Le Siècle* (10 Sept 1909).

122. Ibid.

123. TTLT: Gouverneur-Général de l'Indochine (GGI): F.03: 147: "L'Indochine de 1908 à 1911," 13.

124. TTLT: RST: 38,363: Rapport sur la Service de l'Enseignement du Tonkin par M. Péralle, 18 Apr 1912.

125. TTLT: GGI: F.03: 147: "L'Indochine de 1908 à 1911," 5.

126. CAOM: Indo/GGI: 5934: Copy of "Rapport: Le Commis des Services Civils, faisant functions de Commissaire du Gouvernement à Attopeu to M. le Résident Supérieur de Laos, Vientiane, No. 13, Attopeu, 15 Juillet 1904."

127. Ibid.

128. CAOM: Indo/GGI: 19194: Telegram. Gouvereur-Général to Directeur Cabinet, Hanoi. Saigon, 9 July 1907, 4:55 PM.

129. CAOM: Indo/GGI: 19194: M. le Résident Supérieur en Annam to M. le Gouverneur-Général de l'Indo-Chine, No. 18, Hué, 1 June 1907.

130. CAOM: Indo/GGI: 19194: "Rapport à M. le Gouverneur Général. Hué 25 Octo-bre 1907."

131. See the speeches in *Comité d'érection et d'inauguration du monument Camille Pâris* (Hanoi, Haiphong: Imprimerie d'Extrême-Orient, 1909), 2, 27.

132. For a full description of Sabatier's life and ethnographic work, see Salemink, *The Ethnography of Vietnam's Central Highlanders: A Historical Contextualization, 1850–1900* (London: Routledge Curzon, 2003), chap. 3.

133. CAOM: Indo/GGI: 19194: Délégation à Kontum: Dossier 76.

134. CAOM: Indo/GGI: 19194: Depositions of Yo'n de Dak Drei et Dek de Dak Yo, 5 Sept 1911.

135. CAOM: Indo/GGI: 19194: Kemlin to M. le Délégué, Polei Dodrâp, 10 Oct 1911.

136. CAOM: Indo/GGI: 19194: Guerlach to M. le Délégué, Rohai, 27 Oct 1911.

137. CAOM: Indo/GGI: 19194: M. le Délégué à Kontum to M. le Président du Tri-bunal à Quinhon, Kontum, 28 Oct 1911. Yo'n, however, did not get the justice he sought, as the incident was deemed too old to prosecute. CAOM: Indo/GGI: 19194: M. le Résident de France à Quinhon to M. le Délégué à Kontum, No. 1685, Quinhon, 13 Nov 1911.

138. CAOM: Indo/GGI: 19194: Délégation de Kontum, Dossier 851: Deposition de Nua, Droinh, Nou que le nommé Toh de Kon M'nei, 13 Jan 1912.
139. CAOM: Indo/GGI: 19194: Deposition de 19 Jan 1912 de Huyên H'ma, Nguah, chef, Gih, Menh, Dih, Nol, Nuih de Kon Ko tuh.
140. CAOM: Indo/GGI: 19194: Sabatier to M. le Résident, Quinhon, Konchora 2 Mar 1912.
141. CAOM: Indo/GGI: 19194: Province de Binh Dinh, Délégation de Kon Tum, Tribunal Correctionel, Ministère public et Drio contre Hutinet, Jugement no. 1, Signé: SABATIER et SANDRÉ (n.d.).
142. This was an observation made by the resident-superior of Annam, as well. CAOM: Indo/GGI: 19194: M. le Résident-Supérieur en Annam to M. le Gouverneur Général de l'Indochine, Saigon, No. 512, Hué, 27 June 1912.
143. CAOM: Indo/GGI: 19194: Sabatier to M. le Résident, Quinhon, Konchora, 2 Mar 1912.
144. ASME: 757: vol. 2: Mossard, "Vicariat apostolique de la Cochinchine Occidentale, Compte-Rendu 1905–1906," 1–2.
145. TTLT: RST: 38,363: Rapports sur le Service de l'Enseignement au Tonkin, 1909–1912; Rapport sur la Service de l'Ensiegnement du Tonkin par M. Péralle, chef de Service, Hanoi, 18 Apr 1912.
146. Patrice Morlat, "La Rivalité entre les missions et les loges maçonniques en Indochine durant les annés vingt," in Morlat, ed., *La Question religieuse dans l'empire coloniale français* (Paris: Les Indes Savantes, 2003), 125–73.
147. TTLT: RST: 20,324: Proclamation au peuple annamite a.s. de la déclaration de la Grande Guerre, 1914.
148. CAOM: Indo/GGI: 26608: A.S. des missionnaires à ajoindre aux contingent indigènes expatriés, 1916; Mgr. Bigolles to M.le Gouverneur-Général de l'Indochine, Hanoi, 13 June 1916.
149. CAOM: Indo/GGI: 26608: M. le Gouverneur-Général de l'Indochine to M. le Ministre des Colonies, No. 53, Hanoi, 19 June 1916; and Telegram to M. le Gouverneur-Général de l'Indochine, Pour Bureau Militaire, No. 935, 21 Aug 1916.

Chapter 4

1. On the feminization of Catholicism, see Claude Langlois, *Le Catholicisme au féminin: Les congrégations françaises à supérieure générale au XIXe siècle* (Paris: Les Editions du Cerf, 1984).
2. See, for example, *Annales* 70 (1898): 207; and 71 (1899): 291.
3. Valentine Cunningham, " 'God and Nature Intended You for a Missionary's Wife': Mary Hill, Jane Eyre and Other Missionary Women in the 1840s," in Fiona Bowie, Deborah Kirkwood, and Shirley Ardener, eds., *Women and Missions: Past and Present* (Oxford: Berg, 1993), 89. Cunningham makes the point in regard to British Protestants, but it is equally true of *le missionnaire* of French Catholic origin.
4. *Annales* 69 (1897): 47.
5. Soeurs de Saint Joseph de Cluny, *Après nos fondatrices. Quatre supérieures générales* (Paris, 1936), 289, 295.

6. Ibid., 303.

7. CAOM: FM/G: 495, 2443: Feilles, Gouverneur des Iles de Saint-Pierre et Miquelon, to M. le Sous-Secrétaire d'Etat des Colonies, Saint-Pierre, 7 Jan 1893.

8. CAOM: FM/G: 495, 2443: M. le Sous-Secrétaire d'Etat des Colonies to M. le Gouverneur de Diégo-Suarez, Paris, n.d. (1891).

9. CAOM: FM/G: 495, 2443: Lamothe, Commandant des Iles Saint-Pierre et Miquelon, to M. le Ministre de la Marine et des Colonies, Saint-Pierre, 16 Jan 1887.

10. Julia Clancy-Smith, "Women, Gender, Empire and School: *Laïcité*'s Pre-history in Tunisia, c. 1830–1905" (unpublished paper), p. 2; cited with the author's permission.

11. Even in the 1890s, the number of girls in religious and secular primary schools in France remained fairly evenly divided. See Ministère de l'Instruction Publique, *Statistique de l'enseignement primaire* (Paris: Imprimerie Nationale, 1878–1909), vols. 3, 5, 7.

12. Françoise Mayeur, "The Secular Model of Girls' Education," in Geneviève Fraisse and Michelle Perrot, eds., *A History of Women in the West, vol. 4, Emerging Feminism from Revolution to World War* (Cambridge, MA: Belknap Press, 1993), 245.

13. Linda Clark, *Schooling the Daughters of Marianne: Textbooks and the Socialization of Girls in Modern French Primary Schools* (Albany: State University of New York Press, 1984), 29.

14. Robert Aldrich, *Greater France: A History of French Overseas Expansion* (New York: Palgrave, 1996), 70.

15. On Wallis and Futuna, see Frédéric Angleviel, *Les Missions à Wallis et Futuna au XIXe siècle* (Bordeaux: CRET, 1994).

16. On France's early presence in the South Pacific, see Robert Aldrich, *The French Presence in the South Pacific, 1842–1940* (Honolulu: University of Hawaii Press, 1990), 15–33; on missionary theocracies, see Claire Laux, *Les Théocraties missionnaires en Polynésie au XIXe siècle: Des cités de Dieu dans les mers du sud?* (Paris: L'Harmattan, 2000).

17. Aldrich, *The French Presence*, 23–24.

18. Bernard Gille and Pierre-Yves Toullelan, *De la conquête à l'éxode: Histoire des océaniens et de leurs migrations dans le Pacifique* (Tahiti: Au vent des Iles, 1999), 65.

19. Aldrich, *The French Presence*, 56–57.

20. J. B. Piolet, S.J., ed., *Les Missions catholiques au XIXe siècle, vol. 4, Océanie et Madagascar* (Paris: Librarie Armand Colin, 1902), 48–49.

21. Aldrich, *The French Presence*, 142.

22. The transition to civilian rule under the republic was by no means immediate, as the number of military personnel in the Pacific continued to outnumber colonists and administrators. Naval commandants and rear admirals continued to represent the French government in their work, making up a second, sometimes competing, official presence. Pierre-Yves Toullelan, *Tahiti Colonial (1860–1914)* (Paris: Publications de la Sorbonne, 1984), 189–91.

23. CAOM: Fonds Ministeriels, Série Géographique, Océanie (FM/SG/O): 106, H24:Report, M. le Commandant en Chef, Division Navale du Pacifique, to M. le Ministre de la Marine et des Colonies, No. 190, 19 July 1880.

24. CAOM: FM/SG/O: 98, H32: Réné Robert to M. le Gouverneur, No. 128, Taiohae, 20 Jan 1884.

25. CAOM: FM/SG/O: 106, H24: M. le Gouverneur to M. le Ministre de la Marine et des Colonies, No. 633, 14 Nov 1884.

26. CAOM: FM/SG/O: 106, H24: M. le Contre-Amiral, Commandant en chef, Division Navale de l'Océan Pacifique, to M. le Ministre de la Marine et des Colonies, No. 47, 9 July 1881.

27. CAOM: FM/SG/O: 98, H32: M. le Gouverneur to M. le Ministre de la Marine et des Colonies, No. 95. Papeete, 12 Feb 1884.

28. CAOM: FM/SG/O: 106, H24: Report, 19 July 1880.

29. Ibid.

30. Ibid.

31. CAOM: FM/SG/O: 106, H24: Report, 9 Juillet 1881.

32. Of the 30,000 francs, 24,960 francs went to the Protestant mission, with 6,640 francs paid out to Catholics. Though additional local subventions (especially from Papeete) were often paid to the missions, these figures from the Service local represented the bulk of the subvention the missions received. CAOM: FM/SG/O: 106, H24: Report: "Etablissements de l'Océanie, budget du Service local, exercise 1883, Dépenses, Cultes."

33. Archives de l'Archidiocèse de Papeete (Tahiti) (AAP): 314: E25: 1/32: Mgr. Verdier to M. le Président de l'Alliance française, Tahiti, 4 Nov 1885.

34. CAOM: FM/SG/O: 98, H32: M. le Gouverneur to M. le Ministre de la Marine et des Colonies, No. 122, Papeete, 12 Feb 1883.

35. CAOM: FM/SG/O: 98, H32: M. le Gouverneur to M. le Ministre, 12 Feb. 1883. The concern over the influence of British and American missionaries may well have been coded language that primarily referred to the large number of Protestants on the islands. The London Missionary Society, for example, seems to have had only three roving white missionaries in the Society Islands in the 1880s, but their reach was considerable: in 1884, they distributed 4,000 Bibles translated into Tahitian. Richard Lovett, *The History of the London Missionary Society 1795–1895*, vol. 1 (London: Henry Frowde, Oxford University Press Warehouse Amen Corner, E.C., 1899), 793–97.

36. Georges Goyau, *La Femme dans les missions* (Paris: Ernest Flammarion, 1933), 91.

37. Ibid., 93.

38. CAOM: FM/SG/O: 106, H24: Report, Chessé to M. le Ministre de la Marine et des Colonies, No. 333, Papeete, 15 June 1881.

39. Archives des Soeurs de Saint Joseph de Cluny, Paris (SSJC): Marquises, 2A: L1, "Hommage ou Cinquantième anniversaire des écoles des Soeurs aux îles Marquises," c. 1914, p. 16.

40. CAOM: FM/SG/O: 106, H24: Report from the Commandant en chef, 19 July 1880.

41. AAP: 314: E25: 1/32: Chessé to Mgr. l'Evèque d'Axieri, Papeete, Affaires Indigènes, No. 8. 19 Mar 1880.

42. CAOM: FM/SG/O: 106, H24: M. le Contre-Amiral to M. le Ministre de la Marine, No. 47, 9 July 1881.

43. CAOM: FM/SG/O: 106, H24: Report from the Commandant en chef, 19 July 1880.

44. CAOM: FM/SG/O: 98, H32: M. le Gouverneur to M. le Ministre de la Marine et des Colonies, No. 304, Papeete, 14 May 1884.

45. AAP: 314: E25: 1/32: Mgr. Verdier to M. le Président de l'Alliance Française, 4 Nov 1885.

46. *Messager de Tahiti (Organe des Intérêts Français dans l'Océanie)*, 12 July 1888, clipping in SSJC: 2A: L5: Enseignement—Laicisation: Folder 8.

47. Archives de l'Oeuvre de la propagation de la foi, Lyon (AOPF): H-49: Vicariat Apostolique des Iles Marquises (Océanie), 1891.

48. Ibid.

49. CPGE: 162/1907: Mgr. Olier to Cardinal Giotti, Nukualofa, 7 Sept 1907.

50. Archives of the Congregatio Pro Gentium Evangelizatione, Rome (CPGE): Rubrica 162/1907: Vol. 414; Doc. 53455: Verdier to Cardinal Giotti, Papeete, 20 Dec 1902. Verdier, here, discusses missionary work in the Societies and Tuamotus, though it was true equally across Polynesia.

51. AOPF: H-49: Vicariat Apostolique des Iles Marquises (Océanie), 1891.

52. See, for example, AOPF: H-48: Vicariat Apostolique de Tahiti (Océanie): Verdier, to MM. les Membres du Comité Central de L'OPF à Paris, Papeete, 4 June 1894; and AOPF: V.A. de Tahiti to MM. les Membres du Comité Central de L'OPF, Papeete, 8 Mar 1895.

53. CAOM: FM/SG/O: 98, H32: Report, "La Situation aux Marquises" par l'Inspecteur Salles, No. 24, Papeete, 4 Apr 1903, p. 15.

54. SSJC: 2A: L1: "Hommage ou Cinquantième anniversaire des écoles des Soeurs aux îles Marquises" (no author, c. 1914), pp. 10, 16.

55. Atuona was also the Catholic center of the Marquesas: the apostolic vicar was based there, not, like the administrative resident in Taiohae, on Nuku Hiva. The letters cited in the following section come from SSJC: 2A: L1: Correspondence: Marquises, Atuona, 1885–1913 (C:M/A). The archive has letters written about every two months from the 1880s to 1914. The letters were usually written by the *soeur* who was in charge of the Atuona school at that time (for much of this period it was Soeur Aldegonde). While the letters are rich in detail about the daily life of the school, personal information about the authors is rarely included.

56. SSJC: 2A: L: C:M/A: Sr. Saint Prix Moindrot to "Très-Révérende Bien-Chère Mère Générale," Taiohae, 8 Dec 1885. All the following letters are addressed to the *mère générale* of the Soeurs de Saint Joseph de Cluny in Paris.

57. SSJC: C:M/A: Letter from Sr. Marie Albertine, Atuona, 1 Nov 1886.

58. SSJC: C:M/A: Letter from Sr. Saint Prix Moindrot, Taiohae, 8 Dec 1885.

59. SSJC: C:M/A: Letter from Sr. Aldegonde, Ile Dominique, 17 Nov 1886.

60. Sarah A. Curtis, *Educating the Faithful: Religion, Schooling, and Society in Nineteenth-Century France* (Dekalb: Northern Illinois University Press, 2000), 83.

61. Ibid., 84–88.

62. Isabelle Bricard, *Saintes ou pouliches: L'éducation des jeunes filles au XIXe siècle* (Paris: Albin Michel, 1985), 157.

63. Curtis, *Educating the Faithful*, 95.

64. SSJC: C:M/A: Letter from Sr. Aldegonde, Ile Dominique, 17 Nov 1886.

65. SSJC: C:M/A: Letter from Sr. Aldegonde, Atuona, 15 Dec 1898.

66. SSJC: C:M/A: Letter from Sr. Marie Albertine, Atuona, 1 Nov 1886. Marie Albertine's written French was notably ungrammatical, suggesting minimal education.

67. In the nineteenth century, *canaque* was used as a generic term for Pacific Islanders (it later became more specifically associated with Melanesians). It was spelled in a variety of ways, including *kanaque, kanak,* and so on. SSJC: C:M/A: Letter from Sr. Aldegonde, Atuona, 18 Sept 1901.

68. Ibid.

69. AAP: 314: E25—1/32: "Réglement des Ecoles," 1883, signed by Mgr. Tepano Jaussen.

70. Robert Louis Stevenson, *In the South Seas* (New York: Penguin, 1998), 44.

71. A. C. Eugène Caillot, *Histoire de la Polynésie orientale* (Paris: Ernest Laroux, 1910), 380–81.

72. SSJC: C:M/A: Letter from Sr. Aldegonde, Ile Dominique, 17 Nov 1886.

73. The typical diet consisted almost exclusively of *popoï*. SSJC: C:M/A: Letter from Sr. Prix Moindrot, Atuona, 1 Apr 1887.

74. Stevenson, *In the South Seas*, 45.

75. SSJC: C:M/A: Letters from Sr. Aldegonde, Atuona, 12 Jan 1900, and 30 June 1899.

76. SSJC: C:M/A: Letter from Sr. Saint Prix Moindrot, Atuona, 6 Sept 1889.

77. Aldegonde reproduced the vernacular of her pupils. SSJC: C:M/A: Letter from Sr. Aldegonde, Ile Dominique, 17 Nov 1886.

78. SSJC: C:M/A: Letter from Sr. Aldegonde, Atuona, 30 July 1898.

79. SSJC: C:M/A: Letter from Sr. Saint Prix Moindrot, Atuona, 4 Sept 1887.

80. SSJC: C:M/A: Letter from Sr. Saint Prix Moindrot, Atuona, 30 Aug 1890; and Letter from Sr. Aldegonde, Atuona, 13 Dec 1897.

81. Toullelan, *Tahiti Colonial*, 293.

82. Ibid., 294.

83. SSJC: C:M/A: Letter from Sr. Aldegonde, Atuona, 25 June 1901.

84. SSJC: C:M/A: Letter from Sr. Aldegonde, Atuona, 24 Feb 1898.

85. SSJC: C:M/A: Letter from Sr. Saint Prix Moindrot, Atuona, 30 Aug 1890.

86. AOPF: H-48: Vic Apostolique, Iles Marquises, 1857–1921: Etat des Recettes et Dépenses presumes pour l'année 1894, Vicaire Apostolique des Iles Marquises, Doc. H01802.

87. CAOM: FM/SG/O: 98, H32: Letter from Mgr. Dordillon à M. le Gouverneur, Iles Marquises, Taiohae, 7 Mar 1884.

88. AAP: 314: E25—1/32: Letter from Verdier à M. le Président de l'Alliance Française, 4 Nov 1885.

89. Toullelan, *Tahiti Colonial*, 198.

90. SSJC: C:M/A: Letter from Sr. Aldegonde, Atuona, 13 Dec 1897.

91. SSJC: C:M/A: Letter from Sr. Aldegonde, Atuona, 6 May 1900.

92. SSJC: C:M/A: Letter from Sr. Aldegonde, Atuona, 8 Nov 1900.

93. SSJC: C:M/A: Letter from Sr. Aldegonde, Atuona, 29 Nov 1886.

94. SSJC: Marquises-Tahiti; 2A: L1: Letter from Mgr. Martin to Révérende Mère (of the Soeurs de Saint Joseph de Cluny), Atuona, 11 Jan 1897.

95. SSJC: C:M/A: Letter from Sr. Aldegonde, Atuona, 24 Feb 1898.

96. SSJC: C:M/A: Letter from Sr. Aldegonde, Atuona, 29 Aug 1898.

97. SSJC: C:M/A: Letter from Sr. Aldegonde, Atuona, 30 July 1898.

98. SSJC: C:M/A: Letter from Sr. Aldegonde, Atuona, 28 July 1899.
99. Stephen F. Eisenman, *Gauguin's Skirt* (London: Thames and Hudson, 1997), 156.
100. AOPF: H-49: Doc. 25: Letter from Mgr. Martin to MM. les Membres des Conseils Centraux de l'Oeuvre de la Propagation de la Foi, Marquises, Océanie Orientale, 8 Feb 1900.
101. Piolet, *Les Missions catholiques*, 49–50.
102. SSJC: C:M/A: Letter from Sr. Aldegonde, Atuona, 8 Apr 1899.
103. CAOM: FM/SG/O: 98, H32: Report, Service de l'Instruction publique, par M. Salles, Inspecteur de 1ère classe des Colonies, concernant la verification du service de M. Petithory, Instituteur de l'Ecole primarie supérieure à Papeete, à l'époque du 26 février 1903 et explications fournies par cet agent sur les resultants de sa verification, Mission, 1902–3.
104. Ibid.
105. Langlois, "Catholics and Seculars," in Pierre Nora, ed., *Realms of Memory, vol. 1, Conflicts and Divisions* trans Arthur Goldhammer (New York: Colombia University Press, 1992)," 135.
106. CAOM: FM/SG/O: 98, H32: Report, Service de l'Instruction publique, par M. Salles.
107. Ibid.
108. Legislation passed by the administration dovetails with the "alcoholism, venereal disease, tuberculosis" triptych hotly debated in fin de siècle France. See David S. Barnes, *The Making of a Social Disease: Tuberculosis in Nineteenth-Century France* (Berkeley: University of California Press, 1995), 138–173.

Chapter 5

1. Herman Melville, *Typee: A Peep at Polynesian Life* (New York: Penguin Books, 1996), 12, 17.
2. Ibid., 7, 17. Melville's observations fit into a broader discourse on the unfortunate consequences of Europe's contact with the world. See Patrick Brantlinger, *Dark Vanishings: Discourse on the Extinction of Primitive Races, 1800–1930* (Ithaca, NY: Cornell University Press, 2003), esp. 150–54.
3. Robert Louis Stevenson, *In the South Seas* (New York: Penguin Books, 1998), 33–34.
4. Claire Laux, *Les Théocraties missionnaires en Polynésie au XIXe siècle: Des cités de Dieu dans les Mers du Sud?* (Paris: L'Harmattan, 2000), 291.
5. Bernard Gille and Pierre-Yves Toullelan, *De la conquête à l'éxode: Histoire des Océaniens et de leurs migrations dans le Pacifique* (Tahiti: Au vent des Iles, 1999), 118.
6. Jacques Bund, "Les Iles Marquises," in Jean-Baptiste Piolet, ed., *Les Missions catholiques au XIXe siècle*, vol. 4, *Océanie et Madagascar* (Paris: Librairie Armand Colin, 1902), 50.
7. Henri Jouan, "La Dépopulation aux Iles Marquises" (1891), 197, pamphlet collection, Bancroft Library, University of California, Berkeley.
8. This is based on missionary estimates in the *Annales des Sacrés-Coeurs* (2 Jan 1903): 46.

9. Jean-Louis Rallu, *Les Populations océaniennes aux XIXe et XXe siècles* (Paris: Presses Universitaires de France, 1990), 211.

10. Léon Brunet, *La Race polynésienne; son origine, sa disparition* (Paris: A Parent, 1876), 5.

11. C. de Varigny, *L'Océan pacifique* (Paris: Librairie Hachette et Cie., 1888), 72–73.

12. Robert Hertz, quoted in Joshua Cole, *The Power of Large Numbers: Population, Politics, and Gender in Nineteenth-Century France* (Ithaca, NY: Cornell University Press, 2000), 181.

13. According to Robert Nye, growth between 1872 and 1911 was one-third what it had been between 1821 and 1846. And a number of years leading up to the First World War witnessed negative growth: 1890, 1892, 1895, 1900, 1907, 1911. Nye, *Crime, Madness, and Politics in Modern France* (Princeton, NJ: Princeton University Press, 1984), 134.

14. Dr. Maurice Lutelle coined the expression "terrifying trio"; quoted in David S. Barnes, *The Making of a Social Disease: Tuberculosis in Nineteenth-Century France* (Berkeley: University of California Press, 1995), 138.

15. On the political makeup of temperance societies in the wake of the Commune, see Susanna Barrows, "After the Commune: Alcoholism, Temperance, and Literature in the Early Third Republic," in John Merriman, ed., *Consciousness and Class Experience in Nineteenth-Century Europe* (New York and London: Holmes and Meier, 1979), 210–11.

16. Nye, *Crime, Madness*, 143; on the political divisions over women and reproduction, see Karen Offen, "Depopulation, Nationalism, and Feminism in Fin-de-Siècle France," *American Historical Review* 89, no. 3 (June 1984): 648–76.

17. On the importance of gender and motherhood in the depopulation debate in France, see Cole, *The Power of Large Numbers*.

18. Brunet offers an excellent overview of the accepted wisdom on depopulation in the 1870s. He, however, disagrees with many of these arguments. Brunet, *La Race polynésienne*.

19. CAOM: FM/SG/O: 106, H24: Report, M. le Commandant en Chef, Division Navale du Pacifique, to M. le Ministre de la Marine et des Colonies, No. 190, 19 July 1880.

20. Jouan, "La Dépopulation aux Iles Marquises," 208.

21. CAOM: FM/SG/O: 106, H24: Report, Commandant en chef, 19 July 1880.

22. Jouan, "La Dépopulation aux Iles Marquises," 200–201.

23. Brunet, *La Race polynésienne*, 32.

24. Jouan, "La Dépopulation aux Iles Marquises," 204.

25. Brunet, *La Race polynésienne*, 5.

26. CAOM: FM/SG/O: 106, H24: Report, Commandant en chef, 19 July 1880.

27. Ibid.

28. Bund, "Les Iles Marquises," 52.

29. Eugen Weber, *Peasants into Frenchmen: The Modernization of Rural France, 1870–1914* (Stanford, CA: Stanford University Press, 1976), 309.

30. Ibid., 330.

31. On the philosophical origins of republican education, see Jacques Billard, *De l'école à la République: Guizot et Victor Cousin* (Paris: Presses Universitaires de France, 1998).

32. For parallels in curriculum in Algeria, see Fanny Colonna, "Educating Conformity in French Colonial Algeria," in Ann Stoler and Frederick Cooper, eds., *Tensions of Empire: Colonial Cultures in a Bourgeois World* (Berkeley: University of California Press, 1997), 346–72.

33. Ralph Gibson, "Why Republicans and Catholics Couldn't Stand Each Other in the Nineteenth Century," in Frank Tallett and Nicholas Atkin, eds., *Religion, Society and Politics in France Since 1789* (London: Hambledon Press, 1991), 108.

34. Réné Rémond, *L'Anticléricalisme en France de 1815 à nos jours*, nouvelle édition (Paris: Fayard, 1999), 31.

35. Pierre Chevalier, *La Séparation de l'église et l'école* (Paris: Fayard, 1981).

36. Laux, *Les Théocraties missionnaires*.

37. *Annales des Sacrés-Coeurs* (de Jésus et de Marie et de l'Adoration perpétuelle du très Saint Sacrement, dit *Picpus*), 2e année (1895): 2.

38. Ibid.

39. "Chronique Religieuse," *Annales des Sacrés-Coeurs* (1896): 353.

40. *Annales des Sacrés-Coeurs* (1895): 2–3.

41. *Annales des Sacrés-Coeurs* (1899): 65.

42. "Chronique Religieuse," *Annales des Sacrés-Coeurs* (1896): 352.

43. "Chronique Religieuse," *Annales des Sacrés-Coeurs* (1897): 454.

44. See, for example, "La Nouvelle Année," in *Annales des Sacrés-Coeurs*, 9e année (1902): 3–5; and "Nos Missionnaires," *Annales des Sacrés-Coeurs*, 10e année (1903): 45–49.

45. See "Nos Missionnaires," in *La Croix*, 27 Jan 1903.

46. Laux, *Les Théocraties missionnaires*, 290–91.

47. Archives des Pères Maristes, Rome (hereafter APM): Wallis et Futuna, Mgr. Lamaze, OC 418.1: Letter to Cardinal Simeoni, Préfet de la S. Congregation de la Propagande, Wallis, 26 Feb 1886.

48. CAOM: FM/SG/O: 106, H24: Report extract, Chessé to M. le Ministre de la Marine, No. 333, Papeete, 15 June 1881.

49. Transcripts of the speeches are in *Journal Officiel des Établissements Français de l'Océanie* (17 Sept 1891): 375; a clipping is in AAP: 84–85, B22: 1/45: Mgr. Jaussen.

50. *Journal Officiel des EFO*, 375.

51. SSJC: C:M/A: Letter from Sr. Aldegonde, Atuona, 24 Feb 1898.

52. SSJC: C:M/A: Letter from Sr. Aldegonde, Atuona, 12 Jan 1900.

53. SSJC: C:M/A: Letter from Sr. Aldegonde, Atuona, 1 June 1901.

54. AOPF: H-49: Vicariat Apostolique des Iles Marquises (Océanie), 1892.

55. Loti, quoted in Tzvetan Todorov, *On Human Diversity: Nationalism, Racism, and Exoticism in French Thought*, trans. Catherine Porter (Cambridge, MA: Harvard University Press, 1993), 314.

56. Paul Gauguin, *Noa Noa*, trans. O. F. Theis (New York: Nicholas Brown, 1920), 7, 9, 18.

57. The papers were *Le Sourire* and the Catholic-sponsored opposition newspaper, *Les Guêpes*. Stephen F. Eisenman, *Gauguin's Skirt* (London: Thames and Hudson, 1997), 154.

58. *Les Guêpes*, no. 12, 12 Jan 1900, reprinted in Daniel Guérin, ed., *The Writings of a Savage, Paul Gauguin*, trans. Eleanor Levieux (New York: Viking Press, 1974), 202. On *Les Guêpes*, see Bengt Danielsson and P. O'Reilly, eds., *Gauguin: Journaliste à Tahiti et ses articles des "Guêpes"* (Paris: Société des Océanistes, 1966).

59. CAOM: FM/SG/O: 98, H32: Report: "La Situation aux Marquises," p. 8.

60. Paul Gauguin, *Intimate Journals*, trans. Van Wyck Brooks (Bloomington: Indiana University Press, 1958), 207.

61. Ibid., 76–78.

62. "To the Colonial Passing through the Marquesas," in ibid., 166–70.

63. Gauguin, *Intimate Journals*, 97.

64. Ibid., 26–27, 187.

65. Ibid., 26.

66. Eisenman, *Gauguin's Skirt*, 155, 158–59.

67. Gauguin, *Intimate Journals*, 173.

68. Toullelan, *Tahiti Colonial*, 234, 264.

69. Eglise Evangélique de Polynésie Française (Papeete) (EEPF): SMEP Courrier, 1880–1906: Le Directeur de la SMEP to Viénot, Paris, 13 Jan 1898.

70. EEPF: Procès verbaux, Conférence des missionnaires des Iles de la Société, Session annuelle du 20 au 24 février 1903, pp. 138–39.

71. For example, the Catholic Church in Papeete kept records of who was a member of the local Freemason lodge. See AAPF: 540, K7: 1/13: Franc-maçonnerie.

72. AOPF: H-48: Océanie, Tahiti, Correspondence, 1842–1922: Alazard to M. le Secrétaire de la Propagation de la Foi, Paris, 9 Aug 1894.

73. AAPF: 63, B-13-8: 1/17: Mataiea: M. le Gouverneur p.i. des EFO to Verdier, No. 362, Papeete, 30 May 1899.

74. AAPF: 63, B-13-8: 1/17: "Arguments pour refuter l'opposition des protestants aux processions catholiques" (n.d.); and "Notes sur la procession de la Fête Dieu."

75. CAOM: FM/SG/O: 106, H24: Copy, of a 31 Jan 1900 note by Mgr. Lorenzelli, enclosed in M. le Ministre des Affaires Étrangeres to Decrais, Ministre des Colonies, Paris, 1 Mar 1900.

76. CAOM: FM/SG/O: 106, H24: Gallet, Gouverneur des EFO, to M. le Ministre des Colonies, No. 207, Papeete, 11 Aug 1900.

77. SSJC: Tahiti, correspondence: Sr. Mélanie to "Très Rde chère Mère," Papeete, 19 Dec 1900.

78. Archives of the Congregatio Pro Gentium Evangelizatione, Rome (CPGE): Rubrica 162/1901, vol. 216: Doc. 42574. pp. 729–30: Verdier to Cardinal Ledochowski, Papeete, 19 Dec 1900.

79. CPGE: Rubrica 162/1903, Vol. 265: Doc. 53451, pp. 429–30: Verdier to Cardinal Giotti, Papeete, l8 Dec 1902.

80. Petit's speech was reproduced in *Annales des Sacrés-Coeurs*, 11e année (1904): 209–11.

81. CAOM: FM/SG/O: 98, H32: "La Situation aux Marquises."

82. Ibid.

83. Ibid.

84. Archives territoriales de la Polynésie française, Papeete, Tahiti (hereafter ATPF): Série 17W: ETAT; 137: Correspondence ordinaire, 1904: Cor to M. le Ministre des Colonies, No. 44, Papeete, 27 Feb 1904.

85. See the letters in ATPF: 17W; 137.

86. SSJC: C: M/A: Letter from Sr. Aldegonde, Atuona, 29 Sept 1904.

87. Aldrich, *The French Presence*, 56.

88. AOPF: H-49: Iles Marquises (1838–1923): Mgr. Martin to MM. les Membres des Conseils centreaux de l'Oeuvre de la Propagation de la Foi, Marquises, 30 Sept 1904.

89. CPGE: 162/1905; vol. 334: Doc. 64540, pp. 216–17: Verdier to Cardinal Giotti, Papeete, 30 Dec 1904.

90. ATPF: 17W; 137: M. le Gouverneur to M. le Ministre des Colonies, No. 135, 9 May 1904.

91. ATPF: 17W; 137: M. le Gouverneur to M. le Ministre des Colonies, No. 137, 9 May 1904.

92. *Journal Officiel*, Chambre des Députés, Séance, 3 Feb 1905, 161.

93. Ibid.

94. Ibid., 162.

95. Ibid., 162.

96. AOPF: H-49: Iles Marquises (1838–1923): Bousquet to M. le Président du Conseil Central de l'Oeuvre de la Propagation de la Foi à Paris, Paris, 14 Feb 1905.

97. CPGE: 162/1905: Vol. 334: Doc. 65610, pp. 236–44: *Réponse aux calomnies de M. Dejeante par le RP Ildefonse Alazard, SS. CC. de Picpus: Dépopulation, lèpre, phtisie, ecoles-internats, propriétés, cultures, les trois vicaires apostoliques (1838–1905)* (Paris: Chadenat, 1905), 3.

98. CPGE: 162/1907: Vol. 414: pp. 416–17: Verdier to Giotti, Papeete, 21 Dec 1906.

99. In 1911, for example, with a Protestant governor in power, the colonial regime again tried to take the property but was overruled by the Tribunal Supérieur de Tahiti. ATPF: 17W: 139: Correspondence ordinaire, 1906: Jullien to M. le Ministre des Colonies, No. 66, 19 Feb 1906; and CPGE: 160/1911: Vol. 506: Doc. 108, pp. 514–15: Hermel to Giotti, Papeete, 8 Dec 1910; and Doc. 1306, pp. 554–55: Martin to Giotti. Iles Marquises, 20 Apr 1911.

100. SSJC: Letters from Sr. Aldegonde to Mère Générale, Atuona, 29 Nov 1904; 20 May 1905; 4 Sept 1905; 25 Sept 1906;

101. SSJC: 2A; L1: "Hommage," 23–24.

102. Rallu, *Les Populations océaniennes*, 212.

103. Paul Vernier, "La Situation de la Mission des Marquises. Rapport à la demande du Comité des Missions, Août 1914," *Journal des Missions Évangéliques* (March, 1915): 10, 15.

Chapter 6

1. Archives de la Société des missions évangéliques de Paris (SMEP): 51.245, B.17: Mission de Madagascar, Instructions données le 19 mars 1897 aux mission-naires devant partir pour Madagascar.
2. The phrase is from David Levering Lewis, *The Race to Fashoda: European Colo-nialism and African Resistance in the Scramble for Africa* (New York: Weidenfeld and Nicolson, 1987), 6.
3. Queen Victoria, quoted in G. N. Sanderson, *England, Europe, and the Upper Nile, 1882–1899* (Edinburgh: Edinburgh University Press, 1965), 1; see also Christo-pher Andrew, *Théophile Declassé and the Making of the Entente Cordiale* (London: Macmillan, 1968); the long-held assumption that France and Britain were near the brink of war over Fashoda has recently been challenged. See J. F. V. Keiger, "Omdurman, Fashoda, and Franco-British Relations," in Edward M. Spiers, ed., *Sudan: The Reconquest Reappraised* (London: Frank Cass, 1998), 163–76; and Pas-cal Venier, "French Foreign Policy and the Boer War," in Keith Wilson, ed., *The International Impact of the Boer War* (London: Palgrave, 2001), 65–78.
4. SMEP: 51.245, B.17: Instructions, p. 1; on the replacement of British missionaries with French Protestants, see André Roux, "Comment la Société des missions évangéliques de Paris a été amenée dans le contexte de la colonisation à prendre la relève de missions protestantes d'autres pays," in Guy Duboscq and André La-treille, eds., *Les Réveils missionnaires en France* (Paris: Beauchesne, 1984), 297–320.
5. SMEP: 51.245, B.17: Instructions, p. 6.
6. Throughout this chapter "pacification" should always be read as if it is enclosed in quotation marks.
7. CAOM: Madagascar, Fonds Ministeriels (M/FM), carton 355 / dossier 959: folder "Institute des Frères des Écoles Chrétiennes": Gallieni to M. le Ministre des Colonies, c. 201, Tananarive, 24 Feb 1897.
8. SMEP: 51.245, B.17: Instructions, pp. 6–7.
9. Philip Nord, *The Republican Moment: Struggles for Democracy in Nineteenth-Century France* (Cambridge, MA: Harvard University Press, 1995), 109.
10. Jennifer Cole points out that these ethnic groups were themselves shaped by French colonial ideas of race, in particular the *politique des races* that identified and "essentialized" ethnic groups to ease indirect rule. Cole, *Forget Colonialism: Sacrifice and the Art of Memory in Madagascar* (Berkeley: University of California Press, 2001), 36.
11. Phares M. Mutibwa, *The Malagasy and the Europeans: Madagascar's Foreign Rela-tions, 1861–1895* (London: Longman, 1974), 21–23.
12. Mervyn Brown, *Madagascar Rediscovered: A History from Early Times to Indepen-dence* (Hamden, CT: Archon Books, 1979), 152–59.
13. Bruno Hubsch, ed., *Madagascar et le Christianisme* (Paris: Éditions Ambozontany, Analamahitsy, Antananarivo, 1993), 199.
14. Mutibwa, *The Malagasy and the Europeans*, 25.
15. Stephen Ellis, *The Rising of the Red Shawls: A Revolt in Madagascar* (Cambridge: Cambridge University Press, 1985), 14.
16. Ibid., 15–16.

17. Ibid., 16.

18. Françoise Raison-Jourde, "Mission L.M.S. et Mission Jésuite face aux communautés villageoises Merina. Fondation et fonctionnement des paroisses entre 1869 et 1876," *Africa: Journal of the International African Institute* 53, no. 3 (1983): 57.

19. Ellis, *The Rising of the Red Shawls*, 17–18.

20. Raison-Jourde, "Mission L.M.S. et Mission Jésuite," 66.

21. Archives Jésuites, Vanves (AJ): Fonds Jean-Baptiste Cazet, SJ (FC); Folder 412: Rapport, 1879–1880, Tananarive, 8 Aug 1897.

22. In a letter to the head of the SMEP, the foreign secretary of the LMS noted that even the English interpretation of the treaty differed from that discussed in Paris. SMEP: Madagascar, 1843, 1883–1895, letter from Rev. Wardlaw Thompson to Frank Puaux, M-EP, London, n.d., 1886.

23. See Mutibwa, *The Malagasy and the Europeans*, 303–5.

24. SMEP: Madagascar, 1843, 1883–1895, documents microfichés et non-microfichés: Boegner to M. le Rédacteur, Paris, Apr. 1886; Boegner describes how common, yet unfair, the accusation was in the wake of the first war.

25. A. Adu Boahen, ed., *Africa under Foreign Domination, 1880–1935: General History of Africa (UNESCO)*, abridged edition, vol. 7 (London: James Curry, 1990), 110.

26. Guy Jacob, "Une expédition coloniale meurtière: La campagne de Madagascar," in Marc Michel and Yvan Paillard, eds., *Australes: Études historiques aixoises sur l'Afrique australe et l'océan Indien occidental* (Paris: L'Harmattan, 1996), 155–74.

27. Jean-Jacques Becker states that for every 168 Frenchmen mobilized from 1914 to 1918, 34 died in combat or accidents, or from disease (roughly 20 percent). *The Great War and the French People*, trans. Arnold Pomerans (Leamington Spa: Berg, 1985), 6.

28. Difficulties that the French experienced were largely the result of poor planning. The numbers of deaths suffered on the Malagasy side are impossible to determine, even with Malagasy sources. See Yvan-G. Paillard, "The French Expedition to Madagascar in 1895: Program and Results," in J. A. de Moor and H. L. Wessling, eds., *Imperialism and War: Essays on Colonial Wars in Asia and Africa* (Leiden: Brill, 1989), 168–88.

29. Philip D. Curtin, *Disease and Empire: The Health of European Troops in the Conquest of Africa* (Cambridge: Cambridge University Press, 1998), 177.

30. Raphael Blanchard, "Climat, hygiène, et maladies," in Blanchard et al., eds., *Madagascar au début du XXe siècle* (Paris: Société d'Éditions Scientifiques et Litteraires, 1902), 407–8.

31. See Ellis, *The Rising of the Red Shawls*. Ellis offers a detailed history of the *menalamba*.

32. Ibid., 1–3.

33. For an exhaustive analysis of the role of Christianity in nineteenth-century Malagasy culture and society, see Françoise Raison-Jourde, *Bible et pouvoir à Madagascar aux XIXe siècle: Invention d'une identité chrétienne et construction de l'état* (Paris: Éditions Karthala, 1991).

34. AJ: FC, 412: Cazet to Mon Révérend Père Provincial, Tamatave, 4 Apr 1895.

35. AJ: FC, 412: Cazet to Père Camboué, Tananarive, 25 May 1896.

36. AJ: FC, 412: Cazet to Mon Révérend Père Provincial, Tananarive, 11 June 1896. "Tananarive" is the French name for Antananarivo.

37. For a full account see AJ: 651–60: Documents concernant Jacques Berthieu, 1838, 1873, 1896.

38. CAOM: M/FM, 355/959: article clipping from *Événement* (n.d.).

39. "Necrologie. Mort du P. Berthieu," *Lettres d'Uclès*, IIe série, 4, no. 1 (1897): 94.

40. Ellis, *The Rising of the Red Shawl*, 3.

41. AJ: FC, 412, Cazet to Camboué, Tananarive, 11 Dec 1896.

42. Adrien Boudou, S.J., *Le Père Jacques Berthieu (1836–1896)* (Paris: Gabriel Beauchesne et ses Fils, 1935), 435.

43. CAOM: Madagascar, Gouverneur Gallieni (M/GG), 6(2) D5: M. l'Administrateur-Maire de Nossi-Bé to M. l'Administrateur en chef des Provinces Antankara et Sakalava, no. 628, Hell-Ville, 28 Dec 1898.

44. AJ: FC, 412, Cazet to Camboué, Tananarive, 23 Nov 1896.

45. CAOM: M/GG 4 D 1: Rapport sur la situation politique et administrative des Provinces civiles en 1897, pp. 6–7.

46. CAOM: M/FM, 215/445: Rapport Politique, no. 302, Tananarive, 27 Oct 1896.

47. CAOM: M/FM, 215/445: Rapport Politique, 27 Oct 1896.

48. Ellis, *The Rising of the Red Shawls*, 106.

49. CAOM: M/FM, 348/933: Gallieni to M. le Ministre des Colonies, no. 189C, Tananarive, 26 Feb 1897, attached report from the procurer general, n.d.

50. CAOM: M/FM, 348/932: Gallieni to M. le Ministre des Colonies, no. 423, Tananarive, 12 Mar 1897.

51. CAOM: M/FM, 348/932: P. Raniahatra to Lt-Colonel Borbal Combret, Tsiafahy, 23 Mar 1897.

52. CAOM: M/FM, 348/932: Gallieni to M. le Ministre des Colonies, Tananarive, 28 Mar 1897.

53. London Missionary Society Archives (LMS): Madagascar: Southern Outgoing Letters Box 10, 1897–1900: Cousins to Edmonds, London, 8 Apr 1897.

54. CAOM: M/FM, 348/932: Bertrand to Gallieni, no. 384, Fianarantsoa, 1 May 1897.

55. CAOM: Mad FM, 348/932: Gallieni to M. le Ministre des Colonies, Tananarive, 28 Mar 1897.

56. CAOM: Mad FM, 348/932: Borbal Combret to Gallieni, Tsiafahy, 23 Mar 1897.

57. CWM/LMS: Mad Southern Outgoing Letters 10: Cousins to Edmonds, London, 8 Apr 1897.

58. CAOM: M/FM, 348/932: M. le Ministre des Affaires Étrangères to Lebon, Paris, 24 Mar 1897.

59. CAOM: M/FM, 348/932: M. le Ministre des Affaires Étrangères to Lebon, Paris, 18 Mar 1897.

60. See Hubert Deschamps and Paul Chauvet, eds., *Gallieni pacificateur: Écrits coloniaux de Gallieni* (Paris: Presses Universitaires de France, 1949), 198.

61. Gérard de Puymège, "The Good Soldier Chauvin," in Pierre Nora, ed., *Realms of Memory: The Construction of the French Past, vol. 2, Traditions*, trans. Arthur Goldhammer (New York: Columbia University Press, 1997), 351.

62. AJ: Fma 71: "Extrait d'une lettre aumônier du Corps expéditionnaire de Madagascar," 17 Apr [1896].

63. AJ: Fma 71: "Les Officiers Français et les écoles catholiques" d'après une relation du P. Castets du début de 1897.

64. John McManners, *Church and State in France, 1870–1914* (London: SPCK, 1972), 51.

65. AJ: 252, Catholicisme et Protestantisme, 1882, 1896, 1899, 1904: Cazet circular, Tananarive, 19 Feb 1897.

66. AJ: FC, 412: Copy, Gallieni to Cazet, Tananarive, 26 Feb 1897.

67. AJ: FC, 412: Cazet to Mon Révérend Père Provincial, Tananarive, 8 Nov 1896.

68. CAOM: Mad FM, 355/959: M. le Ministre des Colonies to M. le Résident-Général, Paris, 20 Oct 1896.

69. CAOM: M/FM, 355/959: Camboué to M. le Ministre des Colonies, Direction des Affaires d'Afrique, Bureau de Madagascar, Paris, 15 June 1897.

70. CAOM: M/FM, 355/959: Camboué card and flyer.

71. CAOM: M/FM, 355/959: "Paiement de la subvention accordée à la Mission catholique de Madagascar," signed André Lebon.

72. CAOM: M/FM, 355/959: Telegram, M. le Ministre des Colonies to M. le Résident Général à Tananarive, 15 Feb 1897.

73. CAOM: M/FM, 355/959: Laroche to M. le Ministre des Colonies, c. 352, Tananarive, 25 June 1896.

74. CAOM: M/FM, 355/959: Gallieni to M. le Ministre des Colonies, c. 201, Tananarive, 24 Feb 1897.

75. CAOM: M/FM, 355/959: Files "Mission Catholique, Passage gratuite," 1897, 1898, 1899, 1900.

76. Adrien Boudou, *Les Jésuites à Madagascar au XIXe siècle* (Paris: Beauchesne, 1940), 463–67.

77. SMEP: Mad, 1883–1895: 13e Circulaire aux Comités auxiliaries, Paris, Dec 1892.

78. SMEP: Mad, 1883–1895: Thompson to Boegneur, London, 7 July 1892.

79. SMEP: Mad, 1883–1895: Dahle to SMEP (Boegneur), 1 Aug 1893.

80. *Journal Officiel* (17 May 1893): 1425–30; a copy is in SMEP: Mad, 1843, 1883–1895.

81. Ibid., 1426.

82. Ibid.

83. Ibid.

84. SMEP: Mad, 1883–1895: Boegneur, Thombres, Couve, and Vernes to "Monsieur le Député," Paris, 24 May 1893.

85. Ibid.

86. SMEP: Mad, 1883–1895: Entretien avec M. Alfred Grandidier, Paris, 3 June 1893.

87. SMEP: Mad, 1883–1895: Entretien avec M. Le Myre de Vilers, Paris, 5 June 1893, emphasis in the original.

88. SMEP: Mad, 1883–1895: Entretien avec M. Le Myre de Vilers, 5 June 1893.

89. SMEP: Mad, 1883–1895: "Notes rédigées pour M. Jules Siegfried, et transmises à M. le Président du Conseil, Ministère des Affaires Etrangères," Paris, 19 Jan 1894.

90. SMEP: Mad, 1883–1895: Agent-général de la Société Centrale Protestante d'É-vangélisation to MM. les Membres du Comité de la SMEP, 23 Dec 1895.

91. "La Question religieuse à Madagascar," *Le Temps* (7 Nov 1895), clipping in SMEP: Mad, 1883–1895.

92. "Ibid.

93. Boudou, *Les Jésuites à Madagascar*, 471–72; the report was later published as Henri Lauga and Frédéric-Hermann Kruger, *La Liberté religieuse à Madagascar* (Paris: Maison des Missions Évangèliques, 1897).

94. AJ: FC, 412, letter from Cazet to Père Camboué, Tananarive, 25 Mar 1896.

95. SMEP: Benjamin Escande (1896) letter to M. Boegner, Tananarive, 21 Oct 1896.

96. Ibid.

97. Cazet's phrase was *"bandes des pillards."* AJ: FC, 412: Cazet to Mon Révérend Père Provincial, Tananarive, 16 Jan 1896.

98. AJ: FC, 412: Cazet to Mon Révérend Père Provincial, Paris, 13 June 1895.

99. AJ: FC, 412: Cazet to Mon Révérend et bien cher père, Tananarive, 12 Apr 1896.

100. AJ: FC, 412: Cazet to Camboué, Tananarive, 30 Aug 1896.

101. AJ: 252: Printed letter to "Mes Révérends Pères et mes bien chers frères," by Père R. de Scorraille, S.J., Tamatave, 3 July 1898.

102. AJ: FC, 412: Cazet to Mademoiselle, La Paix de N.S., Tananarive, 25 Jan 1897.

103. AJ: FC, 412: Cazet to Mon Révérend Père Provincial, Tananarive, 12 Dec 1896.

104. AJ: FC, 412: Cazet to Mon Révérend Père Provincial, Tananarive, 12 Feb 1897.

105. AJ: FC, 412: Cazet to Mon Révérend Père Provincial, Tananarive, 12 Dec 1896.

106. SMEP: Escande (1896): Escande to Lauga, Tananarive, 10 Dec 1896.

107. SMEP: 9.495, 51.192, B.46 (1897): no author, "Mémoire relatif aux troubles religieux à Madagascar," 1896–1897.

108. Ibid., p. 5.

109. Ibid., p. 5–6.

110. Ibid., pp. 9, 24.

111. SMEP: Escande (1896): Escande to Lauga, Tananarive, 10 Dec 1896.

112. *Journal des Missions Évangéliques* (1897): 159–162, (hereafter *JME*).

113. Ibid., 160–62.

114. AJ: 252: collection of clippings, with notes; this quotation taken from the 5 Feb 1897 edition.

115. No author, *La Voix de la Montagne*, 12e année, no. 256 (19 Mar 1897): 1–2.

116. "Conférence sur Madagascar à Castres," *La Voix de la Montagne* (19 Mar 1897): 4.

117. CAOM: M/GG, 6 (4) D 6: Cazet to Gallieni, Tananarive, 21 Nov 1896.

118. CAOM: M/GG, 6 (4) D 6: Alby to Gallieni, Antsirabe, 3 Nov 1896.

119. Ellis, *The Rising of the Red Shawls*, 120.

120. SMEP: 62.996; B.218: "Rapport sur l'assassinat de MM. les pasteurs Escande et Minault (21 Mai 1897) à Ambatondrama, by Capitaine Commandant le cercle annexe d'Arivonimamo Schaeffer, Ramainandro, 27 Mai 1897"; see also CAOM: Mad FM, 215/446: Gallieni to M. le Ministre des Colonies, No. 476, Tananarive, 12 July 1897; and SMEP: 62.996; B.218: "Rapport sur l'assassinat de MM. les pasteurs Escande et Minault."

121. In his report to the minister of the colonies, Gallieni stressed this point. CAOM: M/FM, 215/446: Gallieni to M. le Ministre des Colonies, 12 July 1897.

122. SMEP: 62.996; B.218: "Rapport sur l'assassinat de MM. les pasteurs Escande et Minault."

123. CAOM: M/FM, 215/446: Gallieni to M. le Ministre des Colonies, 12 July 1897.

124. CAOM: M/FM, 348/933: Direction des Affaires d'Afrique, Bureau de Madagascar, to Gallieni, C. 504, 24 June 1897.

125. CAOM: M/FM, 215/446: Gallieni to M. le Ministre des Colonies, 12 July 1897.

126. AJ: FC, 412: Cazet to Mon Révérend Père Provincial, Tananarive, 24 May 1897.

127. CAOM: M/FM, 215/446: de Mahy to M. le Ministre des Colonies, No. 1703, Paris, 17 July 1897.

128. SMEP: 62.996; B.218: Copy, Gallieni to M. le Capitaine commandant, le Cercle annexe d'Arivonimano, No. 2244, Tananarive, 30 Aug 1897.

129. CAOM: M/FM, 215/446: M. le Capitaine Schaeffer to M. le Lieutenant-Colonel, commandant le 2e territoire militaire, No. 11e, Arivonimamo, 3 Sept 1897.

130. SMEP: Meyer (1897): Gallieni to Meyer, Tananarive, 7 Sept 1897.

131. See, for example, CAOM: M/GG, 6 (4) D 55: Ormières to Gallieni, No. 71, 10 Jan 1901.

132. CAOM: M/FM, 348/933: Gallieni to M. le Ministre des Colonies, No. 169 GG, Tananarive, 29 Jan 1901.

133. This audience is outlined in the introduction to (no author), *Madagascar et le protestantisme français: Le passé, l'enquête, le devoir* (Paris: Maisons des Missions Évangeliques, 1897), ii, a "supplement" to the Lauga and Kruger report. Despite sharing the title, this was not the same publication as John Viénot's book, discussed later.

134. Lauga and Kruger, *La Libérté religieuse*, 22–25.

135. Ibid., 42–43.

136. Ibid., 42, 44.

137. Ibid., 52.

138. Ibid., 53.

139. John Viénot, *Madagascar et le Protestantisme français* (Paris: Librairie G. Fischbacher, 1897), 14.

140. Here, Viénot quotes Ernest Fallot of the Société de géographie de Marseilles; ibid., 15, emphasis added.

141. Ibid., 16.

142. Elisée Escande, *A Madagascar, hier et aujourd'hui: Essai de vulgarization* (Paris: Librairie Fischbacher, 1898), 205.

143. Elisée Escande, "Le 14 juillet à Fianarantsoa," *JME*, 73e année (1898): 680.

144. Ibid., 681.

145. SMEP: Meyer (1897): Gallieni to Meyer, Tananarive, 7 Sept 1897; and Meyer to Gallieni. Tananarive, 8 Sept 1897.

146. Escande, "Le 14 juillet," 682.

147. Cazet, in *Missions Catholiques* (1897): 3, as quoted in Lauga and Kruger, *La Libérté religieuse*, 23.

148. J. Brucker, S.J., *La Liberté religieuse à Madagascar* (Amiens: Imprimerie Yvert & Tullier, 1897), 7.

149. Ibid., 8.

150. Ibid., 14–15.

151. Gallieni, quoted in CAOM: M/FM, 355/959: Pannequin to M. le Ministre des Colonies, Tananarive, 24 Mar 1901.

152. A. Boegner and P. Germond, *Confidentiel rapport sur la délégation à Madagascar (Juillet 1898–Février 1899)* (Paris: Maison des Missions Évangéliques, 1899), 24.

153. CAOM: M/FM, 355/959: Pannequin to M. le Ministre des Colonies, Tananarive, 24 Mar 1901.

154. Ibid.
155. Sanderson, *England, Europe, and the Upper Nile*, 380.
156. CAOM: M/FM, 348/933: Gallieni to M. le Ministre des Colonies. Cg. 194, Tananarive, 1 Mar 1903.
157. On the inconsistencies between colonial ideology and practice in the 1890s and early 1900s, see Alice Conklin, "Colonialism and Human Rights, a Contradiction in Terms? The Case of France and West Africa, 1895–1914," *The American Historical Review* 103, no. 2 (Apr 1998): 419–442.

Chapter 7

1. Archives of the London Missionary Society (LMS): Madagascar Reports Box 5: Report, J. Rowlands, Ambohimandrosa, 27 Mar 1897.
2. LMS: Mad Personal Box 1: LMS letter "To the Pastors, Evangelists, and Members of the Churches connected with the London Missionary Society in Imerina," Antananarivo, 19 Oct 1897.
3. LMS: Mad Reports Box 5, 1894–1898: Report, J. C. Thorne, Antananarivo, 26 Apr 1897.
4. LMS: Mad Incoming Correspondence (IC) Box 27, 1897: Richardson to Cousins, Antananarivo, 26 Feb 1897.
5. LMS: Mad IC Box 26, 1896: Baron to Thompson, Antananarivo, 24 Feb 1896.
6. LMS: Mad Reports Box 5: Report, D. M. Rees, Ambohimandrosa, 1897.
7. LMS: Mad Reports Box 5: Report, J. Pearse, 27 Mar 1897.
8. LMS: Mad Reports Box 5: Report, C. Collins, Farafangana, 24 Feb 1897. And see E. Malcolm Carrol, *French Public Opinion and Foreign Affairs, 1870–1914* (New York: Century, 1931), 174–75.
9. LMS: Mad IC Box 26: Sibree to Thompson, Antananarivo, 11 June 1896.
10. LMS: Mad IC Box 27: Edmonds to Cousins, Tsiafahy, 26 Apr 26, 1897.
11. LMS: Mad IC Box 27: Letter from C. Jukes to W. Thompson, Antananarivo, 13 Jan 1897.
12. LMS: Mad Reports Box 6, 1899–1902: T. Johnson, Ten Years' Review, 1890–1960; 1901 Report, A. S. Huckett, Fianarantsoa.
13. LMS: Mad Photo 01/009/012/007: "Assembly of students and teachers of LMS High School, Antananarivo, ca. 1900."
14. LMS: Mad Personal Box 1: "A Statement on the Necessity of a Revision of Legislation in Regard to Public Worship in Madagascar" (Imarivolanitra: Imprimerie LMS, n.d., c. 1920), 3. This document provides an excellent overview of LMS attitudes toward French policies.
15. AJ: 412: Cazet to Mon Révérend Père Provincial, Tananarive, 19 May 1901.
16. LMS: Mad Personal Box 1: "A Statement on the Necessity of a Revision of Legislation," 3.
17. Jérôme Braquet, "V. Augagneur et les missionnaires à Madagascar," in Marc Michel and Yvan Paillard, eds., *Australes: Études historiques aixoises sur l'Afrique australe et l'océan Indien occidental* (Paris: l'Harmattan, 1996), 214–15.

18. Clipping from *Le Matin* (22 July 1907), at the Archives du Ministère des affaires-étrangères (MAE): Madagascar Correspondance Politique et Commerciale (Mad CPC): NS 5.

19. *Le Matin* (22 July 1907).

20. Ibid.

21. MAE: Mad CPC, NS 5: Letter from the British Embassy, Paris, 27 May 1908; attached report, "Particulars of the matters complained of by the Missionaries in Madagascar showing the manner in which Monsieur Augagneur's decisions differ from those of his Predecessor."

22. Emphasis in original. MAE: Mad CPC, NS 5: "Particulars of the matters complained of by the Missionaries in Madagascar."

23. MAE: Mad CPC, NS 5: Tralboux to M. le Gouverneur-Général de Madagascar, No. 10-CC, Fort-Dauphin, 26 Feb 1907, attached to Augagneur to M. le Ministre des Colonies, No. 1426, Tananarive, 24 Sept 1907.

24. MAE: Mad CPC, NS 5: Delavaud to Pichon, Christiania, 25 Apr 1908 (Norway). Delavaud quotes from a Norwegian interview entitled "Le Missionnaire Rosaas: La Mission de Madagascar et le gouvernement français; Un gouverneur-général, ennemi des missions."

25. LMS: Mad Personal Box 1: "A Statement on the Necessity of a Revision of Legislation," 3–4.

26. MAE: Mad CPC, NS 5: "Particulars of the matters complained of by the Missionaries in Madagascar."

27. Braquet, "V. Augagneur et les missionnaires," 226.

28. Ibid., 223.

29. LMS: Mad Reports, Box 8, 1908–1912: Report, the Boys High School at Ambatonakanga (Antananarivo), 1908–1909, signed Charles Matthey, Antananarivo, 31 Dec 1908.

30. Braquet, "V. Augagneur et les missionnaires," 221.

31. MAE: Mad CPC, NS 5: "Mission work in Madagascar," British Foreign Office Report, 5 Feb 1908; and LMS: Mad Personal Box 1: "A Statement on the Necessity of a Revision of Legislation," 4–5.

32. LMS: Mad IC, Box 32, 1908–1910: Thorne to Cousins, Antananarivo, 29 Feb 1908.

33. LMS: Mad IC, Box 32: Sharman to Cousins, Antananarivo, 14 Aug 1908.

34. LMS: Mad IC, Box 32: Lester to Cousins, 16 Sept 1908.

35. LMS: Mad IC, Box 32: Thorne to Cousins, Antananarivo, 29 Feb 1908; with attached, "Some particulars of hindrances to missionary work," by Rev. J. Jester, 1907.

36. LMS: Mad IC, Box 32: Lester to Cousins, 16 Sept 1908.

37. LMS: Mad IC, Box 32: Copy, letter from Governor-General of Madagascar, No. 1414, Antananarivo, 15 Aug 1908.

38. LMS: Mad Reports, Box 8: Evans, "Abatonakanga Church and District, Report for 1911."

39. MAE: Mad CPC, NS 5: White to Pichon, Paris, 12 June 1907.

40. MAE: Mad CPC, NS 5: M. le Ministre des Colonies to M. le Ministre des Affaires Étrangères, Paris, 9 July 1907.

41. Braquet, "V. Augagneur et les missionnaires," 231.

42. MAE: Mad CPC, NS 5: M. l'Ambassadeur de France en Angleterre to Pichon, London, 26 Aug 1907.
43. MAE: Mad CPC, NS 5: M. l'Ambassadeur de France en Angleterre to M. Pichon, No. 7, London, 10 Jan 1908.
44. MAE: Mad CPC, NS 5: M. le Ministre des Colonies to M. le Ministre des Affaires Étrangères, Paris, 13 Mar 1908.
45. MAE: Mad CPC, NS 5: Aide-Mémoire, l'Ambassade d'Angleterre, 17 May 1912.
46. LMS: Mad Personal, Box 1: Bianquis to Hawkins, Paris, 18 May 1912 (translation).
47. Ibid.
48. LMS: Mad Personal, Box 1: Bianquis to Hawkins. Paris, 1 June 1912.
49. LMS: Mad Personal, Box 1: Notes of Private Meeting to Foreign Office, 19 June 1912.
50. Ibid.
51. LMS: Mad Personal, Box 1: "Extracts from a letter from Bishop King of Madagascar to the Archbishop of Canterbury, dated June 21, 1912."
52. LMS: Mad Personal Box 1: Notes of Private Meeting to Foreign Office, 19 June 1912.
53. LMS: Mad Personal, Box 1: "Extracts from a letter from Bishop King."
54. LMS: Mad Personal Box 1: Barclay, Re. British Missions in Madagascar, Opinion, 21 Sept 1912.
55. MAE: Mad CPC, NS 5: Minute à Colonies, No. 828, Min. Aff. Etr. Urgent, 16 Oct 1912.
56. MAE: Mad CPC, NS 5: Minute à Colonies, No. 817, Min. Aff. Etr. Urgent, 14 Oct 1912.
57. MAE: Mad CPC, NS 5: Minute à Colonies, No. 828, Min. Aff. Etr. Urgent, 16 Oct 1912.
58. MAE: Mad CPC, NS 5: Note, Ministère des Affaires Étrangères, 25 Oct 1912.
59. MAE: Mad CPC, NS 5: M. le Ministre des Colonies to M. le Ministre des Affaires Étrangères, Très urgent, 5 May 1913.
60. LMS: Mad Personal, Box 1: "A Statement on the Necessity of a Revision," 5.
61. James Sibree, *Fifty Years in Madagascar: Personal Experiences of Mission Life and Work* (London: Allen and Unwin, 1923), 291.
62. "A Madagascar," *Le Siècle*, 4 Nov 1907, clipping at the Archives nationales, Paris (AN): F 19: 6211: Madagascar.

Chapter 8

1. Chambre de Commerce de Lyon à l'Exposition Universelle de Lyon en 1894, *Exposition coloniale* (Lyon: A-H Storck, 1894), 11–12.
2. Ibid., 30–31, emphasis added.
3. See AOPF: Délibérations de Conseil de Paris, 21 Mar 1899 (vols. 15–16), 86.
4. AOPF: Délibérations de Conseil de Paris, 1 July 1907, 185, 4ème annexe, No. 1597, Letter to Conseil Central de Lyon. Paris, le 2 July 1907.
5. For example, in 1886 the *Missions Catholiques* boasted that the chief Catholic newspaper in France, *L'Univers*, had praised the *Almanach des Missions*. Two

years later, it announced the publication of the *Petit Almanach de l'Oeuvre de la Propagation de la Foi*, complementing the existing *Grand Almanach*. Later that same year, *Missions Catholiques* published a letter from Cardinal Lavigerie calling the *Album des Missions* a beautiful piece of work. *Missions Catholiques* (1888): 527, 552.

6. All these annual publications were sold "to profit the Missions." *Petit Almanach de l'Oeuvre de la Propagation de la Foi* (1889).

7. *Missions Catholiques* (1887): 491.

8. "Aimons les missions," *Almanach des Missions* (1885): 9.

9. Ibid.

10. *Almanach des Missions* (Lyon, 1888), "sous le patronage de l'Oeuvre de la Propagation de la Foi." On the cover, an Asian man, with wispy mustache, dons a silk robe with an elaborate dragon embroidered on his chest. Beside him stands a Native American in headdress and a patterned skirt, with a bow and arrow in his hand. Two African figures represent the animist pagan and the Muslim, one with spear, the other in a red fez with a rifle. This cover was a reworking of the original cover on the 1885 *Almanach*, which had six somewhat less specific ethnic types in a similar setting.

11. AOPF: Déliberations de Conseil de Paris, 21 Feb 1907, vol. 16, 136.

12. *Missions Catholiques* 18 (1886): 539.

13. See *Almanach des Missions* (1885).

14. Ibid., 13.

15. L'Abbé Girard, "Les Supplices chinois," *Almanach des Missions* (1887): 19–23. An advertisement in *Missions Catholiques* advised people who were "too impressionable" to pass over without reading this "succession of atrocious scenes." *Missions Catholiques* (1886): 539.

16. "Les Supplices chinois," 19.

17. Ibid., 23.

18. "Peuples anthropophages: Terrible histoire de Bandzinga," *Petit Almanach de la Propagation de la Foi* (1891): 115.

19. On the teaching of patriotism, duty, and other lessons of the nation, see Eugen Weber, *Peasants into Frenchmen: The Modernization of Rural France, 1870–1914* (Stanford, CA: Stanford University Press, 1976), 333.

20. "Je veux être missionnaire!" by Père Le Roy, *Almanach des Missions* (1889): n.p.

21. *Annales* 62 (1890): 59.

22. *Petit Almanach* (1889); *Petit Almanach* (1891): 89–91.

23. *Petit Almanach* (1891), 92.

24. *Petit Almanach* (1899), 72. Weber notes that hygiene was a concern shared by republican schoolmasters as well. *Peasants into Frenchmen*, 330.

25. Roger Dombre, "La Relique," *Petit Almanach* (1899), 108.

26. Ibid., 112.

27. The *Album des Missions Catholiques* was published annually by the *Missions Catholiques* starting in 1888. It was divided into four sections—Africa, East Asia, West Asia, and America and Oceania—and published reports and letters like those found in the *Missions Catholiques*. On its museum-like qualities, see the 1887 advertisement for the *Album* in *Missions Catholiques* (1887): 576.

28. See Charles Rearick, "Song and Society in Turn-of-the-Century France," *Journal of Social History* 22 (Fall 1988): 45–63; Regina Sweeney, *Singing Our Way to Victory: French Cultural Politics and Music during the Great War* (Middletown, CT: Wesleyan University Press, 2001), chap. 1; and Weber, *Peasants into Frenchmen*, chap. 26.

29. As Sweeney shows, politicians were so impressed by the power of music that they were careful to monitor songs for political and immoral content. *Singing Our Way to Victory*, 30–31.

30. Ibid., 33.

31. "Le Désir du martyre," *Almanach des Missions* (1889): n.p.

32. *Missions Catholiques* (1886): 539; the "Chant pour le départ des missionnaires" was published in the following year's *Almanach des Missions* (1887): 12–13.

33. On Botrel, see Sweeney, *Singing Our Way to Victory*, 27.

34. "Le Missionnaire," by Théodore Botrel, *Almanach des Missions* (1901): 22–24.

35. "Chant pour le départ des Missionnaires," *Almanach des Missions* (1887): 12–13.

36. "Le Missionnaire," 24.

37. Ibid., 22.

38. Ibid.

39. Joseph Serre, "Les Grands français," *Almanach des Missions* (1902): 20.

40. Père Lutz, "Massacre conjuré par la courageuse intervention des missionnaires au Rio-Pongo (Côtes Occidentales d'Afrique)," in *Almanach des Missions* (1885): 28.

41. Ibid., 29.

42. Ibid., 30.

43. Ibid.

44. Ibid., 31.

45. Ibid.

46. "Le Missionnaire," no author, in *Almanach des Missions* (1885): 7, emphasis added.

47. "Les Pays de Missions à l'Exposition universelle de Paris: Coup d'oeil rétrospectif," *Almanach des Missions* (1890): n.p.

48. *Annales* 64 (1892): 11, 462.

49. *Annales* (1893): 151.

50. "Civilisons! . . . ," by "Chanaan," in *Almanach des Missions* (1887): 72–78.

51. Ibid., 72.

52. Philip Nord, *The Republican Moment: Struggles for Democracy in Nineteenth-Century France* (Cambridge, MA: Harvard University Press, 1995), 15.

53. The name is ironic on a number of levels. Aside from the fact that the members of this meeting had apparently stripped their African subject of all signs of individual will, many Masonic attacks on religious work in the colonies focused on how religious evangelization threatened the *libre-pensée* of local populations. "Civilisons! . . . ," 73.

54. Ibid., 76.

55. Ibid., 78.

56. "Li pas savoir, li avait pas encore mangé de Français!" in "Récréation," *Petit Almanach de la Propagation de la Foi* (1900): 54.

57. "Aux colonies," *Petit Almanach de la Propagation de la Foi* (1899): 72–73.

58. See Ann Hugone, "Images et messages," in Pascal Blanchard and Armelle Chatelier, eds., *Images et colonies: Nature, discours et influence de l'iconographie coloniale liée à la propagande coloniale et à la representation des Africains et de l'Afrique en France, de 1920 aux indépendances* (Paris: ACHAC, 1993), 53–54.

59. On Victorian interests in cannibalism, see Patrick Brantlinger, "Victorians and Africans: The Geneaology of the Myth of the Dark Continent," in Henry Louis Gates Jr., ed., *"Race," Writing, and Difference* (Chicago: University of Chicago Press, 1986), 203; and Dorothy Hammond and Alta Jablow, *The Africa That Never Was: Four Centuries of Writing about Africa* (New York: Twayne, 1970), 49–113.

60. "Récréation: L'Introduction de la civilization en Afrique," by R.P. Al. Le Roy, in *Almanach des Missions* (1891), n.p.

61. The pot in which the colonist boiled showed a clear "K:W Trademark," enabling the *Almanach* to claim it was not criticizing French colonialism specifically. "Récréation: Le Disciple," *Almanach des Missions* (1903): 31.

62. On representations of urban-rural divisions in nineteenth-century France, see, for example, Alain Corbin, "Paris-Province," in Pierre Nora, ed., *Realms of Memory, vol. 1, Conflicts and Divisions*, trans. Arthur Goldhammer (New York: Columbia University Press, 1996), 427–64.

63. See Susanna Barrows, *Distorting Mirrors: Visions of the Crowd in Late Nineteenth-Century France* (New Haven, CT: Yale University Press, 1981), chap. 2: "Metaphors of Fear: Women and Alcoholics," 43–72.

64. Ibid., 63.

65. *Almanach des Missions* (1885): 5, 7.

66. *Annales* (1896): 347–48.

67. *Annales* 67 (1895): 11.

68. See *Annales* (1898): 11, and 72 (1900): 7.

69. *Annales* (1900): 8.

70. *Annales* 59 (1897): 152.

71. *Annales* 73 (1901): 77.

72. *Annales* (1902): 395.

73. *Annales* (1903): 235.

74. *Annales* (1903): 7.

75. "Les Missionnaires et la science," in *Annales* (1907): 124–34, 266–82.

76. R. P. Cayzac, "Ce que font les missionnaires en Afrique," *Annales* 83 (1911): 238–39.

77. Ibid., 248, emphasis in the original.

78. Robert Gildea, *The Past in French History* (New Haven, CT: Yale University Press, 1994), 34–42.

79. Mona Ozouf, "The Pantheon: The École Normale of the Dead," in Pierre Nora, ed., *Realms of Memory: The Construction of the French Past, vol. 3, Symbols*, trans. Arthur Goldhammer (New York: Columbia University Press, 1998), 326.

80. J. B. Piolet, S.J., ed., *Les Missions catholiques au XIXe siècle*, 6 vols. (Paris: A. Colin, 1901–3); Valérien Groffier, *Héros trop oubliés de notre épopee coloniale* (n.p., 1905).

81. AJ: FC 412: Cazet to Mon Révérend Père Provincial. Fiesole, 31 July 1895. Cazet concluded by suggesting that all material published on Madagascar should cross his desk for approval first.

82. For his six-volume opus, Piolet won the Joest Prize from the Académie française, which habitually promoted missionary publications, and he took a Prix Corbay and a silver medal from the Société de géographie. Jules Pravieux, *A Quoi servent les missionnaires* (Paris: n.p., 1912), 57.

83. Among other works, Piolet published *L'Empire coloniale de la France: Madagascar, la Réunion, Mayotte, les Comores, Djibouti* in 1900; and *Douze leçons à la Sorbonne sur Madagascar, son état actuel, ses resources, son avenir* in 1898.

84. AOPF: Délibérations de Conseil de Paris, vol. 15: 1897–1905: Séance, 24 Jan 1899, p. 77.

85. M. Guasco, "Les Missionnaires et la science," *Annales de la Propagation de la Foi* (1907): 272–73.

86. In 1896, newspaper editorials accused the New Caledonia missions of becoming embroiled in debates between colonists and indigenous communities over the redistribution of land. As in other possessions, the accusations expanded into claims that the missions, under the control of the predominantly French Marist Brothers, opposed the work of the administration and the governor of the colony, a M. Feillet. In response, Mgr. Fraysse, the bishop in Noumea, produced a number of published pamphlets rejecting the claim that missionaries undermined free colonization. APM: New Caledonia: 5 Ca 170; doc. 517: "Extrait d'une letter de Monseigneur Fraysse exposant comment la Mission est accusée d'opposition au Gouverneur, 24 décembre 1896."

87. R. P. Louis Chatelet, "La Nouvelle-Calédonie" in J. B. Piolet, ed., *Les Missions catholiques*, vol. 4, *Océanie et Madagascar* (Paris, 1902), 328.

88. Ibid., 328–29.

89. Ferdinand Brunetière, "Conclusion," in J. B. Piolet, ed., *Les Missions catholiques*, vol. 6, *Missions d'Amérique* (Paris, 1903), 489.

90. Ibid., 490.

91. Ibid., 491.

92. Ibid., 495.

93. Ibid., 496.

94. "What the soldier accomplishes by force, or the financier by the means of money . . . , our missionaries strive for by way of fraternity." Ibid., 498.

95. Ibid., 497.

96. Ibid.

97. AOPF: Procès Verbaux du Conseil Central de Lyon. Séance, 19 May 1905, n.p. Groffier's book was initially called "Pages oubliées de notre épopée coloniale."

98. AOPF: Délibérations du Conseil de Paris, vol. 15, Séance, 22 May 1905, 487.

99. AOPF: Procès Verbaux du Conseil Central de Lyon, Séance, 22 Dec 1905.

100. "Chronique," *Annales de la Propagation de la Foi* 77 (1905): 471.

101. Groffier, *Héros trop oubliés* vii. A copy of the massive, illustrated first edition is located at the library of the Archivio Padri Maristi in Rome.

102. The following analysis is based on a reading of the 1928 edition of the book. The text is entirely the same as the first edition, though the pagination differed in this later, smaller publication. Groffier, *Héros trop oubliés* (Lyon: Librairie Catholique Emmanuel Vitte, 1928), 622.

103. Groffier, *Héros trop oubliés*, 620.

104. Ibid., 544, 137.

105. Ibid., 11.

106. "Gesta dei per Francos," in the context of the Crusades, translates as "the work of God [accomplished] through the French."

107. "Asia Minor was, in the middle ages, a colony of western Europe, and more precisely of France; already our ancestors showed one of the characteristic traits of our national temperament, when they imported completely, in the Holy Lands, their habits and customs from France." Henri Lorin, *La France, puissance coloniale* (Paris: Augustin Challamel, 1906), 4.

108. Groffier, *Héros trop oubliés*, 54.

109. *Annales* 78 (1906): 152.

110. See Appendix.

111. Yannick Essertel, *L'Aventure missionnaire lyonnaise, 1815–1962* (Paris: Les Éditions de Cerf, 2001), 99, 95.

112. Benedict XV, *Maximum Illud*, discussed and quoted in Adrian Hastings, "The Clash of Nationalism and Universalism within Twentieth-Century Missionary Christianity," in Brian Stanley, ed., *Missions, Nationalism and the End of Empire* (Grand Rapids, MI: Eerdmans, 2003), 15.

Index

CPSIA information can be obtained at www.ICGtesting.com
Printed in the USA
LVOW04s2302140815

450135LV00005B/7/P

9 780195 374018